Pitt Series in Composition, Literacy, and Culture
· · · · · · ·

David Bartholomae and Jean Ferguson Carr, Editors

Feminine Principles and Women's Experience in American Composition and Rhetoric

Louise Wetherbee Phelps

Janet Emig

Editors

University of Pittsburgh Press
Pittsburgh and London

Published by the University of Pittsburgh Press, Pittsburgh, Pa., 15260

Designed by Jane Tenenbaum

Library of Congress Cataloging-in-Publication Data
Feminine principles and women's experience in American composition and
    rhetoric / Louise Wetherbee Phelps and Janet Emig, editors.
        p.   cm. — (Pittsburgh series in composition, literacy, and
    culture)
        Includes bibliographical references.
        ISBN 0-8229-3863-4 (cl). — ISBN 0-8229-5544-X (pb)
        1. English language—Composition and exercises—Study and
    teaching—United States.   2. English language—Rhetoric—Study and
    teaching—United States.   3. Women—Education—United States—
    Language arts.   4. Women—United States—Intellectual life.
    5. Feminism and education—United States.   6. Academic writing—Sex
    differences.   7. Women in education—United States.   8. Women—
    United States—Language.   9. Women teachers—United States.
    I. Phelps, Louise Wetherbee, 1940–   .   II. Emig, Janet A.
    III. Series.
    PE1405.U6F46   1994
    808'.042'07073—dc20   94-43034
                                                                        CIP

A CIP catalogue record for this book is available from the British Library.

Eurospan, London

Chapter 3, "Discourse and Diversity: Experimental Writing Within the Academy," by Lillian Bridwell-Bowles, appeared in slightly different form in College Communication and Com-munication *43 (October 1992). Copyright 1992 by the National Council of Teachers of English. Reprinted with permission.*

Chapter 11 quotes lines from Adrienne Rich, "Transcendental Etude," from The Fact of a Doorframe: Poems Selected and New, 1950–1984 *(New York: W. W. Norton, 1984), with the kind permission of the author.*

Chapter 14, "Between the Drafts," by Nancy Sommers, was originally published in College Composition and Communication *43 (February 1992).*

The search for the female subject is simultaneously a quest for a form of inquiry that serves the ends of explanation, understanding, and critique along public and private vectors. This means that the theorist must reject out of hand any mode of explanation which requires or sanctions the imposition upon the female subject of the theorist's own views as to who she is, what she wants, and what she should have in advance of any attempt to probe that subject's self-understanding. To take a human being as the object of political inquiry without patronizing, manipulating, or distorting her world must be every critical feminist thinker's concern. . . . This female subject, as the object of inquiry, must be approached as an active agent of a life-world of intense personalization and immediacy.

—*Jean Bethke Elshtain,* **Public Man, Private Woman**

Contents

Acknowledgments

. . . .

We thank all those who over the years made possible the enactment of this project, from inception through publication. Early on, David Franke of Syracuse University served as a dedicated research assistant. Louise Phelps thanks Syracuse University for a supported research leave in the fall of 1990 to begin work on this text and her colleagues in the Writing Program who made this absence feasible. Periodically, we enjoyed the gracious hospitality of Louise's parents, Virginia and Don Wetherbee, in their Chapel Hill, North Carolina, home.

We are deeply grateful to David Bartholomae, Jean Ferguson Carr, and the University of Pittsburgh Press for accepting a manuscript that violates academic conventions in its mix of contributors and experiments with discourse, in order to breach the walls separating the schools from higher education and both from women's everyday lifeworld. David and Jean understood and enabled our hopes to support a genuinely democratic and inclusive feminism in composition and rhetoric across these contexts. We thank too Jane Flanders, our production editor, and Katherine Kimball Buxton, our copy editor, for whom an experimental venture such as ours presented unique challenges.

We write out of a rich tradition, and we thank all our ancestresses and all our peers who through their thoughts, writing, and actions helped develop and advance our understanding of the roles women play in the learning and teaching of writing and in the practice of rhetoric. We are obliged especially to everyone who sent us abstracts to consider, and we regret that constraints on length kept us in some cases from publishing the work of those who are making and will continue to make major contributions to understandings of feminism and of composition and rhetoric.

And finally we express gratitude for the forbearance of our contributors as well as the encouragement of our families—spouse, partner, parents, and children—who lived with us through a project that proved more arduous, challenging, and satisfying than we could have initially imagined.

Introduction:
Context and Commitment

Janet Emig, with Louise Wetherbee Phelps

Women, for cultural and historical reasons, have seldom enjoyed the opportunity to collaborate on intellectual and imaginative projects exclusively with other women. The constraints have been well rehearsed: women who might have worked together have experienced instead almost systematic separation and isolation imposed by arrangements of class, race, clan, ethnicity, marriage, and child rearing. Written collaborations exclusively between two or more women in almost any mode, from novel to play to script to academic text or project, are rare. Even now, in a climate avowedly friendly to feminism, there are few examples of academic women coediting, much less coauthoring, with other women, particularly in the ragingly individualistic and entrepreneurial world of English studies. Until recently only Sandra Gilbert and Susan Gubar in literary theory and Andrea Lunsford and Lisa Ede in rhetorical studies come readily to mind. Feminist projects, however, provoke, support, or even require such partnerships. One can follow the growth of feminism in composition and rhetoric partly through the increasing number of women engaging in cooperative enterprises; from coediting and coauthorship like ours to feminist workshops, conference sessions, and interest groups like the recently formed Coalition of Women Scholars in the History of Rhetoric and Composition. (Ironically, feminism also enables enduring cross-gender partnerships between coequals: Nancy Mack and James Zebroski are one such pair in composition.)

Perhaps one reason for so few collaborations between women in the past is that the criteria, though hidden, were so stringent. Even now, women who collaborate usually need to be tenured, since they must possess the freedom to arrange time for sustained, shared intellectual inquiry, particularly for the prolonged and intricate conversations that serve as inherent prelude to creating such texts (the one here lasting five years!). If they are geographically separated, or if the project is costly, they must be decently affluent, since few patrons or publishers offer such pairs the inducements or advances that some male teams attract. They themselves must directly honor, or somehow provide the means to honor, commitments and responsibilities represented by ongoing professional duties, as well as by spouses, partners, children, students, family. They must, in a word, be comparatively lucky in the conditions of their lives even while lacking the power and privilege most academic men take as their due.

Are Louise and I saying that within the very privileged population all tenured women faculty represent, we two are among the most privileged? Yes. At the heart of this volume lie five years of conversations held up and down the east coast—in Syracuse, New York; Panther Valley, New Jersey; Chapel Hill, North Carolina; Sanibel, Florida—and sustained in the interim by telephone. It was possible, if not easy, for us to find the funds, steal the time, and balance competing claims on our creative and caring energies in order to bring the project to fruition.

The circumstances in which even privileged women still work, though, lengthened the project beyond our expectation. At one point we faced the classic dilemma of women struggling to reconcile the claims of multiple commitments—the moment when a direct conflict requires them to choose. During the years Louise and I worked together on this project, we also directed programs at our respective institutions that embodied feminist visions and to which we had made enduring ethical commitments. In the last two years of this project, each of us encountered extraordinary crises threatening the health and very survival of our programs, requiring us to respond with every reserve of resourcefulness and care we possessed, at the cost of delaying completion of the volume. This dilemma is one imposed often on women in our field, as it is on so many other women in our society. Women reading this volume as well as our contributors will have made their own difficult choices, situationally different as their feminism is different. They will understand why we see our own choice, agonizing and ambivalent as it was from day to day, as a feminist one.

Why did we elect to work together on a project of this magnitude in the first place—and why this particular project?

It started in September 1987, when at Louise's invitation I visited her, in part to advise on plans she was developing for a new universitywide writing program. As we talked over some of the premises for such a program, we began to discuss the experiences and problems of women in leading such enterprises. Why, we wondered, were these matters not discussed openly as feminist issues? For years, we knew, women in composition and rhetoric had been having underground conversations about gender in relation to genre, the politics of the field, their own experiences as women teachers, scholars, and administrators; yet rarely did they articulate these insights as feminist positions, and almost never in public forums. Without knowing exactly why not, we guessed there was a project there ready to blossom. One of us said, "I've been thinking about editing a book"; the other said, "Let's do it together!" Almost two years later, we would publish a call for papers intended to provoke and reveal the hidden thoughts and writing of women in composition and rhetoric about their experiences, their principles, the history of the field, its topics and issues—all reinterpreted from a feminist perspective.

In retrospect, it is remarkable how quickly we agreed to collaborate on this project. We did not know each other well, and on the face of it, had no reason to be particularly compatible. We were of two generations, only twelve years apart in age but separated by a gulf of social change. I had graduated from college in 1950 and immediately entered a work world not ready for academic women, composition, or feminism. Louise had graduated in the early sixties, married at the start of the sexual revolution, and after working a few years as a high school teacher had not returned to academe as a scholar until almost twenty years later. Formed in sharply different climates for women in American society and education, entering composition and rhetoric around eighteen years apart (though each, perhaps, as pioneers of a sort), we seemed unlikely to share visions of either composition or feminism. I had consciously lived my entire life as a literal feminist: I had been economically wholly self-sufficient since the age of twenty-two, a lifelong lesbian, an early survivor in fiercely male academic settings. I regard my two university graduate programs in English education as conceptually and actually feminist, at a time when, to my knowledge, no others were. Louise, growing up in a close family that valued women's minds and nurtured their strengths, attending women's educational institutions, was late in recognizing that others did not. She consequently traveled a much more complicated and ambivalent route to feminism, taking for granted her commitment to women's rights but not focused on gender as a central issue in her intellectual work. Starting an academic career in composition and rhetoric at almost forty, she came to feminism in part from the need to grasp the complexities of gender for a woman who takes up a leadership role within male-dominated educational institutions. Finally, not the least of our differences were contrasting composing styles and texture of language—my writing poetic, succinct, even telegraphic, Louise's highly elaborated and complex.

Yet over the course of our project—even intuitively in that first conversation—Louise and I came to realize that we shared a vast set of assumptions and beliefs that differed markedly, dramatically, even controversially, from those held, say, by many feminists in literary and cultural theory. For instance, we believe unfashionably that all experience is inevitably embodied and biologically derived and that, consequently, biological-developmental correlates underlie the learning and teaching of all symbolic processes—in this case, writing. We consequently believe in biologically-based innate differences between the sexes that are culturally interpreted, countered or reinforced. Believing also in the biological uniqueness of all individuals, we hold that personal experience uniquely shapes the transaction between any person of either gender and the culture. Few feminists we have read take up this perspective while simultaneously giving the emphasis we would to historical context, material forces, and the role of language and other symbolic processes in forming individual experience and constructing a common world.

How did these assumptions and beliefs develop? By the usual lengthy evolution known to the formulation of almost all complex concepts—by reading, learning, teaching, living (if these four processes can ever in literate lives be teased apart).

Over time, our conversations recursively traced many shared beliefs (cultural critics might say most) to like backgrounds—sometimes uncannily so. Both Louise and I come from intact middle-class WASP families—hers, intensely nuclear; mine, intensely extended. In both families, not unlike, say, Margaret Mead's, strong-minded, capable grandmothers and great-aunts were full-time working women—head nurses, teachers, as well as florists, bookkeepers, and medical receptionists, although, like most women of their respective generations, our mothers stayed home. I am an only, Louise, an eldest, child—and we all know what those facts mean about immense linguistic predilections and advantage. Both of us had rigorous secondary educations. Although neither family was then affluent and sacrifices were necessary, each of us attended a Seven Sisters college on loans and scholarships; and we also know the growing literature about the importance of attending women's colleges for lifelong intellectual assurance. Both of us majored in writing with minors in philosophy. Each entered university life relatively late, Louise raising three sons and me teaching in private and public school and community college. Both, after initially being denied tenure (like many women in composition and rhetoric), persevered to become eventually full professors at major universities.

Louise and I agree, then, that the decision to work together came from our tacit recognition, later made explicit, of personal and professional communalities, as well as the generative frissons, even tensions, our differences assured.

The compatibility of our visions—and their variance from others'—colored our decisions as editors in ways that, even now, are often too deep to recover. The influence is subtle—we did not try to assemble pieces whose feminist positions were the same as ours, or even coherent with one another. In "Editors' Reflections," we offer a fuller discussion of some respects in which our intellectual conceptions influenced the volume itself. Here, we consider how ethical commitments guided our approach and affected the editing process and organization of the book.

More important to this process than common convictions were shared principles. Each of us had been attracted into composition and rhetoric in part on ethical grounds, sensing and responding to its egalitarian and popular roots. We believe in common that all teaching possesses a moral dimension: teaching represents an ethical transaction with the learner, demanding responsibility, scrupulosity, and nurture. Now, perhaps, we would argue this as a feminist position; but we hold this commitment prior to our feminism, because it is made to all learners. Indeed, we each regard the learning and teaching of composition as democratic manifestations of a democratic society requiring serious, courteous, and equitable treatment of all persons across categories of age, gender, ethnicity, race, religion, class, sexual preference, and community status.

How does this feminist populism connect to our editing process? We did not want to construct this book by approaching influential colleagues or friends to solicit predictable, conventional pieces. Not only did we not know the answers we were looking for, we did not even know the questions, nor could we know who had been asking and exploring them in provocative and original ways. We wanted to tap into this subterranean feminism, as a colleague of Louise's called it. We wished to eschew many varieties of subtle but marked snobbism, unfortunately found in composition and rhetoric as well as in more traditional fields, and too common in academic feminism: the snobbism that excludes part-time and adjunct instructors, graduate students, undergraduate students, those who teach the very young and the very old, those whose names we have not heard of, those whose views are thought naive. For all these reasons, we announced as widely as possible (through journals and correspondence as well as two workshops at national conventions) a call for papers that was unique in its democratic ambition and scope. Addressing a broad readership of language arts teachers and scholars of writing and literacy, we welcomed "diverse voices and visions representing all levels of development from early childhood through graduate education and beyond." Holding that there is equity as well among modes of inquiry and discourse, with none more scholarly than any other, we invited "varied forms of inquiry (e.g., case study, theory, historical or biographical studies, critique)" and encouraged experimentation with genre including "narrative, reflective essay, argument, or dialogue."

As Louise explains in the "Editors' Reflections," we fell short of our ambitions in the diversity of voice, topic, positions, and genre that this call attracted (for example, we had few submissions from women of color or on issues linking feminism to race; from teachers at the elementary and secondary levels; and from students in general, with none from undergraduate students). Next time, we will know better how to elicit an even broader range; now we understand better the constraints that might discourage submission from particular groups or on particular topics. Nonetheless, we received over a hundred abstracts, invited forty-five authors to submit manuscripts, and selected about half of these for acceptance or further consideration. Fourteen essays appear in the final volume, including several by authors who do not occupy traditional roles in academe, some by writers we did not know, and a number that violate expectations about "academic discourse."

We chose abstracts, and later manuscripts, on many grounds ranging from potential quality to contrast to freshness of perspective. Throughout the editing process, we worked intensively with authors on revision, especially those who were experimenting with innovative forms.

From the beginning, we wanted the book as a whole to have a fluidity, openness, and intertextuality reflective of our own principles. We needed to find ways to subvert the linearity of the print medium and present the array of pieces not as a fixed sequence but as a kaleidoscope whose pieces could be shuffled by readers to create new patterns and meanings. Editors inescapably provide coherence and guide interpretation in constructing any anthology, whether implicitly, by selecting, ordering, and arranging its pieces, or explicitly by, commenting in an introduction or afterword. As feminists, we did not wish to renounce this real responsibility for an informing vision or to deny or obscure the interpretive power it generates. Yet we rejected imposing any rigid order, category system, or single vision on our readers. Our solution was to multiply interpretations and alternate critical perspectives by incorporating commentary within the volume itself.

After early efforts to categorize and arrange our abstracts and then manuscripts (which turned out to be a rhetorical and feminist problem of considerable complexity), we decided simply to present chapters by alphabetical order of authors' names and to commission others to create alternate tables of contents for the volume. These reconfigurations appear in part 2 of the volume along with other responses reflecting on the volume.

Our invitation to reconfigure the chapters went something like this:

> We ask you to write your commentary on the volume through the device of a common thought experiment: arranging the essays into an alternate Table of Contents according to some principle that reflects a distinct perspective. This device will be the springboard for you to interpret and evaluate or argue with the collected essays and the editorial stance from your own chosen perspective. By juxtaposing different pieces and grouping them under headings according to your own interests and perceptions, you'll convey different ways of interpreting the volume as well as the individual essays. Optionally, we invite you to fill in fictitious titles for essays that your particular angle on feminism, composition, or rhetoric enables you to imagine and call for, as a constructive way of suggesting what the omissions are (in topics, voices, and perspectives) and therefore what work remains to be done and what directions it should ideally take. What you can do, using the device of the alternate Table of Contents and your own category system, is to imaginatively portray the potential richness of feminism in composition and rhetoric at the same time as giving distinctive, complementary interpretations to what we *have* collected.

Two commentators tried this thought experiment, while another wrote a critical reflection on missing voices.

We commissioned two other responses as well. The first is from a graduate student, David Franke, who helped us solicit abstracts and manuscripts. David writes of his efforts to trace sources for feminism in composition and rhetoric through the abstracts and manuscripts for this volume. Mary Salibrici, an experienced college writing instructor, reads the book critically for what it offers her as a feminist and teacher. She fulfills Cynthia Onore's prophecy in a letter evaluating our prospectus: "Teachers will want to know in what ways the understandings in these pieces will affect ... their teaching, their students' learning, their role as a teacher ... their goals for student learning, their conceptualization of student work ... their views of the connections between curriculum and the world, their ability to engage students in a critical reading of the world."

Cindy asked another question that expresses our own hopes for the volume: "Can the modes of inquiry and ways of knowing embodied in these articles be models for teacher-readers? Will they support teachers in their efforts to become reflective practitioners by demonstrating to them ways in which they might find and share their own voices, ways in which they can construct and reconstruct the meanings of their professional lives?" Time will tell. We invite colleagues—teachers, scholars, administrators, writers and students of writing—to discover their own patterns in the volume; to read it instructively and critically; to interpret, appropriate, challenge, revise, and extend the work of its contributors; to write and enact new visions of composition and rhetoric informed by feminism and new visions of feminism informed by composition and rhetoric.

Feminine Principles
and Women's Experience
in American Composition
and Rhetoric

PART I

Essays

Collaboration, Conversation, and the Politics of Gender

Evelyn Ashton-Jones

Any effort to understand how we think requires us to understand the nature of conversation.

—Kenneth A. Bruffee

Since 1984, when Kenneth A. Bruffee's theoretical rationale for collaborative learning ("Collaborative Learning and the 'Conversation of Mankind' ") appeared in *College English,* the issue of consensus in collaborative learning has been much discussed in that journal. John Trimbur's recent attempt there to mediate this conversation describes the turns it has taken and identifies two distinct and disparate critical voices: one emanating from such critics as Thomas S. Johnson, Pedro Beade, and David Foster, who believe that the "use of consensus in collaborative learning is an inherently dangerous and potentially totalitarian practice that stifles individual voice and creativity, suppresses differences, and enforces conformity" (Trimbur, 602); and another voice, emanating mainly from Greg Myers and other "left-wing" critics concerned that collaborative-learning pedagogy conceals the workings of power structures in consensus making—that is, it does not acknowledge "how knowledge and its means of production are distributed in an unequal, exclusionary social order and embedded in hierarchical relations of power" (603).[1] The wide-ranging views represented in this conversation suggest, as Trimbur notes, that consensus is indeed "one of the most controversial and misunderstood aspects of collaborative learning" (602).

Trimbur's own contribution is to dismiss the views of the former critics as baseless but to revise, based on the views of the latter, Bruffee's

conception of consensus as the product of an ongoing, ever expanding
social conversation that "acquires greater authority as it acquires greater
social weight" (602). In its place, Trimbur posits a "rhetoric of dissensus"
that refashions consensus making as the project of identifying and situating particular and discrete differences within the conceptual space oc-
cupied by the idea of difference; thus, its aim is to help students collectively come to grips with difference as a social construct through
explorations of its origins and its impact on lives and communities (610).
As Trimbur puts it in Habermasian terms, this new consensus is not the
end result of collaboration but an "aspiration" that anticipates and continually defers consensus, a project impelled by the goal of creating

> a utopian discursive space that distributes symmetrically the opportunity
> to speak, to initiate discourse, to question, to give reasons, to do all those
> other things necessary to justify knowledge socially. From this perspec-
> tive, consensus becomes a necessary fiction of reciprocity and mutual
> recognition, the dream of conversation as perfect dialogue. Understood
> as a utopian desire, assembled from the partial and fragmentary forms
> of the current conversation, consensus does not appear as the end or
> the explanation of the conversation but instead as a means of transform-
> ing it. (612)

Ostensibly, then, this collaborative process, unlike Bruffee's, foregrounds rather than conceals the workings of power structures and the
role of conflict in meaning making.

Trimbur's emphasis on power, on difference, and, also, on a trans-
formable reality (Bruffee's monolithic and unchanging "real world" presenting another stumbling block for leftist critics, as Myers points out)
would seem to go far toward answering leftist objections to Bruffee's
notion of consensus. Nevertheless, this revised notion of consensus
works from a fundamental assumption that Trimbur doesn't directly address: that those speaking from marginalized and "different" perspectives—be they of race, ethnicity, gender, class, age, sexual orientation,
or occupation—will, in fact, have access to the conversation and, further,
that the dynamics of the conversation itself will remain unaffected by a
given participant's "difference." In the first instance, as Myers has eloquently argued, social factors such as race, ethnicity, and class can determine who is enrolled in a class and, thus, who participates in a collaborative group discussion (167); certainly, many perspectives will not be
represented simply because the students who would or could voice them
are not present. Second, as sociolinguists Candace West and Don H.

Zimmerman note, social factors can also radically influence the dynamics of the conversation itself, determining whether and how a given "voice" is heard and interpreted:

> While one might characterize a conversation as about "nothing," one cannot so easily evade being able to say something about the person or persons one talked to. The sex, age, and race of the one spoken to are, we suspect, accountable features of persons, i.e., *a shared and enforceable social accounting scheme* [italics added]. Insofar as this is so, we might be tempted to say that matters such as gender are always "noticeable" and "salient" in ways that other, more remotely situated identities may not be. (114)

While gender is clearly not the only perspective of difference that operates in conversational dynamics, as West and Zimmerman emphasize, it is the issue I explore in this essay, bringing to the current examination of consensus and collaboration a feminist reading that addresses the role of conversation in reproducing the ideology of gender.[2] It is my belief, too, that gender is a particularly salient variable in conversation and collaborative learning groups and that both activities are profoundly inscribed and influenced by a hierarchy of gender that, in turn, may influence the writing processes and written texts of women students. To explore this topic, I briefly survey the perspectives of feminist collaborative learning advocates, examine several studies of conversational dynamics between women and men, and outline the views of collaborative learning theorists on the nature of the conversation that takes place in writing groups. My aim is not only to argue that the ideology of gender is indeed reproduced in the interactional dynamics of writing groups but also to suggest the extent to which the feminist valorization of collaborative learning in composition leads away from such analysis and, thus, unwittingly colludes in the reproduction of gender structures that feminists seek to disrupt.

Feminist Perspectives on Collaboration

By and large, feminists' commentary on collaborative learning, both outside of and within composition studies, has not yet subjected it to the kind of scrutiny that could show how it, like more traditional pedagogies, may present problems for women students. Rather, the project of this scholarship has primarily been to forge links between feminism and collaborative learning. In their coedited collection on writing and gender, for example, Cynthia L. Caywood and Gillian R. Overing claim that collaborative learning is "compatible with feminism, if not feminist in and of itself" (198), citing the "integral and fundamental relation of equity in the classroom and collaborative learning" (1). As part of this project, others have attempted to establish a causal relationship between feminism and collaborative learning: Pamela J. Annas, for instance, claims that collaborative pedagogies derive from the techniques of feminist consciousness-raising groups of the 1960s (3), and Susan Stanford Friedman attributes the introduction of collaborative techniques into classrooms to the radical feminist agenda of that decade (205).

Although some might question such fundamental links between collaborative learning and early feminism, the impetus behind the correlation is clear. Claiming for feminism such values as cooperation, connection, and validation and linking these values to collaborative pedagogies effectively establishes a binary opposition that frames feminism and collaborative learning in contradistinction to "patriarchal" values: competition, specialization, hierarchy, and more traditional, presentational pedagogies. From this vantage point, feminism and collaborative learning were early on merged in a unified effort to subvert patriarchy in the academy, specifically, as Friedman describes it, to "circumvent the mystique of professional expertise and specialization by emphasizing student 'expertise' based on the authority of their own experience and by de-emphasizing the leadership role the classroom structure demanded" (204–05).

Drawing on this theoretical-philosophical link between feminism and pedagogy, feminist scholarship has been explicit and nearly unanimous in framing collaborative learning as a boon for women students, who have encountered sexism and male bias in more traditional pedagogies and who struggle with the androcentric perspectives that pervade the academy (see, for example, Spender; Spender and Sarah; Rich; Bleich; and Flynn). Describing feminists' enthusiasm for collaborative learning in the 1960s, one such advocate of collaborative learning notes that it seemed an especially appropriate pedagogy for "voicing and exploring the hitherto unexpressed perspectives of women and others" (Maher, 30). More recently in composition studies, Patricia Bizzell suggests that such pedagogical reforms as collaborative learning "promote more equitable relations" (486). This theme also recurs throughout the pages of Caywood and Overing's volume: Wendy Goulston affirms that it "provides the respect and nurturing support that women students especially need" (25); Olivia Frey contends that it is instrumental in creating a "new woman," aware of her own abilities and self-directed (101–02); Annas calls the collaborative learning classroom a "nurturing but rigorous/ tough space" that validates students and encourages them to grow and change (14); and Robert Mielke traces its parallels with women's moral growth (as articulated by Carol Gilligan), suggesting that collaborative learning pedagogies "embrace the web of solidarity with which the young woman begins her moral development" (174).

Carol Stanger's discussion of collaborative learning perhaps best exemplifies the feminist valorization of collaborative learning. She too finds collaborative learning a distinctly feminist pedagogy that subverts gender hierarchy and resituates women and men on equal terms by removing the teacher-authority from the process of composing, thereby allowing students to develop ideas in a way that is not mediated by a dominant "male" culture. That is, "knowledge ... is not being defined as 'fact' handed down by an authority figure; instead, it is something fluid that the group and the teacher create during their interaction" (43). Thus, in Stanger's view, recasting the teacher-authority figure as a collaborating and Bruffeean knowledge-community spokesperson in effect bars the "patriarchal presence" from the scene of composing and redistributes authority such that "power flows from the teacher to everyone in the room, and then from student to student" (43). Within this context, she believes, women can speak and actualize themselves, perhaps even dominate group conversation: "What is happening during a collaborative task is a dialogue between men's and women's language. . . . The new social structure of the peer learning group, the lack of a patriarchal presence 'teaching,' and the presence of strong and vocal women in the group can combine to give women's language the power to surface and replace men's language" (42).

I don't want to overstate the case, for there are hints in feminist discussions of collaborative learning that it may not be quite the boon for women students and teachers that many believe it to be. For example, Friedman speculates that for women teachers collaborative pedagogies ironically reaffirm a basic patriarchal tenet: that "any kind of authority is incompatible with the feminine" (206). Florence Howe suggests that the "group experience . . . is a particularly crucial one" for women students, but she unambiguously defines this experience as an all-woman interaction (864). Marilyn Cooper, speculating on the shape a writing course for abused women might take, likewise asserts the necessity for women to experience the community of work groups, but she also specifies that

"all teachers, aides, and coordinators of the program should be women"
(154). Further, Mary Kupiec Cayton describes a situation where collaboration worked against a student writing on women's communication
patterns: Genelle, she observes, developed a serious writing block because she "consistently had difficulty getting the two (male) members
of her small workgroup to listen. . . . They seemed to ignore her project
whenever the three of them got together to share writing" (326). And
Annas, who admonishes that the collaborative methods and goals developed in women's classes be "mainstreamed"—introduced into mixed
writing classes—remains cautious, citing the productive environment
that her women's classes provided for developing these collaborative
strategies and urging that "feminist scholarship and pedagogy . . . continue to have a separate and uncluttered space of their own" (14–15).

The appearance of such hedges as these in an otherwise largely positive wealth of literature on collaborative learning in composition should
encourage a reexamination of the feminist project's attempts to link feminism and collaborative learning. Perhaps the distance between feminist
theory and practice here derives from the teacher-authority/student-
nonauthority polarization and its concomitant implication that removing
the teacher-authority from the scene of meaning making and redistributing authority among students will, in fact, establish a nonhierarchical
context for learning. The problem with deducing an absence of patriarchal authority in groups is obvious: even if one construes the teacher-
student hierarchy as essentially patriarchal, there is nothing here to suggest that other classroom structures are *not.* That is, it takes a logical
leap of questionable validity to conclude that removing the teacher-authority from the scene of meaning making effectively removes all traces
of the patriarchal presence. Even if one begins from the assumption that
collaborative learning indeed parallels feminist modes of discourse and
holds goals in common with feminism, it remains to be seen whether
men and women function on equal terms within the province of the group
itself.

The feminist valorization of collaborative learning, then, seems to me
surprising, because, with the exception of Stanger's analysis of group
interaction, it does not acknowledge the role that gender may play in
group dynamics. But what happens inside of writing groups? If, as James
S. Baumlin and Tita French Baumlin suggest, a woman faces greater
obstacles in establishing ethos in her communications because she must
"struggle against the projections which 'create' her ethos in an audience's mind" (255–56), then certainly consensus must be acknowledged

as a powerful social influence at play along gender lines. As members of a mixed-gender group interact, for example, male participants may dominate discussion and decision-making processes, perhaps silencing those who speak from the perspective of difference that gender constitutes. That is, group participants, conditioned to interact according to gender-based roles, may well unconsciously reproduce those roles—men subtly encouraging women to adopt the "feminine" postures and display the "nurturing" behaviors that society assigns them; women, in turn, encouraging men to adopt "masculine," more directive behaviors. Paradoxically, such gender-based behaviors have the potential to reinforce (for some) and subvert (for others) the goals of collaborative learning— that is, men may receive the full advantage of learning to negotiate in an open, supportive, nondirective, nonthreatening setting, while women may simply learn to "take advice."

Conversational Dynamics and the Ideology of Gender

That gender is indeed a powerfully operative variable in the dynamics of conversation—an integral part of a "social accounting scheme" in mixed-gender interaction—is the subject of numerous studies, including those conducted by Pamela Fishman.[3] Fishman observes that conversation does not just happen but is, rather, a complex, rule-bound, problematic activity in which conversationalists have the power to initiate a successful exchange or to "stop it dead." Thus, Fishman elaborates, they must "display . . . their continuing agreement to pay attention to one another"— to do the "interactional work" that facilitates conversation (1983, 90–91). This interactional work, she suggests, is to be found in such conversational dynamics as question asking and appropriately timed responses of encouragement.

Fishman's studies, based on her analysis of recorded transcripts of conversations between women and men, confirm significant differences in their conversational behavior. Fishman found, for example, that women ask more questions (including more tag questions) and more often use hedges and "attention beginnings." In addition, she notes that, while women in the studies made the majority of attempts to initiate topics, their efforts were not nearly so successful as those of men. However, women and men showed no difference in the number of minimal responses that they expressed.

While statistics do not tell a story, Fishman's statistics are dramatic and do not deserve to be relegated to a scholarly endnote. To elaborate on her observations: women subjects asked two-and-a-half times more questions and three times more tag questions than men did, (1980, 128); hedged five times more often in one study (129) and twice as often in another (1983, 95); invoked two times as many "attention beginnings" (95); and made 62 percent of the total attempts to introduce topics into a conversation (97). Men's attempts to get topics to become conversations succeeded virtually every time, with a success rate of twenty-eight out of twenty-nine attempts. But women, in contrast, succeeded only 38 percent of the time, despite their more frequent efforts to initiate topics (1983, 97). Interestingly, in an earlier study, women's success rate doubled when they used a question to initiate a topic (1978, 398).

Framing her analysis as a response to Robin Lakoff's speculation that this kind of conversational behavior is the result of insecurity or personality, Fishman extends her analysis beyond frequency to the context of occurrence, speculating on the cause of this behavior. She observes that if personality or insecurity account for women's hedges, then hedges will be distributed throughout their speech; but her study pinpoints their occurrence only in certain conversational sequences: when women unsuccessfully tried to pursue topics and when they received either no response at all or an inadequate response to their statements and questions (1980, 129–30). In addition, she finds that women use the hedge "you know" as a way to verify that they are being heard and to invite response; the preponderance of this expression in their conversation, she concludes, is evidence that their male coconversationalists are not displaying encouraging behavior (131). Like hedges, questions, Fishman suggests, are an interactive strategy for starting and facilitating conversation, and women's frequent question asking highlights the trouble they have when their male coconversationalists, again, do not display encouraging behavior: "Their greater use of questions is an attempt to solve the *conversational* problem of gaining a response to their utterances" (129).

Fishman also examines why women were so unsuccessful at initiating conversation, asserting that the men did not do the interactional work required to make a conversation happen. The men's success, on the other hand, hinged largely on women's efforts to uphold their part in conversational interaction (1983, 97). Fishman elaborates on the implications of this inequity in topic initiation and development, suggesting that women's topics were regarded by both women and men as "tentative" and, thus, "quickly dropped," but men's topics, "treated as topics to be pursued . . . were seldom rejected" (98). The irony of this disparity between women's interactional work and their meager conversational rewards is not lost on Fishman, nor are its implications: "Thus, the definition of what is appropriate or inappropriate conversation becomes the man's choice. What part of the world the interactants orient to, construct, and maintain the reality of, is his choice, not hers. Yet the women labor hardest in making interactions go" (98).

While men's and women's equal use of minimal responses—the "yeahs" and "umms" of conversation that display interest and thereby encourage a speaker to continue—would seem to belie Fishman's thesis, her functional and contextual analysis confirms that women are doing more conversational work. The men's minimal responses, in fact, suggested their lack of interest: "The monosyllabic response merely filled a [conversational] turn at a point when it needed to be filled. For example, a woman would make a lengthy remark, after which the man responded with 'yeah,' doing nothing to encourage her, nor to elaborate" (1983, 95–96). In contrast, the women's skillfully inserted responses indicated the degree of their attention, interest, and support for the speaker as well as their corresponding efforts to facilitate interaction.

The message emerging from Fishman's research is, clearly, that the bulk of interactional work in conversation is shouldered by women. Fishman attributes women's conversational difficulties to men's failure to do the kind of work that facilitates conversations, a failure embedded in "socially structured power relations [that] are reproduced and actively maintained in our everyday interactions"—namely, the social division of labor according to gender, the required "availability" of women to facilitate interaction, and the "maintenance of gender" through socially mandated modes of behavior (1980, 131). She argues that conversation thus becomes a ritualized activity that helps maintain gender hierarchy:

> To be identified as female, women are required to look and act in particular ways. Talking is part of this complex of behavior. Women must talk like a female talks; they must be available to do what needs to be done in conversation, to do the shitwork and not complain. But all the activities involved in displaying femaleness are usually defined as part of what being a woman *is,* so the idea that it is work is obscured. The work is not seen as what women do, but as part of what they are. Because this work is obscured, because it is too often seen as an aspect of gender identity rather than of gender activity, the maintenance and expression of male-female power relations in our everyday conversations are hidden as well. (1983, 99–100)

As Fishman asserts, this division of labor has serious consequences for women, because the conversational " 'goods' being made are not only interactions but, through them, realities" (99). That is, the social division of labor in conversation that requires women to do the work of conversation does not permit them to reap its rewards. Further, she contends, the availability of women to facilitate interactional processes in society at large—the work they "naturally" do because it "is morally required to do so and a highly sanctionable matter not to"—is reproduced in their availability to do the necessary work of conversation (99).

A similar pattern emerges in another area of conversational studies, which focuses on conversational interruptions and overlaps. In an early study, Don H. Zimmerman and Candace West found that participants in same-sex conversations—that is, conversations between women and conversations between men—interrupted or overlapped each other equally. However, in mixed-sex conversations, they observed a significant increase in overlaps and interruptions, nearly all of them by male speakers, who accounted for 96 percent of the interruptions and 100 percent of the overlaps (1975, 116). In a revised version of this study, West and Zimmerman found that 75 percent of interruptions were initiated by males—fewer than before but nevertheless three times more than those initiated by women (1983, 107). Further, the pattern of the violations is illuminating: overlaps and interruptions in same-sex conversations were clustered in only a few conversations but nearly uniformly distributed across mixed-sex conversations. According to Zimmerman and West, this pattern suggests that such violations are "systematic" in conversations between men and women but only "idiosyncratic" in same-sex conversations (1975, 116).

The conversational difficulty male interruptions and overlaps cause are underscored by the response they elicit from women: silence. Zimmerman and West suggest not only that being interrupted or overlapped or not receiving attentive reinforcement elicits immediate silence but that these speech events may elicit silence in women *overall*. Echoing Fishman, they speculate that this silence reflects the speaker's "uncertainty" about her partner's feelings toward the conversation, an uncertainty rooted in his evident "lack of understanding or even disinterest in and inattention to the current talk" (1975, 123).

They conclude that women operate at a strategic disadvantage when they converse with men, that they comprise a special "class of speakers . . . whose rights to speak appear to be casually infringed upon by males" (1975, 117). Because interruptions, they maintain, are "deep incursions" into a speaker's turn that "violate" conversational space, they do not represent the breakdown of conversation, a "non-event," but a "happening" that is constitutive, rather than merely symbolic, of the power differential between men and women (1983, 104–05). In other words, interruptions are power plays that not only reflect gender hierarchy but serve as "reminders" to women of their second-class status. In the final analysis, West and Zimmerman assert, interrupting is "a way of 'doing' power in face-to-face interaction, and to the extent that power is implicated in what it means to be a man vis-à-vis a woman, it is a way of 'doing' gender as well" (1983, 111).[4]

While it seems reasonable to speculate that these conversational patterns might be subverted or reversed in situations where a woman clearly holds power—for example, a female employer conversing with a male employee or a female doctor talking to a male patient—this does not seem to be the case. Candace West, for instance, finds that female physicians use language that minimizes status differences, whereas their male counterparts use language that emphasizes the physician-patient hierarchy—in both cases, regardless of the patient's gender. More to the point, however, Helena M. Leet-Pellegrini's examination of gender and expertise as covariables in mixed-sex conversation shows that, even when women hold positions of power, the conversational advantage that men enjoy is not eliminated. In fact, possessing a higher level of expertise than men did simply reinforced women's supportive work in mixed-sex conversation.

According to Leet-Pellegrini, while both men and women "experts" in her study spoke more than their "nonexpert" partners regardless of gender, male experts talked more when their uninformed partners were female than did female experts with uninformed male partners (101). In addition, women experts exhibited more supportive linguistic behavior than men experts did, but their supportive behavior was more evident when the nonexpert partner was male. Leet-Pellegrini concludes that "when women who are openly acknowledged as experts interact with men who are openly acknowledged as non-expert, the one-up women support the one-down men" (102).

Thus, according to Leet-Pellegrini's study, nonexpert women do not receive, even from other women, the same conversational support that men receive, nor is expert women's assent work with nonexpert men reciprocated. Further, the nonexpert partner, male or female, performed more assent work overall, except in one situation: when the expert was female and the nonexpert was male. And for one particular category of

assent work, moreover, female experts outperformed their male counterparts, but nonexperts, male and female alike, performed this kind of
support work only when their expert partner was male—never when the
expert was female. In other words, in some cases nonexpert women and
men supported expert men but *not* expert women (102).

Concluding that expertise is not a legitimate source of power for
women, Leet-Pellegrini suggests that women and men are consigned, by
virtue of gender, to gender-specific interactive styles, their options fore-
closed in advance of any conversational encounter:

> Perhaps women have to compensate for acquiring this illegitimate
> source of power. Whereas the name of man's game appears to be "Have
> I won?" the name of woman's game is "Have I been sufficiently helpful?"
> While men may pre-empt forms related to power, women may pre-
> empt forms related to support or nurturance, a disservice to them both. . . .
> Effectiveness in human social interaction is based neither upon relation-
> ships of power nor solidarity, but upon having the flexibility to construct
> whatever kind of relationship is appropriate to the immediate encounter
> and not to some restricting notion of gender appropriateness. (103)

Clearly, the findings of these studies have profound implications for
the ways in which writing-group conversations, too, may effectively reproduce the ideology of gender, not simply as a mirror of gender hierarchy but as a dynamic social process that continually constructs and
reconstructs the power and status differential between women and men.
The conversational events that these studies describe are not likely to
disappear magically when the scene of meaning making shifts to collaborative learning groups. On the contrary, it is more likely that in writing
groups women and men's behavior will parallel the conversational events
described in these studies, men interacting as individualists pressing to
get across and win their own points of view—thus controlling the realities
produced in these writing communities—and women shouldering the
major share of the necessary interactional work.

No less troubling is the implication that these gender-linked behavioral patterns in conversation will severely curtail for women the possibilities for intellectual and social development that collaborative learning,
according to its advocates, offers to both women and men. That is, despite their efforts to facilitate the processes of the group, women's own
conversation will not be facilitated by men and only sometimes by other
women, whereas men will receive the full benefit of support from all
participants, men and women alike. In essence, these studies suggest

that collaborative learning groups provide simply one more example of a microinstitution where gender-based patterns of dominance and subordination are reproduced, yet another stage on which the ideology of gender is played out in an almost ritualistic series of gender performances, males acting out what it means to be male in relation to females, and females acting out their supporting role. The pedagogy of "equity" that collaborative learning purports to be thus reveals a very real and potentially invidious male bias. To portray collaborative pedagogies as pedagogies of equity, then, is to perpetuate and collude in the silence that helps to conceal the reproduction of gender ideology.

Conversation as Epistemic and Transformative in Writing Groups

The implications of such gender politics as these become even more disturbing when juxtaposed with the views of collaborative learning theorists on the function of conversation in writing groups. In what is by now a much-cited explanation of conversation's epistemic dimension, Bruffee explains that we learn to think as a result of learning to converse with others, that the act of thinking is a kind of internalized conversation, and that writing is "internalized conversation re-externalized" (1984a, 641). Bruffee's theoretical rationale for collaborative learning is thus premised on three interrelated assumptions: (1) that the ability to think derives from the ability to talk with others, (2) that the kind of thinking a person engages in reflects the quality of that person's conversations with others, and (3) that the way students talk in writing groups influences the ways they will learn to think and write. But that this social process may reflect or reinforce in students' thinking and writing a social consensus on gender-based status differentials is not an issue that Bruffee speaks to.

Reasoning from the same Vygotskian concept of thought as inner speech, Anne Ruggles Gere extends Bruffee's views by drawing on Mikhail Bakhtin's theory of dialogics, which relocates meaning from the interior realm of the psyche to the outer world of social interaction. Gere concludes that Lev Vygotsky's connection of language and thinking and Bakhtin's location of meaning in social interaction together illuminate the epistemic function of conversation and its integral role in learning to write. Writing groups, she observes, "provide a forum in which individuals can practice and internalize" a particular community's language (96). That women practice and internalize the language and the conversational dynamics of patriarchal and sexist society perhaps need not be stated again, but on this point Gere is silent.

Clearly, for both Bruffee and Gere, writing groups are a locus for conversing, for thinking, and for writing—each activity mutually constituting the other. The writing group essentially becomes a microcosm of society, a kind of miniature community in which students learn to converse, internalize their conversations as dialectical thought, and then reintroduce this thought into the social sphere by writing for their peer community. For both theorists, group conversations are the starting point of much more than an exploration of students' written texts; they are the process by which meaning and knowledge are negotiated through linguistic interaction. Given this, then, Bruffee's linking of writing-group conversation to thinking processes begins to sound ominous: "The way they talk with each other," he writes, "determines the way they will think and the way they will write" (1984a, 642). And Gere's assertion of the same assumption is no less discomfiting: "The voices students hear in writing groups contribute directly to what they internalize and later use in writing" (84). The question we must ask is, What, in fact, do women hear?

While Trimbur's vision of the conversation that takes place in collaborative learning more carefully places an emphasis on its transformative capabilities, it perhaps even more ironically underscores implications for women than do Bruffee's and Gere's conceptions of conversation. Under Trimbur's notion of consensus as a tool for critical inquiry, the conversation can be "interrogated" and "interrupted" in order to expose the social injunctions and agents that delimit the act of conversation, that determine what is sayable and who may say it (612). Trimbur's foregrounding of the power relations that constitute difference and structure conversation thus more clearly parallels Freirean aims for transforming the world than do either Bruffee's or Gere's conceptions of collaborative learning:

> By organizing students non-hierarchically so that all discursive roles are available to all the participants in a group, collaborative learning can do more than model or represent the normal workings of discourse communities. Students' experience of non-domination in the collaborative classroom can offer them a critical measure to understand the distortions of communication and the plays of power in normal discourse. Replacing the "real world" authority of consensus with a rhetoric of dissensus can lead students to demystify the normal workings of discourse communities. But just as important, a rhetoric of dissensus can lead them to re-

define consensus as a utopian project, a dream of difference without domination. The participatory and democratic practices of collaborative learning offer an important instance of what Walter Benjamin ... calls the "exemplary character of production"—the collective effort to "induce other producers to produce" and to "put an improved apparatus at their disposal." ... In this regard, the exemplary character of production in collaborative learning can release collective energies to turn the means of criticism into a means of transformation, to tap fundamental impulses toward emancipation and justice in the utopian practices of Habermas' "ideal speech situation." (615)

Again, Trimbur's vision of group conversation presupposes that perspectives of difference will, in fact, be represented in a collaborative learning group, an assumption that doesn't bear up well under scrutiny. Second, I think he underestimates the extent to which a difference such as gender can influence the turns that a conversation takes and, also, the ways in which gender hierarchy in so many ways constitutes the dynamics of mixed-gender conversation. Third, Trimbur's notion that students can, in fact, be "organized non-hierarchically" by breaking down the teacher-authority/student-nonauthority duality does not acknowledge the extent to which gender hierarchy subtly structures the conversation itself. Thus, the "participatory and democratic practices" that he maintains inhere in collaborative learning—the practices that constitute a citizen's role and responsibilities—may be neither participatory nor democratic for women.

Further, the centrality of democratic practices to Trimbur's argument and his close attention to Jürgen Habermas both call for closer examination, an effort facilitated by Nancy Fraser's critique of Habermas. Fraser reconstructs the gender subtext of Habermas's critical social theory, noting that his model of social action reinforces a patriarchal division between public and private spheres because it conceals the fact of women's oppression in both (119). More to the point, she takes issue with his formulation of the "citizen" as a subject who not only has free access to public discourse but also participates in and helps shape it, observing a "conceptual dissonance between femininity and the dialogical capacities central to Habermas's conception of citizenship" (126). This dissonance, she elaborates, is borne in Habermas's failure to recognize the various gender subtexts of the roles that he describes; consequently, his conception of citizenship errs because it "depends crucially on the capacities for consent and speech, the ability to participate on a par with others in dialogue. But these are capacities that are connected with masculinity in male-dominated, classical capitalism; they are capacities that are in myriad ways denied to women and deemed at odds with femininity" (126).

Fraser also points out that while Habermas connects the citizen role to the state and public spheres, he fails to establish other important connections; thus masculinist assumptions pervade his entire conceptual framework. She elaborates on the connections that Habermas makes among his spheres:

> And in every case the links are forged in the medium of masculine gender identity rather than, as Habermas has it, in the medium of a gender-neutral power. Or if the medium of exchange here is power, then the power in question is masculine power: it is power as the expression of masculinity.
>
> ... Because his model is blind to the significance and operation of gender, it is bound to miss important features of the arrangements he wants to understand. By omitting any mention of the childrearer role and by failing to thematize the gender subtext underlying the roles of worker [masculine] and consumer [feminine], Habermas fails to understand precisely how the capitalist workplace is linked to the modern restricted male-headed nuclear family. Similarly, by failing to thematize the masculine subtext of the citizen role, he misses the full meaning of the way the state is linked to the public sphere of political speech.... He misses, too, the way the masculine citizen-speaker role links the state and the public sphere not only to each other but also to the family and the official economy—that is, the way the assumptions of man's capacity to speak and consent and woman's comparative incapacity run through all of them. (127)

Clearly, Trimbur's conception of collaborative learning shares many of the same silences that Habermas's framework contains: in particular, it assumes that society disregards gender in matters of meaning making—that women have unobstructed access to democratic discourse in society at large and in writing groups; it fails to acknowledge, that is, the gender subtext that underscores the role of citizen. Thus, Trimbur's revised notion of consensus does not satisfactorily resolve the concerns of critics like Myers, and we might be reminded of Myers's admonition that progressive pedagogies "may finally support an existing consensus and a conception of reality that supports those now in power" (171). The work of social hierarchies goes on, embodied in the participants, in the process of interaction itself, and in the pedagogy being employed, as

Myron C. Tuman also asserts: "In any pedagogical environment, even one that appears not ... to be under direct control of a supervisor ... classification and framing are nevertheless vigorously at work as agents of social power and control, tying together patterns of economic production and cultural reproduction as effectively as pedagogies based on more openly coercive practice" (46).

Conclusion

Those of us in composition studies must, as Elizabeth Flynn urges, acknowledge that women and men are socialized in different ways—that, as Nancy Chodorow, Carol Gilligan, and Mary Field Belenky and her colleagues suggest, the moral, intellectual, emotional, and social development of men and women differ in distinctive ways. We also need to continue efforts, as Elizabeth Flynn emphasizes, to establish a feminist theory of composing that acknowledges differences in thinking and writing. But we need to be careful. Several studies of gender difference do not address the origin of these differences in gender hierarchy and, thus, can easily be appropriated to serve ends that reinforce, under the label of "difference," women's subordinate status.[5] The mere statement of difference conceals, among other things, the role that gender ideology— the structures of male dominance, the sexual division of labor, and the social rituals that constitute and reinforce both—plays in both creating difference and perpetuating the concept of difference.

Further, the mere fact of difference conceals the extent to which collaborative learning is inscribed by this system and, thus, conceals its complicity in perpetuating it. At issue here is not just difference but status, the power difference that constitutes in part the ideology of gender. For communicative situations such as the conversation of writing groups, this means that the power difference which inheres in gender is a variable that cannot be disregarded. As the studies considered above suggest, the dynamics of conversation are influenced by the gender of the speaker and the gender of the spoken to; the power differential that corresponds to gender thus takes on increasing significance. Given, then, the fact of difference and the fact of status and power difference, we ought not to assume that in writing-group conversations men and women interact in identical or equal ways. The students who engage in such conversations cannot be conflated under the rubric of *student;* as women and men, they are gender-differentiated and, consequently, status-differentiated. Ignoring these issues, then, means that we may be directly instrumental in teaching women a limited subject position from which to write, not only in encouraging them to assume "appropriately feminine" voices and stances as they compose—rhetorical personae that mirror and reproduce the social and political status of women in society at large—but in unwittingly teaching them to accept their subordinate place in the social hierarchy of gender.

Although my focus here has been on gender, I am not denying that other social factors—among them race, ethnicity, sexual orientation, age, occupation, class—influence the idealized conversational space envisioned by collaborative learning proponents; certainly they do, as others have suggested. Nor am I making a case here for returning to traditional, more authoritarian pedagogies that are likewise implicated in the process of reproducing gender ideology. The problems women encounter in the academy and in classrooms, regardless of the particular pedagogy that structures them, are documented in such studies as *The Classroom Climate: A Chilly One for Women?* (Hall and Sandler) and *The Campus Climate Revisited: Chilly for Women Faculty, Administrators, and Graduate Students* (Sandler and Hall). But to remain silent on the ways that writing groups, too, can create chilly conditions for women is to perpetuate the legacy of silence that assures that these processes will continue unchecked. What I would like to suggest is that we begin to acknowledge and examine more closely the ways that gender influences classroom interaction and that we check some of our unfettered enthusiasm for collaborative pedagogies. Even as we continue to try to break down hierarchies and empower students through collaborative practices, we need to remain aware of subtler workings of hierarchy as students interact.

Obviously, the implications of a gender critique of collaborative learning are important for disciplines other than our own. But they are especially important for us in composition studies, a discipline that seeks to teach writers to create the kinds of rhetorical stances and voices that will allow them in writing to interact effectively with others in other discourse communities in other settings—to participate in and even change the written "conversations" of their personal, academic, and professional worlds. We especially need to learn much more about the reproduction of ideology that takes place in educational settings, and our collaborative classrooms are a good place to begin understanding how the socially mandated work of gender ideology continues on, shaping our lives for us and, through us, the lives of others.

NOTES

I would like to thank Gary A. Olson for reading drafts of this article and offering much helpful advice.

1. The views of these critics are also to be found in *College English* (see Bibliography). Other scholars, too numerous to list, have also addressed collaborative learning, but those mentioned here are directly participating in what might be called a conversation, many of their views articulated in the journal's "Comment and Response" section. In addition, an earlier version of Bruffee's article, "Peer Tutoring and the 'Conversation of Mankind,'" appeared in *Writing Centers: Theory and Administration.*

2. While the notion of *difference* that Myers, Trimbur, and others invoke includes such factors as race and class, the focus of this chapter is on gender. Gerda Lerner is helpful on this point:

> The term "oppression of women" inevitably conjures up comparison with the other oppressed groups and leads one to think in terms of comparing the various degrees of oppression as though one were dealing with similar groups.... [This is] misleading and irrelevant. The differences in the status of women and that of members of oppressed minority groups, or even majority groups such as "the colonized," are so essential that it is inappropriate to use the same term to describe all of them. The dominance of one half of humankind over the other is qualitatively different from any other form of dominance, and our terminology should make that clear. (233–34)

3. The studies presented here represent only a sampling of such research. Excellent bibliographies appear in Thorne and Henley; Thorne, Kramarae, and Henley; and Dion. For other helpful overviews, see Graddol and Swann, as well as Poynton.

4. Other sociologists, such as Deborah Tannen and Daniel N. Maltz and Ruth A. Borker, provide alternative explanations for such behavior in conversations between men and women, positing "cultural" difference as the primary factor. Maltz and Borker explain this perspective:

> We place the stress not on psychological differences or power differentials, although these may make some contribution, but rather in a notion of cultural differences between men and women in their conceptions of friendly conversation, their rules for engaging in it, and, probably most important, their rules for interpreting it. We argue that American men and women come from different sociolinguistic subcultures, having learned to do different things with words in a conversation, so that when they attempt to carry on conversations with one another, even if both parties are attempting to treat one another as equals, cultural miscommunication results. (199–200)

This explanation, it seems to me, begs the questions of why these particular cultural differences situate men in a hierarchically superior position and why the interactive problems cited in such conversations take the particular form that they do.

5. Lerner is helpful on this point as well:

> Men and women are biologically different, but . . . the values and implications based on that difference are the result of culture. Whatever differences are discernible in the present in regard to men-as-a-group and women-as-a-group are the result of the particular history of women, which is essentially different from the history of men. This is due to the subordination of women to men, which is older than civilization, and to the denial of women's history. The existence of women's history has been obscured and neglected by patriarchal thought, a fact which has significantly affected the psychology of men and women. (6)

BIBLIOGRAPHY

Annas, Pamela J. "Silences: Feminist Language Research and the Teaching of Writing." In *Teaching Writing,* edited by Caywood and Overing, 3–17. 1987.

Baumlin, James S., and Tita French Baumlin. "Psyche/Logos: Mapping the Terrains of Mind and Rhetoric." *College English* 51 (1989): 256–61.

Beade, Pedro. "Comment and Response." *College English* 49 (1987): 707–08.

Belenky, Mary Field, Blythe McVicker Clinchy, Nancy Rule Goldberger, and Jill Mattuck Tarule. *Women's Ways of Knowing: The Development of Self, Voice, and Mind.* New York: Basic Books, 1986.

Bizzell, Patricia. Review of *Invention as a Social Act,* by Karen Burke LeFevre. *College Composition and Communication* 38 (1987): 485–86.

Bleich, David. "Sexism in Academic Styles of Learning." *Journal of Advanced Composition* 10 (1990): 231–47.

Bruffee, Kenneth A. "Collaborative Learning and 'The Conversation of Mankind.'" *College English* 46 (1984a): 635–52.

———. "Peer Tutoring and the 'Conversation of Mankind.'" In *Writing Centers: Theory and Administration,* edited by Gary A. Olson. Urbana, Ill.: NCTE, 1984b.

Cayton, Mary Kupiec. "What Happens When Things Go Wrong: Women and Writing Blocks." *Journal of Advanced Composition* 10 (1990): 321–37.

Caywood, Cynthia L., and Gillian R. Overing, eds. *Teaching Writing: Pedagogy, Gender, and Equity.* Albany: State Univ. of New York Press, 1987.

Chodorow, Nancy. *The Reproduction of Mothering: Psychoanalysis and the Sociology of Gender.* Berkeley and Los Angeles: Univ. of California Press, 1978.

Cooper, Marilyn M. "Women's Ways of Writing." In Marilyn M. Cooper and Michael Holzman, *Writing as Social Action,* 141–56. Portsmouth, N.H.: Heinemann-Boynton/Cook, 1989.

Culley, Margo, and Catherine Portuges, eds. *Gendered Subjects: The Dynamics of Feminist Teaching.* Boston: Routledge and Kegan Paul, 1985.

Dion, Kenneth L. "Sex, Gender, and Groups: Selected Issues." In *Women, Gender, and Social Psychology,* edited by Virginia E. O'Leary, Rhoda Kesler Unger, and Barbara Strudler Wallston, 293–347. Hillsdale, N.J.: Lawrence Erlbaun and Assoc., 1985.

Fishman, Pamela. "Interaction: The Work Women Do." *Social Problems* 25 (1978): 297–406.

———. "Conservational Insecurity." In *Languages,* edited by Giles, Robinson, and Smith, 127–32. 1980.

———. "Interaction: The Work Women Do." in In *Languages, Gender, and Society,* edited by Thorne, Kramarae, and Henley, 89–101. 1983.

Flynn, Elizabeth A. "Composing as a Woman." *College Composition and Communication* 39 (1988): 423–35.

Foster, David. "Comment and Response." *College English* 49 (1987): 709–11.

Fraser, Nancy. *Unruly Practices: Power, Discourse, and Gender in Contemporary Social Theory.* Minneapolis: Univ. of Minnesota Press, 1989.

Frey, Olivia. "Equity and Peace in the New Writing Class." In *Teaching Writing,* edited by Caywood and Overing, 93–105. 1987.

Friedman, Susan Stanford. "Authority in the Feminist Classroom: A Contradiction in Terms?" In *Gendered Subjects,* edited by Culley and Portuges, 203–08. 1985.

Gere, Anne Ruggles. *Writing Groups: History, Theory, and Implications.* Carbondale: Southern Illinois Univ. Press, 1987.

Giles, Howard, W. Peter Robinson, and Philip M. Smith, eds. *Language: Social Psychological Perspectives.* Oxford: Pergamon, 1980.

Gilligan, Carol. *In a Different Voice: Psychological Theory and Women's Development.* Cambridge: Harvard Univ. Press, 1982.

Goulston, Wendy. "Women Writing." In *Teaching Writing,* edited by Caywood and Overing, 19–29. 1987.

Graddol, David, and Joan Swann. *Gender Voices.* Oxford: Basil Blackwell, 1989.

Hall, Roberta M., and Bernice R. Sandler. *The Classroom Climate: A Chilly One for Women?* Washington, D.C.: Association of American Colleges, 1982.

Howe, Florence. "Identity and Expression: A Writing Course for Women." *College English* 32 (1971): 863–71.

Johnson, Thomas S. "Comment and Response." *College English* 48 (1986): 76.

Leet-Pellegrini, Helena M. "Conversational Dominance as a Function of Gender and Expertise." In *Language,* edited by Giles, Robinson, and Smith, 97–104. 1980.

Lerner, Gerda. *The Creation of Patriarchy.* New York: Oxford Univ. Press, 1986.

Maher, Frances. "Classroom Pedagogy and the New Scholarship on Women." In *Gendered Subjects,* edited by Culley and Portuges, 29–48. 1985.

Maltz, Daniel N., and Ruth A. Borker. "A Cultural Approach to Male-Female Miscommunication." In *Language and Social Identity,* edited by John J. Gumperz, 196–216. Cambridge: Cambridge Univ. Press, 1982.

Mielke, Robert. "Revisionist Theory on Moral Development and Its Impact upon Pedagogical and Departmental Practice." In *Teaching Writing,* edited by Caywood and Overing, 171–78. 1987.

Myers, Greg. "Reality, Consensus, and Reform in the Rhetoric of Composition Teaching." *College English* 48 (1986): 154–74.

Poynton, Cate. *Language and Gender: Making the Difference.* Oxford: Oxford Univ. Press, 1989.

Rich, Adrienne. "Taking Women Students Seriously." In *On Lies, Secrets, and Silence: Selected Prose 1966–1978*. New York: W. W. Norton, 1979.

Sandler, Bernice R., and Roberta M. Hall. *The Campus Climate Revisited: Chilly for Women Faculty, Administrators, and Graduate Students*. Washington, D.C.: Association of American Colleges, 1986.

Spender, Dale. *Invisible Women—The Schooling Scandal*. London: Writers and Readers Publishing Cooperative, 1982.

Spender, Dale, and Elizabeth Sarah. *Learning to Lose*. London: Women's Press, 1980.

Stanger, Carol A. "The Sexual Politics of the One-to-One Tutorial Approach and Collaborative Learning." In *Teaching Writing*, edited by Caywood and Overing, 31–44. 1987.

Tannen, Deborah. *You Just Don't Understand: Women and Men in Conversation*. New York: William Morrow, 1990.

Thorne, Barrie, and Nancy Henley, eds. *Language and Sex: Difference and Dominance*. Rowley, Mass.: Newbury, 1975.

Thorne, Barrie, Cheris Kramarae, and Nancy Henley. *Language, Gender, and Society*. Rowley, Mass.: Newbury, 1983.

Trimbur, John. "Consensus and Difference in Collaborative Learning." *College English* 51 (1989): 602–16.

Tuman, Myron C. "Class, Codes, and Composition: Basil Bernstein and the Critique of Pedagogy." *College Composition and Communication* 39 (1988): 42–51.

West, Candace. "Not Just 'Doctors' Orders': Directive-Response Sequences in Patients' Visits to Women and Men Physicians." *Discourse and Society* 1.1 (1990): 85–112.

West, Candace, and Don H. Zimmerman. "Small Insults: A Study of Interruptions in Cross-Sex Conversations between Unacquainted Persons." In *Language, Gender, and Society*, edited by Thorne, Kramarae and Henley, 102–17. 1983.

Zimmerman, Don H., and Candace West. "Sex Roles, Interruptions, and Silences in Conversation." In *Language and Sex*, edited by Thorne and Henley, 105–29. 1975.

2

Praising Folly: Constructing a Postmodern Rhetorical Authority as a Woman

Patricia Bizzell

This chapter begins in our postmodern climate of skepticism. Although this skepticism has served us well in promoting critiques of prevailing oppressive ideologies, it is becoming dangerous because it is helping to block the possibilities for reconstituting new, more just social orders. To move toward more just social arrangements, I want to find a way to oppose postmodern skepticism with a new kind of ethical authority that does not repeat the oppressive foundational tactics of the ideologies that skepticism has helped to call into question. I am trying to formulate this new kind of authority as *rhetorical authority.*

I came upon a new angle of approach to rhetorical authority while doing historical research for my recent book, *The Rhetorical Tradition,* edited with Bruce Herzberg. When I read *The Praise of Folly* by Erasmus, for some reason I identified with the female persona, named Folly, that he chose to deliver this mock encomium. I was especially struck by the image of her that is presented in Hans Holbein's illustrations for an early edition of *Praise:* a woman in a fool's cap and bells and an academic gown, speaking from a rostrum to an audience of similarly attired men. Perhaps it was this academic connection that made me wonder whether the traditional figure of the fool might provide a means of addressing this problem of skepticism, whether the fool might provide some models for rhetorical authority. Folly's gender, although not much noticed in critical commentaries on Erasmus, also made me wonder whether traditional views of the woman speaking in public are allied to the fool in suggestive ways.[1] By analyzing the image of the foolish woman speaking in public, I hope to sketch a persona for an effective wielder of rhetorical authority.

I see postmodern skepticism as dangerous to the collective life because it tears down but does not build up. This is a skepticism that excels in deconstructing oppressive ideologies or worldviews but despairs of achieving utopian ideologies or framing and propagating egalitarian worldviews. This skepticism no longer acts only as a solvent of received wisdom, creating a principled position from which oppressive structures may be critiqued. Rather, this skepticism has reached the point where the possibility of any kind of wisdom or trustworthy knowledge is disclaimed (see Jeff Smith).

This skepticism creates a dangerous atmosphere in the academy as well. For example, recent discussions of the state of English studies have called attention to our extreme disunity and dissension. Moreover, this condition is often treated as praiseworthy, characteristic of the "best" English departments, those that have kept up with the times by tenuring adherents of all the many warring theoretical schools. Gerald Graff would have us teach these conflicts—make the airing of our differences into a curriculum, but this presents a great challenge when we find it so difficult to air our differences in other than a contentious way. The typical "good" English department today seems to be a place where everyone is constantly, minutely examining everyone else for signs of sins, whether of omission or commission, against the currently correct theoretical positions. Sometimes I feel as if I'm in a medieval monastery where sniffing the bread baking as I walk by the kitchen will get me twenty lashes for gluttony. This is not an atmosphere likely to attract many students to what Graff calls "the life of books" (5).

More important, I'm suspicious of a curriculum purporting merely to teach "difference," because it elides political issues. Skeptical pluralism is not of much use to English studies in combatting what I take to be the radically unjust national and global social order of our day. Jackson Lears remarks, in commenting on the manifestations of postmodern skepticism in popular culture: "We are left with a form of domination that seems at once archaic and peculiarly modern—one that is dependent not on the imposition of belief but on the *absence* of belief, the creation of a void in which only power matters" (60; emphasis in original). And as hegemonic political and economic forces continue to narrow our hopes for decent lives for everyone, with nuclear threats and environmental destruction in the name of national security driving out all thoughts of our need for common security, so too hegemonic cultural forces inscribe divisive, denigrating ideologies into the ethical void of the individual skeptic's consciousness.

This skepticism needs to be countered by a worldview that includes affirmations of egalitarian values; that can be broadly shared among human groups and yet is arrived at consensually, through the participation of as many human groups as possible; and that attracts belief from these groups precisely because it is seen as a collective social construct, not a transcendent system both originating and imposed from on high. The generation and propagation of such a socially constructed worldview would require the operation of an authority powerful enough to resist skepticism yet not operating in such a way as to destroy the consensual processes that are fundamental to that worldview.

In other words, this new authority would have to be antifoundationalist: that is, it would have to be an authority that does not base its credibility claims on possession of any absolute knowledge, the truth of which is presumed to transcend historical circumstances and to compel assent from all normally rational beings. Postmodern skepticism has convincingly argued that foundational authority claims tend to conceal and serve the interests of politically oppressive human groups. I do not want to set aside this argument.

The authority I seek would also have to be antiessentialist, in the sense that it would not base its credibility claims on possession of knowledge that is presumed to be knowable only by one group by virtue of its members' material circumstances, whether these circumstances be, for example, the bare facts of race or gender or the interpretations currently placed on such facts by the dominant culture. An essentialist authority would begin by excluding certain groups from the consensual process, but I am not yet ready to give up the hope of a more inclusive process. In this sense, I am in agreement with one strand of bell hooks's argument in *Talking Back,* where she contends that feminist discourse must not be limited to biological females or discourse on race to so-called people of color.

Some of my recent work (1988, Bizzell 1990) has tried to define this new form of authority under the rubric of rhetorical authority. Rhetorical authority works to gain agreement by pointing out or creating relations between the rhetor's values and the values of his or her interlocutors. For example, a rhetor discussing sexual equality with interlocutors who believe in sexism might ask whether these people also value general human equality and fair play. The rhetor could suggest a contradiction between these values and sexism and argue that sexism must be abandoned. In this example, rhetor and interlocutors already share some values, such as a commitment to general human equality. In the absence of any shared values, rhetorical authority cannot operate; but in their presence, rhetorical authority is freed from the charge of operating manipulatively, because the rhetor participates in and is affected by the worldviews of the interlocutors and is, in theory, as susceptible as they are to change as a result of the rhetorical process. Arguing with someone always entails the risk—or opportunity—of being converted.

This rhetorical process encourages all participants to become conscious of the values they hold and to attempt to construct consistent positions from which to speak, "as a woman," for example, or "as an African-American" (see Alcoff). These positions are related to the individual's membership in some human group but also point outward, to focus on how the individual-as-a-member-of-this-group relates to members of other groups.

It may not be clear at this point how my notion of rhetorical authority differs in its broad outlines from any currently correct postmodern account of persuasion. In general, rhetorical authority partakes of the theory of socially constructed belief; but so far, this definition of rhetorical authority predicts nothing about what values will be constructed. It seems that, in theory, rhetorical authority could work just as well to unite fascists in a project to exterminate racial and religious minorities as it could to unite socialists in an effort to create a more egalitarian economic order. Indeed, rhetoric has often been condemned on grounds that it might be used for immoral ends.

And yet I personally want to foster socialist projects and to rule out those of a fascist nature. I have been told by a man who is an ultracorrect postmodernist that my idea of rhetorical authority is "sentimental." Perhaps he refers to my tendency in recent essays to elide the problem of what values get constructed by loading my perorations with language that evokes projects of a socialist nature, without explicitly showing how rhetorical authority could foster them. Indeed, being in theory, though not in life, a thoroughgoing postmodern skeptic, my friend doubts whether it is possible, or even desirable, to induce belief in anything at all.

I, on the other hand, still hope to find a way to link the notion of rhetorical authority specifically to values I favor, at least a large, loose constellation of values, if not a narrowly specific program. Perhaps the persona of the fool has gathered social implications that would link rhetorical authority—if wielded by a fool—to egalitarian or socialistic worldviews. I have also come to suspect that a woman might be the most effective performer of the fool persona today. Women's suitability to play the fool arises from long-standing prohibitions that brand as unchaste any woman who practices rhetoric in public and from the very recent arrival of a historical moment in which such prohibitions can be deconstructed.

Women and Fools

Women have been virtually prohibited from practicing rhetoric in public, from ancient Greek times to, in some ways, the present day, although there is considerable debate among historians concerning how much education women may have received in a given period, how much women may have known about rhetoric, and how much they may have practiced it in private. At any rate, if one searches the history of rhetoric in all the obvious places for evidence of contributions by women, what one is likely to find instead are explanations as to why there couldn't be any such contributions.

This apparent absence should not be surprising, considering that the usual punishment for defying prohibitions against women's use of rhetoric in public has been to be labeled unchaste. This is an intriguingly gender-specific sanction. On the one hand, one must by definition be a sexed being in order to be susceptible to the charge of unchastity, and this charge is almost always applied only to women. On the other hand, to be charged with unchastity is to be unsexed, in the sense that the unchaste woman has had her sex held up to public scrutiny as worthless. Restrictions on women's use of rhetoric have tended to prohibit public speaking and publishing by women, while permitting private speaking and writing or even defining such private discourse positively as women's sphere (see, for example, Renaissance etiquette books such as Christine de Pisan's). It is precisely the woman's emergence into a public forum that makes her liable to the charge of unchastity, that is, the rendering of her sex as something public and publicly devalued.

For example, in the Renaissance, women, mostly upper-middle-class and aristocratic women, were frequently educated in the new humanist learning along with their brothers (see Bizzell and Herzberg). Women learned mathematics, astronomy, Latin, and Greek—subjects that had been (and would become again) virtually all-male preserves. But as Anthony Grafton and Lisa Jardine point out, humanist educators who advocated this expanded curriculum for women, such as Leonardo Bruni and Juan Luis Vives, nevertheless specifically prohibited the study of rhetoric. Women were to study and practice in all areas of humanist learning except for this central area; and women who attempted to practice rhetoric in public were severely condemned. Woman humanist Isotta Nogarola attempted to enter the public sphere of scholarly correspondence by addressing a letter to male humanist Guarino da Verona. He delayed long enough in answering her letter to make it seem like an improper advance rather than a scholarly inquiry, and Nogarola was attacked in broadsides that accused her of incest and prostitution and averred that an eloquent woman is never chaste.

The only Renaissance women permitted to speak in public were monarchs who happened to be female, such as Elizabeth of England, and precocious young humanist students, such as Cassandra Fedele, who were required to desist upon physical maturity and marriage. Walter Ong's thesis in *Fighting for Life* suggests a possible reason for these exceptions: they applied to women who, by reason of social position or age, could be considered outside the realm of adult male combat played out in rhetoric. The adult woman who entered the arena of rhetorical combat unprotected by great political authority risked being treated like the only female player in a touch football game—and what chaste woman would take such a risk?

The preoccupation with keeping women out of public discourse may have contributed to what Stephanie Jed describes as a Renaissance obsession with Livy's story of the Roman matron Lucretia. The story begins when Lucretia wins a chastity contest. A group of aristocratic husbands, returning home unexpectedly to see what their wives are doing in their absence, find Lucretia the only one not carousing. The sight of her inflames one of the inquisitorial men, Sextus Tarquinius, son of the tyrant then ruling Rome, and he returns later and rapes her. Lucretia then summons a small audience comprising her husband, other male relatives, and male family friends, including Lucius Junius Brutus. Although this audience is assembled in private, she delivers a forensic speech, a public genre, arguing that she, as well as her rapist, must die to avenge this crime against chastity. Lucretia rejects the men's arguments that she should not be punished for a crime of which she was a passive victim. She concludes her oration by stabbing herself. Brutus pulls the knife from her throat and vows to use it to drive the Tarquins from Rome, which he does, thereby inaugurating the Republic. The story concludes by depicting Lucretia as a patriotic heroine, since her death facilitated the establishment of the Republic by inspiring the men who founded it.

Renaissance painters often depicted the story of Lucretia, as art historian Cristelle Baskins has pointed out, on the panels of cassoni, wooden chests presented to women upon marriage. Baskins argues that the wedding-chest evocations of Lucretia are meant to remind married women of the importance of preserving their chastity by remaining in the private, not the public, sphere. Although male humanists commonly composed self-accusatory forensic speeches for Lucretia in rhetorical exercises, women did not see Lucretia speaking on their wedding chests. Rather, in the panels in which Lucretia is alive, she is portrayed in private, at home, being raped or committing suicide. When Lucretia is shown in public, she is shown dead, her body exposed like that of a criminal. Botticelli's rendering of the story of Lucretia uses perspective in two side panels to represent the fatal penetrations of Lucretia's body in the rape and suicide scenes through the invasion of private space by intruding men—her rapist and her forensic audience. In the central panel, Lucretia's limp body is in the foreground, and Brutus, behind her, appears to be standing on her as he orates. (This painting, a triptych, is in the Gardner Museum in Boston.)

A woman would, indeed, have to be a fool to speak in public, if to do so means incurring such sanctions. But suppose she chooses to be a fool. What does it mean to be a fool? William Willeford's cross-cultural study of the fool figure suggests a number of general characteristics. For one thing, the fool must exhibit himself in public. He makes a spectacle of himself, typically dressing in a way that attracts attention. Moreover, his conspicuous dress typically exhibits a lack of all social sense—he happily shows himself in rags a decent person would be ashamed of, or he wears a motley that defies resolution into the pattern of any known garment. He presents as physically or mentally handicapped, as effeminate or actually a woman, usually a whore, or as a character in blackface. He flaunts his ignorance of the social conventions that militate against making an exhibition of oneself. And if we watch with amusement, we permit this violation of convention. This makes us complicit in his exhibition.

In his exhibition, the fool typically acts out mockeries of powerful psychic and social forces. He mocks our anxieties about sexual attractiveness and potency by making exaggerated and always unsuccessful efforts to win someone's sexual favors. He mocks our fear of death by struggling with exaggerated and bathetic forces of dissolution—machines battle him malevolently, chance perches him in positions of extreme danger. He mocks our deference to authority figures in his portrayals of the father, the policeman, the king, and the priest; the devil himself is depicted as a red-faced buffoon headed for a pratfall. In modern terms, we might say that the fool is associated with the discourse of the Other. He is allowed to wander over boundaries supposedly held inviolable; and again, insofar as we watch without preventing the violation, we become complicit in it.

Willeford suggests that the fool's mockeries perform two seemingly contradictory functions. On the one hand, the fool's discourse is an outlet for genuine rebellion, whether psychic revenge taken against the biological forces finite humans are heir to or the expression of social and political views that the authorities would like to silence. A well-known instance of this rebellious function is the fool in *King Lear,* who provides the old man with support in his physical frailty—thus mocking death—while at the same time comes closer than anyone else to letting the king know just how his political policy has gone disastrously wrong—thus expressing views Lear has forcibly silenced in other speakers.

On the other hand, the fool's discourse performs a scapegoat function. Rather than expressing genuine rebellion, however indirectly, the fool staves off rebellion and its potentially dangerous consequences by acting out a mock rebellion that can be seen as ineffectual. According to Willeford, this is why kings kept fools. It is as if the existence of authority automatically invokes rebellion against it, and therefore, the society that wishes to remain stable hastens to fill the role of rebel with someone who is, by definition, incapable of really rebelling—the fool. The public exhibition of a fool who defied him was thus a guarantor of the king's power; conversely, authorities who react with disproportionate violence to mock attacks thereby show their weakness. Here we might say that the discourse of the Other suffers an inevitable co-optation.

Being a fool also usually means being male, as implied in the title of Willeford's study, *The Fool and His Scepter.* Willeford even derives the word *fool* from the Latin for *scrotum* (11). The male fool has special affinities with nonfoolish women, however. Fools and women are associated both with forces of destruction, as represented by the fool's function as a genuine rebel and by women's uncontrolled and licentious sexuality, and with forces of preservation or creation, as represented by the fool's function as a pretend rebel and by women's licit and procreative sexuality. Society allows the fool to display his affinity with these forces while strictly controlling women's association with them, especially through marriage laws. But though the fool never achieves sexual union with a nonfoolish woman, as speakers of cognate discourses of the Other they seem more like coconspirators than erotic combatants. Indeed,

Willeford is much struck by the fact that Lear's fool and his daughter Cordelia are never onstage at the same time, which fact has caused some Shakespeare scholars to speculate that the two characters may have been played by the same actor.

This discursive union of the fool and the woman occurs even more explicitly in the figure of the female fool. One example of the female fool given by Willeford is a figure called Mother Folly. Late medieval and Renaissance carnivals often took the form of systematic mockeries of male religious and secular authorities, each of whom was represented by a burlesque figure. Set over these mock authorities, however, at the top of the mock hierarchy, was Mother Folly (probably enacted by a cross-dressed male). Willeford says that Mother Folly exhibited the characteristics most strongly forbidden to women, and his catalog of these characteristics is interesting: Mother Folly was given to "jealous rage" rather than "selfless maternal compassion," "whorishness" not "chastity," and "mindless chattering" rather than the "silently contained inner knowledge" exemplified by the Virgin Mary at the Annunciation (177). Her impassioned and copious flow of language was associated with sexual misconduct.

Imagine Mother Folly performing both functions Willeford finds typical of the fool figure, expressing genuine rebellion against the natural and social orders and also enacting a mock rebellion that preserves the status quo. Because she is a female, might not her rebellion appear even more rebellious than that of the male fool? For it involves flouting an additional social convention, one he does not have to contend with: the prohibition against women speaking in public for any reason. And might not her sacrificial support of the status quo seem to be somewhat less efficacious than that of the male fool, somewhat more doubtful in its ultimately benevolent effect? For as a woman, a member of an oppressed group, she has less stake in the social order, less to gain from preserving it: as Freud said, woman is a barbarian. And yet, insofar as the female fool can be said to perform this second function at all, she, like the male fool, maintains the possibility of social regeneration in the wake of the criticisms launched in her genuinely rebellious discourse of the Other.

Erasmus's Woman Fool

There is a long-standing interpretive problem concerning *The Praise of Folly:* Erasmus is commenting on his own skepticism here, but what is he saying? The Folly persona is usually identified with the prudence or *phronesis*—that is, reliance on probable knowledge—to which Erasmus's skepticism inclines him; and Folly's rhetorical practice is usually identified with the kind of rhetoric Erasmus sees as a crucial way of constructing probable knowledge and persuading people to action based on probable knowledge. But to call prudence folly and to present rhetoric as the effusions of a loquacious female seems a strikingly vicious attack on these mainstays of Erasmus's skepticism.

More precisely, we are not sure which of two versions of skepticism Erasmus means to endorse. He and other early Renaissance humanists are usually associated with a form of so-called Academic skepticism. Academic skepticism denies the availability of absolute or transcendent truths but asserts that human beings can know probable knowledge, truths that are provisional yet trustworthy enough to be used as the basis for responsible civic action. This probable knowledge is discovered rhetorically, as human beings, who are all assumed to have mental powers capable of making reasonable judgments, review their experience together in light of shared values.

Thus Academic skepticism criticizes received wisdom and destabilizes foundational beliefs so that this rhetorical process can occur, the ultimate justification for which is responsible civic action. Prudence is supposed to equip every citizen to participate in the conduct of a government that will, because of this democratic participation, serve the interests of all. But if political conditions change such that prudential civic action becomes impossible, for example under a dictatorship, then the effort—and risk—involved in destabilizing old knowledge and creating new knowledge may seem not worth incurring.

But even if one feels that it is no longer possible or desirable to undertake the rhetorical process for which Academic skepticism clears the ground, one may still be unable to give up the skeptical, critical turn of mind. Now, however, one's skepticism tears down without building up. Skepticism thus creates an ethical void in which only power matters, a transformation exemplified in later Renaissance rhetorical theory, such as Machiavelli's recommendation that the ruler use rhetoric to subjugate his people, or Montaigne's impotent belletrism. In such a climate, the skeptic may even come to doubt that people share either the mental capacity to make reasonable judgments or the values to interpret experience. In short, the skeptic comes to doubt that people can know anything at all; this is the Pyrrhonistic version of skepticism.

Readers have disagreed as to whether in *The Praise of Folly* Erasmus is endorsing Academic skepticism as usual or veering into Pyrrhonistic skepticism. Folly's praise of prudence and rhetoric is presumably meant to be taken ironically, as blame, since she is by definition an untrustworthy evaluator, a fool. But—if Erasmus is endorsing Academic skepticism—are we to see this blame as merely a joke, a sort of good-natured poking of fun at his own philosophical pretensions? Or—if Erasmus is endorsing Pyrrhonistic skepticism—should this blame be taken seriously?

Most readers experience Folly's mock praise as varying considerably in tone through what seem to be three major sections of the work, making it more difficult to pinpoint what is being endorsed or condemned. In the first section, Folly's praise of her followers among ordinary people puts these adherents of prudence in a pejorative light that, nevertheless, seems warm and indulgent, not really pejorative at all. Prudence is shown to facilitate the enjoyment of life-cycle events, such as courtship, which may be undignified yet make possible the continuation of the species. In the second section, Folly's praise of her followers among religious and secular leaders seems more harsh in tone. But it is not clear whether the leaders are being indicted for their adherence to prudence, with its necessarily limited conception of knowledge, or for their neglect of prudence as it should operate to help them discharge the social responsibilities they flout. Finally, in the third section, prudence seems to be set aside completely, as Folly praises her Christian followers for ignoring social conventions as they seek the disembodied bliss of union with the Divine. Here Folly's tone sounds like sincere, not ironic, praise, and Christ is presented as the prime example of the Christian fool.

One way of interpreting the vacillations of *Praise* is to treat Folly's backhanded endorsement of prudence in the first section as dominant in the entire work. Moreover, the couching of this endorsement in a virtuoso display of ironic rhetoric can be taken to imply an endorsement of rhetoric, or of a particular kind of rhetoric. Folly announces early on that she intends to "play the sophist" (Erasmus 10) and proceeds to demonstrate how to argue all sides of a question and to force the reader who attempts to make sense of her varying tones to see all sides of a question, too.[2] Victoria Kahn suggests, in contrast, that while Erasmus does endorse prudence and rhetoric in the first section of *Praise,* he talks himself out of this endorsement in the second section, in which rhetoric is shown to be inadequate to persuade social leaders to act prudently. It is as if Erasmus comes to doubt human abilities to attain even the limited, probable knowledge his skepticism has already suggested is all we are capable of—in other words, he moves from Academic to Pyrrhonistic skepticism. We might speculate that this transition in Erasmus's thinking reflects political changes in the mid Renaissance toward more authoritarian and militaristic forms of government, in which prudential civic action became increasingly impossible for the ordinary citizen. Hence according to Kahn, in the third section of *Praise,* Christian faith is offered as an alternative to skeptical prudence and wordless bliss as an alternative to rhetoric.

Critics have not much attended to the implications of Folly's gender for interpretations of Erasmus's skepticism. To Renaissance readers, and perhaps others as well, she would be considered unchaste because she is speaking in public. If we adhere to the first reading, in support of Academic skepticism, we might imagine this unchaste speaker as a lovable doxy, a playful illustration of the charms of both the mundane life governed by prudence and the humanistically learned rhetoric that seduces us to prudence. Folly, in this view, is a bit of an actress. Indeed, she bows out of her encomium with a formula often used to conclude a play (see Miller, 138 and n. 1), and theatrical images abound in *Praise* (see Miller, 42–44). The actress Folly perpetrates harmless, enjoyable delusions, that is, the prudential knowledge on which we limited humans must base our lives. Christian bliss, on this reading, is merely one more pleasurable delusion.

If, however, we see Erasmus renouncing Academic skepticism here in favor of the gloomier Pyrrhonistic skepticism and ultimately in favor of a glorified Christianity, Folly looks different. Her unchastity becomes not something she chooses because it is pleasurable but rather a deplorable condition she is forced into, just as Erasmus is forced to abandon Academic skepticism and flee to Christianity, by the extreme human limitations that make the attainment of even probable knowledge impossible. We might imagine, in other words, that Folly is unchaste because she is a victim of rape, an act motivated by another human limitation, lust. Folly, as an unchaste woman speaking in public, emerges in public to use her eloquence only to argue that, because of her condition of impurity, she must be put to death—that is, rejected in favor of Christianity. This view sees Folly as a type of Lucretia.

In this reading there is a tragedy of knowledge of the sort Mario Untersteiner attributes to the early Greek Sophist Gorgias. Moving through increasingly skeptical positions, Erasmus brings himself to the point that he must treat something improbable as proved, that is, he must accept Christ's power as an absolute. He accepts this with full awareness that it marks the suicide of his skeptically inquiring self. He cannot even remain in the realm of probable knowledge, for which there are reasonable grounds for assent, but must make his last reasonable act the assent to an unreasonable position—the self-imposed noble lie—which he now deems necessary in order to have any kind of knowledge at all. He thus creates despairing grounds for faith, a move that, my colleagues at Holy Cross tell me, awakens a shock of recognition in contemporary Christians.

The Woman Rhetor and Postmodern Skepticism

My purpose here is not to decide what form of skepticism Erasmus endorses in *The Praise of Folly* but rather to explore the question of what interest this work might hold for postmodern rhetors committed to left-oriented or liberatory political values. Erasmus is suggestive because his philosophical predicament and his approaches to it seem to have so many affinities with our own. Deconstruction has been our Academic skepticism, criticizing received wisdom and destabilizing traditional foundations of belief. Many of us have experienced the deconstructive perspective as a liberating one, freeing us from traditional forms of discrimination or, if not entirely freeing us, enabling us to distance ourselves from them and create a space in which people who share egalitarian social values can work for change (for an articulation of such a relation between deconstruction and Marxism, see Michael Ryan).

Perhaps like Erasmus, however, we have lived through historical period in which our opportunities for responsible civic action have been diminished radically. Between the 1960s and the 1990s, large-scale political resistance to oppressive ideologies seems to have dwindled to small local pockets or rearguard actions. Democratic protest could once truncate the careers of Lyndon Johnson and Richard Nixon, whereas Ronald Reagan and George Bush recently reigned virtually unopposed. More specifically, we could once see our workplaces, the college campuses, as important sites of egalitarian political resistance; now they are more likely to be stages for the resurgence of oppressive ideologies such as white supremacy. In such a political climate, perhaps we too find ourselves drifting into Pyrrhonistic skepticism. Deconstruction undermines our confidence in the possibility of shared mental powers and egalitarian values that would enable people to work toward a new and more just social order and prompts us to quietism.

Nowadays, of course, unlike Erasmus, we have no ready access to a fool persona. We celebrate no carnivals of social role reversal, and we do not wear motley—though I admit I am tempted to appear at professional meetings in academic gown and cap and bells. I know I often feel

a fool when I get up to speak in public, because the adoption of any kind
of ethical position of the sort I advocate under the rubric of rhetorical
authority appears foolish in the eyes of current theory. Perhaps I need
to appropriate some of the fool's rhetorical advantages—to simply talk
about the egalitarian social order I dream of without worrying about
whether someone will think I am being foundationalist, feigning ignorance of the skeptics all around me waiting to laugh at my moral ear-
nestness. After all, we clowns have always been sentimental. My professional colleagues are fearful as monks in a monastery of committing
some arcane sin. Meanwhile, ethical, cultural, and political leadership is
seized by those who rush in where we fear to tread—E. D. Hirsch, Lynn
Cheney, and others. I say, let's transgress.

But expressing socially rebellious views in the persona of Folly has
other advantages besides simply removing the fear of speaking, potent
though that advantage is, especially for women. The provisional quality
of the fool's speech can be especially helpful in a time of skepticism,
when avowing anything seems foolish. But turned another way, this provisional quality holds the greatest potential for utopian social regeneration. The fool's words are always open to revision, to reconstitution
around the responses of her interlocutors—this is the basis of rhetorical
authority as outlined here. The foolish speaker is different, distractible;
but this means that the other choices ruled out by the adoption of any
authoritative position should have an easier time reasserting themselves
in the interest of justice, if such need comes to pass.

This is what feminist political scientist Kathleen B. Jones describes
as *compassionate authority*. She argues that women have typically been
excluded from the public exercise of authority because of the way authority has been defined, as a social practice that resolves ambiguities
by erasing conflicts of interest in favor of the dominant social group.
Jones argues: "Compassion has the potential for humanizing authority.
If women do not speak authoritatively, perhaps their hesitance reveals
the ambiguity, and the choices, behind all rule systems. By reminding
us of this ambiguity, the voice and gesture of compassion shocks us into
a memory of what has been hidden by the ordered discourse of authority" (131). Jone's characterization of compassionate authority helps us to
understand a final question concerning the persona of Folly, namely, who
would believe a fool? That is, if the woman who adopts a mock-innocent
rhetorical stance is thus enabled to break taboos about what may be
spoken of, she still may not be believed—she may be the sort of fool
exemplified by the Trojan Cassandra. My hope is that the widespread

hunger for compassion and for an expression of compassion in a more just social order will allow this speaker to be heard.

Folly is ineffectual, marginal, not part of the life of the city; but this very fact allows her to see our behavior in ways that we ourselves cannot, unless we put on her persona, and it allows us to accept her critiques. Folly is thus analogous to the early Greek Sophists, who owed their rhetorical success to their wanderings across the boundaries of many city-states (see Jarratt). And in expressing compassion from the margins, a rhetor who speaks as a woman-fool might find ways to make common cause with those who speak from the margins of other racial, sexual, or social-class positions. Exactly what we need now is a rhetorical authority that moves from margin to center, a center reconceived as expanding to the circumference.

NOTES

1. Walter Kaiser compares Folly briefly to "Mother Nature" (94–95) while still associating her fertility connotations with the phallus. Thomas O. Sloane refers to her in passing as "a kind of muse or other traditionally female and therefore nonrational spirit" (67).

2. Thomas O. Sloane argues that humanist rhetoric devoted to the Academic skeptical project of developing probable or prudential knowledge typically proceeds in good sophistic fashion by arguing both sides of a question. Sloane calls this a "Janus-faced" rhetoric, arguing by contraries. For Sloane, Erasmus in *Praise* symbolizes the humanist project by producing an endorsement of prudence out of its contrary, praise by a persona whose praise seems to require being read ironically as blame. Geraldine Thompson has suggested that the shifts in tone over the three sections of *Praise* can be understood as a practical demonstration of the mode of arguing all sides of a question, implicitly endorsed in the opening section. Erasmus refuses to allow the reader to repose in a coherent understanding of the development of his skeptical position, she argues, because he wants to prompt the salutary activity of questioning and reconsidering.

BIBLIOGRAPHY

Alcoff, Linda. "Cultural Feminism versus Post-Structuralism: The Identity Crisis in Feminist Theory." *Signs* 13 (1988): 405–36.

Baskins, Cristelle. "Lucretia or the Virtue of Declamatory Violence." Unpublished manuscript, Holy Cross College, Worcester, Mass.

Bizzell, Patricia. "Arguing about Literacy." *College English* 50 (1988): 141–53.

———. "Beyond Anti-Foundationalism to Rhetorical Authority: Problems Defining 'Cultural Literacy.'" *College English* 52 (1990): 661–75.

Bizzell, Patricia, and Bruce Herzberg. "Christine de Pisan and Laura Cereta." In *The Rhetorical Tradition,* edited by Patricia Bizzell and Bruce Herzberg. Boston: St. Martin's, 1990.

de Pisan, Christine. *The Treasure of the City of Ladies.* Translated by Sarah Lawson. Harmondsworth, G.B.: Penguin, 1985.

Erasmus. *The Praise of Folly.* Translated by Clarence H. Miller. New Haven: Yale Univ. Press, 1979.

Graff, Gerald. "How to Deal with the Humanities Crisis: Organize It." *ADE Bulletin* 95 (1990): 4–10.

Grafton, Anthony, and Lisa Jardine. *From Humanism to the Humanities.* Cambridge: Harvard Univ. Press, 1986.

Hooks, Bell. *Talking Back: Thinking Feminist, Thinking Black.* Boston: South End, 1989.

Jarratt, Susan. *The Return of the Sophists: Classical Rhetoric Refigured.* Carbondale: Southern Illinois Univ. Press, 1991.

Jed, Stephanie H. *Chaste Thinking: The Rape of Lucretia and the Birth of Humanism.* Bloomington: Indiana Univ. Press, 1989.

Jones, Kathleen B. "On Authority: Or, Why Women Are Not Entitled to Speak." In *Feminism and Foucault: Reflections on Resistance,* edited by Irene Diamond and Lee Quinby. Boston: Northeastern Univ. Press, 1988.

Kahn, Victoria. *Rhetoric, Prudence, and Skepticism in the Renaissance.* Ithaca: Cornell Univ. Press, 1985.

Kaiser, Walter. *Praisers of Folly: Erasmus, Shakespeare, Rabelais.* Cambridge: Harvard Univ. Press, 1963.

Lears, Jackson. "Deride and Conquer." Review of *Boxed In: The Culture of TV,* by Mark Crispin Miller. *The Nation* 248 (1989): 59–62.

Ong, Walter. *Fighting for Life: Contest, Sexuality, and Consciousness.* Ithaca: Cornell Univ. Press, 1981.

Ryan, Michael. *Marxism and Deconstruction: A Critical Articulation.* Baltimore: Johns Hopkins Univ. Press, 1992.

Sloane, Thomas O. *Donne, Milton, and the End of Humanist Rhetoric.* Berkeley and Los Angeles: Univ. of California Press, 1985.

Smith, Jeff. "Cultural Literacy and the Academic Left." In *Profession 88,* edited by Phyllis Franklin. New York: MLA, 1988.

Thompson, Geraldine. *Under Pretext of Praise: Satiric Mode in Erasmus' Fiction.* Toronto: Univ. of Toronto Press, 1973.

Untersteiner, Mario. *The Sophists.* Translated by Kathleen Freeman. New York: Philosophical Library, 1954.

Willeford, William. *The Fool and His Scepter.* Chicago: Northwestern Univ. Press, 1969.

3

Discourse and Diversity: Experimental Writing Within the Academy

Lillian Bridwell-Bowles

In classes ranging from Advanced Expository Writing and Women and Writing, at the undergraduate level, to Gender, Language, and Writing Pedagogy and Classical and Contemporary Rhetoric, at the graduate level, I have invited students to imagine the possibilities for new forms of discourse, new kinds of academic essays. I do this because I believe that writing classes (and the whole field of composition studies) must employ richer visions of texts and composing processes. If we are to invent a truly pluralistic society, we must envision a socially and politically situated view of language and the creation of texts—one that takes into account gender, race, class, sexual preference, and a host of issues that are implied by these and other cultural differences. Our language and our written texts represent our visions of our culture, and we need new processes and forms if we are to express ways of thinking that have been outside the dominant culture. Finally, I believe that teaching students to write involves teaching them ways to critique not only their material and their potential readers' needs but also the rhetorical conventions that they are expected to employ within the academy.

Work in composition has been expanded enormously by theories of cognitive processes, social construction, and by the uses of computers and other forms of technology. Yet, as Adrienne Rich writes, "we might hypothetically possess ourselves of every recognized technological resource on the North American continent, but as long as our language is inadequate, our vision remains formless, and our thinking and feeling are still running in the old cycles, our process may be 'revolutionary,' but not transformative" (Rich, 247–48). David Kaufer and Cheryl Geisler argue that "freshmen composition and writing across the curriculum have remained silent about newness as a rhetorical standard, as a hallmark of literacy in a post-industrial, professional age." They do not believe that "this silence can be justified on either intellectual or pragmatic grounds" (309). Others among the composition community (e.g., Alice Calderonello) have also called for challenges to traditional essays.

I am skeptical about whether simply changing the surface of our academic language can give us Rich's "dream of a common language," but I have decided to start where I know how to start—and that is with tinkering on the surface. I have experimented with new forms to match my own changing scholarship, work that has become more and more cross-disciplinary. Just as I have moved from lines of inquiry exclusively based in social science and empiricism to those that are more oriented in humanistic, feminist, and liberation theories, so must my language change. Experiencing what my colleague Lisa Albrecht described as my "own personal paradigm shift," I have sought alternatives—a more personal voice, an expanded use of metaphor, a less rigid methodological framework, and a writing process that allows me to combine hypothesizing with reporting data, to use patterns of writing that allow for multiple truths, what Dale Spender has called a "multidimensional reality" (102), rather than a single thesis, and so on.

This ongoing process has made me realize that students may need new options for writing if they, too, are struggling with expressing concepts, attitudes, and beliefs that do not fit into traditional academic forms. To give them permission to experiment, I simply tell them that they need not always write the standard academic essay and encourage them to write something else. Many continue to write in familiar forms, and I do not require that they do otherwise. They may need to adopt the standard conventions before they can challenge or criticize them (see Bizzell for an account of this position). But increasing numbers of students take me up on my option and learn ways of critically analyzing rhetorical conventions at the same time that they are being introduced to traditional academic discourse communities.

When one attempts to write outside the dominant discourse, one often has to begin by naming the new thing. I have used various terms for our experiments, including *alternative* and *feminist,* but recently we have been using the term *diverse discourse. Alternative discourse* does not allow us to reform thinking, to imagine the possibility that writing choices that are now marginal could someday be positioned alongside, or in place of, the dominant ones. *Feminist discourse* has been my sentimental favorite because feminist theory gave me, personally, new ways of thinking and writing, but many students still feel excluded by this term. I am careful to say here, and in my classes, that even though I use feminist texts as my inspiration, students should feel free to read them as metaphors for their own attempts to write outside a dominant culture, however they define their positions. If they are not attempting to write outside established conventions, I invite them to consider how others might feel the need to do so.

In this essay, I provide a rationale for this experimentation with diverse discourse, examples of the readings that inspire me and students in my classes, and samples of student essays.

Why the Need for Experiments? Or, What Is Your Problem?

Old patterns of argument, based on revealing a single truth (a thesis) using all the available means of persuasion, run counter to new theories of socially constructed knowledge and social change. Sally Miller Gearhart goes so far as to say that "any intent to persuade is an act of violence" (195). She wants to see communication in a more holistic way, as a "womb" or a "matrix . . . within which something takes form or begins" (199–200). She wants an entirely different rhetorical perspective: "We are not the speaker, the-one-with-the-truth, the one-who-with-his-power-will-change-lives. We are the matrix, we are she-who-is-the-home-of-this-particular-human-interaction, we are the co-creator and co-sustainer of the atmosphere in whose infinity of possible transformations we will all change" (200). Susan Meisenhelder also describes rhetorical aggression in her analysis of warlike, pugilistic, and phallic metaphors in writing. I hardly think that all forms of argumentation are passé. What do we do when we describe our positions on issues of social change, when we see a position as clearly wrong, morally, ethically, socially? Obviously, argumentation has a place (even in this essay), but it need not be the only form our scholarly writings take.

Donald Murray, a familiar and respected member of the composition community, appears to support another contested convention when he argues for a distinction between "academic voice" and "personal voice." They are clearly separate for him. According to Murray, academic writing should appeal to reason, maintain a distanced and detached tone, cite outside authority, and be written in response to previous academic writing: "Scholarly knowledge is built in increments of small additional bits added to previous knowledge" (189). Others, who might not make such clear distinctions, pass along similar, conventional academic wisdom for other reasons. Patricia Bizzell, a progressive member of the composition community, argues that students who are politically oppressed must master conventions of academic discourse in order to succeed, but she defines them significantly more broadly. Many students believe that academic "standard" language is the key to their success, perhaps even the key to their very survival, and I try not to debate this point, even though I question whether this key is sufficient for survival and success. We may agree on its necessity, but not on its sufficiency. I also believe that linguistic and rhetorical flexibility may help students to write better conventional prose.

In addition, I know that there are positions other than accommodation to or rejection of the dominant patterns of discourse. Min-zhan Lu takes such a position when she writes about her concern for students in composition classrooms, particularly in the light of her own personal struggle to mediate between the voices of home (English in a Chinese home) and school (Standard Chinese, the official language of New China):

> When composition classes encourage students to ignore those voices that seem irrelevant to the purified world of the classroom, most students are often able to do so without much struggle. . . . However, beyond the classroom and beyond the limited range of these students' immediate lives lies a much more complex and dynamic social and historical scene. To help these students become actors in such a scene, perhaps we need to call their attention to voices that may seem irrelevant to the discourse we teach rather than encourage them to shut them out. . . . We might encourage students to explore ways of practicing the conventions of the discourse they are learning by negotiating through these conflicting voices. We could also encourage them to see themselves as responsible for forming or transforming as well as preserving the discourse they are learning. (447)

Geoffrey Chase, employing the theories of Giroux and Freire, also proposes that students can resist the conventions of academic discourse, analyzing and challenging them, not for the sake of mere opposition but in order to work for social change. On the other hand, I also know that conventional academic discourse can be used in the service of reform.

For a variety of reasons, then, many students welcome the opportunity to critique academic discourse. Instead of adopting prior knowledge in an uncritical way, they establish a dialectical relation with much previous knowledge; they sometimes take a position apart from the established academy. As one student put it, "People like yourself, Robin, Ellen, and others send us the message that WE DO NOT HAVE TO BE COOKIE-CUTTER SCHOLARS. In fact, some of us gave up BAKING long ago and we ARE the products of 20 years of feminist theory. . . . Unlike the traditional angel of the house, we have left the kitchen (KP duty and all) and have a LABORATORY of our own . . . in which we are creating new forms" (Olano 1990, 5).

Any departure from the norm is accompanied by fear, however, and some students are afraid to go too far. Pamela Olano goes on to say that she and her peers

> all have a morbid curiosity about what it is we ARE creating . . . and I can sense a desire to control the unknown . . . to make it "look like" something familiar. . . . This is heady stuff . . . and frightening stuff to fledglings just learning to fly (doctoral students . . . particularly women who are not sure as to their "welcome" into the fold). . . . Sometimes I think the academy and the educational system have done their jobs too well. We (men and women) arrive here believing that there is AN ANSWER KEY (like the one in the back of the teacher's edition), . . . then we run up against the UNDERGROUND that whispers "try it another way." We may in fact resist the voices we hear, but eventually we step off the limb. . . . We write in a new voice, we experiment, we return to the limb. (Olano 1990, 5–6)

Perhaps with time, poststructuralist revolutions in thinking about our culture will influence our language so much that we will come to see personal writing, nonlinear patterns of organization, writing that contains emotion, writing that closes the gap between subject and object, writing that does something "with" and not "to" the reader, and all the other possibilities yet to come as having equal status with carefully reasoned, rational argument.

For now, however, writing in any of these ways clearly suggests Other, and I have tried to explore ways that Other voices could be read and heard in my classes, ways that the Other could be celebrated. I have also included readings that show how successful writers and academics have shared concerns similar to Olano's above.

The Essentialist Problem and Feminist Discourse

Because I often use the term *feminist discourse* and readings from feminist theory are the starting point of my classes, I have to work very hard not to predispose students toward a construction of discourse that invokes the essentialist problem so carefully outlined by Joy Ritchie. I do not want to promote the idea that women, left to their own devices, would all write in a certain way and that this writing would always be different from all men's writing, but neither do I exclude the possibility that there might be significant, socially inherited and constructed contrasts between many women's and men's ways of thinking, their experiences, and their language. Of course, these differences have to be further integrated with race, class, and other differences if we are to fully understand the ways women use language.

I like Carolyn Heilbrun's 1988 discussion of *feminist* with regard to her own and others' writing and her interpretation of Nancy Miller's definition of *feminism:* "a self-consciousness about women's identity both as inherited cultural fact and as a process of social construction" (18). Heilbrun comments, "It is hard to suppose women can mean or want what we have always been assured they could not possibly mean or want" (18). An awareness of the ways our cultural inheritance, embodied largely in language, has limited our vision suggests the need for new ways of writing and the need for experimentation in academic settings.

All of this is complicated, of course, because we are working within a patriarchal, racist, and classist culture and using a patriarchal, racist, and classist variant of language to try to define something outside the culture. It may not be possible to create a feminist discourse with the "father's tongue" (Penelope) or the "master's tools" (Lorde 1981). As Xavier Gauthier puts it, "Perhaps if we had left these pages blank, we should have had a better understanding of what feminine writing is all about" (162). Indeed, silence is a major topic in nearly all feminist theories.

While I have found no simple solutions to many of these problems, I must go on using language. My pragmatic approach is to discuss them directly with students and to invoke an experimental, open attitude. One student speaks for others when she says that an experimental approach is a way of proceeding: "I have said that I find this concept [feminist discourse] stimulating. By that I mean that it works for me as an inspiration, as a metaphor, as an idea fostered by an outrageous, free-roaming imagination." She writes this, even though she herself cannot write her way out of patriarchal language: "And I, at least, can't see how we are to get out of the straitjacket of patriarchal discourse. I have begun to feel as I have grappled with these wonderful ideas that the realization of a woman's voice, the demolition of the straitjacket, is an impossible project" (Ripoll). I responded to her conclusion, and others like it, by saying that I can at least hypothesize the existence of a powerfully diverse theory of discourse, even if I cannot as yet define it or create it.

Reading as an Inspiration for Writing

As a way of beginning, I provide students with dozens of readings and excerpts from feminist scholars and writers who hypothesize diverse forms of discourse. I often begin with Virginia Woolf, who begs us to preserve differences: "It would be a thousand pities if women wrote like men. . . . Ought not education to bring out and fortify the difference rather than the similarities? For we have too much likeness as it is" (91–92). Adrienne Rich captures the essence of so many problems with women and language; here she describes feelings common to many women students and academics: "Listen to a woman groping for language in which to express what is on her mind, sensing that the terms of academic discourse are not her language, trying to cut down her thought to the dimension of a discourse not intended for her" (243–44). Other texts that are invaluable for providing a theoretical background are Dale Spender's *Man Made Language* and Julia Penelope's *Speaking Freely: Unlearning the Lies of the Fathers' Tongue* and essays by Susan Meisenhelder and Sally Miller Gearhart.

The French feminists also give us many tantalizing texts to consider when we allow ourselves to write–or to imagine writing–outside patriarchal, phallocentric discourse. From Julia Kristeva:

> How can we conceive of a revolutionary struggle that does not involve a revolution in discourse (not an upheaval in language as such, but rather a theory of this very upheaval)? (140)

From Helene Cixous, on *écriture féminine:*

> Most women are like this: they do someone else's—man's—writing, and in their innocence sustain it and give it voice, and end up producing writing that's in effect masculine. Great care must be taken in working on feminine writing not to get trapped by names: to be signed with a woman's name doesn't necessarily make a piece of writing feminine. It could quite well be masculine writing, and conversely, the fact that a

piece of writing is signed with a man's name does not in itself exclude
femininity. It's rare, but you can sometimes find femininity in writings
signed by men: it does happen. (qtd. in Moi, 108)

From Moi, writing about Kristeva and Cixous:

> The speaking/writing woman is in a space outside time (eternity), a
> space that allows no naming and no syntax. In her article "Women's
> Time," Julia Kristeva has argued that syntax is constitutive of our sense
> of chronological time by the very fact that the order of words in a sen-
> tence marks a temporal sequence: since subject, verb, object cannot
> be spoken simultaneously, their utterance necessarily cuts up the tem-
> poral continuum of "eternity." Cixous, then, presents this nameless pre-
> Oedipal space filled with mother's milk and honey as the source of the
> song that resonates through all female writing. (114)

Though difficult to read in the ways we typically read discursive
prose, French feminist theories have been interpreted in ways that students and I have found meaningful by Toril Moi (as in the passage
above), Susan Suleiman, Clara Juncker, Robert de Beaugrande, Ann Rosalind Jones, and Elaine Marks and Isabelle de Courtivron. Suleiman,
describing Cixous's dream of writing, says that it would "break open the
chains of syntax, escape the repressiveness of linear logic and 'story-
telling' and allow for the emergence of a language 'close to the body.'
This language, linked, for Cixous, to the voice and the body of the
mother, would allow the 'wildness' of the unconscious to emerge over
the tame reasoning of the superego of the Law" (Suleiman, 52).

When I read many of the texts I have mentioned so far, I am filled
with optimism about the possibilities for a liberating discourse, one that
contains changes in the deep structure as well as obvious alterations in
the surface structure. Though I cannot define it, with feminist discourse
(or "diverse" or "experimental" discourse) I have a name for what I seek,
and that gives me hope. But it is easy to understand a pessimistic perspective. Despite some positive connotations offered by theorists such
as Elizabeth Flynn, we can certainly conjure up the negative connotations
of writing like a woman. This negative semantic space is sometimes at
the heart of what bothers my students when we use the term *feminist
discourse.* Our heads are filled with negative images of what it means to
think, write, drive, throw a ball—anything—"like a woman." Irigaray is
direct on this: "They have left us their negative(s)" (207).

There is perhaps no more discouraging treatise on women's language than Otto Jespersen's chapter entitled "The Woman," in his "seminal" book written in 1922, during the genesis of modern linguistics. A sampling:

> Men will certainly with great justice object that there is a danger of the language becoming languid and insipid if we are always to content ourselves with women's expressions, and that vigour and vividness count for something.... The vocabulary of a woman as a rule is much less extensive than that of a man.... Woman is linguistically quicker than man: quicker to learn, quicker to hear, and quicker to answer. A man is slower: he hesitates, he chews the cud to make sure of the taste of the words, and thereby comes to discover similarities with and differences from other words, both in sound and in sense, thus preparing himself for the appropriate use of the fittest noun or adjective. (247, 248, 249)

Many students are shocked to see the biases in the foundational texts of linguistic "science."

Carolyn Heilbrun provides additional evidence of the powerful lenses through which participants in our culture view women and their writing. She claims that the bonds for women writers are so great that they have suffered from "autobiographical disabilities," unable even to tell their own stories. Before May Sarton's rewrite of her autobiography, in which she attempted to tell the truth about what she had written earlier, most women's stories about themselves are facades, according to Heilbrun, artifices built of what the culture expects of them, including acquired modesty and humility. About Eudora Welty's autobiography, Heilbrun writes, "It is nostalgia, rendered with all the charm and grace of which she is capable, that has produced this autobiography, that same nostalgia that has for so many years imprisoned women without her genius or her rewards" (15). This nostalgia, according to Heilbrun, is a mask for the kind of anger and true emotion that many women suppress when they write.

Because some students, for all these reasons, cannot bring themselves to describe their work as "writing like a woman," I invite them to experiment with what it means to apply feminist theories about difference and diversity to language, hence, our working title for their work: "diverse discourse." Of course, there are other objections to using alternative forms: "it's not scholarly," "it's not objective," "it's too emotional." The discussions of negative writing associated with women provide an occasion for analyzing responses to all kinds of "other" texts. (See Joanna Russ's depressing but informative catalog of the ways women's writing has been positioned as inferior.)

Professional Samples of Diverse Discourse

Not all of the feminist theorists I have quoted write in experimental modes. So we often search beyond feminist discourse theories for samples that can serve as catalysts for our writing experiments. Such writing provokes lively class discussion, and while I don't require students to write in experimental modes, their readings and discussions prompt many students to try their own experiments with writing. (See the section on student samples later in this essay.)

Personal and Emotional Writing

Samples of personal narrative and emotional writing are plentiful in the recent writing of feminist scholars, but it was not always so. Personal journals and diaries have always been an outlet for women and men, but they did not cross over into prestigious academic journals as scholarship. Jane Tompkins describes the price a feminist literary scholar has to pay for violating the expectations of the community of literary critics. Responding to a scholarly article by Ellen Messer-Davidow on philosophy and feminism, Tompkins feels split between the public and the private. She wants to write as a respectable scholar and also as a woman sitting in her stocking feet looking out the window at a red leaf and feeling rage like an "adamantine, a black slab that glows in the dark" (177). She writes with both voices and comments on her ambivalent feelings:

> One is the voice of a critic who wants to correct a mistake in the essay's view of epistemology. The other is the voice of a person who wants to write about her feelings. (I have wanted to do this for a long time but have felt too embarrassed.) This person feels it is wrong to criticize the essay and even beside the point, because a critique of the kind the critic has in mind only insulates academic discourse further from the issues that make feminism matter. That make *her* matter. The critic, meanwhile, believes such feelings, and the attitudes that inform them, are soft-minded, self-indulgent, and unprofessional. (169)

This essay evokes discussions of being silenced. We have many stories to tell each other about the ways we have been too embarrassed to write truthfully. Other outstanding examples of the interweaving of personal and academic voices are Patricia Williams's *The Alchemy of Race and Rights,* Toni McNaron's *I Dwell in Possibility,* and Gayle Graham Yates's *Mississippi Mind: A Personal Cultural History of an American State.*

Breaking the Boundaries of Textual Space

Another of my favorite texts is Judy Chicago's *The Birth Project,* an account of her desire as an artist to produce images of childbirth in designs
stitched by women needleworkers. She chose to work in a unique way,
designing multiple images and employing women working in collectives
across the country to execute her designs. On a typical double-page
spread from her book (154–55), we find multiple voices speaking to us
from the pages. In column one, we read excerpts from her personal
journal during the project. Columns two, three, and four contain excerpts
from a stitcher's journal. In the fifth column, Chicago comments retro-
spectively on the project, and the journal continues in the final column.
Each writer has a different perspective on the project. In fact, Chicago
often discusses their differences and the difficulties they had as feminists
trying to work together on a project that demanded so much of each of
them. Many students find this work helpful as they try to weave together
papers that preserve their own voices alongside the voices of others who
disagree with them or the voices of authorities who might drown out
their own.

Language Play

If my students and I were fluent readers of French, we could turn to
Cixous, Irigaray, and Kristeva for many examples of language play, but
because we are not, I have found that Mary Daly's *Gyn/Ecology* serves
very well for English examples. From the title page to the last page, Daly
emphasizes that we must "dis-spell" the "spooks of grammar," lexicon,
and rhetoric with our own language constructions. She plays with diction,
spelling, punctuation, and other orthographic conventions to develop a
style that signals at every turn that she means something other than
what is typically meant. For example, she reinvests terms such as *crone,
hag,* and *spinster* with positive semantic features. She notes with irony
that Noam Chomsky was "genuinely puzzled and intrigued" by the possibility that there might be connections between language and freedom
when he was asked to speak on this topic (328). Daly argues that "to
break the spell. . . . Croneographers should remind our Selves that the
Newspeak of Orwell's negative utopian tale is patriarchal Oldspeak"
(330). So that we can break the bonds of language, we must invent new
terms, new constructions, new rhetorics:

> This applies to male-controlled language in all matters pertaining to gyn-
> ocentric identity: the words simply do not exist. In such a situation it is

difficult even to imagine the right questions about our situation. Women struggling for words feel haunted by false feelings of personal inadequacy, by anger, frustration, and a kind of sadness/bereavement. For it is, after all, our "mother tongue" that has been turned against us by the tongue-twisters. Learning to speak our Mothers' Tongue is exorcising the male "mothers." (330)

Daly inspires a "serious playfulness" in the writing of many students. Whether or not we can ever find a language other than the "male Mother Tongue" is a topic of much discussion in my classes. Those who are not prepared to use experimental language in their writing often find acceptable models in analyses of male discourse such as those written by Penelope and Spender.

Not the Mythic White Woman

Along with constructions of the Other based on gender, we also consider additional sources of difference for our experimental papers. Even if we are female, we are not writing as "THE Mythic Woman," typically "THE Mythic WHITE Woman," as in much early feminist work. (See bell hooks for an extended discussion of this problem.) We write as individuals participating in various discourse communities. We are social beings, from different racial and ethnic communities, not just two-dimensional versions of "Woman" (or of "Man," trying to "write like a woman"). Moi, in her critique of Cixous, writes, "Stirring and seductive though such a vision is, it can say nothing of the actual inequities, deprivations and violations that women, as social beings rather than as mythological archetypes, must constantly suffer" (123). Rich reminds us that any new theory of "feminist discourse" will have to preserve the differences among women as well as men: "Women both have and have not had a common world. The mere sharing of oppression does not constitute a common world" (203).

Breaking out of Linguistic Prejudice

Throughout the collection of essays *Bridges of Power: Women's Multicultural Alliances,* edited by Lisa Albrecht and Rose M. Brewer, we find the tension between common ground (oppression) and difference (race, class, sexual preference) in women's experiences. Audre Lorde, for example, writing of women of the Black Diaspora, does not assume that women will always share common ground. Differences across languages set up many cultural barriers. She writes, "One of the problems is, we for the most part are very provincial in North America, and we believe that English is the end of all languages. One of the things we need to, I think, start to do as we begin to experience our sisters, is to expose ourselves, open ourselves to learning other languages, so that we can in fact communicate, not only in translations" (1990, 208–09).

Gloria Anzaldua, also represented in *Bridges of Power,* illustrates cross-linguistic tensions. When she writes in English, Anzaldua blends Spanish and Nauhtl terms to make the point that something very important to her is lost in translation. "Oh, white sister, where is your soul, your spirit? It has run off in shock, *susto,* and you lack shamans and *curanderas* to call it back. *Sin alma no te puedes animarte pa'nada.* Remember that an equally empty and hollow place within us allows that connection, even needs that linkage" (229). Even within Spanish, she needs language she does not have and invents the term *lesberadas,* prompted by the word *desperado.* Once we share languages, as Lorde would have us do, we can begin to understand some of the common ground of patriarchal oppression and how it is reflected in each language, but we need to retain our differences as well.

Class Barriers

Other factors, beyond gender, race, and mother tongue, create differences and influence our language. My students and I have just begun to explore the influence of class in this context. Clearly it is a powerful determinant of success and failure within academia and a restrictive force in our linguistic freedom. Standard Written English, with its roots in prestige dialects, does not allow our class roots to show. Our fear of revealing class identities that diverge from the middle restricts our writing options. Writing classes often serve as a gatekeeper, protecting the academy from the infelicities of "errors" generated by differences among dialects that derive from social, racial, and ethnic differences.

Mike Rose's book *Lives on the Boundary* poignantly tells the story of his own fears and his students' fears of being outsiders, mirrored in his response to the image of the medieval goddess of grammar, Grammatica, represented as "severe, with a scalpel and a large pair of pincers. Her right hand, which is by her side, grasps a bird by its neck, its mouth open as if in a gasp or a squawk" (1). Rose writes, "And it's our cultural fears—of internal decay, of loss of order, of diminishment—that weave into our assessments of literacy and scholastic achievement" (7). The academy does not yet have room, except in the rarified atmosphere of "creative" writing, for dialects that differ from "Standard" Written English.

Lives on the Boundary has inspired several of my graduate students to write their ethnographic dissertations in a style that is truer to themselves—and far more interesting to me and to the other members of their committees than some of the pseudoethnographies that have sprouted up in composition studies in recent years. They draw courage from Rose's candid discussions of his own working-class history.

Sexual Orientation

Sexual orientation is another powerful source of difference, and orientations other than the presumed heterosexual are only now becoming somewhat safe topics for discussion in the context of writing classes. This lack of safety is indeed troublesome, given the myth of the academy as the open marketplace of ideas versus the reality of homophobia and violence against gays and lesbians within the academy. Until very recently, very little had been published on the connections between sexual orientation and writing. In some preliminary work on this question, I turned up only one source on the topic of gay and lesbian writing in our university's library: Mark Lilly's edited collection entitled *Lesbian and Gay Writing*. More careful studies of feminist, gay, and lesbian scholarship (e.g., Olano 1991) reveal a growing body of work in specialized journals. The topic is not safe enough, obviously; while gay and lesbian students in my classes have written about the connection between their sexual orientation and their writing, they chose not to give me permission to include samples of their writing in this essay.

Different Composing Processes

Finally, I also encourage students to consider alternative processes for writing their essays. Lisa Ede and Andrea Lunsford's book *Singular Texts, Plural Authors* provides support for the idea of collective, collaborative writing processes. To this I also add many examples of my own from business and industry, as well as from academia. I also share some of the personal difficulties I have experienced as a coauthor doing an unequal share of the work, especially when there were inequities of power in these situations, or as an academic whose coauthored works were not valued as highly as those of colleagues who choose to work alone. We talk about these as a way of committing ourselves to another diverse approach to writing.

The Invigorating Search for Materials

One of the antidotes to the problem of essentialism noted earlier is to analyze the differences among women, among men, and between women and men as well as their shared experiences. Analyses of race, class, gender, language, and sexual preference allow possibilities for all writers who want to create their own divergent, alternative discourses. They extend our thinking beyond earlier feminist analyses of language and discourse. In this section I have shared but a few of the samples that I have been collecting for the purpose of generating more critical readings of patriarchal discursive practices. I have found that searching for language and writing I can use in these ways has reinvigorated me as a reader, as well as a teacher and a writer.

Student Samples of Diverse Discourse

The following examples of student writing represent a range of experiments that students in my classes have produced, inspired by their readings of alternative discourse and their desire to produce something unconventional. Even in the safe space that I work to construct within my classrooms, the signs of student insecurity with experimentation reflect my own. On the one hand, they know that they will write for other teachers, other professors, who are not receptive to these challenges to convention. On the other, they often wonder about the value of conventional writing to reflect their own realities.

Toying with Academic Writing

Many students choose to put themselves back into their learning and experiment with personal voice in academic writing, echoing, for example, Tompkins's dialogue with herself. One undergraduate woman, writing her summa thesis "under my direction" (in quotes for reasons that unfold below), chose to taunt academic discourse. In "Something Like a Preface," she writes:

> I began this project with the intent to write a paper on whether or not there is such a thing as "feminine writing," and if there is, how it differs from the enigma of "masculine writing." It sounds impressive anyway when people ask you what you're up to: *summa thesis....* In any case, it's a paper that by definition "crowns the undergraduate student's work in the University of Minnesota English Department" [and here she cites

our handbook]. Crowns, no less. It's a coronation of sorts, then, with the king and queen waiting anxiously in the wings.

But hold the horns. This prom won't promenade without a pepfest. (At least, none of the ones I ever attended in high school did.) Indeed, a pepfest is absolutely mandatory. But this is a *summa thesis* (need I remind you). We can't just have sophomores bellowing "JUNIORS!" and juniors indignantly bellowing "SOPHOMORES!" right back across the gymnasium floor. In fact, we can't have sophomores and juniors at all (this is a *summa th . . .*). Instead, psychoanalysts, linguists, sociologists, and English professors from around the world have gathered for a pepfest of the magnanimous kind, a stadium of scholars with flags and whistles, hats and cheers, and lips marching in rhythmic unity. (Schubert, 1)

In this passage, Schubert reveals her impatience with the view that she has to please her "masters" and be blessed by those in authority for her work. She also suggests that she cannot write in language that is more immediate to her experience (pepfests). She is supposed to take on the mantle of objectivity. Her paper goes on to reveal very serious scholarship, but the tone throughout is playful and irreverent. The "Review of the Literature" is called "Ancient History" and reveals how irrelevant she finds much that she read about women's voices. At the same time, she lets the reader know when she approves of her reading and by what criteria she makes these judgments. The section in which she comments on what she has read and applies it to people she has known, herself included, is entitled "Unleashed and Raging." She lets her anger shine through the prose, instead of politely maintaining distance as she has been taught to do in academic prose. I responded to her shifts in tone with high praise, but I was not entirely sure what my colleagues would say about it. I should have had more confidence, because this paper won the award for the best undergraduate essay of the year in the Women's Studies Department and satisfied the English Department's requirement for a crowning achievement. I suspect that one of the reasons it was accepted, beyond its insightfulness, was that it was novel, and I have wondered what would happen if more students wrote like this.

The Risks in Challenging Conventions

Another student, at the graduate level, is more fearful about her audience when she writes a paper about her struggles with "feminist reading and writing": "I still fear that it will lack coherence to any reader excluding me, and maybe me, too. . . . This is probably why I feel some discomfort in displaying it to any audience outside of myself. 'Nonsense' they'll

think, 'What jibberish she's written! And a graduate student in English!'
I imagine my readers saying 'Is it too confessional? Too reflective?' "
(anonymous). Even though her classmates and I were the only readers
who would see this paper without the writer's permission,[1] she was still
hesitant to leave behind the objectivity and distance that had served her
well as an undergraduate. Throughout the essay, she weaves concerns
with audience into challenging questions about the material she has
read. It truly is private writing, or "writer-based prose" in the jargon of
composition, but as I had told her earlier, that was what the course was
about: making external knowledge personal. I encouraged her to think
that writer-based prose is not always just a phase that we have to go
through to get to something better, that not all academic writing has to
be "reader-based." At the end of the course, she still held the view that
academic writing should be public and not private, but she said she had
learned something from the experiment.

Another female student, writing in a course in rhetoric, revealed an
awareness of herself as a reader with gender and class as she reacted to
one of the textbooks used in the course. In the paper excerpted below,
she refuses to be left out of the discourse of rhetoric and ultimately
proposes a revisionist's view of *Phaedrus*. Powerfully aware of the restricted view of culture and class revealed in classical rhetoric, she describes some of her reasons for rejecting these traditions:

> I was doing fairly well as a reader of George Kennedy's *Classical Rhetoric*
> although I knew that the world he would describe, and respectfully so,
> would render me invisible; I agreed to read what the Boys were doing
> back then, just one more time. But my self "the reader" slips so easily
> into that imagination: I must have begun to indulge in his account by
> injecting myself into that past life, by imagining myself at least some-
> where in fifth century [B.C. Athens. . . . The Greek harmony is brought
> to, say, undergraduates, and held up as a sublime romance, especially
> according to modern day middle class standards. . . . From whence
> comes the armless, legless, headless, marble Greek woman[?] Yet mar-
> ble women can read noncontextually, so like I said, I was doing well,
> participating in the fantasy . . . though I must have known, at some level,
> that I was not in this course, nor would have been my father. (Bock, 1)

Another student, a man, also felt estranged from the readings in a
course focusing on feminist analyses of language. He wanted to find a
way to connect the theories to his life, so he talked to his friends and
family about them. He introduces himself this way: "I work as a bar-

tender, a stereotypical position of a man who tells dirty jokes, listens to one's problems and gives advice" (anonymous). He writes a one-page introduction, which he calls a "resonating core," and then juxtaposes excerpts from the course readings alongside commentaries about these quotes from regulars at the bar, family members, and friends. The title of the paper is "What the hell are you taking a class like that for???" I believe writing this paper allowed him to process his own personal struggle with that very question.

These few examples illustrate some of the ways students have chosen to put themselves back into their writing. To do so is a risk, and it is not surprising that so many of them write about their fears. Neither is it surprising that some students preferred that I not mention their names in this section.

Writing Without an Argument

One of the men in a graduate class was "persuaded" by Sally Miller Gearhart's essay, "The Womanization of Rhetoric," that argument may not be a mode he wants to adopt in all of his academic writing. Gearhart indicts the discipline of rhetoric because of her belief that "any intent to persuade is an act of violence" (195). The intention to change others, she writes, embodies a "conquest model of human interaction." At least for the week's writing assignment, he chose to write his entire essay as a series of questions. Here is his introduction: "I make no claims to be an expert on the subject [feminist criticism], or even to have a cursory knowledge. I believe I can contribute more by adding questions to the discussion than by asserting opinions or viewpoints. . . . What if questions were answered simply with questions? Imagine the difference in tone!" He then proceeds to ask fifty-eight questions, not in list form but as continuous prose. An excerpt:

> Does a voice that tries "to please all and offend none" boil down to the same as Gearhart's voice that refuses to conquer? Is a voice that refuses either to please or offend a strong voice? What is a strong voice? What does Peter Elbow mean by a voice so strong it scares others? What is "Writing with Power"? Is that what feminist rhetoric is attempting? Is powerful feminist rhetoric a contradiction? An oxymoron? Can the rhetoric of consensus building permit strong, powerful, *individual* voices? Can it permit a strong, powerful, *collective* voice? How is this achieved? If it is achieved, does it contradict the ideology that set it in motion? (Maylath, 2)

In contrast to the writers above, he takes his own opinions out of the paper, except as his questions reveal an underlying position. He could have easily developed a tightly reasoned argument against some of the readings, for he did not agree with all of them. Instead, he chose to think in a new way, to allow himself to ask questions instead of answering them. In the end, he asks, "How do I end this paper???" How, indeed, would he? My hope is that he has not.

Experiments with Form

Many students have experimented with ways to weave their writing together with external sources. With the advent of word-processing packages that make it simple to vary font styles and sizes, as well as to arrange the page horizontally and in columns, my students have been imitating layouts like those in Judy Chicago's *The Birth Project*. One student, Tania Ripoll, included such a figure in a paper she wrote for my Feminist Language and Writing Pedagogy seminar. She uses two columns, lining up the excerpts she finds interesting in one column and commenting on them in the other. In a memo she wrote to students in another class who were reading her paper, she asks, "Does the format work? Since much of the content of the paper is a rejection of linearity as a patriarchal construct, evidently the form had to be adjusted also. How superficial does it seem?" (Ripoll, 2).

Another student decided that she would likewise include a long series of quotes from her readings because "there is an obvious interconnection between all the readings, something I've never experienced so profoundly in my studies; and, most wondrous of all, these writings, these words, are connected to me. They speak to me and for me, in one voice but many. A poly/mono-centered discourse. A collection of interconnected voices. A peaceful cacophony." (anonymous). She arranges these quotes—from writers such as Deborah Cameron, Helene Cixous, Mary Daly, and Dale Spender—in the form of a reader's theater script. Her own ideas are given equal weight as she includes her own name in the cast of characters, the "Voices in Order of Appearance."

Another experiment with form in which students seem to be taking new directions is the addition of a great deal of visual material to their writing. This is easier now that graphics can be easily integrated into word-processed documents. In fact, the advent of icon-driven computers with integrated graphics packages may be a causal factor in this development. These graphics show up frequently in technical writing classes, and they are increasingly present in classes in writing for the arts and in the writing in design disciplines. In classes in landscape architecture, for example, I have found consistent use of drawings and graphics integrated with text. One student included elaborate drawings of Loring Park in Minneapolis, accompanied by her verbal notations in her class journal. These drawings and commentaries eventually became part of a new design and of a report on the design submitted to a jury of landscape architects for a course evaluation. Periodically throughout the journal, she would pause to think only in words, wondering at one point, "What does Loring Park mean?" and then listing all of her possible interpretations. But on most pages, the interplay between visual and verbal images was essential to her process of creating a design that conveyed her sense of the place. These combinations of the verbal and visual illustrate yet another way of avoiding the logocentrism discussed in so many of our readings. In an increasingly iconic culture, students need experience in combining visual images with verbal images in appropriate ways. While this practice is commonplace in many fields, too many writing classrooms have ignored the role of visual symbols in communication.

Differences in Ways of Working

Students in writing classes across the country have begun to explore the possibilities of writing collaboratively, challenging the notion that the individual author must possess all the knowledge, both of content and form, necessary to write well. One of many such collaborative groups in my class was led by a deaf woman and her interpreter, who showed the hearing women examples of signs from American Sign Language that they considered sexist. Not only were the students challenged to exchange their written words in cooperative ways, but they also had to learn new ways of sharing their spoken words, all the while self-conscious that the signs and language they were using constrained their meanings.

Diverse Discourse for Me as a Teacher and a Scholar

I want to end this essay by saying again how invigorating experimentation is for me as a reader, as a writer, and as a teacher. I have read and written more and taught with more enthusiasm as students and I have struggled with genuine questions to which I have no clear answers. They and I have questions and responses, if not answers. In many of my classes, I have felt the balance of power shifting; students have been my teachers in a very real sense, and I theirs, when it was appropriate, which was not always. About my reading and my writing and my teaching, I have felt that I was encountering my work as Gloria Anzaldua describes hers: "an assemblage, a montage, a beaded work with several motifs and with a central core, now appearing, now disappearing in a crazy dance" (66). I find this work much more satisfying than the traditional academic scholarship, social-scientific research on writing that I have been producing. Inter- and cross-disciplinary methods seem much more appropriate for the questions that concern me. A challenge in my future work will be to find ways to integrate this past work with my ways of working now.

I also realize that in many ways I am not like my students and younger members of the profession. I can afford the luxury of experimentation because I am a tenured and reasonably secure member of the profession. During the time when I was establishing my career, I had no rhetorical choices (or thought I had none). I had to write in conventional language, in traditional rhetorical patterns, using accepted research methodologies, if my research articles were to be published. "I" could not be in them at all. For these reasons, I am sympathetic to those who do not feel that they can take risks. But another part of me wants to use the security I have to open doors for others, to consider new possibilities.

I know that this experimentation is important for many students. One former student and composition instructor wrote, in response to this essay,

> In fact, what does go on in freshman composition classes? I would suggest that many of these classes are **HOT-BEDS** of student resistance. The new crop of scholars ... [has] been exposed to feminism in "changed forever" ways. Whether we are resisting the theories or espousing them is really immaterial. . . . We are **ENGAGED** in conversation about them and that creates **NEW MEANINGS**. . . . Meaning about writing, reading, multi-dimensional realities. (Olano 1990, 4)

The real change for me does not lie on the surface of language at all, where I have chosen to begin, but in the deep structure where language and culture interact. In these places, I treasure the new meanings that I and many others have discovered.

NOTE

1. This student has given permission to quote from her essay, so long as she remains anonymous. Several others gave permission to be quoted anonymously;

no student cited anonymously is cited more than once. Others gave permission to me to use their names, and they are cited in the text.

BIBLIOGRAPHY

Albrecht, Lisa, and Rose M. Brewer, eds. *Bridges of Power: Women's Multicultural Alliances.* Philadelphia: New Society Publishers, 1990.

Anzaldua, Gloria. "Bridge, Drawbridge, Sandbar or Island: Lesbians-of-Color Hacienda Alianzas." In *Bridges of Power,* edited by Albrecht and Brewer, 216–31.

Beaugrande, Robert de. "In Search of Feminist Discourse: The 'Difficult' Case of Luce Irigaray." *College English* 50 (1988): 253–72.

Bizzell, Patricia. "College Composition: Initiation into the Academic Discourse Community." *Curriculum Inquiry* 12 (1982): 191–207.

Bock, Mary. "How Do Western Homosociality and Heterosexuality Fit Together? An Invincible Rhetoric for a Vulnerable Cultural Tension." Unpublished student manuscript, n.d., Univ. of Minnesota.

Calderonello, Alice. "Toward Diversity in Academic Discourse: Alice, Sue, and Deepika Talk about Form and Resistance." *ATAC Forum* 3 (Spring/Summer 1991): 1–5.

Cameron, Deborah. *Feminism and Linguistic Theory.* New York: St. Martin's, 1985.

Chase, Geoffrey. "Accommodation, Resistance, and the Politics of Student Writing." *College Composition and Communication* 39 (1988): 13–22.

Chicago, Judy. *The Birth Project.* Garden City: Doubleday, 1985.

Cixous, Hélène, and Catherine Clément. *The Newly Born Woman.* Translated by Betsy Wing. Minneapolis: Univ. of Minnesota Press, 1986.

Daly, Mary. *Gyn/Ecology: The Metaethics of Radical Feminism.* Boston: Beacon, 1978.

Ede, Lisa, and Andrea Lunsford. *Singular Texts, Plural Authors: Perspectives on Collaborative Writing.* Carbondale: Southern Illinois Univ. Press, 1990.

Flynn, Elizabeth A. "Composing as a Woman." *College Composition and Communication* 39 (1988): 423–35.

Gauthier, Xaviere. "Existe-t-il une écriture de femme?" In *New French Feminisms,* edited by Marks and de Courtivron, 161–64.

Gearhart, Sally Miller. "The Womanization of Rhetoric." *Women's Studies International Quarterly* (1979): 195–201.

Heilbrun, Carolyn G. *Writing a Woman's Life.* New York: Ballantine, 1988.

hooks, bell. *Ain't I a Woman: Black Women and Feminism.* Boston: South End, 1981.

Irigaray, Luce. *This Sex Which Is Not One.* Translated by Catherine Porter. Ithaca: Cornell Univ. Press, 1985.

Jespersen, Otto. *Language: Its Nature, Development and Origin.* London: Allen and Unwin, 1922.

Jones, Ann Rosalind. "Writing the Body: Toward an Understanding of l'Ecriture Feminine." In *New Feminist Criticism: Essays on Women, Literature, and Theory,* edited by Elaine Showalter, 361–77. New York: Pantheon, 1985.

Juncker, Clara. "Writing (with) Cixous." *College English* 50 (1988): 424–36.

Kaufer, David S., and Cheryl Geisler. "Novelty in Academic Writing." *Written Communication* 6 (1989): 286–311.

Kristeva, Julia. "La femme, ce n'est jamais ça." In *New French Feminisms,* edited by Marks and de Courtivron, 137–41.

Lilly, Mark, ed. *Lesbian and Gay Writing: An Anthology of Critical Essays.* Philadelphia: Temple Univ. Press, 1990.

Lorde, Audre. "African-American Women and the Black Diaspora." In *Bridges of Power,* edited by Albrecht and Brewer, 206–09.

———. "The Master's Tools Will Never Dismantle the Master's House." In *This Bridge Called My Back: Writings by Radical Women of Color.* edited by Cherrie Moraga and Gloria Anzaldua, 98–101. Boston: Persephone, 1981.

Lu, Min-zhan. "From Silence to Words: Writing as Struggle." *College English* 49 (1987): 437–47.

Marks, Elaine, and Isabelle de Courtivron. *New French Feminisms: An Anthology.* New York: Schocken, 1981.

Maylath, Bruce. "A Question, Please?" Unpublished student manuscript, Univ. of Minnesota.

McNaron, Toni A. H. *I Dwell in Possibility: A Memoir.* New York: Feminist Press, 1992.

Meisenhelder, Susan. "Redefining 'Powerful' Writing: Toward a Feminist Theory of Composition." *Journal of Thought* 20 (1985): 184–95.

Messer-Davidow, Ellen. "The Philosophical Bases of Feminist Literary Criticisms." *New Literary History* 19 (Autumn 1987): 65–103.

Moi, Toril. *Sexual/Textual Politics: Feminist Literary Theory.* London: Routledge, 1985.

Murray, Donald M. *Write to Learn.* 2d ed. New York: Holt, 1987.

Olano, Pamela. "Lesbian Feminist Literary Criticism: A Summary of Research and Scholarship." *Women's Studies Quarterly* 19 (Fall/Winter 1991) 174–79.

———. Letter to the author. Nov. 11, 1990.

Penelope, Julia. *Speaking Freely: Unlearning the Lies of the Fathers' Tongue.* New York: Pergamon, 1990.

Rich, Adrienne. *On Lies, Secrets and Silences: Selected Prose 1966–1978.* New York: W. W. Norton, 1979.

Ripoll, Tania. "Women's Voices?" Unpublished manuscript, n.d.

Ritchie, Joy S. "Confronting the 'Essential' Problem: Reconnecting Feminist Theory and Pedagogy." *Journal of Advanced Composition* 10 (1990): 249–73.

Rose, Mike. *Lives on the Boundary: The Struggles and Achievements of America's Underprepared.* New York: Free Press, 1989.

Russ, Joanna. *How to Suppress Women's Writing.* Austin: Univ. of Texas Press, 1983.

Schubert, Lisa. "The Thing I Came For. . . ." Undergraduate thesis. Univ. of Minnesota, 1990.

Spender, Dale. *Man Made Language.* 2d ed. London: Routledge and Kegan Paul, 1985.

Suleiman, Susan Rubin. "(Re)writing the Body: The Politics and Poetics of Female Eroticism." *Poetics Today* 6 (1985): 44–55.

Tompkins, Jane. "Me and My Shadow." *New Literary History* 19 (Autumn 1987): 169–78.

Williams, Patricia J. *The Alchemy of Race and Rights*. Cambridge: Harvard Univ. Press, 1991.

Woolf, Virginia. *A Room of One's Own*. San Diego: Harcourt, 1929.

Yates, Gayle Graham. *Mississippi Mind: A Personal Cultural History of an American State*. Univ. of Tennessee Press, 1990.

4

Women's Reclamation of Rhetoric in Nineteenth-Century America

Robert J. Connors

Throughout most of Western history, rhetoric was the property of men. The continuing discipline of rhetoric was shaped by male rituals, male contests, male ideals, and masculine agendas. Women were definitively excluded from all that rhetoric implied. Beginning in the nineteenth century, however, with the opening of higher education to women, the theretofore closed field of rhetoric began to shift and change. The shift from a male-dominated rhetoric to one that can encompass other purposes is still taking place, powerfully shaping and changing the discipline over the past two decades and—even more important—shaping us as individuals and teachers. This chapter tells the story of how some of those changes began in the nineteenth century and how they have affected women and men and the ways we think about, use, and teach discourse processes.

The term *rhetoric* is used in this chapter as it would have been used by its practitioners through 1850—that is, as the 2,500-year-old discipline of persuasive public discourse. From its inception in the probate courts of early Syracuse, the techniques of rhetoric were evolved for a single purpose: to create persuasive arguments, to develop and win cases, to put forward opinions in legislative forums, to stake out turf and verbally hold it against opponents in public contest. To use a term popularized by Walter Ong, rhetoric was a quintessentially *agonistic* discipline—concerned with contest. It was ritualized contest, yes, but contest, nonetheless. Argument and debate are verbal agonistic displays, and as Ong has argued, ritual contests of all sorts have been central to Western culture

for as long as we have recorded history. In his book *Fighting for Life,*
Ong traces the strands of agonistic ritual contest between males that
exist in nature and in the convoluted, codified forms of nature we call
culture and civilization. By using Ong's ideas to explore some of what
we know of the history of rhetoric, we can, I think, come to a fruitful
new understanding of why rhetoric assumed the forms it did and how it
has changed and is changing today.

The discipline of rhetoric, as it had evolved from the classical period
through the eighteenth century, was an absolutely male—and thus a
quintessentially agonistic—discipline. Along with logic, its counterpart,
it reified in technical disciplinary form the sometimes inchoate agonistic
longings of a patriarchal society. Classical rhetoric is, plain and simple,
about fighting, ritual fighting with words; this agonistic tone carried over
into all rhetorical study up until the nineteenth century. Feminist scholarship has clearly shown how women had to fight their way into many
intellectual disciplines during the last two millennia of Western culture;
but no discipline was as closed to them as rhetorical study. Through
most of Western history, women were not encouraged to learn to read
or write, though those skills—even the "higher" skills of Latin and
Greek—were grudgingly allowed to women of high social or economic
status. Rhetoric, however, was simply and clearly forbidden to women.
Like battle skills, rhetorical skills were assumed by men to be both beyond women's capabilities and beneath their natures.

This exclusion of women from rhetoric was absolute, and it deeply
affected the discipline. Feminist scholarship in rhetorical history has
scoured all existing records; there are, of course, many women who used
rhetoric, who were known as admirable stylists or influential figures
(Glenn). But we have found not a single woman prior to 1800 who defined
herself, or was defined by those around her, as a rhetorician. This central
discipline, one of the three legs of the trivium of Western knowledge, was
denied women completely. Through the classical era, the idea of women
rhetoricians was either frightening or humorous to male orators. In the
patristic period, Pauline misogyny denied women the right to speak in the
churches, the central rhetorical forums of the time. Throughout the medieval period, the influence of the Church kept women from rhetorical
training or public speaking before mixed audiences.

During the Renaissance, when education for women first came to be
a real issue, we might expect to see a new attitude toward women's
abilities to conduct public affairs, but even such liberal scholars as Leonardo Bruni and Juan Luis Vives worked to close down the emerging

possibilities that women might be taught rhetoric. And through the seventeenth and eighteenth centuries, though colleges developed and became more specialized, women continued to be completely excluded from the capstone discipline of traditional education. Finally, in America during the nineteenth century, women demanded and received access to higher education, and rhetoric changed forever in the face of their determination to have access to it.

Until the nineteenth century, American women shared no higher schooling of any sort with men. There were no colleges for women; education of young women was reserved for the wealthier classes and was carried on, if at all, by private tutors and masters in the parents' home—which was, of course, a young woman's only proper sphere. The strict classical curriculum long taken for granted in all-male colleges was for most of Western history completely unavailable to women, who were shut out even of reading about educational questions and issues because they were seldom taught Latin, the language in which most learned discourse was conducted. Both on the Continent and in the British Isles, women were educationally disenfranchised, and colonial America, where for many years the majority of people of both genders were only minimally educated, merely followed suit in its attitudes.

Even with the establishment after the American Revolution of common grammar schools, higher education for women over twelve years of age was rare. A few female seminaries grew up in the late eighteenth century, but they taught mainly ornamental and domestic skills—sewing, penmanship, music. As American culture matured, however, and the essentially agrarian nature of the society began to give way to manufacturing, a newer urban bourgeoisie evolved, and the status of women in America changed. As Ann Douglas argues in *The Feminization of American Culture,* women in America shifted from producers to consumers during the nineteenth century, from the center of a household-based production economy to the main demand element in a consumption economy based on specialization, industrialization, and nonagrarian extrahousehold workplaces for men (48–68). Women in the American Northeast after 1800 were becoming a more leisured class, and in the egalitarian world of Jacksonian democracy, it was inevitable that institutions would spring up to serve and educate this new class.

The first female academy offering rigorous classical courses was established at Troy, New York, in 1821. The Hartford Female Seminary was established by Catherine Beecher in 1828, Mount Holyoke Female Seminary, in South Hadley, Massachusetts (later Mount Holyoke College), in 1837. Women were demanding their right to an education, and over the next fifty years, the first all-women's colleges were established: Georgia Female College in 1836, Elmira Female College in the mid–1850s, Vassar College in 1860, Smith and Wellesley in 1875, Bryn Mawr and Mount Holyoke in 1888 (Rudolph, 314–19). Separate education for women—including the entire classical course—was a reality by a decade after the Civil War.

More apposite to this study than the general movement for women's colleges, however, is the change wrought on previously all-male colleges by the admission of women. It is in coeducational institutions that we first see truly extraordinary changes in the discipline of rhetoric. The movement toward allowing men and women to go to college together began around the same time the first all-women's colleges were established—the 1830s and 1840s. Oberlin was the first college to allow women to take courses with men, in 1837, but coeducation was a movement slow to be accepted; many educators feared that coeducation would produce "unmanly" men and "unwomanly" women, and fewer than six colleges were coeducational before the Civil War. With the passage of the Morrill Land-Grant Colleges Act in 1862, however, each state was empowered to found an Agricultural and Mechanical College. These schools, especially in the booming Midwest and West, were to become the major state universities. Unshackled by the all-male traditions of many eastern schools, these western universities were nearly all coed from the beginning. By 1872, there were ninety-seven coed schools (sixty-seven of which were in the West). By 1880, 30 percent of all American colleges admitted women, and by the turn of the century this figure had risen to 71 percent (Rudolph, 322).

From no women in colleges in 1830 to three-quarters of all American colleges admitting women by 1900 was a change in educational culture unprecedented in modern history. What we see, within seventy years, is an absolute revision of the all-male enclaves that colleges had been for over a millennium. There were, of course, schools that remained all-male—some even to the present day—but the college experience was ineluctably changed by the gradual influx of young women. This is not the place to detail the horrified objections, the often frantic attempts to safeguard the portals, the manifold arguments advanced against coeducation (Woody, vol. 2). Women were on the move and would not be denied. And where women and men went to college together, the atmosphere and curriculum changed as a result: the atmosphere and tone of life, with startling rapidity; and the curriculum, more slowly but just as certainly. No discipline was as much affected as rhetoric.

Rhetoric entered the nineteenth century as a central argumentative discipline—respected training that was desired by students, was primarily oral, and had a civic nexus. Rhetoric exited the nineteenth century as "composition," a marginalized, multimodal discipline—compulsory training that was despised by most students, was primarily literary, and had a personal, privatized nexus. Coeducation and the decline of agonistic education strongly affected these changes in rhetoric and can be seen to tie together many elements of shifting American discourse education, in particular: (1) the change of student-teacher relationships in rhetoric courses, from challenging and judgmental to nurturing and personalized, a change still in process today; (2) the shift from oral rhetoric to writing as the central classroom focus; (3) the shift from argument as the primary rhetorical genre to a multimodal approach that privileged explanation; and (4) the decline of abstract, distanced subjects for writing and the rise of more personal assignments.

Method: From Agon to Irene

The most general change wrought in the teaching of rhetoric by the influence of women involved the tone and methods of the classroom. From cold, distanced, demanding lecture-recitation teaching and agonistic competition, rhetoric has become, at its most typical, a personalized editorial coalition and, at its most progressive, an irenic, nurturing partnership between teacher and student.

It is difficult for us today to understand what all-male rhetorical education really was like before 1860, because our own experiences are so different. But in an all-male atmosphere, whether the methods were practical or theoretical, rhetorical instruction meant contest—and kinds of contest that had not changed importantly for millennia. In the practical instruction, the methods used were debates and carefully staged persuasive orations—all opportunities for personal display of talent, for contest, for the thrill of victory and the humiliation of defeat. The theoretical instruction, too, was intensely agonistic, using memorization and defense of theses or lecture-and-recitation methods that asked students to take detailed notes of the master's theoretical lecture one day and spit back his own words to him the next in a detailed catechetical recitation. Anyone in a class could be chosen to recite, and woe betide the unprepared reciter, who would be subjected to the severest humiliation and scorn from the master at any hint of error in reciting. "Habitual duel for those in the ranks provided the indispensable sense of security for the men in command," as Laurence Veysey puts it (299).

This constant testing defined the school and college curriculum. It was a tense, rigorous, and demanding curriculum, one that required good students to be perpetually ready to pick up a challenge, answer a point, refute a position, come up with a turn of phrase, and in general protect their vitals from one another and from the master. It is in this kind of agonistic school situation that the long-standing hostility that existed between college faculties and college students grew up.

Education in all-male institutions was set up as a struggle for dominance; one had to wrest authority from the teacher by proving one could "master" the subject—and the proof was by ordeal. The closest comparable phenomena we have today to the older forms of education are probably military boot camps and certain sports rituals; but even these are short-lived reflections of the continuous conduct of all-male education in the past. There was no sense in which student and teacher were assumed to be friends; that is a modern concept. For students of most colleges before 1850, the faculty was the enemy. This may seem a strong statement, but to anyone who has looked into college histories, the dark side of student-faculty relations is very clear.[1] There was no camaraderie and little personal interaction. As W. L. Phelps has testified, the classroom atmosphere was often poisoned by distance, humiliation, and constant testing: "In the classroom, [the faculty's] manners had an icy formality; humour was usually absent, except for occasional irony at the expense of a dull student" (qtd. in Veysey, 295).

The dislike that students often felt for faculty members is not hard to understand, in light of the power of the old-time faculty and the ways they could use it. Before the growth of an administrative bureaucracy in the nineteenth century, all conditions of colleges were set by faculty vote. As Burton Bledstein puts it in *The Culture of Professionalism,* "the tutor played the role of a judge rather than a teacher, and his relationship to the students was normally imperious and unfriendly. The feelings of antagonism were mutual" (229). Of course, this antagonism usually played itself out verbally, and thus rhetorically, in the continuing ritualized test, attack, and defense of the agonistic oral educational tradition. Up until the midnineteenth century, most final exams were oral and public. They were ordeals, and anyone might press the candidate with questions: "College graduates in the audience, like the masters of arts in the medieval universities, were privileged to inject questions of their own or to criticize the answers of the candidates" (Schmidt, 100). This system, which can be traced back to the classical period, often led to lasting distrust and bad feeling between students and teachers. Although students often hated this contestive milieu, faculty members felt that such testing was their only certain method of inculcating knowledge. In the words of Lawrence Veysey, "Only one tactic remained at the disposal of their superiors: the compulsory examination, given at rapid intervals. The continuity of the frequent classroom test in the American system of higher education, from the days of the small colleges down into the period of the new university, revealed a similar continuity of student alienation from the system of which he was supposedly the most essential part" (298). Today, of course, such testing is minimized, and we tend to see professors who engage deeply in it as pathologues; for us, the "defense" of the doctoral dissertation or master's thesis is a curious relic, an atrophied survival of a harder time no one remembers. Few doctoral candidates really have to stand and fight for their theses against determined professorial foes, and it is hard for us to imagine what a student-teacher bond of distrust and hostility might mean.

Among other things, such a relationship meant that the fixed lines of ritual agonism sometimes slipped, and the contest became physical rather than merely verbal. Between 1800 and 1875, there were violent rebellions of students against faculty at Princeton, Miami, Amherst, Brown, the University of South Carolina, the University of North Carolina, Williams, Georgetown, Harvard, Yale, Dartmouth, Lafayette, Bowdoin, City College of New York, Dickinson, and DePauw. Princeton alone saw six violent riots against the faculty between 1800 and 1830. At Virginia, professors were publicly whipped by mobs, and one was shot to death. The president of Oakland College in Mississippi was stabbed to death. At Yale, one tutor was fatally wounded and another maimed by students. Stonings of faculty houses and other minor acts of violence were too common to catalogue. One paradigmatic episode occurred in 1855 at Davidson College, where the students rioted because their mathematics problems were too difficult. They barricaded themselves inside a dormitory and threw rocks at the faculty members who came to investigate. "One of the latter," reports George P. Schmidt, "a West Pointer, drew a sword, and, following his lead, the professors advanced on the dormitory, battered down the door with an ax, and suppressed the rebellion" (82–83).

It is not surprising, in such an atmosphere of persistent anxiety, insecurity, hostility, and contest, that rhetoric and debate would be important subjects. Prior to 1875, almost all students studied rhetoric, and many joined the extracurricular debating societies that were ornaments of almost every college. Such courses and clubs did prepare students for professional life at the bar or in the pulpit, of course, but they were also popular for the same reason that martial arts schools and street gangs now proliferate in tough neighborhoods: if you are liable to attack, self-defense skills are important. Being able to handle yourself verbally was a prime requisite of success in all-male colleges. Life there before 1875 was in many senses a contest (if not a battle), and rhetoric was the primary weapon.

When women entered colleges, this agonistic rhetorical culture was swept away, and rhetoric itself was changed forever. The primary effect of coeducation was the quick decline of public contest as a staple of college life. As Ong argues, the agonistic impulse is a purely male-against-male phenomenon. Males perceive it as honorable to struggle ritually—either physically or verbally—with other males. Even to be bested in such contests preserves honor, if one has obeyed the rules of the contest. The winner and the loser have established a hierarchy they agree on and can shake hands. But to struggle in ritual contest with a *woman?* It was unthinkable. There was no precedent for it, and no psychological rationale (Ong, 51–96). Fighting with a woman, to the agonistically charged male, is ignoble on the face of it. To be victorious in such a contest would confer only slightly less shame and loss of face than to be defeated. Real men don't fight women. Thus, when women entered the educational equation in colleges, the whole edifice built on ritual contest between teacher and student and between student and student came crashing down.

We see evidence of this great change everywhere in reports of college experiences between 1860 and 1900. Living arrangements changed, of course, but of more interest to us are the differences in academic life. The tone of classroom interchange underwent a rapid shift in coed colleges. From having been arenas of contest, the lecture halls and recitation rooms became forums of irenic discussion. The atmosphere changed from one of boredom punctuated by anxiety and hostility to one more decorous. During this period, the lecture-recitation and thesis-defense methods of earlier days gave way to discussion-centered classes, laboratory methods, and seminars—all of which, it will be noted, minimize the agonism inherent in the constant testing of recitation methods. Participation in classes became elective rather than compulsory, and professors' judgments on student work shifted from oral to written.

Thus, the entire contestive edge of criticism was blunted by distance and undermined by teachers' unwillingness to press women with questions in any "ungentlemanly" way. Professors did not wish to humiliate women by forcing them to match wits or publicly prove their knowledge; male students did not want to look churlish or stupid in front of "the girls." Andrew Dickson White notes that life at the University of Michigan, his alma mater, had changed since coeducation: "Formerly a professor's lecture- or recitation-room had been decidedly a roughish place. . . . Now all was quiet and orderly, the dress of the students much neater." When White asked an old janitor, " 'Do the students still make life a burden to you?' he answered, 'Oh, no, that is all gone by. They can't rush each other up and down the staircases or have boxing-matches in the lobbies any longer, for the girls are there' " (400–01). The tone of classrooms changed completely, and this change was most marked in rhetoric classrooms.

Form: From Public Speaking to Private Composition

The most obvious change in rhetorical instruction itself resulting from these changes was the decline of oral rhetoric and the ascent of writing: the shift from rhetoric as public speaking to rhetoric as composition. To understand this shift, we must first look at oral rhetoric as it related to women prior to the changes that coeducation brought. Women, as early as Anne Hutchinson, had demanded the right to be public speakers, but the culture, still held in check by Pauline stricture, consistently placed blocks in their ways. Public speaking was for men, not for women; most women would not imagine their world being any different. The U.S. Supreme Court, denying Myra Bradwell the right to be an attorney, opined that "the natural and proper timidity and delicacy which belongs to the female sex evidently unfits it for many of the occupations of civil life. . . . The paramount destiny and mission of woman are to fulfill the noble and benign offices of wife and mother. This is the law of the Creator" (Bradwell v. Illinois, 16 Lawrence 130 [1873]). Even educated women knew they had no chance of practicing civic oratory, as Molly Wallace's valedictory oration of 1792 at the Young Ladies Academy of Philadelphia shows: "But yet it may be asked, what has a female character to do with declamation? That she should harangue at the head of an Army, in the Senate, or before a popular Assembly, is not pretended, neither is it requested that she ought to be an adept in the stormy and contentious eloquence of the bar, or in the abstract and subtle reasoning of the Senate—we look not for a female Pitt, Cicero, or Demosthenes" (*Rise and Progress,* 74).

We hear over and over again in the nineteenth century the same refrain: the proper province of women is the home, not the public assembly. In 1837, the Congregational ministers of Massachusetts responded with a harsh pastoral letter to abolitionist Angelina Grimke's daring to speak to public mixed audiences. The letter condemned "the mistaken conduct of those who encourage females to bear an obtrusive and ostentatious part in measures of reform, and countenance any of that sex who so far forget themselves as to itinerate in the character of public lecturers or teachers" (Hosford, 82).

The situation of rhetorical instruction for women mirrored these attitudes. The early women's seminaries did teach rhetoric to their charges, but it was a curiously old-fashioned analytical rhetoric, not the praxis-based active rhetoric taught to men. Catherine Beecher's Hartford Female Seminary taught rhetoric in the 1830s using Pestalozzian methods that did not include actual speaking: "In rhetoric and logic, the classes are required to analyze the ideas, arguments, and arrangement of certain pieces pointed out by the teacher. They are also required to compose examples of the various figures of rhetoric, and of the various modes of argument, syllogisms, etc., pointed out in logic" (Woody, I, 433). Rhetoric in the Jacksonian era was still essentially argumentative (and even brawling) and could be fed to women only in harmless bits and pieces, stripped of its popular uses. Though women's academies and colleges were founded in increasing numbers through the 1820s and 1830s, the public arts of oratory and debate were forbidden at many women's colleges; the prospectus of Vassar in 1865 announced that methods of education would be womanly and that "no encouragement would be given to oratory and debate." Debating societies, so popular at men's colleges, were pronounced "utterly incongruous and out of taste" for women (Hosford, 83).

This phenomenon is illustrated by the experience of the women at Oberlin College, the first American college to permit coeducation. In the early years, the women of Oberlin, though trained using Whately's argument-based *Elements of Rhetoric,* were given only written composition to do and were denied oratorical training. As Frances Hosford says in her history of coeducation at Oberlin, "The women of our earlier decades found every approach to public speaking closed to them, because nobody supposed that any woman in her senses would try to become either a minister or a lawyer. . . . Accordingly, the undergraduate men were trained in debate and oratory, the undergraduate women in essay writing" (71–72).

The women formed a Ladies' Literary Society, after being refused permission to join the men's debating society, and read essays and poems to each other at meetings. They were forbidden, however, to conduct debates, either in class or at meetings, and so in the 1840s Lucy Stone and Antoinette Brown formed a clandestine women's debating society. This society met first in the woods, then in the parlor of a local woman's house, and was forced to post sentinels whenever it met. "We shall leave this college with the reputation of a thorough collegiate course," Stone said at the first meeting, "yet not one of us has received any rhetorical or elocutionary training. Not one of us could state a question or argue it in a successful debate. For this reason I have proposed the formation of this association" (94–95).

The gradual admission of women to the mysteries of rhetoric could not, however, be long gainsaid. They were too insistent, and the reasons for denying them were too weak. Women would be given access to rhetoric or they would take it. We see the crumbling barriers clearly reflected in the changing Oberlin commencement ceremonies. Traditionally, each graduate gave a short, carefully prepared oration at commencement, speaking from memory. In 1841, when the first women were graduated, the college faced the question of what to do with them. Clearly, they must get some recognition, yet they could not be allowed to speak or to sit on the stage. The solution, as reported by the college: "To avoid the impropriety of having the young ladies read from a platform arranged for the speaking of young men, and filled with trustees and professors and distinguished gentleman visitors, the essays of the lady college graduates were read by the professor of rhetoric, the young women coming upon the platform with their class at the close to receive their diplomas" (67–68). Here the private, interior, "feminine" world of writing is clearly juxtaposed with the world of rough display allowed the men. The women agitated against this structure, so demeaning to them as scholars, but it was not until 1859 that they were allowed even to read their own essays upon the stage at commencement. This reading of essays by graduating women persisted for a decade; the graduating men continued to declaim their memorized orations, while the women were expected to read their essays in a monotone, hands at sides, eyes on text. Then came Harriet Keeler of the class of 1870, a known suffragette and radical. She did not plead for the right to join the men in oratory at commencement, to the relief of her professors. As Hosford tells it,

She did not raise any issue before the crucial moment—and then she
stormed and took the last line of defense. Demurely she tripped upon
the stage, holding the conventional pages like the other sweet girl graduates. Demurely she read the first sentence, eyes modestly fixed upon
her manuscript—and then the paper was discarded, the brave eyes swept
the rows of startled faces, and the sweet girl graduate addressed the
audience! (102)

The docents of Oberlin held out for four more years and then, in 1874,
gave in and allowed full female participation in graduation oratory. The
days of such oratory were numbered, though, and by 1885 the custom
was done away with completely except for the valedictory address.

As women's colleges became more common and coeducation spread
from Oberlin to other schools, teachers of rhetoric, concerned with protecting and developing their discipline, found themselves in an uncomfortable position. Rhetorical theory, which had since 1783 been led in
the direction of belles lettres and writing by Hugh Blair's *Lectures,* was
beginning by 1830 to turn back toward more traditional oral and argumentative elements under the influence of Richard Whately's *Elements
of Rhetoric* of 1828. Just as it seemed Aristotelian argumentative rhetoric
was picking up steam, however, teachers began to find themselves facing
classes of women. As discussed earlier, argument and debate could not
be major parts of a women's course, and oral thesis defense or thrust-
and-parry was out of the question. A new sort of rhetorical instruction
was needed, one that minimized the agonistic. Women's colleges and
coeducational schools turned increasingly, as had Oberlin, to a form of
discourse that no one found threatening from women: written composition. Composition had been a subject in both grammar schools and academies since the early part of the century, of course, but with the beginning of women's education it was given strong impetus in colleges as
well.[2] Rhetoric needed to be purged of its public and oratorical elements
in order for it to become a safe subject for both men and women. And,
between 1840 and 1890, that is what happened, as rhetoric became composition.

Composition was a safer subject than rhetoric to teach to women or
to mixed classes for several reasons. Unlike the hurly-burly of oral rhetorical praxis, the composition class was quiet. Writing is an essentially
private and interiorized discourse function, and even reading essays
aloud creates a distance between reader and audience that oral rhetorical
speech is deliberately designed to do away with. The intimacy of rhetor-

ical engagement is thus minimized, as is the opportunity for self-display. Composition is contestive only in the most abstract fashion, because it demands from the teacher no public judgments, no invidious comparisons. The judgment of writing was often given in private conferences or in the form of a written comment. The criteria of good performance in writing were easier to objectify; this attempt at objectification characterizes the composition textbooks of the nineteenth century. Composition, usually taught using a plethora of belletristic models, was more culturally oriented, more literary, more in tune with traditional educational goals for women.

This is not to suggest that composition displaced rhetoric only because women threatened male dominance within traditional oral rhetorical training. There were other important reasons for the rise of written-discourse education: the needs of an increasingly far-flung industrial society for cross-continental communication, the rise of an indigenous literary-intellectual culture centered in the Northeast, the egalitarian system of common schooling that guaranteed an increasing percentage of the population basic literacy skills, and the incentive to refine these skills. The culture needed and came more and more to respect writing. However, these reasons for the growth of written rhetoric, real though they are, do not explain the sharp and unprecedented decay of oral rhetoric and of education in oratory, debate, and argument. Why did oral rhetoric, central to education since ancient Athens, the heart of the trivium, one of the first chairs at any university, decline so ruinously in forty years? That falloff can best be explained by the draining away of public agonism in colleges and the consequent collapse of the educational tradition that had grown up to support it. Written composition—private, multimodal, interiorizing—could be the province of both men and women; public oratory, since it could no longer be the province of men only, ceased to satisfy male psychological needs and was allowed to fall into desuetude.

As women were storming and winning the gates of rhetoric, rhetoric could only mutate. More and more textbooks appeared each year with writing, not speaking, as their primary agenda and, eventually, as their only agenda. In Hugh Blair's *Lectures,* and Richard Whately's *Elements of Rhetoric,* the most popular textbooks in the first half of the nineteenth century, we see the increasingly theoretical nature of rhetoric; from this theoretical base, rhetoric became increasingly differentiated from elocutionary training, which was overtly oral in nature. Textbooks in composition and rhetoric like Samuel Newman's *Practical System,* James Boyd's *Elements,* and George Quackenbos's *Advanced Course* were very popular in women's and coeducational colleges. By 1850, rhetoric had bifurcated into two lines: elocution, which declined, and composition, which prospered and strengthened.

Oberlin's division between men's rhetoric classes and women's essay-writing classes is not singular; throughout coeducational colleges, women were encouraged to study rhetoric as writing or as analysis. In 1867, Sophia Jex-Blake, an Englishwoman, visited various American colleges as an observer of this noble experiment. Oberlin was first on her list, but she also traveled to Hillsdale College in Ohio and to the Mary Institute of Washington University in St. Louis, then on to Antioch College. At both Hillsdale and the Mary Institute, the Oberlin procedure of allowing women "exercises in Composition" weekly, while the men were doing "Composition, Declamation, and Extempore Speaking," was followed. The only rhetoric texts in use at the Mary Institute were Newman's and Boyd's composition-oriented rhetorics and Schlegel's *Dramatic Art and Literature*. At Hillsdale, the women got Quackenbos as freshmen and Whately as juniors but no exercise in oral rhetoric. At radical Antioch, she found the situation somewhat more equal. There was no "Ladies' Course," and "Rhetorical Exercises and English Composition" were expected of everyone.

Oral public discourse was no longer a male enclave, and, its secret agonistic agenda attenuating, it slowly withered. This is not, however, the place for a complete discussion of the decline of oral discourse teaching in America during the latter part of the nineteenth century. Marie Hochmuth and Richard Murphy, writing from a speech-communications point of view, clearly demonstrate how obvious was the decline in elocution. Up until 1825, rhetoric had encompassed writing and its oral delivery, but after 1830 or so the oral aspect of rhetoric, elocution, was increasingly treated as a separate subject. Elocution, which was launched in American colleges around 1825 by the texts of Ebenezer Porter, Jonathan Barbour, and James Rush, hit a tremendous peak of popularity around 1850 and declined thereafter—in almost exact correlation with the entry of women into colleges. Rhetoric was gradually dissociated from the oral agonistic skills of elocution, however, and as Warren Guthrie states, professional connections were shifting as college departments formed: "By 1850 the grouping was not so frequently 'Rhetoric and Oratory' as 'Rhetoric and Belles Lettres' or 'Rhetoric and Composition,' with delivery now relegated to the tremendously popular 'Elocution' " (69).

After the Civil War, however, elocution—especially the old agonistic sort—fell on hard times, for reasons discussed above. It was demoted from a requirement to an elective at most colleges and lost prestige rather sharply, except in the traditionalist (and all-male) colleges of the East, where elocution held on longest. During this time, oral rhetoric and elocution were also changing character, as the old persuasive orations gave way to multimodal and literary effusions in oral, as well as written, discourse. Especially influential in this movement were the theories of the French actor and music teacher François Delsarte (1811–1871), under whose influence "public speaking" began to have a more aesthetic and literary character. From the old, stern Ciceronian tradition of civic oration, public speaking gradually became histrionics, dramatic readings, "interpretations" of poetry, and a host of other completely non-agonistic performances (Shaver, 210). In these, of course, women could share much more easily, and they did.

Earlham College, a coeducational Quaker school, established in 1888 the first speech department in America. Speech contests Earlham was involved in included both orations and dramatic readings and interpretations, but after 1883 there were more dramatic interpretations, as the Quaker ban on dramatics broke down. Such readings as "The Guardian Angel" and a pantomime called "The Romance of Mary Jane" were common, and eventually readings from Shakespeare became most popular. Debating began in 1897, but, in spite of women being allowed in oratorical contests, all debate team members mentioned in Earlham records are men (Thornburg, 216–17).

The last hurrah of oral agonistic rhetoric was, in fact, intercollegiate debate. George Pierce Baker of Harvard was instrumental in setting up these debates in the late 1880s, but the vogue for them was brief. We might view intercollegiate debating as a hothouse flower, a forced blossom of agonism made to grow artificially in a place where it no longer took natural root. As at Earlham, college debating in general was overwhelmingly male-dominated. It never made much headway, however. Bliss Perry describes his own attempts to popularize debate at Princeton during the fin de siècle: "Oratory was beginning in the eighteen-nineties to lose vogue in all the eastern colleges, and the best I could do at Princeton in that field was to prop up for a while a building that was doomed to fall" (135). By the turn of the century even the brief revival of oral agonistic discourse provided by the intercollegiate debate movement was expiring.

Meanwhile, the composition strand of rhetorical studies was rapidly gaining strength at all institutions. Written composition had absolute predominance in actual teaching time after 1870, and college composition courses became an almost universal requirement at exactly the same point when elocution courses were being remanded to elective status. Between 1870 and 1900, rhetoric became, for all intents and purposes, composition. As Albert Kitzhaber shows, after around 1850 most rhetoric texts concentrated on composition, with oratory mentioned, if at all, only as one of the various types of composition (138). By 1885, the term *rhetoric* had begun to give way to the term *composition* at most schools, and we seldom see it in textbook titles after 1895. The Harvard Reports and the uproar over "illiteracy" sealed the fate of the older oral rhetoric, already on the decline. Composition, that quiet, multimodal, private, nonthreatening discourse that could be the province of both men and women, ruled the day.

Mode: From Argument to Multimodality

In addition to the change from oral to written discourse, the latter part of the nineteenth century saw a startling decline in the importance of argument and a corresponding rise in interest in other sorts of expression. This transition began long before women entered higher education, of course; multimodal perspectives on rhetoric can be seen as far back as Augustine's *De Doctrina,* and serious modern discussion of nonargumentative modes of discourse began with Adam Smith's rhetoric lectures in 1749 (Connors 1984). The idea that discourse could have ends more valuable than mere persuasion gained credibility from George Campbell's *Philosophy of Rhetoric* of 1776 and was popularized—at least tacitly—by Blair's *Lectures* of 1783, which concentrated on written genres as much as on the traditional oration.

Under Blair's influence, multimodal rhetoric became theoretically very influential in the first three decades of the nineteenth century. Richard Whately's *Elements of Rhetoric* of 1828, however, denied that rhetoric should be "the Art of Composition, universally," and proposed "to treat of Argumentative Composition, generally and exclusively" (6). Whately's book was, next to Blair's immensely popular lectures, the most widely used rhetoric text in American colleges between 1835 and 1865, going through at least fifty-one American printings, and between 1840 and 1850 it began to displace Blair's as the most popular rhetoric text. Under Whately's aegis, it seemed that argument as the primary genre of rhetoric might reappear. We see from the National Union Catalogue records, however, that the popularity of *Elements* diminished substantially after the Civil War, and though it was in print until 1893, only a few colleges used it as a text after 1870.

The reason for the rejection of Whately's text was the increasing popularity of rhetoric textbooks proposing several different modes of discourse. Beginning with Newman's *Practical System* of 1827, American rhetoric textbooks—increasingly and obviously composition text-books—were supplementing Whatelian argumentative rhetoric with other modes. Teachers were coming to prefer books that offered concrete treatments of the different sorts of communication aims writing obviously served. As writing displaced oral rhetoric, the older insistence on a single argumentative purpose did not serve, and in 1866 the desire for a multimodal rhetorical system was met by Alexander Bain, whose *English Composition and Rhetoric* provided the multimodal system that remains definitive to this day (the "forms" or "modes" of discourse): narration, description, exposition, and argument. Bain's modes by no means constituted the only multimodal system—between 1850 and 1880 more than a dozen modal systems were advanced—but his was the most popular. It advanced unstoppably into almost absolute acceptance. Within three decades, argument had been displaced; from being the heart of rhetoric, argument became merely one of its forms (Connors 1981). After 1885, the modes of discourse and their related subset, the "methods of exposition," held complete sway. Rhetoric would never again be taught solely as argument, and in fact, expository discourse would gradually come to be the prime desideratum of composition courses.

Like the reasons for the displacement of oral rhetoric by writing, the reasons for the demotion of argument are not singular. Rhetorics that took nonargumentative forms as important had been around for years, and their acceptance and growth merely confirms the validity of nonargumentative aims and their growing importance to a pragmatic and education-minded culture. Even so, however, acceptance of the Bainian modes—of modal rhetoric in general—is so startling and sudden in the years after 1870 that it gives us pause. At least one important reason for the decline of unimodal rhetoric is the decline of public agonism in colleges and the resultant lack of interest in agonism's central genre, argument.

This decline worked itself out quite pragmatically. As women entered colleges, the older rhetoric courses organized around argument and public contest made men (and some women) uncomfortable. Agonistic behavior directed against women during these Victorian times was really disquieting to many. Part of the reason that oral rhetoric declined at coeducational schools was that many *women* did not want it. President Mahan of Oberlin, whose rhetoric course used Whately's *Elements,* sincerely believed in coeducation but found that many women in his first coeducational class, even with his encouragement, refused to face the men in public contest (Bledstein, 133). Elsewhere, the argument-based courses caused similar discomfort, as college men were asked by professors to do the ungentlemanly, unthinkable act of verbally attacking young women. Argumentative battle that had been psychologically meaningful in all-male courses was now, to many men, dishonorable. The overt agonism of rhetorical argument was more than could be borne, and the only solution was to demote argument and allow for other aims within rhetoric.

Assignment: From Abstract to Concrete

Related to the decline of argument was the slightly later change in the kinds of writing and speaking assignments teachers gave to students. Between 1820 and 1900 the sorts of knowledge that a student in a rhetoric class was expected to command changed radically, in ways that reflected declining agonism (Connors 1987). Students in the older oral rhetoric classes were given abstract, impersonal subjects on which to write and orate. Before 1860, such subjects as "The Baneful Effects of Indulgence" and "The Happiness of Innocence" were commonly assigned—subjects that assumed considerable previous cultural knowledge and had tacit but clear bases in argument. After 1860, however, such abstract topics were increasingly supplanted by subjects based in personal observation—"A Pleasant Evening" or "Of What Use are Flowers?" These descriptive essays were finally joined in the late 1880s and 1890s by assignments that were concrete and overtly personal in nature—"When My Ship Comes In" and "An Incident From School Life." The rhetorical tasks assigned students during the nineteenth century are indeed one long retreat from abstraction and from subjects based outside of immediate cultural and personal experience.

In part, of course, the rise of personal subjects is explicable as further evidence of romanticism as it entered and came to dominate the psychic climate of the century. Personal writing reflected the literary writing and personally based essays that became popular during the first third of the nineteenth century—exemplified in the work of Lamb, Hazlitt, and Carlyle. It can also be understood as a result of the change from oral- to written-discourse education. It is only natural that as oral-discourse education—public by nature—gave way to writing, the subjects of rhetoric would become smaller scale, more private, more personal. But this change can also be seen as evidence of the decline of agonistic discourse that resulted from women's entrance into the colleges. Personal writing, for whatever reason, had not been a part of rhetoric for twenty-four hundred years, and its admission to rhetoric corresponds exactly to the admission of women to rhetoric courses.

Why might this be? Abstract subjects of the older sort are inherently related to agonistic contest. A large part of dealing with nonpersonal subjects involves the obvious deployment of hard-won extrapersonal knowledge; even if the discourse aim is purportedly explanatory, the most effective rhetor is the one who seems to know the most about the world. That is one important method of establishing ethos, the reputation for good character, knowledge, and perspicacity central to any effective appeal. Indeed, this question of ethos and how much a speaker had to know (or seem to know) was a central issue for both Cicero and Quintilian. They were aware that careful use of abstract knowledge—from maxims to precedents to witness to myth—was the very cornerstone of ethos, which was the heart of rhetoric.

Public display of extrapersonal knowledge is agonistic, as every political debate shows and as every serious player of the board game Trivial Pursuit knows well. Even if such fact-based discourse is not explicitly argumentative, it has as a part of its agenda serious display of self. Dazzling listeners with wit, command of facts, and impressive analysis has been a traditional part of ritual male attitudes toward other males. All of the contemporary male verbal agonistic rituals—fliting, the dozens, trading sports statistics, rapping—are displays of skill with facts and knowledge, not merely displays of argument. While they may sometimes seem to be personal, these rituals actually put fictive personae in play in fictive contests. What is at stake here is the ability to manipulate the stuff of language and of the world. Personal interests and personal confession have to do with these contests only tangentially.

In rhetoric, personal observation writing assignments grew out of teachers' frustrations with the paucity of traditional abstract knowledge noted in college students after 1870, as an ever growing percentage of Americans attempted college. In place of the truly abysmal writing that increasingly resulted from assignments like "Filial Affection," teachers came to ask for and accept writing based on personal observation. But as opposed to neutral observation, personal narrations and personal feeling assignments were something new in rhetoric, and such a concession

cannot be completely explained without looking at the rise of coeducation. There were elements of confession, of intimate personalism, and of
antiagonistic admission of weakness in the new topics that could not have
existed prior to women's entrance into higher education. "The Loneliness of Freshmen," a suggested topic of 1912, would have been unthinkable half a century earlier; even admitting such a feeling as loneliness
would have been hooted at as unmanly in the all-male college of 1860.

Personal writing has been traditionally, though not exclusively, associated with women more than with men. Carol Gilligan, Belenky and
her colleagues, and many other feminist critics and scholars have remarked on the commitment to personal feelings and individual emotional
reality found in women's writing, and although that case is not accepted
by all feminist scholars, it is taken very seriously. Less investigated by
scholarship has been the degree to which males are uncomfortable with
personal effusions, but evidence does exist in the journal analyses of
Cinthia Gannett, who found a clear dichotomy between the full, rich,
personal lives recorded in the women's journals in her freshman class
and the narrow, uncomfortable, agonistic mentality found in most male
journals. The rise of personal subjects in composition is related strongly
to women's colleges and to coeducation. Although coeducation was only
one influence among many on the changing of rhetorical assignments
between 1870 and 1900, if women had not entered the world of higher
education, we would today inhabit a very different rhetorical world.

Epilogue: The Creation of the Present

The entry of women into higher education had a profound effect on
college rhetoric. In 1870, 1 percent of college faculty were women; by
1890, that figure had risen to 19 percent. By 1920, 33 percent of all bach-
elors' degrees were awarded to women. Although the early 1920s were
a high point for the percentage of women undergraduate and graduate
students—after that time, their numbers lagged and at times declined
until the 1970s—the great changes in American education had been
wrought by 1900. No more was it, or would it be, an all-male world. And
composition, more than any other one of the humanities, was influenced
by women at all levels. By 1900, over 90 percent of high-school English
teachers were female, and when the *English Journal* was begun in 1911
by the fledgling NCTE, women were substantial contributors to it. (By
1920, more than 50 percent of *English Journal* essays were written by
women.) During this century, the influence on composition teaching

style and methods of these ever larger groups of women teachers and students has been immeasurable.

I do not mean to suggest that the teaching of composition has ever been completely feminized, or that agonistic elements have been purged from writing instruction, or that the feminization of rhetoric has created a perfect world. No one could claim that composition since 1900 has been an irenic love feast or that many of its conditions have been satisfying for teachers or students. However, composition as it has developed is vastly less agonistic than the rhetorical instruction that preceded it; composition has been and remains one of the most feminized college-level disciplines.

It is also, unfortunately, true that composition has been marginalized by the academy, in part at least because it has been so heavily staffed by non-Ph.D.s, especially women. During the first three decades of the twentieth century, between 7 and 16 percent of men in graduate school achieved Ph.D.s within a decade, but that figure never rose from between 3 and 5 percent for women (John 1935, 13–19). Despite the rise in absolute numbers of women in graduate school and the absolute number of female Ph.D.s, there were vastly larger percentages of uncompleted female than male Ph.D.s. Since the Ph.D. was a virtual prerequisite for promotion from instructor rank, most of these women, if they chose to remain in college teaching, were forced to settle into the rank of permanent instructor. And, indeed, Warner Taylor's study in 1929 shows that, of all composition instruction nationwide, 38 percent was being conducted by female instructors (22). This is certainly the highest percentage of female instruction found anywhere in colleges, with the exception of the home economics and nursing departments, and it has surely risen since 1929 (Connors 1990).

The relation between composition theory and women teachers and students during the twentieth century is a fascinating subject, but it cannot be taken up here. Suffice it to say that the current whole-language, writing-process, and social-construction models of teaching seem to be continuing the retreat from agonistic rhetoric that began with coeducation over a century ago. The teaching of composition has been in the hands of women for a long time, but in the last three decades it has evolved into a truly feminized and academically equal discipline—probably the most feminized discipline outside of women's studies. Until the 1970s, the majority of composition theorists were male, but since then a clear preponderance of the most interesting young voices in the field have been women's. No one looking at Ph.D.s in composition since 1980 can doubt that the future of the field—already highly feminized—will be increasingly in the hands of women. So, too, the actual teaching of writing and the direction of that teaching on both secondary and college levels are coming increasingly into the hands of women.

As feminist scholars have pointed out, agonism is not gone from the teaching of writing, and in a pedagogically pluralistic world, it can never—and should never—be gone. Argument and debate, teacher criticism, hierarchies, and personal contest of all subtle sorts will always be with us. But they are no longer at the heart of our discipline, because we have ceased excluding the other half that each man and woman possesses—the nurturing, supportive, interiorized, personal elements in human character that were so long ignored or sneered at while rhetoric was exclusively male ritual. The task remains ahead of us to develop rhetorical pedagogies that give students access to both sides of themselves, that shortchange neither the outer world of demand, action, struggle, and change nor the inner world of feeling, introspection, and the myriad meanings of the self. Only by nurturing the abilities to deal in both worlds will we be able to say we have been teachers of the whole person.

NOTES

1. I do not, of course, want to claim that all teachers were hated, that all students disliked teachers. There were always, as there are today, extraordinary teachers who were beloved and remembered fondly by their students. Indeed, the fond and nostalgic reminiscences such teachers often provoked from their students years later have grown into a sizable subgenre of literature—a subgenre, I would claim, that has perhaps blinded our eyes to the majority of teacher-student relations that were not eulogized by loving disciples. But these teachers have been the exceptions, not the rule.

2. It is interesting to note that Writing and Composition were at first separate subjects in the women's colleges, the former an adult literacy course involving penmanship and word forms, the latter a course in written rhetoric. Woody shows a steep decline in writing courses after 1830 in female seminaries and a strong increase in rhetoric courses, as the women's schools gave less attention to "practical" educational goals like penmanship and turned to courses patterned on those of the male colleges (418).

BIBLIOGRAPHY

Adams, Charles Francis, E. L. Godkin, and Josiah Quincy. "Report[s] of the Committee on Composition and Rhetoric." Reports no. XXVIII, XLIX, and

LXXI. In *Reports of the Visiting Committees of the Board of Overseers of Harvard College,* 117–57, 275–87, 401–24. Cambridge, Mass.: Harvard University Press, 1902.

Bain, Alexander. *English Composition and Rhetoric.* London: Longmans, Green, 1866.

Belenky, Mary Field, Blythe McVicker Clinchy, Nancy Rule Goldberger, and Jill Mattuck Tarule. *Women's Ways of Knowing: The Development of Self, Voice, and Mind.* New York: Basic Books, 1986.

Blair, Hugh. *Lectures on Rhetoric and Belles Lettres.* London: W. Strahan, 1783.

Bledstein, Burton J. *The Culture of Professionalism.* New York: W. W. Norton, 1976.

Boyd, James. *Elements of Rhetoric and Literary Criticism.* New York: Harper and Brothers, 1844.

Campbell, George. *The Philosophy of Rhetoric.* London: W. Strahan and T. Cadell, 1776.

Connors, Robert J. "The Rise and Fall of the Modes of Discourse." *College Composition and Communication* 32 (1981): 444–55.

———. "The Rhetoric of Explanation from Aristotle to 1850." *Written Communication* 1 (1984): 189–210.

———. "Personal Writing Assignments." *College Composition and Communication* 38 (1987): 166–83.

———. "Overwork/Underpay: The Labor and Status of Composition Teachers Since 1880." *Rhetoric Review* 9 (1990): 108–26.

Douglas, Ann. *The Feminization of American Culture.* New York: Knopf, 1977.

Gannett, Cinthia. *Gender and the Journal: Diaries and Academic Discourse.* Albany: State Univ. of New York Press, 1992.

Gilligan, Carol. *In a Different Voice: Psychological Theory and Women's Development.* Cambridge: Harvard Univ. Press, 1982.

Glenn, Cheryl. *Muted Voices from Antiquity through the Renaissance: Locating Women in the Rhetorical Tradition.* Ph.D. diss., Ohio State University, 1989.

Gordon, Ann D. "The Young Ladies Academy of Philadelphia." In *Women of America: A History,* edited by Carol Ruth Birkin and Mary Beth Norton, 68–91. Boston: Houghton Mifflin, 1979.

Guthrie, Warren. "Development of Rhetorical Theory in America, 1635–1850." *Speech Monographs* 15 (1948): 61–71.

Hochmuth, Marie, and Richard Murphy. "Rhetorical and Elocutionary Training in Nineteenth-Century Colleges." In *History of Speech Education in America,* edited by Wallace, 153–77. 1954.

Hosford, Frances Juliette. *Father Shipherd's Magna Charta: A Century of Coeducation at Oberlin College.* Boston: Marshall Jones, 1937.

Jex-Blake, Sophia. *A Visit to Some American Schools and Colleges.* London: Macmillan, 1867.

John, Walton C. *Graduate Study in Universities and Colleges in the United States.* Washington, D.C.: U.S. Government Printing Office, 1935.

Kitzhaber, Albert R. *Rhetoric in American Colleges, 1850–1900.* Ph.D. diss., University of Washington, 1953.

Newman, Samuel. *Practical System of Rhetoric.* New York: Mark H. Newman, 1846.

Ong, Walter. *Fighting for Life: Contest, Sexuality, and Consciousness.* Ithaca: Cornell Univ. Press, 1981.

Perry, Bliss. *And Gladly Teach.* Boston: Houghton Mifflin, 1935.

Quackenbos, George. *Advanced Course of Composition and Rhetoric.* New York: D. Appleton, 1854.

The Rise and Progress of the Young-Ladies' Academy of Philadelphia. Philadelphia: Stewart and Cochrane, 1794.

Rudolph, Frederick. *The American College and University: A History.* New York: Knopf, 1962.

Schmidt, George P. *The Liberal Arts College.* New Brunswick: Rutgers Univ. Press, 1957.

Shaver, Claude L. "Steele MacKaye and the Delsartian Tradition." In *History of Speech Education in America,* edited by Wallace, 202–18.

Taylor, Warner. *A National Survey of Conditions in Freshman English.* Research Bulletin 11. Madison: University of Wisconsin, 1929.

Thornburg, Opal. *Earlham: The Story of the College 1847–1862.* Richmond, Ind.: Earlham College Press, 1963.

Veysey, Lawrence R. *The Emergence of the American University.* Chicago: Univ. of Chicago Press, 1965.

Wallace, Karl R., ed. *History of Speech Education in America: Background Studies.* New York: Appleton-Century-Crofts, 1954.

Whately, Richard. *Elements of Rhetoric.* London: John W. Parker, 1846.

White, Andrew Dickson. *Autobiography.* New York: Century, 1905.

Woody, Thomas. *A History of Women's Education in the U.S.* 2 vols. New York: Science Press, 1929.

5

The Role of Vietnamese Women in Literacy Processes: An Interview

Mary Kay Crouch, with Son Kim Vo

Son Kim Vo is a Vietnamese refugee, one of the boat people who left her country for political reasons. However, when she arrived in the United States in 1981, she was entering it for the fourth time. She came first in 1961 to study for a master's degree in botany at Washington University in St. Louis, having earned her bachelor's degree in biology and education at Saigon University. On her second trip in 1970 she went to the University of Oklahoma for training in the teaching of biology. On her third trip she pursued her Ph.D. in education at the University of Southern California. Her dissertation centered on the role of the community college in Vietnam. When she returned to her country in November 1974, she expected to use her knowledge to implement a community college system in the south, but in April 1975 Saigon fell, and she had no opportunity to pursue these plans. At that time she was a professor of education at Saigon University. With the North Vietnamese takeover, she was forced to spend two years in a "reeducation" program required of all university professors of social sciences. After completing this, she taught educational psychology briefly before she was transferred to the ESL (English as a second language) program at Saigon University.

With no hope of effecting any changes in her country's educational system—the communists, she says, destroyed the morale of both teachers and students—in 1981 Son left Vietnam by boat with her father and husband and arrived at Pulau Bidong Refugee Camp in Malaysia. There she volunteered as education coordinator to work with Australian and

American volunteers to revise the cultural orientation programs and the training programs for the Vietnamese teacher aides. She was also elected refugee camp leader, the first woman to hold this position in the modern history of refugees. As leader, she was in charge of the welfare and security of 14,000 refugees, working in cooperation with both the United Nations and local Malaysian government officials.

On her arrival in southern California, Son joined an established Vietnamese community that now numbers over 100,000 people in Orange County alone. The major shopping and cultural area, known as Little Saigon, draws Vietnamese from all over California and the nation. Son has been immersed in work with this community and its refugee population from the beginning. Within a week of her arrival in the United States, she was employed as a social worker. A year later she was hired to direct a center providing cultural orientation, vocational training, and employment services for new Indochinese refugees. Since 1984 she has served as special consultant on refugee affairs for the California State Department of Social Services. In this position she acts as liaison between social services and refugee communities in Orange and San Diego counties, and she frequently speaks on cultural issues before governmental agencies and nonprofit organizations that provide services to refugees.

In 1988, Son and I met when she added to her state job the position of director of the Intercultural Development Center of Cal State University at Fullerton. As director of the developmental writing program, I had been working with the many nonnative speakers who make up about 60 percent of the basic writing classes taught through this program. The Writing Center on campus, which I also direct, had become, and continues to be, a locus of help for many ESL students. Our mutual interests in assisting Vietnamese and other immigrant students with their language difficulties brought us together initially as professional colleagues; through our continuing concerns for these students, we have also become strong allies and friends. As IDC director, Son serves as an advisor to Vietnamese and foreign-born students, counseling them on adaptation skills for campus life. She also consults with various faculty, staff, and student groups on campus and is an invaluable resource for those of us whose classes and programs serve Asian and international students. In her spare time Son teaches courses in the Vietnamese language at a local community college. This year I have become her student in these courses and have experienced firsthand her practice of education.

Although her life in the United States involves her intensively in refugee and educational activities here, she is still vitally concerned with the state of education in Vietnam. In April 1990, she returned to Vietnam as a consultant to California Congressman Art Torres to negotiate plans for an educational conference that will help facilitate exchanges between Vietnamese and American professors and students. In July and August 1991 Son and I joined several other Cal State professors in a series of ESL workshops held in Hanoi and Ho Chi Minh City.

While she is deeply respectful of and faithful to her Vietnamese culture, Son's academic and professional life can be characterized in part by its positive resistance to that culture. To understand this irony, one must understand something about the role of women in Vietnamese society. In this culture women traditionally hold a special place as the moral educators of the family, ensuring that the children learn about filial piety, respect for elders, honesty, and so on. In the past, many Vietnamese women, especially those living in rural areas, never had the opportunity to attend school beyond the third or fifth grade; they often married at age seventeen. Son, on the other hand, is highly educated; she married much later than was traditional, and she carved out a career for herself in a country where professional women were rarities. Her resistance was a legacy from other women in her family. Son's grandmother had been a successful entrepreneur, bought land in the Delta, and was literate in both Vietnamese and Chinese. Her mother was sent to school and was taught to play musical instruments. Son recalls that both her grandmother and mother were avid readers of Vietnamese and Chinese novels. Son's own womanliness and her ability to span two cultures form the ethos that allows her to marshal her education and knowledge so successfully in so many different areas. She acknowledges that much of her success with students, for example, stems from their perception of her as both an educated woman and an older, trusted woman—in effect, an educator-mother. This was as true with her students in Vietnam as with her students here.

In the United States, the role of Vietnamese women has changed: without the large family network of support they were virtually guaranteed in Vietnam, women now feel it very important to earn degrees, to work, or, at the very least, to be trained for a job. Son compares this changing role with that of other American women who are also finding ways to combine work and family responsibilities successfully. Vietnamese women, too, are in transition. They remain, as mothers, the traditional moral educators of the family, but they also set the tone for a community ethic that places great value on education for females as well as for males.

Son has crossed gender, as well as geographical, boundaries, helping to open doors and providing a model for other Asian women who wish to take up professional careers. In addition, her literacy in three languages (Vietnamese, French, and English), her educational and professional background, her teaching, her efforts to provide refugees access to higher education, her status in the Vietnamese community through her involvement with refugee affairs—all place Son Kim Vo at the center of many issues taken up in this volume.

The following interview with Son Vo addresses several areas. The first concerns her acquisition of English literacy and her composing in English. Second, we discuss literacy and culture with special reference to Vietnamese literacy. Next we talk about the role of Vietnamese women and the impact literacy has had on their lives in this country. Finally, Son discusses her role as what I term an *educator-mother,* who addresses for Vietnamese and international students the problems and disjunctions of living in two cultures.

Son as a Writer

Mary Kay: Let's begin by talking about your language experience. Since you received two degrees in this country, would you tell me about how you learned English?
Son: I don't know if I should disclose that. When I was in Marie Curie High School my last year, I took Vietnamese as a foreign language because this school belonged to the French system of education. Other students took German, English, or Spanish, but I chose Vietnamese because I didn't have time to focus on language study. All my time was focused on my science courses.

Then when I went to the university and was in the School of Education, I was required to have two foreign languages. Vietnamese was not recognized as a foreign language because this was the Vietnamese system. I had French, which was no problem, but English was the other language I had to take. At the university level, they taught only reading comprehension. They expected the students to read English books as course texts. For the first year I learned just basic English, but I had a double major: I was in the School of Education, but I was also in the School of Science, so I spent much of my time in both courses of study.

I confess I neglected English. When I began to study at the university, the Vietnamese system of education was just getting started, and I came with a background of the French system. There were only four students with my similar background; others came from the Vietnamese background. At the beginning, to take notes in the Vietnamese language in science—I was lost in some courses. Though the professors spoke Vietnamese and I could write it, I didn't understand what my notes meant. Working on my notes took a lot of time. But in compensation, when we had a professor from France, another student and I took notes and printed them for the Vietnamese students, because they couldn't take notes at all from the French professor. Doing this, along with taking a double major in education, kept me from studying English as I should have.

At the end of the year, I had to take the language exam, just like everyone else. The professor gave us a book in English and said we had a choice of any text in that book. Fortunately, there was one about the life of Madame Curie, and because I liked the high school I came from and was interested in Madame Curie, I had read a lot of books about her. He asked us to read the text for about ten minutes and then summarize what it meant.

Mary Kay: In English.

Son: No, in Vietnamese. And I didn't read the text at all. I cheated. I didn't study anything because I had all the information. I already knew enough about Madame Curie to write what was necessary. I was so ashamed because the professor gave me eighteen out of twenty possible points on the test.

Mary Kay: So then, how *did* you learn English?

Son: After I graduated from the University of Saigon, I got a scholarship from U.S. AID to study at Washington University. Before coming here, I had to pass a test of English. From July to November I took an intensive class. I studied English grammar for three hours in the morning and conversation in the lab for two hours in the afternoon. In November they sent me to Georgetown University's Institute of Language, and I went through an orientation program for foreign students. We spent three hours every day to learn English. Then I went to Washington University. For the first semester, I was in two programs: English program in the evening and master's program in the day.

I remember an incident about my limited English at that time. One of my professors had a very bad reputation for being most difficult, but I didn't know it when I signed up for his class. Only three of us took his course; I got a *B* and the other two got *C*s. And one of the students who hated him so much used me by telling me to go tell Dr. Wilson, "You're a nut." And I loved all kinds of nuts, so for me that meant "I like you." That was my interpretation. I went to him and I said, "Dr. Wilson, you're a nut." So he asked, "Who taught you that?" And I said, "Doesn't it mean 'I like you'?" and he said no. But because he liked me and was my mentor, what I'd said to him wasn't a problem.

Mary Kay: Still, it had to be terribly difficult for you when you went to Washington University and you didn't have that good a grasp of English. Obviously you had to write lab reports and papers. How did you manage?
Son: It was difficult, since no one really understood my situation, but thanks to science terminology and to my French background, except for some pronunciation of the words I understood things right away. And the science reports didn't have to be so fancy—just write up the experiment, hypothesis, and results. It was very easy to say things in this manner.

Mary Kay: Naturally you continued to use English. How did you improve your use of the language?
Son: I lived in the dorm, and that helped a lot. I lived with the American girls and learned the good as well as the bad things in English. I found out I had improved tremendously in one semester. And then the next year I moved out of the dorm and shared an apartment with an American girl who corrected me and helped me learn appropriate science terminology. Also, I learned how to cook American food.

Mary Kay: In my field we talk a lot about how we go about writing, about our composing process. When I talk to you, however, I'm talking about three languages and perhaps three composing processes. Let me ask you first about French. Do you use it much anymore?
Son: No, only maybe in my thinking. When I try to find an English word, usually the French word comes out—not the Vietnamese, not the English, but the French.

Mary Kay: Given your schooling in the French system through high school, what did you learn about composing in that language?
Son: When I was in the third grade, I began to learn French formally, but because my sister had been tutored privately and I had sat in on that, I already knew enough that I could write from dictation. In tenth grade we began to learn French literature, and I loved to read. And I loved to go to movies and to go to theater, and so my French improved. But in terms of writing, I didn't like it because of the way it was taught.

My ninth-grade year in the boarding school, I had French from a Catholic nun. She brought in models. For example, to describe a house, she took samples from a book. These didn't tell the strategies for describing a house but were real compositions describing a house. She asked the students to memorize the compositions—hundreds and hundreds of them. She thought these models would help us internalize the style, so when we began to write we would pick up a phrase, a sentence, thinking in the French way. I wanted something original, not that. But she used this method because at the end of ninth grade we had to take an exam. And her students might fail in other subjects, but never in her subject. I rebelled. I left her class after that year.

Mary Kay: We still use models in English classes, but we certainly don't ask students to memorize them. Did you ever have a formal class in English composition?

Son: When I went back home after my master's work, I enrolled in the School of Letters and took a formal course in writing, like English 101 here. I got a good teacher, an American teacher, and so the course was very helpful.

Mary Kay: What sort of differences do you find between writing in English and Vietnamese? You've listed a lot of pieces on your resume that you've written for various service programs. You write a column each month for an international Vietnamese Catholic magazine [*Trai Tim Duc Me*]. As you compose in the two different languages, do you see any differences in composing in Vietnamese and composing in English?

Son: Other than differences in the words themselves, I don't think so. I think my background in science dictates most of my style of writing.

Mary Kay: Okay. Tell me a little bit about that.

Son: I must be clear and concise. I am careful about the structure. The introduction should motivate the reader to go through the article, so I bring in some facts here and there, bring up the problem or the issue, explain it, then describe what the issue is, and finally analyze the issue and come to a conclusion. It is like a dissertation or a science report.

Mary Kay: You do essentially the same thing in both languages. Do you usually think a lot about what you're going to say before you write?

Son: I usually think about what I'm going to write before I go to sleep. When I write the column for the magazine, I do that on the plane or at the airport, because I thought of it before. Or I read the newspaper, and from that I get ideas. Or when I watch TV, I get ideas about what I should write.

Mary Kay: What sorts of TV programs do you get ideas from?
Son: Usually *Eyewitness News,* even Oprah Winfrey for the magazine column.

Mary Kay: How do you do that? Do you see something that takes place, a situation, and then go from there?
Son: That's why the readers like my column. I don't make up the stories; they're real. Then I write the facts and use my psychology books as reference and analyze the situation.

Mary Kay: Give me an example of what you write about in the column.
Son: One day when I was home sick, I watched a program on Oprah about sex education, debating whether we should offer sex education or not. There was a group of young people, and Oprah asked them what they knew about sex. And they talked about how they learned about sex. I reported this, where the children learned about sex education, and from there I analyzed which one would be the best resource—friends, parents, experimentation, and so on.

Mary Kay: It sounds as if you're doing a couple of things with that column. First, you're talking to the parents and children about family education. But a topic like sex education seems cultural, too. I want to be very careful here because I may be dealing in stereotypes, but I understand that many Asians don't talk easily about this topic, and here you are in a Catholic paper that goes to readers throughout the world writing about something like sex education. It seems fairly radical to broach this topic with such a large and diverse audience. Are you therefore using your writing to bring in some cultural things that parents need to know about their children? And what kind of reception does this receive?
Son: Yes, parents need to know about this, particularly the older generation. It is my background in both science and education that allows me to discuss this topic in the column.

Mary Kay: And you write this column once a month.
Son: Yes, and after three years or so they will put these columns together into a book.

Mary Kay: Because you also give so many talks to different groups, I'd like to turn to that kind of composing. Do you go about writing these in the same way?
Son: This is a problem for me. Usually groups ask me to write down what I'm talking about. I write this out, but I give a totally different talk. I think that if I put down what I'm talking about, they don't need me

there. I can just give them the paper. So I always consider the papers as a supplement to my talk.

Mary Kay: So you prepare a handout, and you don't talk the handout; you talk the ideas that aren't in the handout.
Son: The organization doesn't need me there if what I say is already written for them.

Mary Kay: You've talked about helping students with their writing projects for the master's thesis here at Fullerton. Surely, this comes from your own experience as a writer.
Son: Yes. When I wrote my dissertation, it was so easy because in all the classes I wrote papers in that direction. It took me only nine months to write my dissertation, since I had done all my literature research already. By the time I wrote, I was ready to do it. I feel that students might as well draw on something they already know about for their writing, rather than having to create an entirely new project.

Usually for the graduate students, the advice I give comes from my own experience. But the professors here, sometimes they don't do that. For one graduate student, I encouraged him just to have a broad view at the beginning, so in that case all the papers would be in that direction. He could focus his readings in that direction then narrow down to the topic of the thesis. That saves time.

Mary Kay: Often professors don't know how to tell students how to go about writing a thesis, yet they need to help students in that way. Because the professors know how to write, they don't consider that someone else needs help in learning how to write this kind of paper.
Son: The professor of the student I mentioned took the task as a very simple one, because he is too high in terms of academics and he cannot go down to the student level. Students spend the most time on the literature research, and if they don't prepare ahead, it will take them a long time.

Culture and Literacy

Mary Kay: Now, let's move our discussion to the implications your three literacies have on you as a Vietnamese. You're literate in Vietnamese; in French, although you don't use it much anymore; and you're obviously literate in English. Sometimes I've asked my writing classes to read a book by Richard Rodriguez, *Hunger of Memory,* in which he says that in order to gain a place in American culture it was necessary for him to give up his own Hispanic culture. He did that. He put away his Hispanic heritage. Much to my surprise, often students agree with Rodriguez rather than arguing with his view.

You went to a French high school. You took Vietnamese as a foreign language. You learned English to complete your master's degree. You have two degrees from American universities, and your work now requires you to spend much of your time speaking and writing English. Do you feel any conflicts between your own Vietnamese culture and American culture with all these experiences?

Son: No. But I think it depends on the individual. If you think multicultural means a melting pot, then you have to melt in order to blend in with the others. But if you think multicultural means a salad bowl, you don't have to forget your own culture, because in a salad bowl each piece still keeps its own identity.

Mary Kay: So you haven't felt any conflict about being Vietnamese in American society or about being Americanized?

Son: No, I don't think so, because as I told you there was inside of me a rebel. For example, when I was in the French school the administration didn't like my long hair—I usually kept it very long—and they gave personal hygiene as a reason to cut my hair. I put my hair into a French braid, and then they had nothing they could say to me. I didn't want to cut my hair.

Mary Kay: It sounds as if you adapted to the school but kept what was important to you. I've talked to some of my own students who've been in this country for ten or more years about conflicts they experience between their home culture and the American culture they've learned through school, TV, their contact with American friends, and so on. For example, one student, whom I'll call Hung, had a hard time with his college major because his father decided he should be an engineer so Hung could make good money when he finished college. First Hung wanted to study music and then business, but he didn't feel he could refuse his father's demands. For over a year he wrestled with this problem, until he moved in with his brother, who talked to their father about the situation and got him to agree that Hung could study business. Taking the Vietnamese students you know as an example, are they also feeling conflicts between their home culture and the larger American culture they're immersed in every day?

Son: Let me answer in this way: When I ask the students if they are interested in taking a course if we offer one about Vietnamese culture on this campus, they all say yes. They say they go into the community and they feel left outside because they don't know how to behave or to act properly. They even make their parents embarrassed when the parent's friends come to their house. They don't want to create that kind of situation anymore. One of the students in our Vietnamese class thanked me because she now understood about the use of *chung no* ["they," which actually refers to inferiors]. Her parents' friends called on the phone, and she referred to her parents as *chung no,* not as *Ba Me,* the proper, respectful form. The friends reported this to her parents, and then her parents yelled at her for being impolite. But she said she didn't mean anything impolite.

Mary Kay: Traditional Vietnamese culture and its language are undergoing changes here in their translation to America. For example, recently you showed me an ad that appeared in a Vietnamese newspaper for a business that will deliver food to the home every day. You mentioned that the ad made you bitter. Why?

Son: This ad reflects the history of Vietnam. If you look, there are some words that are of Chinese origin: *phan luong* and *chuyen nghiep.* Then there is *boong,* which is transcribed from French, but it has become Vietnamese. And of course *gout* is a French word. And *tech-ke* is English. The expression "take care" has been transcribed into Vietnamese and is pronounced much like it is in English. This reflects the history of Vietnam. These words—sometimes I try to see them in a positive way, as a way we can increase our language. But in another way, we are losing words. If we try to translate "take care" into Vietnamese, it is *cham soc,* but if I say "cham soc" with the students, they can't understand it.

Mary Kay: But they understand *tech-ke.*

Son: Yes. I'm bitter in the sense that we are losing something; the language is losing something.

Mary Kay: I was surprised in the fall semester, when we had Vietnamese students in your language class at the community college.

Son: There have been at least six in my classes in the past three years. The young people don't know how to write Vietnamese, which way to put the accent marks. [Vietnamese has five accent marks that affect both pronunciation and meaning.]

Mary Kay: That brings up the fact that you say many of the Vietnamese students can't speak very good Vietnamese, and they also can't read it.

Yet you said there are a number of newspapers available in the community. That fact indicates a high literacy rate among Vietnamese immigrants.

Son: Yes there is, and people want to express themselves. To be the editor or staff writer of a newspaper proves they have education, that they are scholars. So they have pride in working for the paper.

Mary Kay: These papers are free for the taking, a very interesting phenomenon. In America, as you know, newspapers aren't free of charge. Are newspapers also free in Vietnam?

Son: No. In Vietnam, newspapers are sold. But here if they are sold, the papers won't get many readers. So the only way the papers survive and make money and cover costs is to sell the advertisements.

And when I visited some of them, most of them use the garage as the office. But they don't know how to get organized. On one visit I made, someone on the telephone asked the editor, "I'd like to have the same kind of advertisement I used before," and he had to go from wall to wall to see where they have a sample of the old copy. They don't even save an issue from time to time for themselves, and sometimes I can't get a copy of an article I need. When I was at the Orange County *Register* once and saw that operation, I really admired the courage of the Vietnamese newspapers.

Mary Kay: About how many papers are produced every week in the community?

Son: I think now we're over twenty. On Saturday in Little Saigon, you should see the people with the shopping bags, big ones, to collect the newspapers so they can read for a week. That's how they entertain themselves, especially the older people.

Mary Kay: You did say that a lot of the younger people can't read Vietnamese.

Son: Unfortunately, only about 25 percent can read it. I brought some newspapers into school, and I tested by watching the students to see how many would pick them up, but almost none do. It's so sad. The newspapers often print this message: "Don't worry that your children cannot speak English, but worry that your children cannot speak Vietnamese." Even for the Vietnamese Student Association newsletter—I just had to write two articles for them in Vietnamese because they can't do it themselves.

Mary Kay: What about language classes? The Chinese community and the Japanese have Saturday school for their children so the children won't lose the language and culture. You did say one time that some of the young parents are not encouraging their children to learn Vietnamese and retain the culture because they want them to learn American culture.

Son: That was in the first stage of resettlement. The young parents took pride of having children who speak fluent English in a short time. In the beginning, the young parents were not motivated to send their children to these schools. They argued that, since we live here, we have to adopt the new traditions and new customs; they don't want to confuse their children with two cultures. And they felt proud of having their children adopting the new culture rather than preserving the old one. We are in the second decade of living here, so parents now want their children to learn the language and culture.

One thing I had in mind was to write the experiences of the refugees so we don't forget these.

Mary Kay: Of course, this situation you describe is typical of most refugee groups that have come in the past. The first generation of young people want to be so American that they put their parents' culture and language behind them.

Son: There are other factors, political and economic. But when we came here, the American culture seemed superior to the Vietnamese, and that's why the parents took pride in having their children learn English.

Mary Kay: Can you say now that the parents are seeing the value of Vietnamese culture, that American culture isn't superior, just different from Vietnamese?

Son: My niece and nephew at first had a problem of identity. They didn't want to be identified as Vietnamese for two reasons: one, to be Vietnamese means to be a welfare recipient. Two, to be Vietnamese means to be a dog eater, as many Americans assume. They don't want to be identified as Vietnamese. But I told them, if you don't respect yourself, how can you expect others to respect you. And you're Vietnamese; you have to be proud of yourself before you can get respect from other people. Now my niece, a senior in high school, is on a soccer team, and she is very proud of being the only Vietnamese on the team.

I was surprised when a nineteen-year-old boy said to me, "I would like to learn Vietnamese culture because in the future, when I have children and they ask me about Vietnamese culture and life, I will feel ashamed because I don't know it." I was so shocked for a young boy to tell me that. He thought of the next generation.

Women, Education, and Culture

Mary Kay: That comment makes me wonder about who is preserving the culture. Are men as interested as women in doing that, or do men find their place in work here and women retain their traditional role as the transmitters of culture?

Son: Men preserve certain customs, such as ancestor worship and Tet [the New Year celebration]. But the women put all the culture and tradition together. However, women are torn between our culture and the American culture, between the past and the present. In Vietnamese we have a book called *Gia Huan Ca,* which trains a female for her role in the family. It is a poem. In the past every Vietnamese woman had to know what the poem contains. It asks women to think of their main responsibilities: to be a housewife, to be pleasant with the family, with the husband, and to educate the children. This book is part of the culture.

Mary Kay: In what sense do you mean "educate"?

Son: To educate means to instruct the children about being honest, being humanitarian, being unselfish, making the distinction between the wrong and the right, teaching about filial piety, respecting the elders.

Mary Kay: So women teach morality and tradition. Is that still a part of what young women would be expected to do here in this country?

Son: Yes.

Mary Kay: How do they learn that? They go to school longer, many graduate from college. How is it now that the young Vietnamese women learn to be the moral educators of their families in this country?

Son: Through handing the tradition from generation to generation. And if they don't have their mothers or their grandmothers here, they learn it from friends. The media, the Vietnamese magazines and newspapers, are also very important in the family education. They have a column once a week or once a month on family education. And also they try to incorporate traditional sayings, poems, and proverbs into the media. They try to tell people how to cook some special dish for meals that is traditional.

Mary Kay: It seems there is also a strong Vietnamese community ethic that children be academically educated.

Son: Yes. The first question parents ask when they get together is which college are your children in. They feel ashamed if their children aren't in college.

Mary Kay: How do families foster this ethic?

Son: They require the children to study. For example, a group of Vietnamese lived in a certain area we economically call "Villa Park." [The reference here is ironic, since Son is referring to a poor area in Garden Grove, whereas Villa Park is a very well-to-do area.] About 120 families negotiated with the manager for their children to use the conference room of the apartment complex to study and do their homework, because, with so many people living in the apartments, it is hard for the children to study. The children have to show that they've done the assignments, even if the parents don't understand the homework.

Mary Kay: With all the Vietnamese valedictorians at local high schools every June, it seems that all the studying pays off. As part of the community ethic, I assume that young women who are here are also encouraged to get an education. I've had a number of Vietnamese women in my classes, but I find they face conflicts about working and one day being wives and mothers. Is the role of women in Vietnamese society here different from what it was in Vietnam?

Son: In Vietnam we see the future of the woman is to support the family. She is not the primary wage earner, because either she can rely on her husband or on her parent's heritage for support, and life is not under so much pressure as here. Here, we have to work because there is so much demand for material goods. When women come here, they see the relation between education and income, and they know they need to get an education in order to get a better salary and particularly better living conditions.

Mary Kay: So it is fairly well accepted that Vietnamese women can be independent, not marry at a young age, that they can work for a while before they marry.

Son: I think the spirit of independence underlines women's motivation to get an education and work. And here, they work even when they get married. Here, women can lose their husbands any time. Husbands can get killed, and women have no one to rely on except themselves, so they have to prepare for the future.

Mary Kay: Could you make a broader comparison with other Southeast Asian groups and their feelings about women being educated, now that they are here in this country? Is it just as important for the Cambodians, the Hmong, the Laotians to educate women as it is for the Vietnamese?

Son: The Hmong are a special situation. Unfortunately, there are not many role models of educated women among them. The wife is not encouraged to go to school, because the husband fears losing his wife, as I understand it. The husbands try to use the idea that less-educated women are more content to continue their traditional role of wives. The less-educated Cambodians have the same idea. However, the younger Cambodian women have begun to bring some reform in their community.

Through the Department of Social Services and a federal grant, I will bring education to these women, whom I call "homebound wives." They need ESL, but, as an excuse for not going to school to learn English, they say that they don't have transportation and they have to take care of their children and can't leave their homes. To eliminate these variables I am trying to get a place within walking distance so they can go to class. I will schedule the classes while their children are at school. You can call the program "ESL on Wheels." I want to bring the women out of their homes and expose them to the opportunities given to them here in Orange County.

Mary Kay: It seems that the children will leave their mothers behind if they don't know something about the lives their children are leading here. The children will know so much more than their mothers about education, life in America, about getting along, that I wonder if education will become a barrier between the mothers and their children eventually. *Son:* Yes, especially regarding language. But even if they speak English, sometimes real communication doesn't exist. That's why I encourage the Vietnamese to get an education, learn to communicate for a job or at least to communicate with the children. I encourage them not only to learn the language but also about things like sports, so they can keep their children close to them. When a boy begins to talk about baseball or basketball, they will understand.

Mary Kay: Getting back to you and your attitude, you seem to have had an independent spirit even when you were living in Vietnam. You must have been an anomaly there. You were a highly educated woman. You traveled around the country working with educators and schools. Part of the time that you spent in Saigon, your husband was living in the Delta. You left Vietnam shortly after your marriage to get your Ph.D. How did you fit into a society that valued women who stayed at home rather than someone like you who was attempting to reform the educational system in the South? *Son:* I was considered . . . too pushy. Even when I was teaching in high school, I wasn't obedient to the administration; my teaching methods weren't traditional. In my thinking too, I was considered liberal, and that's why I attracted the university students. When I was in the School of Education, I spent lunchtime with students, and they shared with me all kind of intimate stories that they could not share with their parents at home. So if they have a conflict in their family, when the students ask my opinion, they accept what I say about it because they knew I'm not too conservative.

Even here in the IDC at Fullerton, the same happens. For example, when the students have a dance, I write some letters to the parents and explain that we need to help their children to develop socially as well as academically. The parents think I may be conservative so they listen to me. At the same time, I encourage the students to help me by being home on time, not doing anything wrong.

Son as Educator-Mother

Mary Kay: It seems, then, that you take your role as an educator seriously. You educate the parents about the needs their children have, but you also educate the children to respect your willingness to help them and to meet their parent's wishes. While you have no classroom at the university, you use the center as a way of educating the students.
Son: Right. I have to build their trust in me, and, once I have that, they will take my advice. It will be easier for me to do my job.

Mary Kay: In a sense, do you think it's easier for you—that the students listen to you in some ways—because you're a woman and you're acting in a way that women have traditionally always behaved in Vietnamese society? I ask this because sometimes my students talk about their mothers. In fact, they seem to talk only about their mothers: "My mother gave me the money. My mother bought me this car." And sometimes I've asked, "Is you father dead?" because they don't mention their fathers much. But no, their fathers aren't dead, yet the person they talk about all the time is their mother as the one who takes care of everything.
Son: Not only that, but the mother is a woman who understands. And they can be close to her because she doesn't represent an authority. In the family the father is the authority, but the mother is the source of love.

Mary Kay: So the fact that you're not only an educated woman and an educator but that you are a woman helps in what you do here with the students?
Son: I think all [of those]. Because of my education, especially my education from this country, they think that I know everything. [Here Son laughs.] I am mature enough and a woman, so I get their respect, and I

also earn their love. They don't consider me as too conservative, because I encourage them to socialize and their parents don't. I understand them as whole individuals. The Cambodian students and sometimes the Vietnamese, in the morning they just come and give me a hug and then leave. Others give me food—an apple or something like that—to show their appreciation, and a lot of them put their arms around my shoulders and say, "I wish you were my mom."

Mary Kay: So, in effect, you're like a mother to a whole lot of students, or you seem to function in that way.

Son: To the Vietnamese and the international students, I do. For example, one Iranian student was so depressed about his financial situation—he didn't have money to pay his tuition, and he came here crying and said that I understand him without words. Sometimes [when] I was about to close the center . . . he would leave work five minutes early to come here and tell me how he was. I feel blessed for being here to understand students like him.

Mary Kay: If I may, in a sense, have the last word here, using your words, I'd like to quote from the speech you gave when you won the Women's Foundation Progress for Women Award in 1988. You said, "I always believe that each woman . . . has a special value and is assigned to certain responsibilities. A privileged woman should therefore assist an underprivileged one to develop her special talent and dormant abilities, so that she can successfully perform her role in society." It seems that you've lived and you continue to live the philosophy of those words in all the areas you find yourself engaged. Women *and* men benefit from the understanding you have of your role and responsibilities.

6

The Stories of Our Lives Become Our Lives: Journals, Diaries, and Academic Discourse

Cinthia Gannett

Since the 1960s, journal writing has become an increasingly significant part of many English studies curricula and is a central strategy of writing across the disciplines pedagogies (see Burnham; Fulwiler; Fulwiler and Young; Young and Fulwiler). Innumerable articles and books testify to the popularity of the journal as a prewriting tool that develops fluency and generates the habits of observation and reflection, analysis and synthesis.

Yet even as journals ride this recent wave of pedagogical popularity, their buoyancy—their legitimacy in the classroom—is being challenged by more than one strong wind. There is actually an antijournal movement, composed in large part of parents and groups affiliated with the political and Christian Right, which has attacked the use of journals in academic settings as being too personal, for constituting a threat to families by invading their privacy, and for failing to foster correct language use (see Autry; Fulwiler "Guidelines"; Macrorie; Schinto; Schlafly). Many academics as well have questioned the appropriateness of journal keeping in school, sharing some of the concerns of the parent groups. Some question whether journals foster the same intellectual "habits of thought" that other academic writing tasks presumably require (Bizzell), whether their use might sponsor writing that is mechanically or grammatically sloppy or incorrect (Hollowell and Nelson), and whether some topics students might raise in journal should be considered overly personal for school use (Heath; Hollowell and Nelson). But neither those who find journals a panacea nor those who find them problematic have

generally sought to understand the "short happy life" of the journal in
its fuller cultural or historical contexts.

Consider the word *journal*. As a college English teacher, when I think
of that term, several images come to mind. Students freewriting for the
first ten minutes of class or working at some informal in-class assignment, each in his or her own book; one in a bound, yellow spiral notebook, one on a green legal pad, another using lined theme paper in a
blue three ring binder. Or three students in a group sharing entries that
respond fully, spontaneously, and yet thoughtfully to an excerpt from
Machiavelli, an essay by C. P. Snow, a poem by William Carlos Williams.
Or one student, at home some autumn evening, sipping cocoa, brain-
storming or drafting or rereading an earlier entry and making thoughtful
new connections between texts.

Now consider for a moment the word *diary*. What associations does
that word carry? Private, personal, introspective? The diaries of Anne
Frank, Anais Nin, and May Sarton come to my mind. I imagine someone
like my grandmother Grace or my great-grandmother Hilda Carolina
committing to paper the retelling of a family event, a birth or death, some
private thought—maybe a religious meditation, even a recipe, or a list of
work to be done in the garden. Or possibly a young girl confiding to her
diary about a problem at school, planning her future, meeting an "awe-
some" young man, or just wondering about her life—considering her
clothes at one moment, her conscience at another. Too personal for the
classroom? Too subjective to cultivate the appropriate habits of thought
required for rigorously objective academic work?

Indeed, much of the controversy surrounding the use of journals in
college writing may well be related to their close implicit affiliation with
our current notions of the diary, which we tend to perceive as nonacademic, nonintellectual, overly personal, and importantly, as a feminized
discursive form. The notion that the diary is a kind of "girl's writing"
may be a demonstration of what may be identified as an intuitive grasp
of the obvious, but what is obvious is also often invisible, because we
look through it and not at it.

Indeed, if the terms were not similar or overlapping, most teachers
would not need to spend so much time explaining to students how journals and diaries are different. This implicit tension between the *journal*
and the *diary* is prominently displayed in the "Guidelines for Using Journals in School Settings," approved by the National Council of Teachers
of English and published as the introduction to Toby Fulwiler's *The Journal Book*. The guidelines stress the distinction between journals as ap-

propriate academic writing and diaries as writing inappropriate for school. The introduction to the guidelines states, for example, "Because journals provide students considerable freedom to express their thoughts and feelings, students often write about private and intimate subjects—subjects that more properly belong in *personal diaries* than *school journals*" (Fulwiler, 5; emphasis added). The final suggestions exhort us to explain to our students that journals are not like diaries, although they borrow certain features, such as being written in the first person (see also Fulwiler 1982, 17). Clearly, the effort here is to legitimize and ameliorate the use of the term *journal* by dumping all its undesirable cargo of association onto the decks of the term *diary*.

Yet despite various efforts at clarification, many students sense that both journals and diaries belong, in part, to a set of gendered traditions of discourse that lie at best at the margins of the academic discourse community and are, therefore, neither appropriate nor particularly valuable. No wonder students are often confused when asked to keep a journal. Putting journals and diaries back into some of their larger social and historical contexts, including an examination of the ways in which gender marks their development, might serve to clarify and reconnect teachers' and students' perceptions of these literacy practices.

This chapter will provide some provisional contexts for the gendering of journal and diary traditions and consider the manner in which these gendered traditions surface in the journal writing our students produce in our classes and in their attitudes about journals. The gendering of the journal exemplifies the larger issue of the tension between marginalized and muted discourse communities, specifically those of women, and the traditionally dominant discourse communities of public and academic life, which were constructed historically by men and for men using their own models of language and epistemology. These muted discursive forms and practices can and should be reclaimed as powerful and intellectually valuable types of writing.

Historical Contexts and the Gendered Heritage of the Journal

Although journals were promoted as prewriting tools by researchers like D. Gordon Rohman and Albert O. Wlecke in the early 1960s, along with the introduction of writing process or expressivist pedagogies, compositionists sometimes forget that they were not *invented* in the 1960s. Rather, journals, diaries, and logs have a long complex history dating from at least 56 A.D. (Lowenstein 1987), and flourishing in a variety of forms and traditions both within and outside of the academy.

Indeed, until roughly a hundred years ago, the words *journal* and *diary* were in many respects synonymous, coming from similar Latin roots meaning *daily* and referring to almost any kind of daily or periodic writing. The chimerical terms *journal* or *diary* have encompassed everything from the tenth-century pillow book of Sei Shonagon to fourteenth-century Irish scribes' jottings and personal marginalia in Celtic on the Latin texts they were transcribing, commenting on a great phlegm that came upon them or how much wine was available to drink during religious holidays. The development of the various forms of the journal-diary stretches procrustean to fit over and across ancient public journals of accounts and daybooks; travel journals; expedition and military logs; the journey of the spirit as documented in the countless spiritual journals and diaries born of the Protestant Reformation; and the rich and varied entries in fifteenth-century manorial commonplace books and assorted domestic chronicles. With the epistemological shift of the Renaissance toward valuing the individual knowing self, these multiple strands transform and coalesce (although they each continue to develop separately as well) over the next few hundred years into the secular personal journal or *book of the self* that is the primary popular meaning of the term today (Dobbs; Fothergill; Gannett 1987, 1992; Kagle; Lowenstein 1982, 1987; Mallon; Ponsonby; Shields).

While most of us are generally not aware of the complex origins or early history of journals and diaries, many of us are familiar with the journal as a minor literary genre populated primarily by a few good men like John Evelyn, Samuel Pepys, and the early Puritan fathers in the seventeenth century, James Boswell in the eighteenth century, and trancendentalists like Henry David Thoreau and Ralph Waldo Emerson in the nineteenth century. Yet, women have for centuries kept journals or diaries of many types as well (see Begos 1987, 1989; Blodgett 1988, 1991; Bunkers 1987, 1990, 1993; Bunkers and Huff, forthcoming; Cooper 1987, 1991; Culley; Franklin; Huff 1985, 1989; Hoffman and Culley; Moffat and Painter; Ranier; Schlissel; Simons; Sterling) Thus while well-known Puritan and Quaker men, such as John Winthrop, Samuel Sewell, and John Wesley, were practicing their journals of conscience, women like Lady Margaret Hoby, an early Puritan diarist (1599), were keeping their own "account of each day's stewardship" (Fothergill, 19). And by the time Pepys was finishing the engaging secular diaries, replete with sexual candor, that would make him the paradigmatic secular diarist in the eyes of the largely male Victorian audience that discovered him, Celia Fiennes (born in 1662) had started a lively travel and personal journal of her own during her solitary wanderings through the northern England and Wales of the late seventeenth century. Noblewomen, such as Lady Frederick Cavendish, Mary, Countess Cowper, and the duchess of Northumberland, kept entertaining and thoughtful court diaries throughout the eighteenth century.

And while the eminent Samuel Johnson was penning a series of travel diaries during his trips to Wales (1774) and France (1775) in the company of the Thrale family, Mrs. Hester Thrale (later Mrs. Piozzi) was herself composing what would become a very popular social diary based on Johnson's bon mots, *Johnsoniana.* She was also keeping a more personal (and more powerful) diary, *Thraliana.* And a little girl named Fanny Burney, whose family belonged to the same social circle as Johnson and the Thrales, was learning to keep a journal whose form and strategy she would draw on later as she wrote one of the very first novels, *Evelina* (Blodgett, 1–62; Gannett *Gender and the Journal,* 124–41).

The tendency to associate the development of the journal with Pepys, Sewell, and Thoreau rather than Hoby, Fiennes, Thrale, and Burney, to canonize male journal keepers (Blythe 1989; Fothergill 1974; Kagle 1979) but not to canonize, criticize, or even preserve women's journals in a similar manner, signals the common historical practice of muting or silencing women as writers, speakers, and knowers. That women have had a privatized and marginalized relation to language generally and to the various forms it takes both in speech and writing, is well documented by linguists and literary critics. The work of these scholars and many others has exhaustively probed the ways in which women as a group have been muted or silenced; women have been hindered by a public language that frequently distorts or elides their experience, making it difficult for women to name or know themselves or the world as they see it. In addition, women's speech styles and modes of writing have often been devalued or restricted to the private sphere by tradition, by limited access to education, and by the presence of implicit and explicit sanctions against those who ignore cultural norms (Benstock 1987, 1988; Coates; Ehlstain; Frank and Treichler; Kramarae; McConnell-Ginet, Borker, and Furman; Miller and Swift; Nilsen, Bosmajian, Gershuny and Stanley; Olsen; Showalter 1977, 1985; D. Spender 1980, 1986, 1989; L. Spender; Thorne and Henley; Thorne, Kramarae, and Henley).

It comes as no surprise, then, that women have historically tended not to see themselves (or to be seen) as public writers or public knowers.

Indeed, until recently, simple literacy was beyond the reach of most women. Marie de Jars (1565–1645), a protege of Michel Montaigne, considered the father of the essay, writes: "Even if a women has only the name of being educated, she will be evilly spoken of" (Partnow, 129). Even in the middle of the nineteenth century, as John Stuart Mill pointed out, "women who read, much more, women who write, are in the existing constitution of things a contradiction and a disturbing element" (qtd. in D. Spender 1980, 192). Anne Finch, a seventeenth-century writer, summarized the plight of women who would be writers so eloquently she has been often quoted in the twentieth century: "Alas! A woman that attempts the pen, / Such an intruder on the rights of men" (qtd. in Goulianos, 71).

Given these restrictions, it is no wonder that women have been attracted to the journal-diary as a genre (or set of genres) historically available for their attempts at written expression. Indeed, literate women throughout the centuries have created a rich tradition of journal writing and related forms of personal and domestic writing, not only as forms of accommodation to the restrictions they have faced as public writers and generators of language and knowledge but also as forms of resistance to the powerful external and internal discursive constraints placed upon women. Over time, these forms took on their own value and meaning for women. Joan Goulianos writes:

> There exists a rich and complex literature by women that goes back to the Middle Ages, a literature that consists of diaries, of autobiographies, of letters, of protests, of novels, of poems, of stories, of plays—a literature in which women wrote about their lives and from which women and men today can draw insights about theirs. . . . When women wrote they touched upon experiences rarely touched upon by men, they spoke in different ways about these experiences, they often wrote in different forms. Women wrote about childbirth, about housework, about relationships with men, about friendships with women, as wives, mothers, thinkers, and rebels—and about the discrimination against them as writers and the pain and courage with which they faced it. (xi)

Interestingly, journal traditions, which tend to flourish at the margins of public and private discourse, still show clearly the pattern of marginalization and privatization in women's discourse. Women, particularly since the eighteenth century, when they began to be literate in substantial numbers, kept diaries and journals—in large part because domestic correspondence, letter writing, household accounting, and journal keeping had become a required part of women's domestic responsibilities (Ardener, 25). Many of these journals were thus undertaken at the request of, or on behalf of, others in the family or immediate social circle. But while historically considered trivial or mundane, these journals served several important functions in the maintenance of domestic and social life and proved valuable to women's discursive, emotional, and intellectual needs, as well.

While women have tended to write in these privatized (familial, social, personal) forms of the journal, men have more often chosen to employ its more public forms. Penelope Franklin found, in her search for women's diaries for her book, *Private Pages: Diaries of American Women 1830s–1970s,* not only that the vast majority of published diaries were by men, but also that "the men's diaries published were often the tales of exploration, literary or historical figures; or were those of famous literary or historical men," while published women's diaries tended to be those of the "wife, mother, or sister of a famous man" (xiv). (These journals were considered valuable enough to publish because of the light they shed on the famous male, not on the female relation who held the pen.) Margo Culley, in her excellent historical introduction to her anthology of American women's diaries from the eighteenth to the twentieth century, *A Day at a Time: The Diary Literature of American Women from 1764 to the Present,* explains some of the critical differences between the forms and functions of men's and women's journals during this period:

> Many eighteenth- and nineteenth-century diaries were semi-public documents intended to be read by an audience. Those kept by men, in particular, record a public life or are imbued with a sense of public purpose or audience. . . . Women diarists in particular wrote as family and community historians. They recorded in exquisite detail the births, the deaths, illnesses, visits, travel, marriages, work, and unusual occurrences that made up the fabric of their lives. Women for whom that fabric had been torn, who emigrated to this country, traveled as part of the westward migration, joined their husbands on whaling ships, or went to distant lands as missionaries, used journals to maintain kin and community networks. The diaries kept by those women functioned as extended letters often actually sent to those left behind. (3–4)

Certainly many of the women's diaries that create, share, and preserve familial and social information can be seen, in part, as forms of domestic verbal housework that served the interests of the dominant discourse community, not only by freeing up males to do other kinds of writing but also by socializing females and males to their very different roles and discursive positions. Thus, while eighteenth- and nineteenth-century university students, for the most part male, were keeping commonplace books (filled with quotes, witticisms, responses to reading, observations, and apprenticeship writing) as essential supplements to the university curriculum that would prepare them for public life and a life of the mind, many of the females in women's finishing schools were more likely to be taking courses or reading etiquette books on how to keep personal or domestic journals, in order to be proper ladies, good wives, and effective mothers (Blodgett; Culley; Morgan; Solomon).

At the same time, however, in addition to the social and cultural value of the journals themselves, journal or diary keeping has helped women negotiate the relations of language, society, and self by sustaining and nurturing women's otherwise muted discourse networks and communities. Indeed, throughout the eighteenth and nineteenth centuries, American women "created a network of correspondence and mutual support that stretched from North Carolina to Massachusetts and was based on a shared interest in journal writing" (Ranier, 11). Most important, journals have offered women the opportunity to negotiate the claims of language, self, and society by allowing women to be what Margo Culley calls " 'remark'able" (8) on their own terms, particularly since the nineteenth century, as the main strand of the journal-diary tradition came increasingly to be defined as a *book of the self*. Culley explains some of the forces that transformed the nineteenth-century diary into the gendered genre we recognize today:

> In the course of the nineteenth century, as a split between the public and private spheres came increasingly to shape the lives of women and men, those aspects of culture associated with the private became the domain of women. Simultaneously, changing ideas of the self, influenced by romanticism, the industrial revolution, and the "discovery" of the unconscious, contributed to changes in the content and function of the diary. As the modern idea of the secular diary as a "secret" record of an inner life evolved, that inner life—the life of personal reflection and emotion—became an important aspect of the "private sphere" and women continued to turn to the diary as one place where they were permitted, indeed encouraged, to indulge full "self centeredness." American men, unused to probing and expressing this inner life in any but religious terms, found, as the secular self emerged as the necessary subject of the diary, the form less and less amenable to them. (3–4)

In addition to being a valued part of women's muted discourse traditions, the journal has the potential to operate in what Showalter calls the "wild zone" of discourse, outside the purview of dominant discourses (1985, 262). In the journal, women have for nearly five hundred years explored their private worlds and *the* world. The fragmented, recursive, cumulative, and fluid form of the journal has often fit the rhythms of their lives. In this sense the journal may function in part as a kind of *ecriture feminine,* a way of writing, healing, and knowing that acknowledges the lived experience of women and women's bodies. Women have discovered themselves as thinking subjects and inscribed themselves onto a world that has offered fewer opportunities for women than for men to leave their verbal imprint. Thus, Adrienne Rich calls the journal "that profoundly female, and feminist genre" (1979, 217). Women have used it to "read" and "write" themselves into critical self-consciousness, to listen to and develop their own possible voices (Bowles; Sciwy; Bunkers 1993; Cooper 1991; Huff 1991; Myerhoff and Metzger). Many women, over many centuries, have felt like Molly Dorsey Sanford, who writes in her journal in 1859, "I am sure I shall never pose as an author or writer. But I do often wish that I might be something more than a mere machine" (98). Listen to this small sampling of women diarists testifying to the intellectual and emotional life they found in their journals. A much larger sample of these voices can be found in the appendix to this chapter and in *Gender and the Journal* (Gannett, 1992, 142–45).

Fanny Burney, writing on March 27, 1768:

> To have some account of my thoughts, manners, acquaintance and actions when the hour arrives in which time is more nimble than memory, is the reason which induces me to keep a journal. . . . I must imagine myself to be talking to someone whom I should take delight in confiding and remorse in concealment. (Qtd. in Dobbs, 186)

Charlotte Forten, writing on December 31, 1856:

> Once more my beloved Journal, who art become a part of myself,—I say to thee and to the Old Year, Farewell. (Qtd. in Culley, 11)

Marie Bonaparte:

> In writing [the notebooks] I found unspeakable relief, a supreme catharsis. I fled into an imaginary world, far from this world with its tor-

ments, its conflicts and its disappointments. . . . This habit of taking refuge in writing whenever I have been hurt by life has remained with me. (Qtd. in Spacks, 281)

Mary MacLane:

I write this book for my own reading. It is my postulate to myself. As I read it, it makes me clench my teeth savagely; and coldly tranquilly close my eyelids: It makes me love and loathe Me, Soul and bones. (Qtd. in Culley, 13)

Marion Taylor:

How nice a diary is. I could not get along without one. I enjoy writing what has happened as much as I enjoy the happenings themselves almost—thinking about them—living them over again and putting them in words. (Qtd. in Franklin, xvii)

Anais Nin writing in November 1945:

The real Anais is in the writing. (Qtd. in Mallon, 85)

Playing so many roles, dutiful daughter, devoted sister, mistress, protector, my father's new found illusion, Henry's needed all purpose friend, I had to find one place of truth, one dialogue without falsity. This is the role of the diary. (Qtd. in Moffat and Painter, 14)

Margo Culley sums up the views of countless women who have kept diaries with this simple sentence: "I write, therefore I am" (8).

The Gendering of Student Journals

Since 1985, I have been studying the journal writing of women and men in academic settings (Gannett 1987, 1992; Lowenstein, Chiseri-Strater, Gannett 1994). What I have discovered to date suggests that students coming into our composition and literature classes are not *tabulae rasae* with respect to journals. They have inherited, consciously and unconsciously, the complex legacies of these gendered strands of the journal-diary tradition, just as they have inherited their larger gendered discursive positions, and they bring these traditions and positions with them into the classroom in significant ways.

When given the task of writing a journal that was not strictly defined, the men and women in my expository prose class were inclined to create journals consonant with their gendered heritage. The men tended to use their journals as daybooks in which to log, identify, and vent about school assignments in the venerated tradition of the daybook or events log. Each of the three men whose journals I analyzed more closely also had entries reminiscent of an adventure or expedition-travel journal. These extended, three-to-four-page entries, about road trips to Dartmouth or excursions to Boston to see the Celtics, inevitably involved risk, the exploration of new territory, and the possibility (and attendant excitement) of personal danger. Two other men in the class, both of whom had writerly aspirations, used their journals in the Baconian commonplace tradition, interlarding their observations with important quotes and drafts of writing in progress.

As a group, the men made a deliberate effort to stay away from the more obviously personal uses of the journal and were not generally interested in creating texts about their lives. They were also more likely than the women to comment that using the journal to connect their learning with their lives was a chore. One student, Ted, starts his journal in this way:

> 9/24   After an unbelievable start—actually the entire month of September, I am sitting down to my homework assignment—my daily journal. It's been eight years since I've kept any kind of a journal, since seventh grade English. I can't say that I missed doing it—I used to hate it—five pages a week. I think that class is what made me dislike writing. I'm feeling very lost right now in the art of journal writing. (Qtd. in Gannett 1992, 160)

To the extent that these young men saw the journal as "like a diary," which to them meant a place for self-disclosure and introspection, they tended to shun it, seeing it explicitly as gender-inappropriate behavior. A student in another class graphically articulates his view of the feminized nature of the journal assignment this way:

> Sure, I keep a journal too, but I fear it has almost degenerated into a Diary (a label which has always suggested to me something an emotional pre-adolescent keeps, furiously writing out her thoughts every time the captain of the football team looks at her or whenever she develops another pimple). (Qtd. in Gannett 1992, 181)

The men's attitudes also clearly showed in the lengths of the journals they kept. The average length of the men's journals was 48 pages, while the women's journals averaged 119 pages. Indeed, two of the six men who finished the course registered their antipathy or discomfort simply by not writing in their journals outside of class at all after midterm.

The women in that class, as might be expected, although not always sure that journals belonged in the college classroom, felt considerably more comfortable with the overlapping of the journal and diary traditions. Although a few women tried hard not to let "diary" writing (personally connective writing) seep into their journals, most of the women in that class integrated their academic writing with writing on family and friends and domestic and social relationships, in keeping with the earlier women's journal traditions of maintaining domestic verbal networks and chronicling family and social history. The women also actively used their journals as places to define themselves, to construct themselves in texts, as women diarists have done for centuries, demonstrating an implicit sense of the deep connections between access to language and the development of agency, reflexivity, and active thinking. The importance of connecting ideas and language with lived experience and interpersonal realities for women, often described as "connected knowing," has been explored by researchers such as Belenky and her colleagues in *Women's Ways of Knowing*. Several of the women in the class remarked explicitly about using their journals for this purpose. Christina expresses this view thus:

> Writing. A release. A desire to express captured feelings, verbalized thoughts. I need to write. I need to correlate my thinking and my acting—on paper the two seem to flow together. (Qtd. in Gannett 1987, 102)

And Jennifer, in an entry about working in a bookstore:

> I just got the inspiration I think I need to keep a journal. I've been waiting for something related to my writing or reading to note in here—I want it to be "relevant." But isn't everything I do or hear or say relevant to my life and therefore to my writing? (Qtd. in Gannett 1987, 109)

And Cathy:

> I love my journal because it helps me put my struggles, my anxiety, my pressures, my feelings, my good times into perspective. (Qtd. in Gannett 1987, 78)

My women students were clearly working in a journal-diary keeping tradition, albeit one historically outside of academic discourse communities. Indeed, at the time of the study, seven of the eleven women were keeping what they called personal journals or diaries in addition to the class journals. Of the six males, only the two who kept writer's journals had ever kept any kind of journal outside of class, and they kept the same journal for classwork and self-sponsored writing.

This pattern was confirmed in a larger study conducted in four sections of freshman English the following year. In that study, twenty-eight of forty women reported having kept a personal journal or diary outside of school, while only four of the thirty-five men reported keeping something they would identify as a diary or journal. Of those four, one student had misresponded, writing about a required school journal rather than a self-sponsored one; the journals of two others were actually logs, one a climbing log and the other a running log, both undertaken specifically to monitor and improve physical performance. In short, only one of the thirty-five men kept what might be called a personal journal or diary, while nearly four-fifths of the women did.

A critical finding for instructors who assign journals was that the men's and women's attitudes about keeping personal journals carried over into their attitudes about keeping class journals. Of the students who reported having kept any kind of writing journal in school, only 20 percent of the men gave fully positive responses, while 67 percent of the women made only positive remarks. On the other hand, a full 50 percent of the men made only negative evaluations, while only 13 percent of the women responded negatively.

Part of what sustains women's journal keeping is the greater availability of published models by young female diarists and references to diary keeping in popular culture. Female readers of the twentieth century have Anne Frank, Anne Morrow Lindbergh, May Sarton, and Anaïs Nin as real-life models as well as many fictional representations of diary keeping, such as the chapter book novel by Joan W. Blos, *A Gathering of Days: A New England Girl's Journal, 1830–32* and the popular *Babysitter's Club* series by Ann Martin. (One rare exception of popular culture modeling for males is the television series *Doogie Howser* in which the central character, a child prodigy and physician, keeps an electronic journal.) In the same fashion, girls and young women had Marie Baskirtseff and Mary MacLane as models of the intimate journal in the late nineteenth century, and the endearing childhood diaries of Fanny Burney and the feisty little Scottish girl, Marjorie Fleming, in the early part of the nine-

teenth century. More important, girls see journal keeping actively mod-
eled by the girls and women around them. Many of the women I surveyed reported that their mothers, grandmothers, sisters, or friends had
also kept diaries. Girls are also more often recipients of the ubiquitous
flowered or paisley-covered blank books, well over a million of which are
sold each year, as active inducements to initiate diary keeping.

These attitudes and practices appear to be established very early.
Some of the college women I surveyed mentioned that they started their
journals as soon as they could write, that is, by age five or so. The teacher
in my son's combined fourth-fifth grade class, Joan Zelonis, remarked to
me that she had tried to auction off (for good behavior tokens) some blank
books for students to keep for themselves. When she held the books up,
someone called out that only girls would want them, because the boys
would certainly *not* be interested. There was a chorus of agreement. With
her permission, I surveyed the class informally to elicit their definitions
of and attitudes toward journal keeping. I found that elementary school
kids already know a considerable amount about the complex and confusing ways in which journals and diaries are distinct and yet related. To
some students, the terms are still synonymous, but to others, the journal
is already associated with more academic writing, the diary with "secrets."
Below are some representative definitions given by the boys.

> Journal: "A book that you put things you knew for yourself."
> Diary: "It is personal."
>
> Journal: "It's something you write all your thoughts in."
> Diary: "It's the same."
>
> Journal: "A story about yourself."
> Diary: "It's about yourself and it's personal."
>
> Journal: "One kind of journal is where you write about a book you
> read."
> Diary: "A diary is something you write in a book about yourself. And
> I'm not really sure what a journal is."

Here is a sampling of the girls' responses.

> Journal: "Something you keep your thoughts in."
> Diary: "A diary is a book you keep your ideas, feelings, or anything
> you want in. A diary is more private."

Journal: "I think it's a paper that the teacher wants you to write or you may want to write about something."

Diary: "A diary is personal writing you do. It's different because in a journal you write just about what happened and in a diary you write about you or your friends in a personal way."

Journal: "It's something you can tell about, like a trip somewhere, and how you felt about it."

Diary: "I think a journal is things that happened and your reaction and a diary is for feelings and secrets."

Journal: "A book people write personal things in."

Diary: "I don't really think there is a difference."

These elementary school students were quite certain about one thing, however: that girls do (read "should") keep diaries, and boys don't (read "shouldn't"). Jared is very explicit: "Well, the easiest kind of writing for me is about myself. But I don't like diaries." Or, as another boy put it succinctly, "Diaries are sissy things" (Begos 1987, 69).

Importantly, both males and females identified only females (sisters, mothers, or friends) as people they knew who had kept or were keeping a personal journal. Not one of the six boys responding to the survey reported keeping a journal, while six of the nine girls in the class had already begun to do so. These gendered extracurricular literacy traditions, linked with issues of muteness and voice, permeate the journal traditions even in the early years, as exemplified by a journal entry by a nine-year-old girl, the daughter of a colleague of mine, who wrote the following in her school journal on October 27, 1987:

> I think the best part of school is our log books. It's where I keep what I think about school, what we do, and why we have the feelings we have.
>
> I love my log book because I have a way of telling my feelings *without using my voice* [emphasis added]. Another reason is that I can remember what we have done in school and my thoughts.
>
> I think it's a very good idea to have a log book in school.

Final Thoughts: Two Steps Forward, One Step Back

Elizabeth Flynn, in her important article on the connections between composition studies and feminist studies, "Composing as a Woman," writes: "A feminist approach to composition studies would focus on questions of difference and dominance in written language" (114). This chapter attempts to pull back a few of the complex layers of "dominance and difference" that have grown, or have been constructed, around journals and diaries, particularly those associations that collect around the intersections of gender and school writing.

In the university, women have begun to valorize and reclaim the discourse traditions they have historically found empowering, whether or not those forms have been accorded academic or literary status. They have also continued to develop discursive power in ways traditionally reserved for men, particularly elite groups of men. The dramatic increase of women as scholars and teachers in higher education over the span of the nineteenth century participated in, and may have, in part, precipitated significant modifications in the privileged discourses of the academy based on agonism, ritual combat, and strict hierarchies of speaking rights, such as debate, defense, declamation and oratory, lecture and recitation (Connors; Ong; Peaden).

More recently, writing process and associated liberatory pedagogies introduced in the 1960s and 1970s, which promote journaling and other process-based writing and acknowledge the self as the matrix of learning, have also benefited women and included them as learners in important ways (Caywood and Overing; Flynn). Yet various subtle biases remain. For example, Pamela Annas has shown that, while many composition teachers allow, even encourage, some forms of personally connective writing, they order assignments so as to " 'wean' students from subjectivity into objectivity," thereby implicitly reasserting the traditional hierarchy of academic discourse (1985, 360). In this model, journals are relegated to the position of prewriting, not writing; of warm-up exercises rather than the intellectually and emotionally empowering activity of writing they have often been for innumerable women and men through the ages.

The gendered differences observed in the student journals and the controversy surrounding the use of journals in academic settings are indicative of the complex and shifting dominant and muted positions women and men have held in relation to language, society, and schooling. Indeed, many of the discursive practices of the academy continue to alienate, trivialize, and derogate women as speakers, writers, and learners, but those practices are now being identified and called into question. These critiques are increasingly accompanied by the development of pedagogies intended to make literacy education more responsive to all students, including women and other muted or marginalized groups (Annas 1985, 1987; Aronson; Barnes; Bolker; Cambridge; Cayton;

Caywood and Overing; Chiseri-Strater; Frank and Treichler; Gabriel and Smithson; Heilbrun; Mccracken and Appleby; Meisenhelder; Pigott; Sadker and Sadker 1990, 1994; Sandborn; Whaley and Dodge. See also the extended bibliography in Thorne, Kramarae, and Henley).

As for the future of journaling in the academy, it is uncertain. Several journal types, including the more objective forms such as class or reading logs, science lab books, observation notebook in sciences like ecology or forestry, or even sketchbooks in the fine arts, have been accepted practices in the academy at least since Bacon promoted their use to cultivate the habit of regular observation and reflection in young Renaissance gentlemen. Commonplace books have been considered legitimate educational adjuncts since the classical period. These types of journals are in no danger of being expunged. But some forms of the journal introduced (or reintroduced) in the 1960s inadvertently and serendipitously brought certain language practices associated with marginalized communities, particularly women, into composition and other academic classrooms, thus creating, or rather exposing, some of the complex tensions between the dominant-masculine and marginalized-feminine discourse communities (Autry, Mahala, Price).

My preliminary studies with student journals suggest that, while some of the women were at first confused by the confluence of journal writing (which they tended to associate with a set of important discourse practices not necessarily related to formal schooling) and academic writing, most of them got over their initial confusion and created significant texts connecting their lives to their learning. Many of the men, however, were less comfortable with, and sometimes even irritated at, the prospect of writing a *journal,* which they generally felt was doublespeak for *diary,* a genre they perceived as an inferior, inappropriate and "feminized" type of writing, although they, too, implicitly called upon certain journal traditions they found valuable.

Students aren't the only ones confused or alarmed by the use of journals or diaries in schools. As Ken Macrorie writes in the foreword to *The Journal Book,* parents' groups and even some educators are convinced that "journals are dangerous" (3). Some parents' groups have even gone so far as to testify against their use in congressional hearings on abuses of privacy in education (Schlafly) and to sue school districts to prevent them from assigning journals (Melichar). In fact, the primary "danger" posed by the journal appears to be that students might tell the truth about their experience—"Children spill everything in writing" (Melichar, 55)— or that they might ask troubling questions. Also, much of the anxiety seems to center on the possibility that taboo or "secret" subjects, like sexual abuse, incest, or violence against women might surface in the journals. Arguing for the abolishment of personal journals in composition at the secondary level, John Hollowell asks: "Do you really want to read entries on child abuse, group sex, alchoholism, or wife beating?" (Hollowell and Nelson, 14). Or consider the explicitly misogynist assertion in a critique of the Dartmouth curriculum made in the *Hopkins Bulletin* recently. In its condemnation of of the whole women's studies program, the column asserts that women students are required to keep journals that document their "sexual and man-hating development" ("A Look at the Dartmouth Curriculum," 4).

To the extent that these attacks are taken seriously, women's discourse traditions and women's experience and knowledge will continue to be muted or silenced in the academy. Child abuse, and incest, and other forms of violence against women will not disappear just because they can't be written about, nor will those experiences stop having profound effects on students as learners. Indeed, writing about the events that silence and fragment children (female or male, minority or white) can help them heal sufficiently to see themselves as knowers once again. And if that writing makes us as teachers uncomfortable, we must remember how much more uncomfortable these events must be to endure, and we must at least acknowledge the courage it takes to break those silences, to try for the truth. While teachers may legitimately feel that they cannot take on the roles of professional healers, they should not deny the curative potential of writing itself and its relation to knowing (Baumlin and Baumlin).

While it should be acknowledged that the journal-diary, as a locus for personal writing, can encourage reflection, reflexivity, and the development of critical consciousness, the multiple strands of the journal-diary tradition can be utilized in a variety of pedagogical applications. Indeed, the history of the journal-diary and the texts of the students' journals themselves demonstrate that men and women both have many intellectually valuable journal traditions to draw upon, some of which overlap, others traditionally associated more with one gender that the other. Teachers can help students consciously locate themselves in, connect with, and tap into those traditions. They can offer excerpts of particular diaries or journal types for students to read, as well as having students reread and comment on their own journals or those of their peers (see, for example, McKuen and Winkler). Knowledge of the various journal traditions, including their gendered associations, can also help instructors identify and clarify the

kinds of journal writing they feel is most appropriate for particular pedagogical purposes. Above all, teachers can begin to take into account the
kinds of traditions and experience of journals and diaries that men and
women bring to school with them, which inform their experience and
attitudes toward school journals in powerful ways.

Instructors can assign journals as a way of initiating a discussion of
canonicity and marginality in academic discourse and the politics of discourse generally. Why are journals and diaries marginalized forms? How
might race, ethnicity, class, bilingualism and multilingualism, and other
social constructions intersect with or reconfigure journal and diary
traditions (Mlynarcyzk)? Why is the feminized form *diary* the one we
load with negative associations, in order to legitimize the term *journal?*
Why have forms associated with women's discourse traditions often been
trivialized or ignored in the academy? As a student, I read the diaries of
Evelyn, Pepys, and Boswell in literature classes. Yet, the diaries of Nin,
Sarton, and Woolf encountered on my own have empowered me intellectually far more. I had kept a journal-diary off and on since the sixth
grade, but never connected the intellectual and affective power of that
diary with the academic journals I was asking my students to keep until
I began this study.

Furthermore, women in the academy have always had to work in
both dominant- and muted-language communities, speaking, reading,
and writing through and around the discourses and discursive models
constructed by and for men. Hence their "double voice," actually a multiple voice, as Elaine Showalter calls it (1985, 263). Indeed, it might be
educational for men, particularly white, middle-class men, to work in
discourse forms not historically of their making. It might help them become more multivoiced, expand their language conventions and, thus,
their world view, as well as those of the academy itself.

Finally, many students, but particularly marginalized students, and
especially women, have found the journal a place to connect with possible
literary, public, and academic possibilities for their own voices. By voice,
I refer not simply to the sometimes reductive expressivist notion of *personal voice,* but rather to the effort to *give voice* in the difficult social and
historical conditions that have governed the possible voices for women
and other muted groups. It is now a commonplace for many types of
feminisms (Anglo, French, post-structuralist, psychoanalytic, social constructionist, and new historicist) to invoke the body "coming to voice"
as a primary metaphor for women's intellectual development and social
empowerment. Adrienne Rich refers to this struggle to become articu-

late, to become a knower, when she writes in a poem on the astronomer Caroline Herschel (1979, 48):

> I am an instrument in the shape
> of a woman trying to translate pulsations
> into images for the relief of the body
> and the reconstruction of the mind.

Pamela Annas reminds us, "Women students need to stop learning primarily how to translate their own experience into a foreign language and instead spend some time learning their mother tongue" (1985, 371). Evelyn Scott, an early twentieth-century writer, remarks in her diary:

> When I am convinced of something, I am convinced with my whole self, as though my flesh had informed me. Now I *know.* Knowledge is the condition of my *being.*" (Qtd. in Moffat and Painter 90, emphasis in original)

Adrienne Rich puts it simply, "The stories of our lives become our lives" (qtd. in Hubbard, Henifen, and Fried, 4). What better place to write ourselves, women *and* men, into knowing, into being, than in "a book of our own"?

APPENDIX
Women Diarists on the Value of Journal-Diary Keeping

Sei Shonagon (966/67–1013?)
If writing did not exist, what terrible depressions we should suffer from. (Qtd. in Partnow 39.12)

Louisa May Alcott (1832–1888)
I wrote in my Imagination Book, and enjoyed it very much. (Qtd. in Moffatt and Painter, 31)

Anne Frank (1929–1944)
In order to enhance in my mind's eye the picture of a friend for whom I have waited so long, I don't want to set down a series of bald facts in a diary like most people do, but I want a diary itself to be my friend, and I shall call my friend Kitty.
Thursday 16 March 1944: But still, the brightest spot of all is that at least I can write down my thoughts and feelings, otherwise I would be absolutely stifled! (Qtd. in Moffat and Painter, 35)

Marie Baskirtseff (1860–1884)

[Marie started her journal as a young child. She was always afraid that her journal would be destroyed.]

And in a short time, of me there would remain nothing. . . . This is the thought that has always terrified me; to live, to be so filled with ambition, to suffer, to weep, to struggle, and at the end oblivion! oblivion! as if I had never existed. (Qtd. in Moffat and Painter 46–47)

Nelly Ptaschinka (1903–1920)

February 23, 1918: How much I wanted to write yesterday! How I longed for my diary. But I could not write. Today there is no one at home and therefore I can put my time to good use. When I am excited or sad nothing soothes me like my diary. I find when I am very happy my joy calms down, subsides whilst I write. My diary has become indispensable to me. (Qtd. in Moffat and Painter, 56)

Hannah Senesch (1921–1944)

[Hannah was born in Hungary, escaped to Israel, then returned to Hungary to help her mother escape. She was subsequently caught and killed.]

September 19, 1945: Or do I bear this sorrow from the time when—at the age of seven or eight—I stood beside my father's grave and began to write poems about the hardships of life. I feel I am just chattering. However, this is necessary too. Amid essays, speeches and silence it's good to converse sometimes even if only with oneself. (Qtd. in Moffat and Painter, 72)

Anna Dostoyevsky (1846–1918)

[Anna started her diary while in Europe in 1867, escaping creditors.]

I could record freely; for now I knew that no one but myself could read what I put down in shorthand. (Qtd. in Moffat and Painter, 131)

Sophie Tolstoy (1844–1919)

October 8, 1862: A diary once again. It makes me sad to go back to the old habits which I gave up when I got married. I used to take to writing whenever I felt depressed, and I am probably doing it now for the same reason. . . .

February 25, 1865: I am so often left alone with my thoughts that the desire to write my diary is quite natural. Sometimes I feel depressed but now it seems wonderful to be able to think everything over for myself, without having to say anything about it to other people. (Qtd. in Moffat and Painter, 139, 142)

Ruth Benedict (1887–1948)

October 1912: I want it [my diary] for my very own: I want it to help me shake myself to rights during the next few months. . . .

October 1920: The greatest relief I know is to have put something in words. (Qtd. in Moffat and Painter, 150, 160)

Alice James (1848–1892)

May 31, 1889: I think that if I get into the habit of writing a bit about what happens or rather doesn't happen, I may lose a little of the sense of loneliness and desolation which abides with me. . . . I shall at least have it all my own way and it may bring relief as an outlet to that geyser of emotions, sensations, speculations and reflections which ferments perpetually within my poor carcass for its sins; so here goes, my first Journal! (Qtd. in Moffat and Painter, 192)

Virginia Woolf (1882–1941)
Easter Sunday, April 20, 1919: . . . I got out this diary and read, as one always does read one's own writing, with a kind of guilty intensity. I confess that the rough and random style of it, often so ungrammatical, and crying for a word altered, afflicted me somewhat. I am trying to tell whichever self it is that reads this hereafter that I can write very much better. . . . And now I may add my little compliment to the effect that it has a slapdash and vigour and sometimes hits an unexpected bull's eye. But what is more to the point is my belief that the habit of writing thus for my own eye is good practice. It loosens the ligaments. . . . Moreover, there looms ahead of me the shadow of some kind of form which a diary might attain to. I might in the course of time learn what it is that one can make of this loose drifting material of life; finding another use for it than the use I put it to, so much more consciously and scrupulously in fiction. What sort of diary should I like mine to be? Something loose knit and yet not slovenly, so elastic that it will embrace anything, solemn, slight, or beautiful that comes into my mind. . . .
Monday, October 25, 1920: Melancholy diminishes as I write. (Qtd. in Moffat and Painter, 226–27, 229)

Katherine Mansfield (1888–1923)
October 14: I have been thinking this morning until it seems I might get things straightened out if I try to write. . . . Ah, I feel a little calmer already to be writing. Thank God for writing! (Qtd. in Moffat and Painter, 330)

Joanna Field (Marion Taylor)
[Marion was an English psychologist who wrote *A Life of Her Own* in the 1930s on using the journal as a psychological tool.]
October 10: I began to try and observe what happened when I wrote my thoughts freely without any attempt to control their direction. . . . Only the first sentence or two were concerned with the present and then I plunged into memories of fifteen or twenty years ago, memories of things I had not consciously thought of for all those years, memories that I never knew I had remembered. . . . It seemed that I was normally aware of the ripples on the surface of my mind, but the act of writing a thought was a plunge which at once took me into a different element where the past was intensely alive. (Qtd. in Moffat and Painter, 352)

Florida Scott-Maxwell (1883–?)
[Florida started her journal at age 82.]
As I do not live in an age where rustling black skirts billow about me, and I do not carry an ebony stick to strike the floor in sharp rebuke, as this is denied me. If a grandmother wants to put her foot down, the only safe place to do it these days is in a notebook.

[My notebook] is more restful than conversation, and for me it has become a companion, more a confessional. It cannot shrive me, but knowing myself better comes to that. (Qtd. in Moffat and Painter 362, 364)

NOTE

This essay draws on research and writing from my dissertation, "Gender and Journals: Text and Life in College Composition," University of New Hampshire, 1987, which has been published in revised form as *Gender and the Journal: Diaries and Academic Discourse* (Albany: State University of New York Press, 1992).

BIBLIOGRAPHY

Annas, Pamela. "Style as Politics: A Feminist Approach to the Teaching of Writing." *College English* 47 (1985): 360–71.
———. "Silences: Feminist Language Research and the Teaching of Writing." In *Teaching Writing,* edited by Caywood and Overing, 3–17. 1987.
Ardener, Shirley. *Defining Females.* New York: Wiley and Sons, 1978.
Aronson, Anne. "Remodeling Audiences, Building Voices." Paper presented at the Conference on College Composition and Communication, Atlanta, March 1987.
Autry, Ken. "Toward a Rhetoric of Journal Writing." *Rhetoric Review* 10 (1991): 74–90.
Barnes, Linda Laube. "Gender Bias in Teachers' Written Comments." In *Gender in the Classroom,* edited by Gabriel and Smithson, 140–59. 1990.
Baumlin, James S., and Tita French Baumlin. " "Psyche/Logos: Mapping the Terrains of Mind and Rhetoric." *College English* 51 (1989), 245–61.
Begos, Jane DuPree. "The Diaries of Adolescent Girls." *Women's Studies International Forum* 10 (1987): 69–74.
———, ed. *A Women's Diaries Miscellany.* Weston, Conn: Magic Circle Press, 1989.
Belenky, Mary Field, Blythe McVicker Clinchy, Nancy Rule Goldberger, and Jill Mattuck Tarule. *Women's Ways of Knowing: The Development of Self, Voice, and Mind.* New York: Basic Books, 1986.
Benstock, Shari, ed. *Feminist Issues in Literary Scholarship.* Bloomington: Indiana Univ. Press, 1987.
———. *The Private Self: Theory and Practice of Women's Autobiographical Writings.* Chapel Hill: Univ. of North Carolina Press, 1988.
Bizzell, Patricia. "What Happens When Basic Writers Come to College?" *College English* 37 (1986): 294–301.
Bleich, David. "Gender Interests in Reading and Writing." In *Gender and Reading,* edited by Flynn and Schweickart, 234–66. 1986.
Blodgett, Harriet, ed. *Capacious Hold-All: An Anthology of English Women's Diary Writings.* Charlottsville: Univ. Press of Virginia, 1991.

————. *Centuries of Female Days: Englishwomen's Private Diaries.* New Brunswick: Rutgers Univ. Press, 1988.

Blos, Joan W. *A Gathering of Days: A New England Girl's Journal, 1830–32.* New York: Aladdin, 1979.

Blythe, Ronald, ed. *The Pleasures of Diaries: Four Centuries of Private Writing.* New York: Pantheon, 1989.

Bolker, Joan. "Teaching Griselda to Write." *College English* 40 (1979): 906–08.

Bowles, Gloria. "Going back Through My Journals: The Unsettled Self: 1961–86." *National Women's Studies Association Journal* 6 (July 1994).

Bunkers, Suzanne L. "Diaries: Public and Private records of Women's Lives." *Legacy* 7 (1990): 17–26.

————. " 'Faithful Friend': Nineteenth-Century Midwestern Women's Unpublished Diaries." *Women's Studies International Forum* 10 (1987): 7–17.

————. "What Do Women *Really* Mean? Thoughts on Women's Diaries and Lives." In *The Intimate Critique: Autobiographical Literary Criticism.* Diane Freedman, Olivia Frey, and Frances Murphy Zauhar, eds. Durham: Duke University, 207–21. 1993.

Bunkers, Suzanne L., and Cynthia Huff. *Inscribing the Daily: Critical Essays on Women's Diaries.* Amherst: Univ. of Massachusetts Press, 1995.

Burney, Fanny. *Evelina, or, The history of a young lady's entrance into the world [by] Frances Burney.* Edited and introduced by Edward A. Bloom. London: Oxford Univ. Press, 1968.

Burnham, Christopher C. *Writing from the Inside Out.* San Diego: Harcourt Brace, 1989.

Cambridge, Barbara. "Equal Opportunity Writing Classrooms: Accommodating Interactional Differences Between Genders in the Writing Classroom." *Writing Instructor* 7 (1987): 30–39.

Cayton, Mary Kupiec. "Women's Initiation into Academic Discourse Communities." Paper presented at the Conference on College Composition and Communication, St. Louis, March 1988.

Caywood, Cynthia L., and Gillian R. Overing, eds. *Teaching Writing: Pedagogy, Gender, and Equity.* Albany: State Univ. of New York Press, 1987.

Chiseri-Strater, Elizabeth. *Academic Literacies: The Public and Private Discourse of University Students.* Portsmouth, N.H.: Heinemann Press, 1991.

Coates, Jennifer. *Women, Men and Language.* London: Longman, 1986.

Connors, Robert. "The Feminization of Rhetoric." Paper presented at the Conference on New Directions in Composition Scholarship, University of New Hampshire, Durham, October 1986.

Cooper, Joanne E. "Shaping Meaning: Women's Diaries, Journals, and Letters—The Old and the New." *Women's Studies International Forum* 10 (1987): 95–99.

————. "Telling Our Own Stories: The Reading and Writing of Journals and Diaries." In *Stories Lives Tell: Narrative and Dialogue in Education,* edited by Carol Witherell and Nel Noddings, 96–112. New York: Teacher's College Press, 1991.

Culley, Margo, ed. *A Day at a Time: The Diary Literature of American Women from 1764 to the Present.* New York: Feminist Press, 1985.

Dobbs, Brian. *Dear Diary . . . Some Studies in Self Interest.* London: Elm Tree, 1974.

Ehlstain, Jean Bethke. *Public Man, Private Woman: Women in Social and Political Thought.* Princeton: Princeton Univ. Press, 1981.

Field, Joanna. *A Life of One's Own.* Los Angeles: Tarcher, 1981.

Flynn, Elizabeth A. "Composing as a Woman." In *Gender in the Classroom,* edited by Gabriel and Smithson, 112–26. 1990.

Flynn, Elizabeth A., and Patrocinio P. Schweickart, eds. *Gender and Reading: Essays on Readers, Texts, and Contexts.* Baltimore: Johns Hopkins Univ. Press, 1986.

Fothergill, Robert A. *Private Chronicles: A Study of English Diaries.* London: Oxford Univ. Press, 1974.

Frank, Francine Wattman, and Paula A. Treichler. *Language, Gender, and Professional Writing: Theoretical Approaches and Guidelines for Nonsexist Usage.* New York: MLA, 1989.

Franklin, Penelope, ed. *Private Pages: Diaries of American Women 1830s–1970s.* New York: Ballantine, 1986.

Fulwiler, Toby. "Guidelines for Using Journals in School Settings." Introduction to *The Journal Book,* edited by Toby Fulwiler, 5–8. 1987.

———. *The Journal Book.* Portsmouth, N.H.: Heinemann, 1987.

———. "The Personal Connection: Journal Writing across the Curriculum." In *Language Connections,* edited by Fulwiler and Young, 15–32. 1982.

Fulwiler, Toby, and Art Young, eds. *Language Connections: Writing and Reading across the Curriculum.* Urbana, Ill.: NCTE, 1982.

Gabriel, Susan L., and Isaiah Smithson, eds. *Gender in the Classroom: Power and Pedagogy.* Urbana: Univ. of Illinois Press, 1990.

Gannett, Cinthia. "Gender and Journals: Life and Text in College Composition." Ph. D. diss., University of New Hampshire, 1987.

———. *Gender and the Journal: Diaries and Academic Discourse.* Albany: State Univ. of New York Press, 1992.

Goulianos, Joan. *By a Woman Writt: Literature from Six Centuries by and about Women.* Baltimore: Penguin, 1973.

Heath, Gail. "Journals in a Classroom: One Teacher's Trials and Errors." *English Journal* (Feb. 1988): 58–60.

Heilbrun, Carolyn G. "The Politics of Mind: Women, Tradition, and the University." In *Gender in the Classroom,* edited by Gabriel and Smithson, 2–40. 1990.

Hoffman, Leonore, and Margo Culley, eds. *Women's Personal Narratives: Essays in Criticism.* New York: MLA, 1985.

Hollowell, John, and G. Lynn Nelson. "Bait/Rebait: We Should Abolish the Use of Personal Journals in English Classes." *English Journal* (Jan. 1982): 14–17.

Hubbard, Ruth, Mary Sue Henifin, and Barbara Fried, eds. *Women Look at Biology Looking at Women.* Boston: G. K. Hall, 1979.

Huff, Cynthia. *British Women's Diaries.* New York: AMS Press, 1985.

———. "That Profoundly Female, and Feminist Genre: The Diary as Feminist Practice." *Women's Studies Quarterly Journal* 3–4 (1989): 6–13.

Kagle, Steven. *American Diary Literature 1620–1799.* Boston: Twayne, 1979.

Kramarae, Cheris. *Women and Men Speaking.* Rowley, Mass.: Newbury, 1981.

Kramarae, Cheris, and Paula A. Treichler. "Power Relationships in the Classroom." In *Gender in the Classroom,* edited by Gabriel and Smithson, 41–59.
1990.

Lifshin, Lyn, ed. *Ariadne's Thread: A Collection of Contemporary Women's Journals.* New York: Harper and Row, 1982.

"A Look at the Dartmouth Curriculum." *Hopkins Bulletin* 2 (March 1989): 1–4.

Lowenstein, Sharon Sondra. "The Personal Journal–Journal Keeper Relationship
as Experienced by the Journal Keeper: A Phenomenological and Theoretical
Investigation." Ph.D. diss., Boston University, 1982.

———. "A Brief History of Journal Keeping." In *The Journal Book,* edited by
Fulwiler, 87–98. 1987.

Lowenstein, Sharon Sondra, Elizabeth Chiseri-Strater, and Cinthia Gannett. "Re-
Envisioning the Journal: Writing the Self into Community." In *Writing and
Reading (in) the Academy: Pedagogy in the Age of Politics,* edited by Patricia
A. Sullivan and Donna Qualley. Urbana, Ill.: NCTE, 1994.

Macrorie, Ken. Foreword to *The Journal Book,* edited by Fulwiler, i–iii. 1987.

Mahala, Daniel. "Writing Utopias: Writing across the Curriculum and the Promise of Reform." *College English* 33 (1991): 773–86.

Mahl, Mary R., and Helene Koon. *The Female Spectator: English Women Writers
before 1800.* Bloomington: Indiana Univ. Press, 1977.

Mallon, Thomas. *A Book of One's Own: People and Their Diaries.* New York:
Penguin, 1984.

McConnell-Ginet, Sally, Ruth Borker, and Nelly Furman, eds. *Women and Language in Literature and Society.* New York: Praeger, 1980.

McCracken, Nancy Mellin, and Bruce C. Appleby, eds. *Gender Issues in the
Teaching of Composition.* Portsmouth: Boynton/Cook, 1992.

Meisenhelder, Susan. "Redefining 'Powerful' Writing: Toward a Feminist Theory
of Composition." *Journal of Thought* 20.3 (1985): 184–95.

Melichar, Don. "A Leap of Faith: The New Right and Secular Humanism." *English
Journal* (Oct. 1983): 55–57.

Miller, Casey, and Kate Swift. *Words and Women: New Language in New Times.*
Garden City, N.Y.: Doubleday, 1976.

Mlynarczyk, Rebecca. "Conversations of the Mind: A Study of the Reading/Writ-
ing Journals of Bilingual Students." Ph.D.diss., New York University, 1993.

Moffat, Mary Jane, and Charlotte Painter, eds. *Revelations: Diaries of Women.*
New York: Vintage, 1975.

Morgan, Bob. "Three Dreams of Language: Or, No Longer Immured in the
Bastille of the Humanist Word." *College English* 49 (1987): 449–58.

Myerhoff, Barbara, and Deena Metzger. "The journal as activity and genre: Or,
listening to the Silent Laughter of Mozart." *Semiotica* 30 (1980): 97–114.

Nilsen, Alleen Pace, Haig Bosmajian, H. Lee Gershuny, and Julia P. Stanley, eds.
Sexism and Language. Urbana, Ill.: NCTE, 1977.

Olsen, Tillie. *Silences.* New York: Delacorte/Seymour Lawrence, 1979.

Ong, Walter. *Fighting for Life, Contest, Sexuality, and Consciousness.* Ithaca: Cornell Univ. Press, 1981.

Partnow, Elaine. *The Quotable Woman from Eve to 1799.* New York: Facts on File
Publications, 1985.

Peaden, Catherine Hobbs, ed. and intro. *Nineteenth-Century Women Learn to Write: Cultures and Practices of U.S. Women's Literacy.* Norman: Univ. of Oklahoma Press, forthcoming.

Pigott, Margaret B. "Sexist Roadblocks in Inventing, Focusing, and Writing." *College English* 40 (1979): 922–27.

Piozzi, Hester Lynch. *Johnsoniana; or supplement to Boswell: being anecdotes and sayings of Dr, Johnson, collected by Piozzi [and others].* London: J. Murray, 1836.

———. *Thraliana; the diary of Mrs. Hester Lynch Thrale (later Piozzi) 1776–1809.* Edited by Katharine Canby Balderston. Oxford: The Clarendon Press, 1942.

Ponsonby, Arthur. *English Diaries.* London: Methuen, 1923.

Price, Gayle B. "A Case for the Modern Commonplace Book." *College Composition and Communication* 31 (1980), 175–82.

Ranier, Tristine. *The New Diary: How to Use a Journal for Self-Guidance and Expanded Creativity.* Los Angeles: Tarcher, 1978.

Rich, Adrienne. *The Dream of A Common Language: Poems 1974–1977.* New York: W.W. Norton, 1978.

———. *On Lies, Secrets, and Silence: Selected Prose 1966–1978.* New York: Norton, 1979.

Rohman, D. Gordon, and Albert O. Wlecke. *Prewriting: The Construction and Application of Models for Concept Formation in Writing.* East Lansing: Michigan State Univ. Press, 1964.

Sadker, Myra, and David Sadker. "Confronting Sexism in the College Classroom." In *Gender in the Classroom,* edited by Gabriel and Smithson, 176–87. 1990.

———. *Failing at Fairness: How America's Schools Cheat Girls.* New York: C. Scribner's Sons: 1994.

Sandborn, Jean. "Blocked by the Academic Essay: Case Studies of 'Misfits.' " Paper presented at the Conference on College Composition and Communication, Atlanta, March 1987.

Sanford, Mollie Dorsey. *The Journal of Mollie Dorsey Sanford in Nebraska and Colorado Territories 1857–1866.* Lincoln: Univ. of Nebraska Press, 1976.

Schilb, John. "The Usefulness of Women's Nontraditional Literature in the Traditional Literature and Composition Course." In *Women's Personal Narratives,* edited by Hoffman and Culley, 115–23. 1985.

Schinto, Jean. "Private Lives: Why We Keep Diaries." *Boston Globe Magazine,* Nov. 8, 1987, 22–38.

Schiwy, Marlene. "Taking Things Personally: Women, Journal Writing, and Self Creation." *National Women's Studies Association Journal* 6 (July 1994).

Schlafly, Phyllis, ed. *Child Abuse in the Classroom.* Alton Ill.: Pere Marquette, 1985.

Schlissel, Lillian. *Women's Diaries of the Westward Journey.* New York: Schocken, 1982.

Shields, David. *A History of Personal Diary Writing in New England, 1620–1745.* Ann Arbor, Mich.: University Microfilms, 1982.

Showalter, Elaine. *A Literature of Their Own.* Princeton: Princeton Univ. Press, 1977.

————, ed. *The New Feminist Criticism: Essays on Women, Literature, and Theory.* New York: Pantheon, 1985.

Simons, Judy. *Diaries and Journals of Literary Women from Fanny Burney to Virginia Woolf.* Iowa City: Univ. of Iowa Press, 1990.

Smithson, Isaiah. "Introduction: Investigating Gender, Power and Pedagogy." In *Gender in the Classroom,* edited by Gabriel and Smithson, 1–27. 1990.

Solomon, Barbara Miller. *In the Company of Educated Women: A History of Women and Higher Education in America.* New Haven: Yale Univ. Press, 1985.

Spacks, Patricia Meyer. *The Female Imagination.* New York: Alfred A. Knopf, 1975.

Spender, Dale. *Man Made Language.* London: Routledge and Kegan Paul, 1980.

————. *Mothers of the Novel: 100 Good Women Writers Before Jane Austen.* New York: Pandora, 1986.

————. *The Writing of the Sex? or Why You Don't Have to Read Women's Writing to Know It's No Good.* New York: Pergamon, 1989.

Spender, Lynn. *Intruders on the Rights of Men: Women's Unpublished Heritage.* London: Pandora, 1983.

Sterling, Dorothy, ed. *We are Your Sisters: Black Women in the Nineteenth Century.* New York: W.W. Norton, 1984.

Thorne, Barrie, and Nancy Henley, eds. *Language and Sex: Difference and Dominance.* Rowley, Mass.: Newbury, 1975.

Thorne, Barrie, Cheris Kramarae, and Nancy Henley, eds. *Language, Gender, and Society.* Rowley, Mass.: Newbury, 1983.

Young, Art, and Toby Fulwiler, eds. *Writing Across the Disciplines: Research into Practice.* Upper Montclair, N.J.: Boynton/Cook, 1986.

Whaley, Liz, and Liz Dodge. *Weaving in the Women: Transforming the High School English Curriculum.* Portsmouth, N.H.: Boynton/Cook, 1993.

Winkler, Anthony C., and Jo Ray McCuen. *The Journal Reader.* Fort Worth, Tex.: Harcourt Brace, 1993.

7

Writing a Life: The Composing of Grace

Myrna Harrienger

This chapter presents an ethnographic case study of Grace, an eighty-year-old woman institutionalized after suffering right frontal lobe damage caused by two slight strokes. Grace's oral and written discourse spanned a sixty-two year period, from her eighteenth year until she died in 1988. I am currently studying this work in relation to medical views of old, sick women. Here, I offer a portrait of Grace as a writer, because she used language to control and to name her life in every detail—and to narrate it as well. The sketch illustrates what our composition research has not yet studied, composing as its everyday experience becomes a life-defining practice: it describes the role played by composing through the stages in one woman's adult life, including illness in old age. Janice Lauer correctly notes that "our field knows very little about writing in old age, and nothing about writing in illness." Yet in light of our aging, medicalized society where the majority of the old are women, we have a great need to understand what people like Grace can tell us (see Kahana and Kahana; Riley).

Because Grace's writing extends over the sixty-two years of her adulthood, it illustrates what often eludes shorter-term studies, namely, the enormous potential of rhetoric, especially in its written form, to construct, empower, and validate the ordinary life. Written discourse was central to Grace's mode of life, her self-concept, and her sense of worth and defined her relationship with the persons and events of her lived experience.

Having cared for my mother before she died and later for a friend whose rare disease required constant patient care, I came to Grace's illness keenly aware of what Adrienne Rich notes: "The powerful decide for the powerless . . . the well for the ill" (39). What I now know about medicine, illness, and caregiving began then, with reading, listening to patients, interviewing doctors, and observing caregivers. I was struck by the tendency to treat the chronically ill and the old as if they would become well and by the extent to which health care workers, family, and others attended to the voice of medical authority while being relatively deaf to the discourse of the ill (see Stoeckle; Kleinman). I remain incredulous that the central and often insurmountable difficulty of being old or sick—the sense of loss—goes virtually unnoticed (see Cassell; Zaner).

I first met Grace in April 1987 when her niece Mary, a colleague at a midwestern university, moved her aunt from Florida to a nursing home in the city where Mary lives. After her arrival, Grace and I visited at the nursing home three or four times each week. I found Grace alert, intelligent, articulate, and talented. We shared a no-nonsense approach toward life, perhaps because, as oldest daughters, we had each had to assume early family responsibility. We both enjoyed reading, sewing, and needlework.

"Some things you do because you love to; I guess I have always loved words." Grace's own literacy accounts, frequent and intense, suggested what her writing assured, that composing was a centripetal force in her adult life. Her writing evidences an enormously literate, broadly educated person, even though Grace lacked a college education and had not held the type of job whose work-related writing compositionists currently study. A brief overview of her adulthood writing gives a sense of how language and Grace composed each other.

Three interrelated aspirations—literacy, independence, and relationships—characterize Grace and explain her self-defining involvement with language and the fundamental role of discourse in her personal and professional life. These values are the reasons she wrote. Grace often wrote to share literacy events. She did not write to learn. For persons of her age cohort educated in current-traditional curricula, writing is evidence of, not a means to, literacy. Learning experiences provided purpose and content for much of her completed discourse. Writing allowed her to share these experiences and information while also maintaining relationships with her friends and relatives. Finally, she wrote to maintain that control we associate with independence. For Grace, order and organization were critical elements of this control. Until her illness, Grace's writing included travel booklets and scripts for slide presentations, letters, organization-related writing including club minutes, a dictionary of unfamiliar words, newspaper articles, a eulogy for a friend, and post-cards, as well as several kinds of what Shirley Brice Heath calls jottings, including labels, lists, and files.

Until recently, Grace's discourse would have fallen outside the scope of composition studies. However, Louise Wetherbee Phelps, in her influential work *Composition as a Human Science,* argues convincingly for a broader notion of composition. Defining writing as the practice of composing meaning, a function of reflection as complement to experience, Phelps identifies composition as the potential for such meaning and assigns to composition studies the responsibility for attending to that reflection (65, 67). Using Heath's term, "literate behavior," Phelps includes within the domain of composition the broad panoply of such practices as "writing, reading, speaking, listening, inner speech" (67). This chapter affords us an on-line/off-line reading of one person's composing of meaning and meaning of composing. It illustrates Phelps's view of the dynamic interplay between composition and life "outside the text." Grace exemplifies the intertextual character of a life imbricated in discourse.

Whereas today camcorders and thirty-five-millimeter cameras record and store our memories, memories of the 1930s come to us in neatly labeled albums of black-and-white photos and in scrapbooks. Even in the thirties, though, Grace's travel books were unusual. She produced a travel book for each of twelve auto trips taken with friends during the thirties and early forties to such places as New England, various national parks, Mexico, and world's fairs. For each, she transcribed and typed shorthand notes taken throughout the trip. She then bound each text into a fifty-page booklet nine inches square, which she machine-stitched at the spine and glued to a stiff, blue cover. On the front of each, thin cork letters identify the trip. Besides text, these books include photos, pertinent information from magazines or brochures, and an appendix with a distance and mileage chart, addresses, and a list of tour guide books. Grace's copies also contain an itemized list of her expenses and, occasionally, one or two personal comments. This is where I learned, for example, that she had been more impressed by Mount Rushmore (where only the head of Washington was completed at the time) than by Yellowstone and that, at the Grand Canyon, "having stolen out into a predawn hush before the world had wakened, [she] stood wide-eyed before the rising sun."

Like most of her personal writing, these booklets address a specific, known audience, those who shared the group experiences the piece records. The collective nature of the pieces, then, may account for the lack of self-reference. Almost as an observer, Grace built her narratives around what the group did, where they went, and how much it cost. Rarely did she provide a personal view, thought, impression, or reaction. Even telling about the Mexico trip when her luggage never arrived, Grace's writing is subdued: "I was this side of panic. Here I was with only the clothes on my back with a three week Mexican tour just starting. . . . Make the best of a bad situation and hope. . . . Spent a warm and worried night." This tendency to avoid self-revelation, of course, is more evident in these booklets than in her letters, though her writing generally exhibits the reserve and dry humor interviewees identified with Grace. In such audience-directed prose, the rare, inadvertent self-reference catches one unaware. The sudden shift in tense of this remembrance jettisons the reader into an event fifty years past: "Here I am using Arlie's hair appointment, sitting under a dryer writing my impressions." Through the inadvertent inclusion of shorthand marginalia, the reader is momentarily privy to Grace talking to herself: "Remember when you get home to write Christina a note" or "Have Mom order one of these."

These books also include significant amounts of geographic, historical, or demographic information, duly credited to sources Grace either used to prepare the trip or acquired en route. Like most of her writing, factual information overshadows both particulars about the trips and personal reflections. On one trip, Grace and a companion both wrote travel accounts. They told similar versions of evenings with the cowboys during a stay at a dude ranch near Yellowstone, but how the stories are told contrasts sharply. Louise's account is witty, informal, and written in a familiar style that employs slang, while Grace's references are less direct and less personal, even though she is the anonymous traveler involved in several described incidents. She uses first-person plural pronouns but refers to herself as "Grace" when using the singular. While Grace admits playing the piano most of the evening, we learn from Louise that she played until after midnight to avoid one of the cowboys. Grace also provides more factual information: numbers, names, and times. Louise, though, provides a view of Grace as writer: "There's Gracie writing in the car, at the picnic table, and propped up in bed. She'll turn squiggles into stories, memories of fun in the sun, wait 'n see."

At about the same time Grace was writing about these vacations, her composition also turned an artistic project into a public presentation. A course in puppetry led Grace and her two sisters to make several marionettes for which they developed skits to entertain their nieces. Using these skits as a basis, the sisters organized an act divided into scenes, and Grace wrote the scripts for the marionettes: a clown whose trained seal dances while juggling a ball on its nose; a pair of Spanish dancers; a tall, frail, white-haired pianist who shares his piano with a torch singer; a ballerina; and three marionettes whose faces and clothes match those of Grace and her sisters. The three performed this act locally for several years.

During her marriage of the next fifteen years, Grace photographed but did not write about trips, since, as she explained, "Jack and I could talk about them." Their move from city to farm brought a halt to entries in the notebook listing both movies and plays Grace had attended and over a thousand books she had read during the previous twenty years. "I have new records to keep," Grace wrote then. "My writing has always been tied to what I'm doing, you know," she continued. Too busy for extensive writing, "I stitched curtains instead of pages." "Except for letters, mostly to Ellen after she moved [west], my writing dealt with the farm and the house. Maybe you and Mary wouldn't call it real writing, though." Many of the jottings mentioned below date from this time on the farm. My favorite example, reflecting the frugality of people from Depression years, is a three-by-five-inch notebook whose current label covers another label that reads, "Eggs Sold: 1951–52."

In later years, as a widow living and working again in the city, Grace replaced travel booklets with written scripts to accompany slide presentations she arranged for friends. Those trips to places in Europe, Canada, Mexico, and Japan were also literacy events for Grace. "What I enjoyed most about these trips," she writes to a friend, "is learning all I could about the place and the people." Following the trip's chronology but no longer intended as a record for the travel group, these scripts are filled with information about places and events. Meticulous about details, Grace carefully credits her sources, whether tour guide, residents of countries visited, or printed material.

Because Grace was socialized at a time when Americans used long-distance telephone only for emergencies and depended upon written correspondence to maintain family ties and friendships, letters make up the largest category of her writing. In early adulthood, Grace corresponded with her mother's family in Pennsylvania. (The earliest sample of her writing, though, a kind of journal entry, tells about being graduated from business school, a two-year program Grace completed in six months, and finding a job the next week.) Besides family, friends prompted Grace to write. Interestingly, notes as follow-ups to chance meetings initiated several long-term friendships. To Grace, such follow-ups were part of being literate, which she took to include being cultured: "It's important to be thoughtful, and people appreciate it when you take time to write." "It takes a great deal of time to maintain friendships, and much of that goes into correspondence."

Written first in shorthand and then typed single spaced, Grace's letters average two pages, becoming shorter after she retired. By then, her correspondence list had grown and she was very busy. As well, she had always valued exactness and succinctness. Length was not a value in itself, as Grace notes in a letter to her sister: "When you have something to say, say it. I don't think going on and on is a virtue. No one has time for that and few the interest." Always personal and thoughtful, Grace's letters ask about family members, remember special days, comment upon previous correspondence, and respond to problems. Often she encloses some remembrance—a photo, slide, article, or gift. "One reason I've done so much tatting in Florida," she told me, "is because it fits so well in an envelope." "Remembering is so important to people; I try never to forget a birthday, anniversary, or what have you." Her small, thirty-year-old datebook is filled with dates significant to friends, co-workers, club members, and their families.

Whereas most letters depict Grace as friend, letters to Ellen, her youngest sister and seven years her junior, portray her as an oldest sister. In these, the caring interest and warm concern common to all her letters are more explicit, probably because in them Grace is somewhat less reserved. They express a clear, preferential love for her "baby" sister. "I'm so proud of you; you looked beautiful," Grace wrote. "Just the thought that you made it! Thank you." "Finally, others recognize your artistic ability." "How far your candle throws its light." In these letters, too, can sometimes be heard the impatient, even abrupt, sound of authority that punctuates my own interaction with my youngest sister. Orders: "Get your rest. . . . Don't waste your time . . . [or] want to accomplish too much in one day"; opinions: "You must decide . . . [it] isn't very reasonable"; and impatience: "Of course, I know what calligraphy is" are offered out of sisterly concern: "Sorry I sound harsh, but it's out of love I write to you this way."

Except for a few years during her marriage, Grace worked all her adult life as an executive secretary, retiring at age seventy. In 1925, secretarial work was considered a suitable job for women—as were library and clerical work, nursing, and nonuniversity teaching. Basically scribal work, they required language ability of a functional, noncreative sort.

Women in these jobs copied, documented, recorded, and filed the language and discourse produced by others, nearly always men. But Grace did more than move around the words of male-dominated language and tidy up a corner of the masculine work world. If rhetoric deals with the functionality of language in context, Grace's job was as discursively constructed as her personal life. "I guess I've worked with words all my life," she told me. "I loved my job for that reason." Grace voiced satisfaction: "My secretarial friends at other companies made more money, but, you know, I never felt I was only working with someone else's words; they were. It may be a man's world, but not all of it. My old boss used to tell me that the King's English is sometimes owned by queens."

Co-workers concurred. "Grace had such a command of English, she certainly made Mr. Hires look great on paper. Foreign-born and self-made, Jack Hires knew his trade better than his English." "You know, if 1930 had been 1990," another colleague laughed, "Grace would've been company president." "She did not just type and take shorthand," Betty assured me. "Whether Jack just outlined its contents, which he usually did, or actually dictated it, Grace really composed nearly every document. She loved words, you know, and never let an unfamiliar word go unnoticed. She knew all the technical language of the production end."

"I still wrote, typed and filed, but at home," Grace said of her retirement. She continued to type ninety-two words a minute and to use shorthand "for everything—phone messages, composing letters, taking notes at a meeting or on a trip." In Florida, she wrote a weekly social column for a local paper, was secretary for the local chapter of the Federal Mobile Home Owners' Association, and wrote a piece for *Needlework* (November 1987), the journal of the Embroiderers' Guild of America. Her move to Florida also occasioned continuous correspondence. In fact, a record of her correspondence for the two years before her strokes indicates that Grace wrote an average of three letters a day.

Jottings, lists, labels, and files were extremely important to Grace, for they satisfied her desire and ability to maintain order and organization in every facet of her life. Her upbringing by German parents, her training and employment, and her own artistic talent all contributed to her equating order with control. A brief tour of her house convinced me that Grace had kept a list of, a label on, or a file about everything important to her.

A jar of rice, for example, was labeled and the recipe taped to the top. Tiny labels atop spice containers facilitated identification. A typed list of foodstuffs to be found in the cupboard sat on one shelf. On another kitchen cupboard, one envelope read "large plastic bags," another, "small plastic bags." On the inside edge of each curtain was printed "left" or "right." Labels also identified boxes, utensils, and appliances. Attached to several utensils, small cards explained cleaning procedures; taped to the back of the television set, a label noted its make and serial number and the date, place, and circumstance of its purchase. Music boxes, unusual dishes, and handmade items also bore labels. A handwoven basket, for example, was "made in 1964, by Evelyn Stoner from Madagascar pine needles."

A bedroom drawer held important examples of Grace's composition. She was especially proud of the black leather-covered dictionary she had begun in high school and added to throughout her life. It contained an alphabetical listing of unfamiliar words and definitions of each word in perfectly formed miniature print. Among those words are "accouchement," "*muliebrile*," and, my favorite, "perspicacious." Snippets of paper throughout the house held words, some with definitions, awaiting inclusion in this marvelous collection. In that drawer also was a small blue notebook holding another list, begun in 1932, of handmade items given as gifts. One page begins, "1939, Mary, Christmas, yellow mittens w crocheted flowers." A folder of needlework in an adjoining cupboard held directions and a sketch of those mittens.

Accompanying nearly everything Grace had saved—photos, slides, handiwork, writings—were written explanations, labels, and entire scripts, all meticulously noted, identifying the item and giving pertinent information, which Grace surely knew because she had told it to me. Needlework items were labeled, grouped into labeled boxes, and placed on labeled shelves. Linens were identified by size, condition, and age. A walk-in closet housed two file cabinets filled with updated printed material dating from the early 1930s: bills and receipts; lists of household items with prices, places, and dates of purchase; appliance warranties and instructions; and articles from magazines.

Yet from years in the business world, Grace knew that she did not need to keep most of this material. She must have realized, too, that the labels told what she already knew. Ironically, it was as if her composing formed a discursive blueprint from which she could reconstruct and resume her life, should a catastrophe, like a stroke, occur. Certainly the linguistic display of her house epitomizes the extent to which discursive composition unified, constructed, and validated Grace and her way of life. Gerontologists tell us that old persons control death and assure remembrance by ordering their possessions, specifying gifts, composing

value statements, or leaving visible examples of their life's work. I suspect that the addressivity of Grace's composition, a continuously constructed value statement, included the hope that readers would realize
how much it revealed about a woman who never kept a diary because
"someone might read it."

The two strokes Grace suffered, in October 1986 and March 1987,
and her subsequent illness affected her composition and altered that life,
which had been continually enlivened by discourse. Neither stroke,
though, damaged areas of the brain most responsible for reading and
writing processes. The lesions occurred in the right frontal lobe, which
performs the high-level synthesis that coordinates, mediates, and integrates such processes (Gardner, 168, 275). These operations enable abstract thinking and spatial-temporal functions. Thus, despite left-side
muscle weakness, Grace remained articulate and intelligent, but, while
she could perform a delimited task, she displayed other poststroke difficulties, in relating goals to plans, discerning relationships and timing
involved in making and executing plans, and recognizing when plans
required change (Gardner, 270). The effects on her life were obvious;
less obvious were its effects on her language use.

Since daily routines involve complex planning, Grace could no longer
live alone, and, like most childless widows needing assistance, she found
herself in a nursing home (see Hess; Riley). Relocation a thousand miles
from her home and personal belongings underscored the rupture in the
life that composition had helped to build. Following her strokes, the
order Grace had obtained through composing no longer provided control. Grace composed no jottings, since the world she had used them to
order was gone. "I had a place for everything, kept track of it all, but
that's all down the drain." Gone, too, was Grace's belief that she had any
world to control. "You live in someone else's world here, and abide by
their rules," she wrote. Finally, strokes had short-circuited her ability to
plan or to dream, in Gardner's words (269). Less able to employ that
simple yet profound complex of skills, Grace had difficulty grasping a
picture of her life big enough to require jottings.

This loss had also disrupted the continuity of her relationships (Cassell, 44). Carol Gilligan notes that being old, sick, and a woman is especially difficult, since women "define themselves in context of human
relationships and judge themselves in terms of ability to care" (171). Not
only had Grace's personal support shrunk to Mary and me, but her social
interaction with other patients was severely limited. Nearly every patient
was hearing-impaired, deaf to Grace's quiet voice, and most had greater

cognitive impairment than she. Territorial claims of long-term patients also thwarted her efforts to socialize (Hooyman and Kiyak, 368). "The first roommate wouldn't talk to me, said I didn't belong in her room. Now, this one can't hear me and insists I'm plotting against her. All I want is to be heard so I can converse with someone who lives here."

The nursing home afforded Grace few opportunities to compose or to participate in literacy events. These events were often for lower-functioning patients, although Grace did attend the monthly poetry readings and recitals. Understandably, she enjoyed literacy events employing various forms of composition, since she herself was an accomplished pianist, an avid photographer who had developed her own work, and, despite being color blind, an expert at several forms of needlework. At one such event, Grace and Mary gave a slide presentation of their trip to Germany using material Grace had prepared some years before. Hesitant about this public display, Grace was also pleased. She and Mary decided that she would read for about five slides. Two of the five were out of order, but Grace did not notice the first and was unable to adjust her response to the second. However, she did supply unwritten information about other slides, telling, for example, about the autobahn.

"All this makes me wonder if who I have always thought I was is who I am," Grace confided. Since her strokes, besides language use, she had retained only the ability to write shorthand and to tat. "Thank God," she added immediately, her voice vigorous, "I can still read and write." When I asked if she did those as well as before her stroke, she nodded happily. "Hm, hm, sure. Except for my handwriting which is awful, so small and cramped." Looking up, she asked, "What would I do if I couldn't read or write?" "I can't tell you how much I miss my friends. They've been my day-to-day family since my sister died four years ago, you know." Even in illness, Grace continued to correspond with over a hundred persons "because communication is the only means I have now of relating with my friends and family." In fact, difficulty formulating, altering, and executing elaborate plans necessarily affects complex processes like composing (Gardner, 365). Both Grace's reading and her writing evidenced stroke effects. She was less selective about what she read, always beginning short-story collections, for example, with the first piece. Often not able to recall the contents of an article, she could tell from its title whether she had read it. In general, her letters during her illness became shorter and less developed and exhibited problems with sequence, organization, and conventions.

Yet Grace was unaware that her language skills were affected, because right-hemisphere strokes inhibit the patient's awareness of her illness effects and their implications. For Grace to have been cognizant of such deficits, she needed the very synthesizing ability the strokes had affected. In ordinary terms, Grace had more trouble getting things through her head than holding them there. Reading difficulties, then, were less a problem of recall than an inability to synthesize complexity with the rapidity required for the kind of material she read. The strokes, the illness context, and Grace's fluctuating health accounted for the differences between previous work and her illness writing, differences that became more noticeable over the nine months during which I observed Grace's discourse practices. However, fairness to her composing requires acknowledging that these factors alone do not account for the considerable variation existing among her illness writings. For example, except for handwriting, several pieces equal the quality of retirement letters. While most letters of this quality occurred early in her illness and while most letters with unmistakable impairment effects were written near the end of the study, this progression is not absolute. Sometimes only a day separated a "healthy" letter from a stroke letter.

Given the complexity of the human experience, including that of the human brain, medicine can identify only some of the factors impinging upon impairment and illness. Two additional factors bear mentioning. First, the human factor was incalculable. The encouragement of the two persons who accepted Grace's dissonance while affirming her integrity—what Sacks calls existential medicine (248–51)—helped to bridge the stroke-related disruption in integrity: they sought to reflect to Grace the strength and wholeness she possessed but could neither see nor confirm in herself without such mirroring. Second, Grace had maintained the cognitive ability to access writing schema culled from long-term, extensive, conscious use of discourse. This allowed her to use language tacitly, that is, to run partly "on automatic" after her strokes impeded access to explicit knowledge. Tacit skills undoubtedly contributed to those textual features of her writing that showed little impairment, for example, word choice, phrasing, and audience awareness. It is fortunate that Grace's tacit skills were well developed, given the complexity of composing and the nature of her impairment. Composition is, after all, so complex that psychology avoids its study. In fact, this is why few have studied stroke writing beyond such sentence dyads as question/answer or two-person conversation, and virtually no one has related composing to right-hemisphere stroke.

Grace had little difficulty with either word choice or phrase formation. Some examples—"bring me up to date," "you might want to,"
"thank you profusely," "I'm sure Ellen would add her thanks," "I, too,
would like to"—are only standbys, occurring often in previous writing.
Other phrasing examples, like "safely ensconced," "gourmet-style meal,"
"arrived like a whirlwind," or "exchange pleasantries," indicate an ac-
cessibility to word choice and phrasing, as does, "I went today to a book
review on Bess Truman which was quite worthwhile."

We may safely assume, likewise, that tacit skills contributed to the
high degree of audience awareness maintained in Grace's illness writing.
However, there were also indications that Grace directed conscious attention to this effort. Often she sat with the letter being answered in her
lap for quick reference. Still very attuned to the events and people in her
friends' lives, she asked Helen about her daughter, reminded Ellen of
Mary's birthday, and commiserated with Dolly over her husband's death.
In addition, her self-references were often audience-specific. To her traveling companion Lucille, for example, Grace wrote about missing her
car, her freedom, and her travel. However, since Aileen, Grace's Florida
neighbor, "wouldn't understand because she doesn't drive, and was
home with her husband," Grace wrote about missing her home and playing cards.

Of course, diminished capacity to plan had the most noticeable effect
on Grace's writing. Planning relates to spatial-temporal functions and to
diminished duration of cognitive engagement. Because short-circuited
planning abbreviates the duration of cognitive engagement, persons like
Grace tend to be more easily disengaged, more given to impulse: that
is, they become more easily distracted and spontaneous and less attuned
to appropriate behavior or established protocol. These planning-related
features of composing and behavior are reflected in problems of sequence, organization, and development and with attention to conventions. Grace's prestroke writing has privileged specific detail, description, and factual information, but in her illness writing, she often provides
less development for topics and had difficulty organizing material. We
can see this deprivation of topic and development in a letter to a cousin.
Although each of its eight paragraphs deals with a single topic, six contain only one sentence; the other two each have two sentences. In another letter, several unrelated topics occur in a single paragraph. These
problems with development and organization affect coherence, as, for
example, when a letter of four paragraphs contains a paragraph of ten
sentences with seven different topics or when an entire letter is a single

paragraph of twenty-three sentences covering seven topics, only two consecutive pairs of which are related.

Organization is further affected by Grace's tendency to repeat a topic, reintroducing it elsewhere in the letter. For example, having written, "Mary is so good to me" near the beginning of one letter, seven sentences and five topics later, she reintroduces it with "Mary visits whenever she can." Sometimes, in a single letter, Grace returns three times to the same topic. Those topics to which she consistently returns were, of course, those that most concerned her: the thoughtfulness of her niece, Mary; her own lack of improvement; her new friend, Myrna; and her loss of lifestyle, personal surroundings, and social interaction. The stroke had made Grace less attentive to linguistic and genre conventions and to the general appearance of items she prepared for mailing. For example, she was less deliberate in her selection of paper, often beginning a letter on the same paper on which she had already jotted down a small segment of something she had overheard, like a bit of conversation, or an item from a television show. When I pointed this out once, Grace registered surprise, "Where'd I get that?" Toward the bottom of that letter, she unwittingly includes two sentences of a conversation between her roommate and the woman's son. Grace may have been distracted by the angry tone of the conversation or engrossed in her own letter, but she did not recall she had written those two sentences.

In contrast to prestroke discourse, these letters illustrate some difficulty with usage and genre conventions. Occasionally, misspellings such as "geriatrik," "enuff," and "allways" occur, this from a woman who found the facility's spelling bee boring because, "Who doesn't know how to spell 'ukulele'?" Finally, Grace often addressed envelopes upside down or, after folding the letter itself into thirds, wrote the address on a folded portion of the letter. Previously meticulous about observing protocol, Grace was less aware of convention and, at those times she was aware, less concerned about following its directives. The few times she seemed to notice those problems addressing letters, she never related them to protocol: she never questioned their being mailed.

Difficulty with spatial relations affected Grace's handwriting. Once small, neat, and uniform, it had become tiny, cramped, and unevenly spaced. Because her visual awareness was affected, the left margin of each written page grew wider as it meandered down the page. Spatial deficits accounted, too, for misplaced genre conventions: greeting, closing, and signature sometimes appeared at unconventional places on the line. Grace also had consistent difficulty addressing envelopes, because

placement in an open space burdens visual representation in stroke victims. This inability to relate things spatially explains why she could not
follow patterns, even those whose steps she had explained to me.

A few months before she died, I observed Grace writing three letters
at the same time. This fascinating episode epitomizes the role and the
power of composing in her life. Grace had started a letter to a niece when
she paused to glance at things on her desk; focusing momentarily on a
newspaper article sticking from a book, she then reached for a pink pad
and began writing. She worked alternately on these two pieces for about
fifteen minutes—writing, reading what she had written, and occasionally
looking out the window. Then, reaching for a card her niece had sent,
she noticed, picked up, and read another card, which prompted her to
reach for a second pink pad and to begin her third letter. When I asked
later if she usually did "that," Grace replied, "What? Get right to it and
write? Yes, usually, if I'm alone and don't get distracted. You're not a
distraction." When I specified her writing of three letters at once, she
said she didn't "usually do that, but the ideas came, so I dashed them
off." Those letters were among the "healthy" group mentioned above.
Incredibly, each was two full pages, developed, coherent, and contained
different contents. Two, though, do mention the papal visit occurring at
the time. The article that had prompted the second letter was about the
pope's stop in Detroit; remembering a friend who had seen the pope in
Miami, Grace decided to write to her.

This episode illustrates Grace's skill at composing, though not in the
obvious ways her previous writings suggest. Her stroke writing lacks the
controlled skill we recognize in her bound books, the intricacy of the
blackwork composition now hanging in Mary's home, and the complexity of a multiple composition like the script, music, and marionette now
safely stored in glass case and on videotape. This episode, in fact, reveals
impulse intruding as distraction and raises questions about control. Yet
neither impairment nor tacit knowledge can account for the more important element of this episode, namely, the underside of impulse, only
rarely seen as a positive force—intense, though impermanent, concen-
tration and deep, though not comprehensive, thought. For neither Grace
composing nor the letters themselves evidence impulsiveness. Grace
showed no signs of being agitated, flustered, or fidgety; her actions were
deliberate, their steady rhythm quickened briefly twice as she took up
additional paper. In fact, she sat with composure and gave every evidence
of concentrating on what she was doing, even to ignoring my presence.

Her composing that day made visible the lithe, brilliant execution of balance, which all her writing necessarily had become, between the limits and unsteadiness of impairment and the assets still available to her—conscious, tacit, and relational. For Grace, the stakes of composing were high: to lose balance would have been to lose "the living 'I' " (Sacks, 251). It would have been to lose reflection, the complement to the composing experience that defined her. It is impossible to overestimate the role of language in Grace's life, a role radicalized by her illness. For her, everything else about being sick was a disappointment and a frustration. Yet each time I observed her reading or writing and each time we talked about language use, she was at ease, helpful, articulate, and content. Her satisfaction and pleasure increased, of course, when we talked about her own practices or those of her niece. She "couldn't ever remember [having been] more proud than when Mary honored [their] family by writing a book." "Her life is *also* filled with writing," Grace affirmed.

Though her composing skills were limited as a result of the strokes, Grace's continued ability to write affected her experience of illness. Because she lacked sufficient synthesizing ability to make sense of her illness, Grace had to live in a more-or-less permanent state of disease. Implicated in this loss, of course, was everything about Grace. Relatively unable to com-pose, in the sense of bringing together, of constructing and integrating meaning, her composing had become necessarily less complicated, her constructions partial, and her meanings less adequate. Yet, within these constraints, composing and construction had been possible. For Grace, discursive composition, especially writing, had remained an enactment of literacy, of ordered experience, and of maintained relationships. While stroke effects prevented Grace from composing herself or her illness world, her acts of composition, being dramatic in nature, composed—however tenuously, inadequately, temporarily—what otherwise would have remained centrifugal and fragmented. While composing could not com-pose her life to the degree it had before, it remained the greatest force for empowering, validating, and affirming Grace and her self-worth. It allowed her to maintain a modicum of control and provided her a means of salvaging her life and herself from an otherwise unbearable situation.

BIBLIOGRAPHY

Cassell, Eric J. *The Healer's Art: A New Approach to the Doctor-Patient Relationship.* New York: Lippincott, 1976.

Gardner, Howard. *The Shattered Mind: The Person After Brain Damage.* New York: Vintage, 1974.

Gilligan, Carol. *In a Different Voice: Psychological Theory and Women's Development.* Cambridge: Harvard Univ. Press, 1982.

Haug, Marie R., Amasa B. Ford, and Marian Shaefor, eds. *The Physical and Mental Health of Aged Women.* New York: Springer, 1985.

Heath, Shirley Brice. "Being Literate in America: A Sociohistorical Perspective." In *Issues in Literacy: A Research Perspective,* edited by Jerome A. Niles and Rosary V. Ladi, 1–8. Rochester, N.Y.: National Reading Conference, 1985.

Hess, Beth. "Aging Policies and Old Women: The Hidden Agenda." In *Gender and Life Course,* edited by Alice Rossi. New York: Aldine, 1985.

Hooyman, Nancy, and H. Asuman Kiyak. *Social Gerontology: A Multidisciplinary Perspective.* Boston: Allyn and Bacon, 1988.

Kahana, Eva, and Boaz Kahana. "Institutionalization of the Aged Woman: Bane or Blessing?" In *Physical and Mental Health,* edited by Haug, Ford, and Shaefor.

Kleinman, Arthur. *Illness Narratives: Suffering, Healing, and the Human Condition.* New York: Basic Books, 1988.

Lauer, Janice M. Personal interview with author, Oct. 25, 1987.

Phelps, Louise Wetherbee. *Composition as a Human Science: Contributions to the Self-Understanding of a Discipline.* New York: Oxford Univ. Press, 1988.

Rich, Adrienne. *Of Woman Born: Motherhood as Experience and Institution.* New York: W. W. Norton, 1976.

Riley, Matilda White. "The Changing Older Woman: Cohort Perspective." In *Physical and Mental Health,* edited by Haug, Ford, and Shaefor.

Sacks, Oliver. *Awakenings.* New York: Summit, 1973.

Stoeckle, John, ed. *Encounters Between Patients and Doctors: An Anthology.* Cambridge: MIT Press 1987.

Zaner, Richard. *Ethics and Clinical Encounter.* Englewood Cliffs, N.J.: Prentice-Hall, 1988.

8

Intellectual Parenting and a Developmental Feminist Pedagogy of Writing

Janice Hays

In 1989, at a symposium I attended on current work in life-span development, a psychologist reported her research about gender differences in students' epistemological growth during the college years, research growing out of her own interest in intellectual development in general and women's sociocognitive development in particular. Her study suggested that some stylistic characteristics of women's reasoning patterns temporarily inhibit college women in their development of higher-level intellectual complexity, and she discussed some implications of these findings for pedagogies that would foster such growth in women. One woman in the audience, an English professor at a small eastern college, raised her hand and said, with evident emotion, "But why would you want to change our thinking and speaking in our own unique voices?"

The presenter thought for a moment and then responded, "I don't want to stifle anyone's unique voice, but I also assume that more intellectual complexity is preferable to less." In addition to what this interchange may tell us about differences in disciplinary perspectives, it echoes some of the discussion taking place around issues of women's epistemology and discourse. The interchange raises questions about whether women reason in unique ways and, if so, whether those ways are innate or acquired and whether they should be encouraged or questioned—or both (Kerber et al.). Current interest in the nature and development of women's intellectual growth has been stimulated by publication of Carol Gilligan's *In a Different Voice,* a study of patterns of women's moral development, and,

more recently, of *Women's Ways of Knowing,* by Mary Belenky, Blythe
Clinchy, Nancy Goldberger, and Jill Tarule, a book that explores women's
epistemology. Both these works grew from earlier studies of adult development, a relatively new field emerging as a continuation of Jean Piaget's
work on child development and the subsequent recognition that sociocognitive development does not end at the age of fourteen but continues
throughout human life. Concurrent with this understanding was the
awareness that logical-formal reasoning is not the apex of cognitive development and that formal operations are followed by postformal ones,
complex modes of reasoning more systemic and dynamic than formal
operations. (In his late work [1972], Piaget himself reached some of these
conclusions.)

Erik Erikson, Lawrence Kohlberg, Jane Loevinger, and William Perry
are the names most commonly associated with studies in adult development, although many others could be added to this list. These four
writers describe constructionist patterns in the domains of psychosocial,
moral, ego, epistemic, and ethical development during the college years.
They trace growth through a predictable sequence of "positions" that
move from less to more complex functioning, from rigid and dichoto-
mized to contextually contingent and "dialectical" reasoning, from global
to differentiated feeling and judgment, and so on. Such models also suggest that growth in higher-order functioning is not automatic. Rather, it
results from readiness for such growth in combination with environmental challenges to deal with multiple and often conflicting perspectives on
reality, through processes analogous to Piaget's characterization of as-
similation and accommodation (1968). Such growth is the product of a
complex interaction between individuals and their social contexts, during
the course of which each is changed. Because epistemology has so many
implications for the construction of discourse, Perry's model of epistemic
development is particularly germane to a consideration of women's intellectual growth (1968). This discussion includes work with the Perry
scheme following Perry's initial studies, especially work with women's
development. It also refers to other models of adult development and to
psychoanalytic perspectives that contribute insights about women's
growth as thinkers.

Numbers of studies utilizing Perry's and related models show that
most students enter college with dichotomous rigid or conventional
stances toward knowledge and learning. Perry (1968) calls this position
dualism; it is characterized by rigid, binary thought that frames ideas
and experience in either/or, true/false terms. Over the college years,

most students become aware of competing perspectives on reality but as yet lack the tools to evaluate such conflicting realities. Rather, they fall back upon hunch and intuition or upon a facile consensus that avoids conflict—the position of *multiplicity.* Unfortunately, many learners leave college not having advanced much beyond this level of reasoning. Those who do move further achieve the position of *relativism,* a socially contextual position in which the thinker recognizes that, although there are many ways of viewing any reality, not all ways are equally valid; thus the basis for justifying and evaluating ideas and beliefs becomes paramount.

Finally, in Perry's model are positions that Perry terms *committed relativism* and that others refer to as *critical* or *dialectical epistemology.* (By *dialectical,* developmentalists do not mean Hegelian dialectic, with its synthesis of polarities, but a more complex process; see Basseches; Perry 1981). In these positions, a learner realizes that all "truth" is socially constructed, dependent upon context and perspective, in constant flux, and thus subject at all times to revision. But the thinker also recognizes that one cannot live without making commitments and taking action and that the process of arriving at and acting upon those commitments can be among the most meaningful human activities, one that expresses the self and shapes the direction of the individual's life. The person holds this knowledge in tension with the recognition that such commitments must be rethought again and again in the light of new knowledge, experience, and constructions of meaning (Perry 1968). Studies show that in this country most learners do not achieve these positions as undergraduates but move into them in graduate school (Mentkowski, Moeser, and Strait; Benack and Basseches). Current work with adults suggests that for some people the work world can also provide the challenges that produce such growth (Zachary).

In the research leading to *Women's Ways of Knowing,* Belenky and her colleagues studied both college and noncollege women and identified important patterns associated with women's reasoning. Contrary to popular opinion, their findings do not invalidate Perry's model as it applies to women but rather suggest that these patterns are variations and elaborations of basic structures identified by the earlier researchers. Perry has commented on recent gender studies, noting that the Perry scheme may indeed require alteration to accommodate findings from "different populations and different contexts" but also cautioning that "in particular, changes in nonstructural areas are more likely than structural changes to reflect influences of gender and social class" and stressing the importance of not confusing structural with stylistic change (1989,

2). That is, if structural patterns—such as dichotomous thinking in dualism—remain constant although subject and style vary, then the overall
model is sound, although perspectives and particulars within structural
positions change with changing contexts. In conversation, Perry has likened his model to a Swiss cheese, the cheese representing the structure,
and the holes, individual and contextual variations within the structure
(personal communication, 1990).

Numerous studies following Perry's, one of which was conducted in
a women's college (see Mentkowski, Moeser, and Strait), have found
gender not to be a significant factor in developmental position, as scored
by nationally validated Perry scheme instruments. (The Perry scheme
is shown in the appendix to this chapter; see Perry 1981.) In a longitu-
dinal study of men's and women's reasoning patterns, Marcia B. Baxter-
Magolda finds no significant gender differences between men's and
women's structural positions during year one of the college experience;
however, men advance more rapidly than women in cognitive position
during years two and three. By the end of the junior year in college,
however, the results for women and men again even out. This study also
identifies distinctive stylistic differences within structure between men
and women. In this study, Baxter-Magolda found that 25 percent of each
gender resembled the other, and vice versa (personal communication,
1989); Gilligan's colleague Nona P. Lyons found similar ratios in a lon-
gitudinal study of moral development.

In studying poor rural blacks, Carol B. Stack discovered little difference between men's and women's styles of moral reasoning. Learning-
style research with Mexican-American children and with other indigenous minorities has identified reasoning styles in both sexes like those
characterizing traditionally feminine patterns of reasoning—field sensitivity, cooperativeness, and relationality; such studies imply that gender
and ethnic differences in cognitive style are linked to socialization practices (Ramírez and Casteñeda, 76). Robert L. Durham, Janice Hays, and
Rubén O. Martinez report no significant differences in Perry scheme
positions between junior-level Chicano students and a matched group of
Anglo students. However, the variables associated with epistemic levels
in the two groups differ significantly and suggest that cognitive style may
be a factor. David Kolb (1981) finds that learning-style preferences cause
people to gravitate toward particular fields and professions, which then
reinforce the learning style. He contends that learning styles are also
developmental: as people mature, they cultivate and integrate those
modes of learning earlier neglected. Lyons notes that, as the men and

women in her study grew older, their reasoning styles became more like that of the other gender (138). Together, these findings suggest that women's ways of reasoning are often stylistically different from men's, but not structurally so, and that they are thus flexible and subject to expansion and change—as also, of course, are men's styles.

Lyons calls women's moral justification pattern "connected." It is more social and contextual than the "separate" style associated with men and involves responding to others on their terms and sustaining caring and closeness in relationships. Grounded in an awareness of interdependence, it is a collaborative stance—as distinct from the more individualistic and task-oriented posture of separate reasoning, which experiences relationships in terms of reciprocity mediated through rules and grounded in obligations and commitment (Lyons, 134). In studying epistemology, Belenky and her colleagues have adopted Lyons's term to refer to women's ways of thinking. Clinchy writes: "The heart of connected knowing is imaginative attachment. . . . It is a personal way of thinking, and it involves feeling" (651). Some of Baxter-Magolda's interview excerpts illustrate such stylistic differences between men and women rated at the same structural levels. For example, within position three on the Measure of Epistemological Reflection (a Perry-derived instrument), she finds gender differences in every domain generally coded for epistemic development. Concerning the role of classroom peers in the learning process, women typically see the function of peers to be "talking to create a more relaxed atmosphere and asking questions to relieve pressure on others to talk." Women also stress the importance of getting to know other class members so that they can feel closer to them, understand their personalities, and thus be more comfortable asking questions. By contrast, men see their peers as partners in argument, in "quizzing each other in order to further learning." One man comments "We put our minds together and get the problem. I also have somebody in the class ask me questions—they ask questions I didn't think to review. Then I do the same for them" (11).

These comments illustrate the relational focus of many women students—that it is important to establish a trusting, interconnected environment in which everyone feels safe to participate—and the separate or reciprocal style of many men—that peers are part of a task orientation in which individuals take turns helping one another to achieve their performance goals. Yet both the men and women cited above are rated at the same structural level in intellectual development, one at which peers are not yet seen as sources of learning, as they will be in subsequent development. Treating connected and separate knowing as styles within epistemic structures, Joanne G. Kurfiss has formulated a model that integrates the work of Belenky and her colleagues with the Perry scheme; in this model, for example, Perry's "dualism" becomes "dualism/received knowledge," and so on (52–54; see also appendix to this chapter).

Questions about women's intellectual development and reasoning styles are important in current discussions among feminist scholars about the nature of women's thought and expression and their relationship to language and discourse (see Marks and de Courtivron; Hawkesworth). This colloquy has arisen in part from studies of women's psychological, moral, and epistemic development as well as from postmodernism in general and French feminist writing in particular. Central to this discussion is the premise that the dominant reasoning and linguistic modes of Western society have been male-patriarchal ones that reify meaning and valorize individuality, competitiveness, binary thinking, analytic separation of experience into its constitutive parts, and emotionless rationality and abstraction. All of these are "hard," unitary, phallocratic ways of functioning that exclude communality and cooperation, caring, multiple meanings, holistic thinking, emotion—and women.

Some theorists ground their conclusions in social and political conditions—for example, dichotomies between public and private life: women, exiled to the private dimension because of their roles as mothers, have developed expressive, relational, collaborative, and connected ways of being associated with caretaking, ways that have excluded them from full participation in public discourse. Other theorists base their analyses in biopsychological domains, attributing the dichotomization of thinking styles between men and women to the fundamental conditions of child rearing in white Western culture, suggesting that the closeness between mothers and their daughters may well give rise to women's relationality and connected learning styles (Chodorow; Dinnerstein). Some theorists valorize this relationship as enabling women to develop unique and humanly valuable ways of being in the world—the ethics and expression of care (Belenky et al.; Gilligan; J. Miller; Noddings; Ruddick; Surrey). But other sociopsychological analyses suggest that the close relationship between many mothers and daughters is a highly ambivalent one, producing not only strengths but also deeply conflictual difficulties for women's development (Eichenbaum and Orbach 1987b; Lerner; Westkott). By contrast, French feminists suggest analogies between women's reasoning and the nature, meaning, and expression of female sexuality and desire, described as various, fluid, unfocused, and interior (see, for example, Irigaray).

In the domain of epistemology, as noted above, learning-style studies, the fact that some men are connected and some women separate knowers, and stylistic differences between racial and ethnic groups together suggest that the patterns characterized as women's reasoning styles are indeed stylistic rather than structural. The dominance of one style over another doubtless issues from socialization patterns, especially as mediated through child-rearing practices, as well as from cultural contexts and individual temperament (Ramírez and Casteñeda, 76–78; 83–102). Such learning styles probably also reflect responses to social and political powerlessness, for if the disenfranchised are to survive, they must be more interpersonally sensitive than those who have power over them. There are also dangers in this kind of categorizing, for it seems to suggest that people are exclusively separate or connected knowers, when in fact they are more apt to be combinations of the two or to function differently in different domains. Manuel Ramírez and Alfredo Casteñeda advocate a "bi-cultural" or bimodal style, which integrates field sensitivity and independence for all learners (129f), while scholars in the area of intercultural studies contend that an "ethnorelativistic" style is the ideal (Bennett, 46).

What attitude, then, should a feminist pedagogy assume toward women's reasoning styles and the discursive patterns that express them? The problem of formulating a feminist pedagogy of discourse may lie in assumptions that polarize the available options and so unwittingly continue the dichotomous thinking that has for so long characterized Western culture, especially in its attitudes about gender, race, and class. The choices are not between public discourse and private language—between, on the one hand, an abstract, excessively emotionless scientific discourse stripped of affective, moral, or personal dimensions and, on the other, an excessively private, affect-based language that eschews hierarchy, analysis, and establishing propositions and is in danger of becoming inchoate and incoherent, apolitical and theory-repudiating. A developmental perspective informed by psychoanalytic thought can integrate these polarities and offer a feminist pedagogy for teaching writing.

Michael Basseches suggests that mature epistemology is dialectical, an interactive process in which the ground of reality is process itself: change and modification of a multisystemic reality that constantly requires reshaping and redefining. For such an orientation, any "reality" is part of a larger structure rather than separate and fixed, and thus is basically interconnected. Psychoanalytic thought suggests that human development toward this point begins with a dialogic process between infant and caretaker, taking place in the context of a culture. Each participant is attuned to the other to create shared affect states and experiences and later, with the infant's acquisition of language, to construct shared meanings that validate the infant's developing sense of a cohesive self (not the "unitary self" of liberal humanism but that which experiences itself as "going on being" [Stern, 162 passim; Winnicott, 183–90]). The emergence and meaning of the self, or subject, are grounded in the connectedness associated with mother-child relatedness, broadened over time to include interactions with an increasingly complex world of others and with the experiences and culture that they mediate.

But the self and its meaning are also separate, for the infant experiences personal affect states, private and initially preverbal—affective knowledge that both can and cannot be communicated to others. These separate experiences are necessary for the construction and consolidation of a cohesive self—that which has continuity in time. Language itself can act as an agent of separation, for much of what the self experiences cannot be communicated in words, although connection can also occur in silence. Yet individuals must construct and share meaning in interaction with others in order to experience who and what they are (Stern, 162–84). Robert Kegan's model of human development views the evolving self as oscillating, along a continuum he visualizes as an ascending spiral, between two orientations—one toward the self (compare separate knowing) and one toward others (compare connected knowing)—in an increasingly complex process that culminates in an integration of both. Such integration moves beyond the limitations of both separate and connected knowing, experiencing each as part of a larger whole and utilizing both in thinking that is interactive and complementary.

Developmental theories suggest that we do not mature as thinkers simply by willing ourselves to do so but rather we achieve maturity through a whole series of meaning-constructive activities, each at a more complex level than that which has preceded it. At every point in this process, we need the presence of facilitating others who guide and support us and who can also grow and change with us. The analogy to responsible parenting is obvious, and an ideal feminist pedagogy assumes a parental stance toward students, one that envisions the student's full intellectual growth as its goal and works to facilitate it. Intellectual parents are attuned to students' needs, "holding" them when to do so is appropriate, urging them to progress when they need urging, and entering with them into the interpersonal process of making meaning (see Winnicott 1988, 126–30, for the analogue with the "good enough environment" in childhood).

In teaching writing, such a pedagogy would regard discourse as a meaning-constructive activity, dialogic, a mutual construction of "truth"; included in this dialogic process is the instructor's parental status as one who has greater knowledge and experience to share with students, while recognizing mutual participation in the process and mutual transformation by the process. (Wolfgang Loch suggests that psychoanalytic discourse between analyst and analysand is such a dialogic process, in which both participants must construct consensual truth about the analysand's life.) With their vision of the full scope of intellectual development, the instructors see more clearly than students what circumstances can stimulate growth, but they can only facilitate, not coerce. I am deliberately adopting the term *parental* rather than *maternal* to characterize a feminist pedagogy, in order to avoid the dichotomizing gender-role attributes that the term *maternal* inevitably evokes. Because women have always been children's primary nurturers, the association between feminism and a maternal or parental response is a natural one. But *intellectual parenting* suggests that men also can and do nurture and facilitate the growth of both children and students and looks forward to the time when more men will do both. This posture in many ways resembles that which Sara Ruddick ascribes to maternal thinking.

Some feminist scholars urge women to abandon logical, hierarchical, and argumentative discourse as patriarchal and exclusively to embrace nonlinear, associative, and inchoate forms of expression (see, e.g., Cixous). In contrast, I suggest that a feminist pedagogy of writing should help students compose discourse that constructs meaning, expressed with sound reasoning and the concerned voice of the writer, in those forms appropriate to the kind of writing in question and to its context, occasion, and audience. The final view of reasoning in this definition perceives experience and ideas as multiple rather than binary, arrayed along a continuum, complex, and continuously in flux. Such a perspective does not abandon rationality or eschew the expression of meaningful conclusions about ideas and experience. Rather, it posits that claims must be supported with evidence and that, though they will always be partial rather than conclusive, containing within themselves the possibility of their own negation, it is nonetheless possible to make judgments with respect to the relative validity of claims and their support. Such a perspective also recognizes that we must draw tentative conclusions and act on them, if we are to function as subjects in a complex world; such conclusions include not only the products of rational, conscious thought but also of intuitive processes, emotions, and an awareness of the irrational, unconscious forces that shape much of our thinking. Such awareness of the unconscious does not mean that the resulting discourse must be irrational; but part of the purpose of making the unconscious conscious is to understand it by means of both reason and emotion, subjecting the conclusions of intuition to rational verification, deconstructing rationalizations that masquerade as rationality, and articulating meaning in both transactional and expressive modes.

We can, of course, remain stuck in more limited postures, from which we view reality in dualistic or multiplistic ways and with only separate or connected perspectives. But if it is limiting to think only in binary, linear, analytic, classificatory, hierarchical, and logical- "objective" ways, it is equally limiting to think only in ways that are diffuse, multifaceted, co-ordinate, associational, and intuitive-"subjective." And if stylistically it is limiting to function in exclusively individualistic, task- and goal-directed orientations, it is equally limiting—for women, even more so—to function only with interpersonal, other- and group-oriented perspectives that are frequently self-abnegating.

In looking at (largely white) women college graduates, Clinchy and her colleagues observe that all too few of them leave college having moved into commitment in relativism, or what Belenky and her colleagues term *constructed knowledge.* Rather, they are more apt to disso-ciate themselves from the intellectual life, to give up on themselves as thinkers, to regard their college work as simply so much mechanistic ritual that they have to perform in order to get a degree, and to dissociate thinking and feeling in order to preserve the feeling side of themselves (Clinchy, 1989, 654–55 passim; see Weiss for similar observations about many minority women). The loss, both to women and to society, from such alienation is profound. In constructing a feminist pedagogy of discourse that will help women to avoid such alienation, we need to find ways to integrate reason and emotion, self and other, concrete particularities and abstract generalizations along varying points of a continuum extending between these polarities. As Tarule notes: "We [college teachers] are faced with honoring the personal while still inviting students to learn the more objective methods with which much of the thought of the culture is constructed. If we do not do both kinds of teaching, we toss the metaphorical baby out with the bath water" (23). Engaging in such integrated discourse will help students—men as well as women—advance to higher levels of epistemic development. Yet before students can reason dialectically, they must think multiplistically and relativistically, and the problems of teaching discourse will vary according to where students are in their journeys of intellectual growth (Beers)—and, for that matter, according to where instructors are in their own journey; at least one study suggests that many college professors adhere to epistemologies that fall short of dialectical reasoning (Beers and Bloomingdale). The important thing for us as teachers is to facilitate and enhance growth, taking care not to abort or stunt it. Instructors also need to recognize that when their learning styles do not match those of their students, they must compensate accordingly.

Further, we need to remember that intellectual and emotional functioning are intertwined. Impediments to epistemic growth are not simply cognitive, for emotional responses can make movement forward seem so threatening as to be untenable. Here again, we benefit from a perspective on both epistemology and discourse that unites all aspects of human functioning. Finally, it is important to remember that, while we can generalize about structures and styles of thought, each student we teach will experience and express these structures and styles in different ways and to differing degrees. We can discern the areas of commonality—for example, patterns of dualism in a group of students—but we also need always be alert to the differences between group members and resist rigid categorizing.

In constructing a developmental course in any area, an instructor must focus first on the student, not simply on the content to be learned. Instructors who have worked in women's studies programs are familiar with student-centered approaches, as indeed are composition teachers who follow process and/or social-contextual models. However, more traditionally oriented instructors may find shifting the emphasis from content to students and to the process by which one facilitates learning a new and often threatening experience. Yet study after study demonstrates that, in general, students learn more effectively from a developmentally structured class than from more traditional lecture approaches. (See, for example, Clinchy, Lief, and Young; Widick and Simpson; Stephenson and Hunt. Since most of these studies have involved classes in discipline-specific courses rather than in composition, we badly need studies of developmental approaches in the teaching of writing.) A developmental instructor must consider where students are epistemically and what their dominant learning styles are. To determine learners' developmental levels, it would be ideal to administer measures of epistemological position and learning-style preference to all students, but to do so is usually costly in terms of both time and money. However, one can rely on well-conducted studies for a rough idea of where students are apt to be in their intellectual development. On the most widely used Perry measure of intellectual development, nationally normed studies from both public and private colleges and universities show that freshmen generally arrive at college as dualistic reasoners moving toward multiplicity (Moore, 26). In terms of learning style, most women will be connected knowers and most men separate knowers, although the percentages of each will likely vary from discipline to discipline and according to racial and ethnic group.

The first premise of developmental education is that it must, on the one hand, challenge learners to move to a more complex level of functioning while, on the other, offering them support systems appropriate to their present levels (Sanford). Challenges must be sufficient to stimulate growth but not so great as to overwhelm it; research has shown, for example, that learners tend to regress and become more entrenched in current ways of functioning when asked to function at epistemic levels too far beyond their present positions, than when they are simply left unchallenged (Stern and Cope). Dualistic learners can effectively be challenged to perform in multiplistic ways, but not in relativistic ways. For example, Janice Hays, Kathleen Brandt, and Kathryn Chantry found that multiplistic students were effectively challenged to increased dialectical reasoning, a characteristic of relativism, by supporting a position before an audience likely to disagree with that position. Dualistic writers, on the other hand, were apparently overwhelmed by this assignment and often lapsed into a moralism and didacticism that interfered with their writing effectively.

Thus an instructor needs to understand what generally characterizes reasoning at different developmental positions and how gender and ethnically associated learning styles are expressed within those positions. And in teaching written discourse, it becomes important to know what generally typifies the writing behavior of students at differing levels of development. With such understandings, the instructor can design a curriculum that will challenge students to intellectual growth, building upon students' present strengths and working to strengthen their weaknesses. A "connected" dualist, for example, may generate abundant, if somewhat general, material on a "turning point" or "meaningful experience" essay but may need structured help in making that material more specific, focusing and organizing it, and explaining its importance. On the same assignment, a "separate" dualist may state an experience's significance clearly but have little else to say about it; this writer will need structured help generating the particulars that make the experience vivid and credible for a reader. And both separate and connected dualists will find it hard to articulate the reasons for the experience's significance, to connect its events to its importance in ways establishing causality. It is here that the instructor can structure a developmental challenge.

As important as challenges are support systems designed to make students feel safe as they move into new intellectual territory. Research suggests that support is even more important for most women than for most men students, since women need to feel secure in developing their own voices and opinions. If women students feel invalidated, they are more apt than men to retreat into silence, conformity, and withdrawal from the intellectual enterprise. Numbers of publications have identified the general factors in traditional college classrooms that can provide a "chilly climate" for women students, factors ranging from outright sexism and sexual harassment to subtle denigrations of women's academic work (Cook; Hall and Sandler 1982, 1984; Sandler and Hall). In addition, instructors who want to establish a hospitable, growth-enhancing atmosphere for women students need to design courses and strategies where connected learning is deemed as valuable as the separate knowing most often characteristic of men.

These remarks need, however, to be qualified: in the above statements and in most of the studies to date on women's epistemology *men* refers to white men. Recent studies on minority students and self-esteem suggest that in a public domain setting where values are predominantly white-male oriented such as the classroom, minorities of both sexes suffer from a diminishing of self-esteem even greater than that of white women in similar settings—and, in the cases of black, Chicano, and Native American men, lower than that of their women counterparts (Martinez and Dukes 1987, 1991; also, see Fleming for similar patterns among black students in white colleges). Clearly, in constructing support systems for students, instructors need to be sensitive not only to epistemic and gender issues but also to class, racial, and ethnic issues, seeking ways to construct intercultural learning environments.

Newer paradigms for teaching writing stress process and strategy and adopt a workshop approach in the classroom. Cynthia Caywood and Gillian Overing suggest that such approaches are more hospitable to women's learning styles than are "current-traditional," product-oriented models. They are also usually individualized and collaborative and often include inquiry-learning tasks. (Probably many readers of this volume are familiar with such models, but those who are not might want to consult Bruffee, Flower and Hayes; and Hillocks. Lindemann describes these and many other current approaches to teaching composition, and Donovan and McClelland survey a number of recent directions in composition scholarship and research. In a developmental-feminist pedagogy of discourse, many of these process-centered strategies would be used, but they would be applied in differing ways and proportions at different levels.)

L. Lee Knefelkamp and Ron Slepitza suggest a paradigm for constructing a developmentally oriented course that uses the Perry scheme as a metatheoretical "general process model" (54), providing "a framework for viewing an individual's development in reasoning about many aspects of the world" (Knefelkamp, Widick, and Stroad, 17). This model incorporates assumptions about conceptual, ego, epistemic, identity, and moral development and is applicable to any content area; L. Lee Knefelkamp, Carole Widick, and Barbara Stroad have, for example, applied it to the ways in which a woman may think about her role as woman and to the implications for counselors working with women; other instructor-researchers have used the paradigm in constructing courses in history, psychology, and literature, and their results consistently find that students both learn more in such courses and make greater epistemic advances than in traditionally constructed classes (Touchton et al.; Widick and Cowan; Widick, Knefelkamp, and Parker; Widick and Simpson).

Knefelkamp and Slepitza list nine areas in which one may expect to see qualitative change within a developmental sequence: locus of control (i.e., internal or external), analysis, synthesis, semantic structure, self-processing, openness to alternative perspectives, and the abilities to assume responsibility, to take on new roles, and to take risks. In designing a developmental course, one tries to provide challenges and supports that will produce change in the appropriate qualitative areas (some have been identified as being more compelling for dualistic thinkers and others for multiplistic or relativistic thinkers). Research also suggests that an optimum balance in challenges and supports is achieved by varying four aspects of instruction: structure, personalism, experience, and diversity.

In a lower-division writing class, an instructor can generally expect that students will be in transition to multiplistic thinking while retaining significant elements of dualistic thought. Dualistic learners reason dichotomously; there is only one right view on any subject, only one right solution to any problem. Knowledge is externally given, and the learner's task is to receive, memorize, and regurgitate it. Dualistic thinkers have trouble analyzing material and find synthesis very difficult. They also find it hard to cope with differing or conflicting opinions and to do "original work," often not having any idea of what is meant by the term. They engage in a minimum of self-processing or metacognitive activity (see Schrader for a developmental perspective on metacognition). In learning situations, they want clear directions and procedures for what they are supposed to do and clear criteria for evaluation; they want to be told what to learn. They do not regard peers as a source for learning and, in fact, may criticize the instructor who requires them to engage in small-group collaborative work.

Many of these characteristics are true for both men and women dualistic thinkers, but there are also differences in gender-associated styles within dualism that suggest structures for writing courses to meet women's needs. Belenky and her colleagues characterize women who reason dualistically as *received knowers,* and their term suggests the incorporative nature of women who reason from this perspective: they learn by listening, by taking in; consequently, they do not speak much and, in fact, lack confidence in themselves as speakers and knowers. They do not articulate their opinions, as do men dualistic thinkers: dualistic men talk, dualistic women listen, especially, in my experience, women who come from highly traditional family or cultural settings. Further, unlike their men counterparts, dualistic women tend not to align themselves with the authorities whom they so respect (Belenky et al., 37–44). Perry describes dualistic thinking as "Authority-right-we," whereas the women in Belenky and her colleagues' study seem to adhere to the view of "Authority-right-they" (44); perhaps women have been outside society's power structures for so long that they cannot imagine themselves aligned with its authorities.

Baxter-Magolda finds that this learning style especially handicaps women in their transition to more complex reasoning. "By passively receiving knowledge women take less initiative to explore the ramifications of uncertainty than do men via their active approach" (19–20). Clearly, received knowers need to be empowered, but the received knowers Belenky and her colleagues studied feared developing their own power at the expense of others, most specifically family members; rather, they felt that they should selflessly devote themselves to the care of others (46). This is a hazardous position for women who see themselves as disenfranchised, and the attitude is in danger of being exacerbated by instructors who too globally advocate an ethic of care and thus unwittingly appear to validate the very powerlessness that received knowers suffer from, for the received knower will invest the professor with an authority that renders everything that instructor says as true in all circumstances and for all time. Received knowers need permission and encouragement to develop their own voices, their own identities and sense of self-worth—and, during a certain period of their development, to place their own needs ahead of others'.

In constructing challenges and supports for the lower-division writing class, an instructor also needs to be aware of the writing behavior of dualistic students. Left to their own devices, dualists tend, in their analytic writing, to make flat, unqualified, and unsupported statements; they do little elaborating either on their assertions or on the evidence supporting them, and virtually no weighing or evaluating of ideas and evidence. Their uncoached writing contains an abundance of absolutes and a minimum of comparatives, general word choices, and heavy reliance on slogans, cliches, and commonplaces (see Hays, Brandt, and Chantry; Hays and Brandt; Hays et al., 1990b). Although dualists are usually comfortable with narrative writing, their narrative productions are often over-general, lacking in the nuances and rich particularity that characterize sophisticated narrative. Their syntax is relatively simple—often either simple or compound sentences or simple subordinated structures with little end modification and less embedding than found in more complex writing (Haswell; Weathermon).

Developmental educators suggest that the primary challenges in teaching dualistic learners involve introducing them to diversity and engaging them in large amounts of experiential learning; suggested supports focus on providing them with a high degree of structure and a personal atmosphere in the classroom (Touchton et al., 45). Introduction to diversity, however, does not mean requiring dualistic students as yet to evaluate conflicting perspectives; the mere awareness of more than one legitimate viewpoint is threatening to many dualistic thinkers, and they will cope with this awareness by compartmentalization: "Some authorities are misguided"; "In some areas, the truth is not known yet (but someday it will be)"; or "They want us to work on these things so that we can discover how to find the right answer." The challenge in teaching dualistic learners is to help them to recognize that there are legitimate differences on important issues and to qualify and particularize their writing. Another challenge is to help them develop analytic abilities, an area of development also crucial for multiplists.

A particular challenge for dualistic women students is the authentication of themselves as knowers and learners; Belenky and her colleagues note how crucial such growth is for their transition to more complex thinking (54). A response journal to the course's content and work can be one of its most important tools, providing both challenge and support, for it requires active response from each learner and encourages her to formulate and explore her own ideas about what she is learning and thus discover that she indeed has ideas. For example, a learning unit on gender roles might begin by asking each student to write several journal entries about experiences she has had on the basis of being a woman. Or she might write about a day's activities and, later, note all those that were gender-influenced, from blow-drying her permed hair to fixing dinner for her family. These items could become the basis for further journal entries in which she might draw inferences about gender roles. A journal can also be a place where students are encouraged to reflect upon their own thinking and learning, an activity that helps build metacognitive complexity; an entry can be assigned, for example, in which students reflect on and describe some aspect of their writing process, an activity dualists find difficult but one at which they can, with practice, become more adept. Needless to say, journals should not be "corrected," and the instructor must make the notebook a safe and supportive place where the student can take risks in finding her voice and authenticating her own experiences and ideas. I assign checks rather than letter grades to journals, but I also make them a course requirement; the journal has to "count," or dualistic students will not take it seriously.

The instructor also needs to engage the student, as she reveals herself in the journal, in a supportive dialogue, using her comments to ask questions that will draw the student out, validating writing that is moving in directions of growth, and avoiding criticism of what is not done so well. For example, with a student who needs to develop more detail in her writing, an instructor might refrain from comment on general passages that say little but respond to the occasional concrete detail: "I really like your use of specific detail here. It helps me to see the place you're describing," or "This is vivid descriptive writing! I'd like to see more of it." Belenky and her colleagues note how important praise is to received knowers and how destructive criticism can be if it makes them feel that they and their ideas are worthless (49); journals are a good place for generous amounts of praise. Since many received knowers have internalized a "good girl" orientation that requires them to mirror and please others at all costs, it is important that the instructor encourage any expressions of what seem to be a student's own ideas, especially including any disagreements with the instructor herself. I also try to support expressions of ambiguity in dualists' journals, perhaps with a comment noting that "your recognition of the contradictions in these experiences shows that you're thinking in complex ways about the matter. I'd like to know even more about these contradictions." Given dualistic learners' needs for structure, it is also a good idea to suggest topic areas about which they can write in the notebook and to model some journal entries for them. On the other hand, some students will take these suggestions as commands and dutifully write on every topic area suggested; the instructor will need to point such writers in personally more meaningful directions.

Since women students are often alienated by what they perceive as the excessively abstract and impersonal thrust of academic knowledge, it is crucial for the instructor to help them find personal points of connection with what they are studying; this is true in every subject and at every level of development. Probably most, if not all, of our own academic work has begun with some question or problem related to our own lives; only later in the scholarly process do we generalize about the issue and deal with it at a more public level. We need to make students aware of this connection between the private and the public and encourage them to take advantage of it, instead of pretending that we investigate areas of knowledge with complete objectivity, in a personal vacuum. Again, relating the course's content to students' lives is an old given of women's studies; many readers of this volume are probably already engaging students in such processes.

With dualistic learners, the major challenge is to present students with diversity, and in the writing classroom there are many ways to do so. (For further suggestions on how to structure writing classes for students at this level, see Hays 1988, 1990.) Sources of diversity include short readings written from various (not necessarily contrary) perspectives—for example, autobiographical excerpts about similar key experiences, written by both men and women, working-class as well as middle-class writers, and by members of different ethnic groups (with dualists, one probably would not want to deal with all these at once). A number of anthologies that include intercultural and cross-class writings are now available. Students can also write about their own similar experiences with key events and engage in structured collaborative work with all these writings, moving then to compare-and-contrast assignments that require low-level analysis and generalization. In a literature class, it is easy to find short fiction from a multitude of backgrounds.

Asking students to do interviews in conjunction with a paper topic can also be a valuable source of diversity if the instructor plans the exercise so that students interview people from different backgrounds and helps students develop questions and strategies; students can later write up their results to share with each other, ideally as a common "data base," in preparation for a more analytic paper that will present conclusions about the interviews and use material from them to support the conclusions. As Tarule suggests, such assignments not only promote active learning but also help students to see that academic issues develop out of life experience (19–20). For received knowers, the interview provides support, for it takes advantage of the received knower's inclinations to listen while also actively involving her in asking questions. Further, she becomes an expert on the views of those whom she has interviewed; this helps to build her confidence in herself as a thinker. Interviews also provide a second area of challenge for received knowers, for they involve experiential learning. Dualistic thinkers need to work from the data to the concept, rather than vice versa—the usual rule in college classrooms—and this means hands-on activities that lead students gradually into forming and verifying concepts. Many of the strategies already discussed are experiential, and to these can be added such standard writing-class activities as collaborative work on generating ideas, revising sections of writing, analyzing readings, working on a variety of rhetorical and syntactical exercises, and so on (see Hawkins; Hillocks; Lunsford, for suggestions about inquiry-learning activities).

Many of these approaches not only challenge dualistic learners but also provide them with support in the form of personalism. Received knowers especially value small groups as a way of creating a relaxed atmosphere in the classroom; they are more comfortable when they know who their peers are, and one way of supporting students at this level can be through class activities to help them learn about each other, activities that can easily include writing components. Although one way of using small-group work to promote diversity is to shift group makeup from assignment to assignment, it can also be supportive for received knowers to have a "home group" to which they return regularly. These home groups should probably be established so that students with similar learning styles are grouped together (Ramirez and Casteñeda, 141). Received knowers find it comforting to discover others with whom they can identify, and their comfort enables them to feel freer to venture their own ideas (Belenky et al., 38). If at this point in their development they are placed in groups in which separate knowers predominate, they may simply retreat into silence; in the beginning, it may even be easier for dualistic learners to work with a single partner, rather than in a group.

Another major source of support for dualistic learners is a high degree of structure, for they need to feel that they are doing what they "should." Dualists do not respond well to looser "write about what interests you" approaches. They need concrete guidelines about how to discover writing material, shape and focus it, and so on. Structure can take the form of detailed assignments with specific and limited rhetorical frameworks, due dates, clear statements of evaluation criteria, and points for assignments. Structure is especially important with small-group work, where discussion will diminish into silence or transform itself into a rap group if it is not carefully designed and monitored. Numerous materials discuss how to design inquiry-learning collaborative groups (for example, Bouton and Garth). Collaborative learning should be structured to utilize connected as well as separate knowing—as, for example, in group tasks that ask students to understand a text rather than challenge it; such groups can also share members' feeling responses to the text, responses that have first been noted in each learner's journal. With received knowers it is especially important to establish a climate of sharing rather than one of confrontation and argument (Belenky et al., 40).

Another strategy to establish connected knowing is to have students pair up with a partner and teach each other about something. It has long been an axiom in the peer-tutoring movement that tutors learn as much as those being tutored; Belenky and her colleagues note that discovering that they have something useful to share with someone else—in the context of a peer self-help group, for example—often enables received knowers to start believing in their own worth and thus to move toward the more self-affirming position of multiplicity (47). In the writing classroom, that Old Faithful assignment the process paper, in which a writer explains how to engage in some process or activity, can also be a vehicle for students' teaching each other. Everyone is an expert on something, from washing the dog to, in the case of a student in one of my classes, dissecting a cadaver. The process assignment can be constructed so that the learners share their expertise and enthusiasm (or loathing) with others in the class.

The transition into multiplicity is crucial in students' progress to intellectual maturity. This is the position at which at least half of American students complete college; in it, students come fully to recognize the existence of multiple perspectives on any issue and the legitimacy of these perspectives, although students cannot as yet comfortably evaluate this diversity, which is a long developmental journey from the dualistic thinker's certainty that there is only one right view of any topic. Belenky and her colleagues refer to women's epistemology at this level as "subjective knowing," and for women, this transition is facilitated by their turning away from external authority and coming to trust their own internal "voices" (54). This move from being externally to internally directed is extremely important for growth, although it can leave the learner temporarily dependent upon intuition and hunch for evaluating ideas and experiences. For women to advance to multiplicity in the academic environment, they must cultivate their inner voices and feel sufficiently connected to their peers, in an atmosphere of safety, to safely confront diversity (Baxter-Magolda, 21). Personal narrative and "life story" can be powerful tools for facilitating women's growth at every point in their development, but especially as they approach multiplicity. Baxter-Magolda finds that women students at this level especially value hearing the ideas and experiences of others (14). Virtually every study of women's development mentions the importance of women's stories for women's growth, and many women's studies courses are predicated upon that importance.

"Life-as-text" researchers have emphasized that we construct and reconstruct our lives by the ways in which we interpret and formulate the truth of those lives at different points in our development (Snoek; Loch). In writing about and trying to understand their experiences, students make meaning and develop self-processing abilities. Having moved away from external authority and from received definitions of themselves, multiplistic women are often redefining who they are (Knefelkamp, Widick, and Stroad). Thus writing about their lives helps them construct the new selves toward which they are evolving: Belenky and her colleagues note the extent to which subjective knowers look inward and reflect upon their lives as ways of understanding all kinds of experience (85). In the classroom, sharing life experience papers can also be the basis for drawing more general conclusions about women and thus also can lead to analytic assignments.

In some writing classes it is appropriate to use personal material for the course's content, and students' experiences can be a rich source of data, provided a climate of safety has been established. However, many subjective knowers will not wish to disclose their often painful experiences to peers, although they may comfortably share more neutral material. They may want to write about conflicted events in a paper that only the instructor reads or in their journals, and indeed, for subjective knowers, the journal comes into its own as a site for constructing meaning. Others, multiplistic learners, will be eager to write about their own lives and to share their writing. It is also important to treat these papers primarily as writing and not get into the group therapy business in the classroom; the instructor will need to lay the ground rules accordingly. No student should be required to write personal papers, but doing so can be one option among several in a given topic area. Again, students can read and write about autobiography and biography, including accounts from various historical periods; they will still be learning about constructing meaning out of experience. To facilitate epistemic growth at this point, it is important that writing assignments require some analysis, some shaping to emphasize the meaning that emerges from the story. The use of personal narrative as topic material or as a springboard for more analytic writing can ensure that students do not find analytic writing irrelevant and dull, even though it may be general or abstract.

Some subjective knowers come from dysfunctional families in which they have been emotionally, physically, and/or sexually abused by male authorities (54). As a consequence, subjective knowers often turn for guidance not only to their own authority and wisdom but also to women's nurturance, with a sense that, if men can't be counted on, women can (60–62). This sense appears to go back to the earliest connection to one's mother and to the care that she provided; mother-daughter relationships are undoubtedly a major origin of connected knowing. Some theorists and practitioners postulate a "relational" psychology for women, born out of the mutuality of the mother-daughter bond, a relationality in which mother and daughter nurture each other; for the daughter, this connectedness forms the basis for subsequent relationships (see Chodorow, Surrey, J. Miller). Followers of such theories encourage this maternal caring as ideal for women and, ultimately, for society.

But there is a negative side to this relationship, which has serious implications for women's intellectual development. Drawing upon Karen Horney's late work, Marcia Westkott has described the adverse consequences for women of having been called upon to nurture—most often their own mothers—before their own needs for nurturance have been met. Westkott anchors this phenomenon in nineteenth- and twentieth-century Western culture's construction of women's roles as exclusively nurturers of men and children, leaving them with no source of care for themselves. Thus they often turn to their daughters to meet their own needs, and the daughters must care for others before they have been adequately cared for themselves. Such relationships promote in women deep overconcern for others' welfare, at bottom a conviction that a woman is responsible for others, that her own needs and wishes are unimportant, and that in effect she can never leave home (123–39; also see A. Miller). Drawing upon object-relations psychoanalytic theory and practice, Eichenbaum and Orbach describe these "merged relation-ships" and their consequences at length: women fear that to move toward autonomy and concern for themselves is to betray their mothers. Along with this guilt comes fear that leaving the caretaking role will mean aban-donment, for it is this role, in patriarchal culture, that defines women and their relationships (1987a, 51–71 passim; 1987b; for a general intro-duction to object-relations theory, see Eagle; Greenberg and Mitchell).

For women, the questioning of authority entailed by movement into multiplicity can symbolize saying no to their mothers: in effect, "No, I see it differently." Such assertion of one's selfhood can provoke both guilt and anxiety, especially for those subjective knowers whose moth-ers, perhaps because of their own sense of deprivation, powerlessness, and need, have been unable to validate their daughters' separation and individuation. Since mothers often project their idealized selves onto their daughters, expecting those daughters to be everything that the mother is not, daughters feel they do not have a right to their own lives. For such women, loosening adherence to one's family's ways of defining reality and recognizing that there may be other avenues of knowing can be a deeply troubling development, not only cognitively but also emo-tionally (Lerner, 146). This dynamic may partly explain why subjective knowers need the assurance that forward movement will not threaten present relationships (Baxter-Magolda, 20); they need to feel firmly con-nected to others with whom it is safe to share and with whom they can identify, whose ideas can therefore be accepted, and who will likewise accept them and provide them with a supportive matrix.

Perhaps similar dynamics contribute to the behavior of those subjec-tive knowers whom Belenky and her colleagues call "hidden multiplists." Frequently such women come from outwardly advantaged backgrounds where they have been rewarded for obedience, conformity, and adher-ence to middle-class values. Such women often feel stultified by their own conformity, which they come to recognize as a "false self" (45–47; Westkott, 145–51). Yet instead of moving forward toward more authentic subjecthood, they retreat into silence, unresolved conflict, and often de-spair. One danger for the woman student is that she may use relation-

ships with others to remain at conformist levels in order to maintain the
approval and acceptance of those upon whom her very existence seems
to depend; she may also be defending herself against recognizing the
rage she feels because of her own devaluation (Westkott, 136).

Because much of this struggle takes place unconsciously, women
students may simply experience the idea of recognizing the legitimacy
of contrary viewpoints as unthinkable. For some women, the struggle is
replayed in the present and thus compounded by immediate constraints
and consequences—for example, in the lives of reentry women for whom
legitimizing viewpoints different from their husbands' may be highly
threatening, or a student from a fundamentalist background for whom
listening to any perspective contrary to the fundamentalist view may at
first seem anathema. Such students do not survive in college unless they
resolve these dilemmas, and the support of peers can be crucial at this
point. A woman instructor can also provide support for students who are
grappling with such transitions by the posture that she assumes, one in
which she herself is able to accept the legitimacy of many diverse ideas
while nevertheless adhering to her own reasoned views, including her
qualifications of and doubts about them; as Belenky and her colleagues
note, "the significant educational action is the reassurance and confir-
mation that 'maternal authority' provides a woman that she, too, can think
and know and be a woman" (62). It is also helpful to articulate for students the difficulty of this movement into the wider world of ideas and
on occasion to share with them personal struggles with and resolutions
of these dilemmas.

Yet women instructors also need to be careful that such sharing is
not a replay of mother-daughter overinvolvement. In a study done in the
1970s, Norma Haan, M. Brewster Smith, and Jeanne Block found that
women college students who had reached the highest levels of moral
development often came from families in which mothers were not overly
involved with their children's welfare but had busy and active lives of
their own and even, on occasion, voiced their annoyance at having to
extend themselves on their children's behalf—a posture contrary to the
usual maternal stereotypes. The implications for women faculty as role
models are clear: women faculty need to nurture and support but also to
convey the message that they themselves are strong and autonomous
people and that they have confidence that the student too will achieve
strength and independence. This same study also found that students
with the highest levels of moral development came from families in
which they had been allowed to express their own ideas freely, where

parents could disagree with their children without requiring conformity to their own views; Belenky and her colleagues also discuss the importance for women's development of having mothers who can allow their daughters to disagree with them (176–80).

In my own experience, among the most helpful things I have done for women at this point in their development is to encourage them to disagree with me and then to validate their courage in taking on the instructor. A woman instructor also needs to be prepared for hostility from some of her women students, for whom she can be an object of maternal transference, and to demonstrate through her handling of such hostility that it is safe to get angry at maternal figures—and that the student-teacher relationship can survive the anger. Belenky and her colleagues point to the significance for women's development—and to the relative rarity—of interactions with fathers who permit their daughters to disagree with them, to challenge them, without retreating to an authoritarian stance of "I'm right, and you're wrong" (183–85). These latter findings have important implications for men instructors in their interactions with women students. There is some reason to believe that once a woman has grown into multiplicity, she may move more rapidly than a multiplistic man into relativism (Baxter-Magolda, 21)—perhaps because having symbolically loosened her primary attachment to her mother, a woman can more easily question other goddesses and gods.

Multiplistic learners must also develop the ability to support the ideas they now intuitively adhere to and to learn that one needs grounds for one's beliefs. Since many subjective knowers repudiate abstract theory and academic authority, they may be resistant to looking at such grounds. However, subjective knowers enjoy exchanging ideas and like to learn about practical matters and to accumulate facts, data, and information. They are often more ready to act than to reason about actions (Belenky, 71–75). Tarule writes about students who can implement ideas in action before they can fully articulate and support them, a phenomenon probably grounded in "tacit knowledge" or "felt sense" (Polanyi; Gendlin; also, see Gelwick). We need to respect the validity of such ways of knowing and utilize them to help students develop beyond the hunch-and-intuition stage of thinking. Creativity studies certainly establish that intuition is often valid, but intuitive insights need to be checked with rational verification—something the multiplist does not yet do. Yet at this developmental point especially, action can often lead to reflection and understanding, and we can take advantage of this phenomenon to encourage further intellectual growth.

Problem-solution or proposal assignments can be useful here, for they are practical, action oriented, and at the same time analytic; further, the proposal's feasibility analyses require evaluating proposed actions in practical yet reasoned ways. Jeanne Fahnestock and Marie Secor have an excellent framework for such papers (263–90), one that can be scaled down for freshman-level courses or used as is in advanced writing courses. Multiplists will tend to slight full analysis of a problem's causes and will find the proposal's feasibility section the most difficult part of the assignment to do effectively: they will be apt to slide over or dismiss problem areas and to paint utopian pictures in which all aspects of a problem can be perfectly solved. Nevertheless, they will come up with some ingenious ideas and will often develop proposals that they then carry into the college or community, another important connection between learning and experience. Often these proposals will grow out of problem areas in the student's own experience. Causal analysis, especially multiple causation, can also be an important challenge for multiplists and is, in any event, a necessary foundation for a problem-solution paper.

This is also an appropriate point for students to play Peter Elbow's "believing game"—advancing all the reasons why a position might be so—which Blythe M. Clinchy suggests is the quintessence of connected knowing. Other challenges for multiplists include encouraging students to try out unaccustomed roles, perhaps through role-playing exercises; to continue to explore their own thought processes; to take more responsibility for their own learning; and to increase the complexity of their language, semantically, in terms of comparative and qualifying terms, and syntactically, through practice with embedding and end modification. The latter also helps increase depth of elaboration in writing.

Support for multiplists would stress "a cooperative, peer-oriented classroom"; as students move into multiplicity, they come increasingly to value peers as sources of learning (Kurfiss, 65). Students at this level want to know *how* to learn (as distinct from the *what* to learn of dualists) and expect the instructor to provide such information. In some cases, the instructor should simply do so; in others, she may find it more productive to engage students in the process itself. For example, students can work together to develop criteria for evaluating papers, ideally through analyzing sets of student essays that range from ineffective to effective; students can be given a skeleton evaluation matrix to elaborate on. Papers from prior classes or other sources should be used for constructing the evaluation rubric but not those of the students involved in the present class, although the rubric itself will later be applied to class members' papers.

Many American college students finish their undergraduate education still in multiplicity, and women especially are liable to remain at this position (Clinchy and Zimmerman 1982). Their interpersonal sharing of subjective experience can also become a defense against moving forward into relativism, autonomy, and competence. In this culture most men get stuck at the separate knowing position of procedural knowledge, or what Kegan calls "the institutional balance," that position in which one becomes a person in one's own right, gains admission to a societal arena, and seeks achievement, usually through a career (222–53). It is this position that the culture reinforces, and feminist critiques are an important corrective to this overemphasis. However, such criticism goes too far when it asserts that the values of procedural knowledge are exclusively masculine values and therefore to be eschewed. Many women want an opportunity to perform in public domains, and indeed, securing such opportunities has been a major goal for the women's movement. It is when procedural knowledge becomes the end point, not a way station, of development that its orientations need to be questioned. We need to encourage women to struggle toward autonomy rather than to avoid it (see Clinchy and Zimmerman 1985).

In order to grow past procedural knowledge, one must move through it, neither remaining in nor avoiding it on the grounds that it is counterproductive—grounds that for women are often defenses against fears that one cannot safely individuate or achieve selfhood. We need to remember that the goal for both men and women is to unite and integrate separate and connected knowledge in what Kegan calls the "interindividual balance" (102), Belenky and her colleagues, constructed knowledge, and Perry, committed relativism. This developmental step need not mean embracing competitive, aggressive individualism; Belenky and her colleagues note that women's styles in achieving procedural knowledge are more connected than men's. A feminist pedagogy will support students as they develop rational skills, learn procedures that enable them to achieve intellectual and professional mastery, and make judgments about a wide range of issues, judgments that are both intellectually sound and ethically committed, both reasoned and caring.

In the writing classroom, the challenge is not only to help students learn to make reasoned arguments that view issues in broad social and historical contexts and acknowledge the relativism of any viewpoint, including the writer's own. Students must also recognize that some positions are more tenable than others and that there are ways of determining why they are so. At this point in their writing development, students are ready for rigorous argumentation and the understanding that it need not lead to hostile confrontation. Rather, it can mean making a plausible case about an issue, to discover common ground upon which writer and reader can consider issues that concern both and to find some basis for cooperative action, accommodation, or respectful disagreement. Espousing thoughtful positions is especially important for women, who are prone to gloss over differences in favor of an easy consensus that avoids the risk of disagreeing with those they care about (caring they depend on to feel whole), never fully realizing who they are and what they believe (Lerner). Often in constructing argument, students can work out ideology; this work too is especially important for women, who need encouragement to claim entry into the wider arena of discourse and action that ideology addresses.

Students need to meet several discursive challenges as they move into and through relativism: learning the conventions and vocabulary of a discipline or orientation and, in the process, understanding both the strengths and the weaknesses of such orientations; developing and implementing ways of weighing and evaluating competing claims and evidence, while still recognizing the legitimacy of those claims; synthesizing and integrating material from disparate sources into coherent wholes; learning to assume the perspective of others, especially those who may differ from the self; and (later, in relativism) seeing ideas and experiences as parts of larger, interconnected systems, recognizing that all knowledge is contextual and provisional.

These challenges can be broken down into action-learning tasks, many of which can be conducted in small groups. Collaboration can now mean genuine discussion rather than simple sharing of unsupported opinions. In a disciplinary class, the subject matter will govern what is discussed. In an advanced writing class, issues of general disciplinary, social, or cultural concern will generally be the focus. It is important at this point to move students to wider frames of reference than those of their own milieus, but once again the personal should be connected to the more general, and once again the response notebook can be one valuable facilitator of such connections. Women who have been victims of abuse can move from their own experiences to consider the psychological and social forces that result in abuse and to explore ways of dealing with the problem. Students who value the out-of-doors can connect their own experiences to wider concerns about environmental safety and preservation, and so on. In short, this is the optimum developmental point for establishing discourse communities: groups of students can investigate an area, discuss the implications of the emerging material, play devil's advocate or the believing-doubting game with one another, coach one another as they develop papers, perhaps collaborate on a paper, and so on (see MacGregor 1988, 1987). More specific tasks can include work on reciprocal causation (as preparation for the later dialectical orientation); weighing and evaluating claims and their support or, conversely, deciding what responsible claims can be extrapolated from collections of information and data; and placing phenomena within systems, perhaps through the use of Richard Young, Alton Becker, and Kenneth Pike's tagmemic heuristic, especially its field perspective (121–36).

Much of the class activity should concentrate on challenging students to understand contexts and orientations different from their own so that they can develop mature empathic skills, including the ability to both identify with and differentiate oneself from the thought and emotions of others (Benack). Both aspects of empathy are important components of writing effectively for readers: without identification, writers cannot understand their reader's perspective on an issue; without differentiation, they cannot recognize points at which writer and reader lose a common context or body of assumptions that has allowed them genuinely to understand and address those points (Hays and Brandt). Benack's study indicates that identification develops early but differentiation is a later phenomenon, and Eichenbaum and Orbach suggest that women have difficulty with the differentiation aspects of empathy because they find it hard to separate and achieve autonomy (1987a, 69).

Readings and written responses to them, both affective responses and reflective preparation for discussions, can form one large source for broadening perspectives, for students at this point are ready for more emphasis on the vicarious experience of reading, as distinguished from the hands-on experiences they needed at earlier points. Role-playing and simulations can be another way to extend perspectives and strengthen differentiating competencies. To perform these activities, students must understand how those whose roles they play differ from them, and why. An environmentalist could write several journal entries or a paper from the perspective of a lumber-mill owner; a woman opposed to abortion could write as a thirty-seven-year old divorced woman who has just started job training in order to get herself and her children off welfare and discovers that she is pregnant. Obviously, some reading and research need to precede the writing. After some preparation, students could pair up and take turns playing these roles with one another. Such activities offer both the protection of play and the vicarious working through of problems and issues (Waelder). They increase flexibility of thought, help students understand other perspectives, and at the same time (usually) avoid hostile confrontations.

Students will find it difficult fully to assume the perspective of someone on the other side regarding issues on which they hold strong opinions. They will tend to give lip service to that person's viewpoint and then rush to dismiss it (Hays and Brandt). It is important that they come to understand, at an emotional as well as an intellectual level, why those with differing perspectives believe and feel as they do. Here a Rogerian rhetorical perspective that tries to enter into another person's thought and feelings in order to understand their anxieties about and resistances to change can be helpful and can also keep discussions from polarizing into right-or-wrong dichotomies (see Young, Becker, and Pike, 273–90). For women, an additional challenge comes with committing to and supporting a position on an issue and then learning how to concede and accommodate to other perspectives without abandoning one's own convictions. Such activities really involve a dialogic way of thinking and recognition of gradations of validity. The instructor can move students gradually into greater complexity by increasing the number of perspectives they are asked to deal with.

Support for students moving into and through relativism can come from peers, for students can now discover the pleasure of being connected to others in order to engage in the learning process (Clinchy et al.) and can appreciate the extent to which their own thinking is refined by discussing ideas with others. The response notebook continues to be a source of support as well as a place for the student to connect what has been learned in one class with problems in another discipline or in the world outside school. Women students who are struggling with issues of autonomy need encouragement and emotional support from the instructor, who once again can share some of her own experience with this struggle as well as point to more general knowledge about what women must deal with in making this transition. In some courses, students at this point may be interested in material about women's development as part of the assigned reading.

Few students move through relativism as undergraduates. Those who do are generally older students in colleges with nontraditional populations. However, an intellectual parent needs to remember that further growth awaits the student and to hope that, in experiencing a facilitating environment at every point during the undergraduate experience, the student has internalized a paradigm for continued intellectual and social development. This chapter suggests ways in which writing instructors can make their classrooms such environments and indicates a parental perspective from which they can assist students in their growth, while always recognizing that it is the students themselves who construct meaning and find their own particular ways through the developmental process. Like good parents, good instructors both challenge and support their students and, in good time, let them go—perhaps later to see them return as friends or colleagues. Watching students as they grow, mature, and take their places as our peers rather than our students is among the most satisfying aspects of a feminist orientation toward teaching, just as watching one's children grow into likable and competent adults who are friends as well as offspring provides the reward for the hard work of parenting—and is probably the basis for all human connectedness.

Appendix. **Perry Scheme of Cognitive and Ethical Development**

Dualism modified	Position 1	Authorities know, and if we work hard, read every word, and learn Right Answers, all will be well.
	Transition	But what about those Others I hear about? And different opinions? And Uncertainties? Some of our own Authorities disagree with each other or don't seem to know, and some give us problems instead of Answers.
	Position 2	True Authorities must be Right, the others are frauds. We remain Right. Others must be different and Wrong. Good Authorities give us problems so we can learn to find the Right Answer by our own independent thought.
	Transition	But even Good Authorities admit they don't know all the answers *yet!*
	Position 3	Then some uncertainties and different opinions are real and legitimate *temporarily,* even for Authorities. They're working on them to get to the Truth.
	Transition	But there are *so many* things they don't know the Answers to! And they won't for a long time.
	Position 4a	Where Authorities don't know the Right Answers, everyone has a right to his own opinion; no one is wrong!
Relativism discovered	Transition *(and/or)*	But some of my friends ask me to support my opinions with facts and reasons.
	Transition	Then what right have They to grade us? About what?
	Position 4b	In certain courses Authorities are not asking for the Right Answer; They want us to *think* about things in a certain way, *supporting* opinion with data. That's what they grade us on.

Appendix. **Continued**

. . . .

	Transition	But this "way" seems to *work* in most courses, and even outside them.
	Position 5	Then *all* thinking must be like this, even for Them. Everything is relative but not equally valid. You have to understand how each context works. Theories are not Truth but metaphors to interpret data with. You have to think about your thinking.
Commitments in relativism developed	Transition	But if everything is relative, am I relative too? How can I know I'm making the Right Choice?
	Position 6	I see I'm going to have to make my own decisions in an uncertain world with no one to tell me I'm Right.
	Transition	I'm lost if I don't. When I decide on my career (or marriage or values) everything will straighten out.
	Position 7	Well, I've made my first Commitment!
	Transition	Why didn't that settle everything?
	Position 8	I've made several commitments. I've got to balance them—how many, how deep? How certain, how tentative?
	Transition	Things are getting contradictory. I can't make logical sense out of life's dilemmas.
	Position 9	This is how life will be. I must be wholehearted while tentative, fight for my values yet respect others, believe my deepest values right yet be ready to learn. I see that I shall be retracing this whole journey over and over—but, I hope, more wisely.

BIBLIOGRAPHY

Basseches, Michael. *Dialectical Thinking and Adult Development.* Norwood, N.J.: Ablex, 1984.

Baxter-Magolda, Marcia B. *Knowing and Reasoning in College: Gender-Related Patterns in Students' Intellectual Development.* San Francisco: Jossey-Bass, 1992.

Beers, Susan E. "An Analysis of the Interaction Between Students' Epistemological Assumptions and the Composing Process." Paper presented at the Conference on College Composition and Communication, New York, 1984.

Beers, Susan E., and John R. Bloomingdale, Jr. "Epistemological and Instructional Assumptions of College Teachers." Paper presented at the meeting of the American Educational Research Association, Montreal, April 1983.

Belenky, Mary Field, Blythe McVicker Clinchy, Nancy Rule Goldberger, and Jill Mattuck Tarule. *Women's Ways of Knowing: The Development of Self, Voice, and Mind.* New York: Basic Books, 1986.

Benack, Suzanne. "Postformal Epistemologies and the Growth of Empathy." In *Beyond Formal Operations: Late Adolescent and Adult Cognitive Development,* edited by Michael L. Commons, Francis A. Richards, and Cheryl Armon, 340–56. New York: Praeger, 1984.

Benack, Suzanne, and Michael Basseches. "Dialectical Thinking and Relativistic Epistemology: Their Relation in Adult Development." Document BENASB-87A0292. St. Paul, Minn.: Perry Network Copy Service, 1987.

Bennett, Milton J. "Towards Ethnorelativism: A Developmental Model of Intercultural Sensitivity." In *Cross-Cultural Orientation: New Conceptualizations and Applications,* edited by Michael Paige. Lanham, Md.: University Press of America, 1986.

Bouton, Clark, and Russell Y. Garth, eds. *Learning in Groups.* New Directions for Teaching and Learning 14. San Francisco: Jossey-Bass, 1983.

Bruffee, Kenneth A. "Collaborative Learning and the 'Conversation of Mankind.'" *College English* 46 (1984): 635–52.

Caywood, Cynthia L., and Gillian R. Overing. Introduction to *Teaching Writing: Pedagogy, Gender, and Equity,* edited by Caywood and Overing, xi–xvi. Albany: State Univ. of New York Press, 1987.

Chodorow, Nancy. *The Reproduction of Mothering: Psychoanalysis and the Sociology of Gender.* Berkeley and Los Angeles: Univ. of California Press 1978.

Cixous, Hélène. "The Laugh of the Medusa." Translated by Keith Cohen and Paula Cohen. *Signs* (1976): 875–93.

Clinchy, Blythe M. "The Development of Thoughtfulness in College Women." *American Behavioral Scientist* 32 (1989): 647–57.

Clinchy, Blythe M., Mary F. Belenky, Nancy Goldberger, and Jill M. Tarule. "Connected Education for Women." *Journal of Education* 167 (1985): 28–45.

Clinchy, Blythe, Judy Lief, and Pamela Young. "Epistemological and Moral Development in Girls from a Traditional and a Progressive High School." *Journal of Educational Psychology* 69 (1977): 337–43.

Clinchy, Blythe, and Claire, Zimmerman. "Epistemology and Agency in the Development of Undergraduate Women." In *The Undergraduate Woman: Issues in Educational Equity,* edited by Pamela J. Perun, 161–81. Lexington, Mass.: Lexington Books, 1982.

Clinchy, Blythe, and Claire Zimmerman. *Growing Up Intellectually: Issues for College Women.* Work in Progress 19. Wellesley, Mass.: Stone Center for Developmental Services and Studies, Wellesley College, 1985.

Cook, Kay K. "Equity in the Classroom: An Issue for Both Sexes." *The Tutor-Graduate Teacher Program Newsletter* 4 (1988). University of Colorado, Boulder.

Dinnerstein, Dorothy. *The Mermaid and the Minotaur: Sexual Arrangements and Human Malaise.* New York: Harper and Row, 1976.

Donovan, Timothy R., and Ben W. McClelland, eds. Eight Approaches to Teaching Composition. Urbana, Ill.: NCTE, 1980.

Durham, Robert L., Janice N. Hays, and Rubén O. Martinez. "Socio-Cognitive Development, Social Economic Factors, and the Writing of Chicano College Students." Unpublished manuscript, University of Colorado, Colorado Springs, 1990.

Eagle, Morris N. *Recent Developments in Psychoanalysis: A Critical Evaluation.* Cambridge: Harvard Univ. Press, 1987.

Eichenbaum, Luise, and Susie Orbach. *Between Women: Love, Envy, and Competition in Women's Friendships*. New York: Penguin, 1987a.

Eichenbaum, Luise, and Susie Orbach. "Separation and Intimacy: Crucial Practice Issues in Working with Women in Therapy." In *Living with the Sphinx: Papers from the Women's Therapy Centre*, edited by Sheila Ernst and Marie McGuire, 49–67. London: Women's Press, 1987b.

Elbow, Peter. *Writing Without Teachers*. New York: Oxford Univ. Press, 1973.

Erikson, Erik H. *Identity: Youth and Crisis*. New York: W. W. Norton, 1968.

Fahnestock, Jeanne, and Marie Secor. *A Rhetoric of Argument*. 2d ed. New York: McGraw-Hill, 1990.

Fleming, Jacqueline. *Blacks in College: A Comparative Study of Students' Success in Black and in White Institutions*. San Francisco: Jossey-Bass, 1984.

Flower, Linda S., and John Hayes. "A Cognitive Process Theory of Writing." *College Composition and Communication* 32 (1981): 365–87.

Gelwick, Richard. "A Case of Complementarity: William Perry's Model of Cognitive Development and Michael Polanyi's Philosophy of Commitment." Perry Network Copy Service Olympia, Washington, GELWRA83A0202.

Gendlin, Eugene. *Experiencing and the Creation of Meaning*. New York: Free Press, 1962.

Gilligan, Carol. *In a Different Voice: Psychological Theory and Women's Development*. Cambridge: Harvard Univ. Press, 1982.

———. Reply. See Kerber et al.

Greenberg, Jay R., and Stephen A. Mitchell. *Object Relations in Psychoanalytic Theory*. Cambridge: Harvard Univ. Press, 1983.

Haan, Norma, M. Brewster Smith, and Jeanne H. Block. "Moral Reasoning of Young Adults: Political-Social Behavior, Family Background, and Personality Correlates." *Journal of Personality and Social Psychology* 10 (1968): 183–201.

Hall, Roberta M., and Bernice R. Sandler. *The Classroom Climate: A Chilly One for Women?* Washington, D.C.: Association of American Colleges, 1982.

Hall, Roberta M., and Bernice R. Sandler. *Out of the Classroom: A Chilly Campus Climate for Women?* Washington, D.C.: Association of American Colleges, 1984.

Harris, Barbara. "The Woman Student in the 1980s: A Developmental and Sociological Perspective." Perry Network Copy Service, Olympia, Washington, HARRBA83A0082.

Haswell, Richard H. "The Sentence: Studio and Free." Unpublished manuscript, Washington State University, 1989.

Hawkesworth, Mary E. "Knowers, Knowing, Known: Feminist Theory and Claims of Truth." In *Feminist Theory in Practice and Process,* edited by Micheline R. Malson, Jean F. O'Barr, Sarah Westphal-Wihl, and Mary Wyer. Chicago: Univ. of Chicago Press, 1989.

Hawkins, Thom. *Group Inquiry Techniques for Teaching Writing*. Urbana, Ill.: ERIC/RCS and NCTE, 1976.

Hays, Janice N. "Socio-Cognitive Development and Argumentative Writing: Issues and Implications from One Research Project." *Journal of Basic Writing* 7 (1988): 42–67.

———. "The Teaching of Basic Writers: Developmental Perspectives." Paper presented at the Conference on College Composition and Communication, Chicago, March 1990.

Hays, Janice N., and Kathleen S. Brandt. "Socio-Cognitive Development and Students' Performance on Audience-Centered Argumentative Writing." In *Constructing Rhetorical Education: From the Classroom to the Community,* edited by Marie Secor and Davida Charney, 202–29. Carbondale: Southern Illinois Univ. Press, 1992.

Hays, Janice N., Kathleen S. Brandt, and Kathryn H. Chantry. "The Impact of Friendly and Hostile Audiences on the Argumentative Writing of High School and College Students." *Research in the Teaching of English* 22 (1988): 391–416.

Hays, Janice N., Robert L. Durham, Kathleen S. Brandt, and Allan E. Raitz. "Adaptations to Friendly and Hostile Readers in the Argumentative Writing of Students at Three Levels of Adult Development." Paper presented at the Fifth Annual Adult Development Symposium, Society for Research in Adult Development, Cambridge, July 7, 1990a.

Hays, Janice N., Robert L. Durham, Kathleen S. Brandt, and Allan E. Raitz. "Argumentative Writing of Students: Adult Socio-Cognitive Development." In *A Sense of Audience in Written Communication,* edited by Duane Roen and Gesa Kirsch, 248–66. Newbury Park, Calif.: Sage, 1990b.

Hillocks, Jr., George. *Research on Written Communication: New Directions for Teaching.* Urbana, Ill.: NCTE, 1986.

Horney, Karen. *Our Inner Conflicts: A Constructive Theory of Neurosis.* New York: W.W. Norton, 1945.

Irigaray, Luce. *This Sex Which Is Not One.* Translated by Catherine Porter. Ithaca: Cornell Univ. Press, 1985.

Kegan, Robert. *The Evolving Self: Problem and Process in Human Development.* Cambridge: Harvard Univ. Press, 1982.

Kerber, Linda K., Catherine G. Greeno, Eleanor E. Maccoby, Zella Luria, Carol B. Stack, and Carol Gilligan. "On *In a Different Voice:* An Interdisciplinary Forum." *Signs.* 11 (1986): 304–33.

Knefelkamp, L. Lee, and Ron Slepitza. "A Cognitive-Developmental Model of Career Development—an Adaptation of the Perry Scheme." *Counseling Psychologist* 6 (1976): 53–58.

Knefelkamp, L. Lee, Carole Widick, and Barbara Stroad. "Cognitive-Developmental Theory: A Guide to Counseling Women." *Counseling Psychologist* 6 (1976): 15–19.

Kohlberg, Lawrence. "State and Sequence: The Cognitive-Developmental Approach to Socialization." In *Handbook of Socialization Theory and Research,* edited by David Goslin, 347–480. Chicago: Univ. of Chicago Press, 1969.

Kolb, David A. "Learning Styles and Disciplinary Differences." *The Modern American College: Responding to the New Realities of Diverse Students.* Edited by Arthur W. Chickering and Associates, 232–52. San Francisco: Jossey Bass, 1981.

Kurfiss, Joanne G. *Critical Thinking: Theory, Research, Practice, and Possibilities.* Washington, D.C.: Association for the Study of Higher Education, 1988.

Lerner, Harriet E. "Internal Prohibitions Against Female Anger." *American Journal of Psychoanalysis* 40 (1980): 137–48.

Lindemann, Erika. *A Rhetoric for Writing Teachers.* 2d ed. New York: Oxford Univ. Press, 1987.

Loch, Wolfgang. "Some Comments on the Subject of Psychoanalysis and Truth." In *Thought, Consciousness, and Reality,* edited by Joseph H. Smith, 217–55. Vol. 2 of *Psychiatry and the Humanities New Haven: Yale Univ. Press, 1977.*

Loevinger, Jane. *Ego Development.* San Francisco: Jossey-Bass, 1976.

Lunsford, Andrea A. "Cognitive Development and the Basic Writer." In *A Sourcebook for Basic Writing Teachers,* edited by Theresa Enos, 449–59. New York: Random House, 1987.

Lyons, Nona P. "Two Perspectives: On Self, Relationships, and Morality." *Harvard Educational Review* 53 (1983): 125–45.

MacGregor, Jean. *Intellectual Development of Students in Learning Community Programs 1986–87.* Occasional Paper 1. Olympia: Washington Center for Improving the Quality of Undergraduate Education, 1987.

———. "Design and Implementation of Four Learning Community Models." *Washington Center News* 3 (1988): 7–10.

Marks, Elaine, and Isabelle de Courtivron, eds. *New French Feminisms: An Anthology.* New York: Schocken, 1981.

Martinez, Rubén, and Richard L. Dukes. "Race, Gender, and Self-Esteem Among Youth." *Hispanic Journal of Behavioral Sciences* 9 (1987): 427–43.

Martinez, Rubén, and Richard L. Dukes. "Ethnic and Gender Differences in Self Esteem." In *Youth and Society,* 22 (1991): 318–38.

Mentkowski, Marcia, Mary Moeser, and Michael J. Strait. *Using the Perry Scheme of Intellectual and Ethical Development as a College Outcomes Measure: A Process and Criteria for Judging Student Performance.* Vols. 1 and 2. Milwaukee: Alverno College Productions, 1983. 6 vols.

Miller, Alice. *Prisoners of Childhood.* New York: Basic Books, 1981.

Miller, Jean Baker. *Toward a New Psychology of Women.* Boston: Beacon, 1976.

Moore, William S. "The Measure of Intellectual Development: An Instrument Manual." Olympia, Wash.: Center for the Study of Intellectual Development. Unpublished manuscript, 1989.

Noddings, Nell. *Caring: A Feminine Approach to Ethics and Moral Education.* Berkeley and Los Angeles: Univ. of California Press, 1984.

Perry, William G., Jr. "Cognitive and Ethical Growth: The Making of Meaning." In *The Modern American College: Responding to the New Realities of Diverse Students and a Changing Society,* edited by Arthur W. Chickering and Associates, 76–116. San Francisco: Jossey-Bass, 1981.

———. *Forms of Intellectual and Ethical Development in the College Years: A Scheme.* New York: Holt, Rinehart, and Winston, 1968.

———. "William Perry's Reflections." With Madeleine Van Hecke, in "The Evolution of Meaning: 20 Years Later." *Perry Network Newsletter* 11 (1989): 1–2.

Piaget, Jean. "Intellectual Evolution from Adolescence to Adulthood." *Human Development* 15 (1972): 1–12.

———. "The Role of the Concept of Equilibrium in Psychological Explication." In *Six Psychological Studies,* edited by David Elkind, 100–16. New York: Vintage, 1968.

Polanyi, Michael. *Personal Knowledge: Toward a Post-Critical Philosophy.* Chicago: Univ. of Chicago Press, 1962.

Ramírez, Manuel, III, and Alfredo Castañeda. *Cultural Democracy, Bicognitive Development, and Education.* New York: Academic Press, 1974.

Ruddick, Sara. "Maternal Thinking." *Feminist Studies* 6.2 (1980): 342–67.

Sandler, Bernice R., and Roberta M. Hall. *The Campus Climate Revisited: Chilly for Women Faculty, Administrators, and Graduate Students.* Washington, D.C.: Association of American Colleges, 1986.

Sanford, Nevitt. *Self and Society: Social Change and Individual Development.* New York: Atherton, 1966.

Schrader, Dawn E. "Case Analyses of Differences in Moral Metacognition in Adolescence and Adulthood." Paper presented at the Fourth Annual Adult Development Symposium, Society for Research in Adult Development, Cambridge, July 29, 1989.

Snoek, Diedrick. "A Case of Feminist Transformation: A Constructivist-Developmental Perspective." In *Representations: Social Constructions of Gender,* edited by Rhoda K. Unger, 77–96. Amityville, N.Y.: Baywood, 1989.

Stack, Carol B. "The Culture of Gender: Women and Men of Color." In "On *In a Different Voice,*" edited by Kerber et al., 321–24.

Stephenson, Bud W., and Christine Hunt. "Intellectual and Ethical Development: A Dualistic Curriculum Intervention for College Students." *Counseling Psychologist* 6.4 (1977): 39–42.

Stern, Daniel N. *The Interpersonal World of the Infant: A View from Psychoanalysis and Developmental Psychology.* New York: Basic Books, 1985.

Stern, George G., and Alfred H. Cope. "Differences in Educability Between Stereopaths, Non-Stereopaths, and Rationals." *American Psychologist* 11 (1956): 362.

Sullivan, Harry S. *The Interpersonal Theory of Psychiatry.* New York: W. W. Norton, 1953.

Surrey, Janet L. *Self-in-Relation: A Theory of Women's Development.* Work in Progress 13. Wellesley, Mass.: Stone Center for Developmental Services and Studies, Wellesley College, 1985.

Tarule, Jill M. "An Exploration of the Inner Voice in Learning: Definitions and Pedagogical Implications." Paper presented at Project Match, Davidson College, Davidson, N.C., 1985.

Touchton, Judith G., Loretta C. Wertheimer, Janet L. Cornfeld, and Karen H. Harrison. "Career Planning and Decision-Making: A Developmental Approach to the Classroom." *Counseling Psychologist* 6 (1977): 42–47.

Waelder, Robert. "The Psychoanalytic Theory of Play." *Psychoanalytic Quarterly* 2 (1933).

Weathermon, Karen L. "Where Two Schemes Meet: An Analysis of the Correlation Between the Perry Scheme of Intellectual Maturity and Christensen's Generative Rhetoric." Unpublished manuscript, Washington State University, Pullman, 1989.

Weiss, Lois, ed. *Class, Race, and Gender in American Education.* Albany: State Univ. of New York Press, 1988.

Westkott, Marcia. *The Feminist Legacy of Karen Horney.* New Haven: Yale Univ.
    Press, 1986.
Widick, Carole, and Michael Cowan. "How Developmental Theory Can Assist
    Facilitators to Select and Design Structured Experiences." In *Exploring Con-
    temporary Male/Female Roles: A Facilitator's Guide,* edited by Clarke Carver
    and Sarah McMahon. La Jolla, Calif.: University Associates, 1977.
Widick, Carole, L. Lee Knefelkamp, and Clyde A. Parker. "The Counselor as a
    Developmental Instructor." *Counselor Education and Supervision* 14 (1975):
    286–96.
Widick, Carole, and Deborah Simpson. "Developmental Concepts in College In-
    struction." In *Encouraging Development in College Students,* 27–59. Minne-
    apolis-St. Paul: Univ. of Minnesota Press, 1978.
Winnicott, David W. "Communicating and Not Communicating Leading to a
    Study of Certain Opposites." In *The Maturational Processes and the Facilitat-
    ing Environment,* 179–92. New York: International Universities Press, 1965.
———. *Human Nature.* New York: Schocken Books, 1988.
Young, Richard E., Alton L. Becker, and Kenneth L. Pike. *Rhetoric: Discovery
    and Change.* New York: Harcourt, 1970.
Zachary, Lois J. "An Analysis of the Relevance of the Perry Scheme of Intellectual
    and Ethical Development to the Practice of Adult Education." Ph.D. diss.,
    Columbia University Teachers College, 1986.

9

Teaching Other People's Children

Emily Jessup and Marion Lardner

Our Children, Other People's Children: Marion

The year Sam was born, my teaching changed. The baby in my arms was my first grandchild; he was precious, vulnerable, the realization of a dream for our daughter, Emily. And in five years that same precious and vulnerable Sam would walk into a kindergarten classroom. Multiply vulnerable times twenty, times forty or fifty given two sessions, and these are our students. What kinds of feelings do these children bring with them, along with the new shoes and the box of crayons, as they enter the classroom? And as the wooden door to the classroom closes on the moms, the grammies, the aunties, the dads, what fears about schooling remain unspoken by the children and by the people who bring them to school for the first time? Recognizing that all children are as precious and as vulnerable as this one grandchild, I have to think again about the kind of responsibility we as teachers assume when we close that door and face the children. It is surely a responsibility that goes deeper than the plan book, the schedule, the educational rhetoric or theory of the moment. It is a responsibility that grows out of loving observation, the same kind of attentiveness that we offer our own grandchildren.

Remembering baby Sam in my arms, I urge us to examine our new kindergarten students as one studies a grandchild. Imagine what would happen in our classrooms if we could learn to be as caring, as tender, as responsive to the needs of those children as we might be to a first grandchild. For real learning to occur, a great deal of listening must happen: we need to listen as children find ways to tell us who they are, what is important in their lives, what they worry about, what they are interested in. Embracing the concept that our rooms are full of first grandchildren with some thoughtful ideas of their very own is the first step in the process of teaching and learning. If we as teachers skip that crucial step of listening, of understanding and being attentive to the individuals in our classes, we may find that our whole language, our new math manipulatives, our socialization games become a thin veneer encapsulating the child. The best stories, songs, and writing corners won't carry the curriculum if the children do not feel that they are indeed a very important part of its creation; they become a part of that creation only as they share their hopes and aspirations with their new friends and their teacher, only as they are listened to. When we welcome our students as first grandchildren, we put children first, curriculum second, and learn to work the curriculum around the children in our classroom.

We spend a great deal of time in kindergarten asking children to think away from the big "I," to consider the feelings of others, the workings of the class as a group—those things that make the classroom work. It is important that in teaching these socialization skills we remind the children that each of them as an individual is important, has a contribution to make, even while they have a responsibility to listen to and be concerned about the ideas of their peers. Our ultimate goal is to raise up students who have compassion as well as curiosity, who listen to others and know that others will listen to them. Bridging that splendidly secure feeling about "I" with a bigger idea, "us," marks an important turn in the path toward successful citizenship. And if we have five year olds who may never have experienced that unconditional love or who experienced it only in infancy, so early that it is a shadow memory, then we as teachers get the double responsibility of helping children feel loved even as we try to teach them to care for others.

Sam is five, has been since last February. In September he will enter kindergarten. I know he has some special gifts, some insecurities. As his grandmother, I would like to enter the classroom at his side, to protect him from those practices that are so much a part of traditional kindergartens and so far removed from Sam. Will Sam be made to color the ball red and to stay within the lines? Probably. Will he learn that the sticker on his paper is the prize to achieve, rather than learning to value the work itself? Quite likely. Will someone insist that his exuberance be calmed, his voice softened, his curiosity stifled? This little boy who has grown up with tall grasses and black-eyed Susans, peach trees and bees—will he be made to draw tulips in regiments of green stems? How will he do sitting on a chair at a table waiting his turn when he has spent the summer wading with crayfish and following his baby goat? I am not unique in my fears—look at the line outside the door after the first session of any kindergarten. The people who care for the students in our classes know that what goes on in school is typically far removed from the children they love, that too often, teachers ask children to accommodate themselves to the curriculum rather than finding ways to work curriculum around the particulars of each child.

Kindergarten is hard work. It can be the most valuable experience in a student's education, the first big step toward civilizing wonderful pieces of humanity and guiding them toward good feelings about themselves, concern for their peers, and an eagerness to learn about everything. A successful kindergarten experience is the promise of all the good things school has to offer down the road and an enormous responsibility. As we look at the faces of Sam this fall—faces that have come from under the hood of their daddy's stock car, from the playground of the project, faces of kids who have lived with single moms not much older than themselves, faces that reflect material indulgence and emotional starvation, faces of kids who have been loved and cherished—hold dear your own Sam, your classrooms of Sams. Teach with the compassion of a first-time grandmother and the objectivity of an old-time teacher. And rejoice in the opportunity.

Listening Lessons: Emily

Journal notes, 12/9/90:

> *Eileen M. came into the writing workshop today in great distress. She had taken an exam on the history of the English language and felt she had been graded unfairly. We went over the exam together, looking at what Eileen had written and at her teacher's comments. She had been to see the instructor to discuss the exam, and the conversation had been awful. According to Eileen, the teacher told her that she didn't "sound" like she was supposed to, like the other students in the class or like the teacher herself. "I can't sound like that," she told me. "And I don't want to."*
>
> *Her voice—the voice of a woman in her forties, married to a lineman, mother of two daughters (one grown and one nearly grown), returning to the university, after a year at the "feeder" campus, to get a degree in English because she loves to read and write—is inaudible in that classroom. We talked about what she might do to get a fair hearing. I suggested that she talk with the appropriate administrator. I wondered, though, as she left my office, if this administrator, an Oxford-educated scholar fluent in seven lan-*

guages, tenured in the University of Michigan's English department, would hear her.

Another woman has been coming into the writing workshop regularly this term. Patty has been writing a "portrait" to fulfill an assignment she received in a sophomore seminar—a curricular innovation intended to give lower-level undergraduates the opportunity to become acquainted with a professor. Patty's portrait was about her older sister, Kelly. Upon discovering that her father was not the father of her brothers and sisters, Kelly dropped out of high school, began to use and sell drugs, resorted to stealing and prostitution to support her habit, and finally became pregnant and moved back in with her family in Detroit when her friends in Los Angeles refused to support her. Patty was writing about a time when Kelly had left her son with her siblings, on a day when one of her sisters was scheduled to attend an academic honors banquet with her parents, her other sister was supposed to take part in a friend's wedding, and her brother had planned to go to church with his girlfriend. Kelly walked out, leaving her sibs with the baby, Brandon. Patty was trying to describe Kelly's selfishness without judging her. Patty's teacher found this portrait of a sister, this story of loss, success, and family, "uninteresting" and "flat," a mere "summary of events." He wrote nothing to Patty that spoke to the story itself. He seemed only to see her "irregular" word choices, her occasional lapses into shifting verb tenses.

Patty couldn't make her writing, herself, heard. After meeting with her teacher to talk about the next assignment, she learned that he had called her academic counselor and suggested that she take a speech class as well. He liked the way she talked no better than the way she wrote.

My three-year-old daughter Becky is playing by herself on the tire swing down on the beach. Suddenly, she calls out: "Look at me. Hey, everybody, look at me." I turn, startled by her willingness to call out for an audience, particularly in this fairly public space. She is standing on the back of the swing, which, in her mind, is the same as "doing a trick." "Look at me!" As I watch her do her trick, I wonder about what we are doing—her request that I watch her, my decision to do as she asks and give her my attention. For me, this is what teaching, especially teaching writing, is about. I write best when I know someone else will pay attention to what I'm trying to say. My most important need as a writer is an attentive reader; my most basic need as a learner is an attentive teacher. What I seem to be learning about teaching and about parenting is that the most important aspect of either practice is learning to be attentive: to see clearly the concerns of someone else and to respond to those concerns, rather than imposing my own concerns upon my children or my students (Tronto).

Journal notes, 3/20/90:

I am all the things I do: I walk, I garden, I tend goats; I am a daughter, a granddaughter, a mother; I teach writing to college students. Through all this, I learn to listen. I learn to be quiet. I've tried yelling at the goat when she refuses to get on the milkstand. I've cursed at the weather. I've tried yelling at children. I've tried yelling at students in a figurative sense—haranguing them with things they need to do, issuing orders for writing assignments and paper topics, removing myself from the kind of closeness with them that leaves me vulnerable. None of this works very well. "Yelling" at students is ineffective. I can't teach from such a distance. Yelling at the children causes one to retreat into splendid five-year-old isolation, another to burst into tears. When I yell at the goat, she gets even balkier. Yelling at the weather, or at the weeds, or at the tomato horn worms or the raspberry cane borers or the aphids eating the apple tree buds, does no good either. So I listen. I work, I do; I learn to be quiet.

In the theory of teaching we are proposing, teachers must learn to quiet their own concerns and listen to their students. When I am at my best, I become the attentive listener-observer that my daughter needs. A small point, a radical turn, because much of the time it seems I am asked to listen to others talk about what my children or my students need to do or to write. This is not a call back to romantic notions of children and students—not to child-centered or student-centered teaching, completely removed from context. Rather, I envision teachers who are more aware of the multitude of contexts in which they and their students work, of the rich set of experiences that each of us brings with us; who acknowledge that to write is to put something from those selves on display; and who use that awareness to help themselves shape constructive responses to the individual voices of their students. Before I can shape a response, though, I have to learn to be attentive, to listen carefully, to be quiet, so that I can hear not what I expect students to say but what they actually are saying. In *To Know as We Are Known,* Parker Palmer describes his temptation as a teacher to speak, to prove his authority: "So often, I speak to solve problems for people, to give them definitive answers to their questions. Frequently, I rush to respond in order to prove my authority or relieve a moment of classroom tension. I forget that tension can be creative; I fail to give it a chance to draw us into the learning space. I do not allow my students' problems and questions to deepen within them, to do their own educative work" (81–82).

Journal notes, 5/10/89, on listening:

I just read Donald Hall's essay called "The Wild Heifers," in String Too Short to Be Saved. It's about a kid who recognizes finally that his grandfather is dying and doesn't quite know what to do. The grandfather is telling stories, not talking about dying: "He was giving his life to me, handing me a baton in a race, and I took his anecdotes as a loving entertainment when all of them, even the silliest, were matters of life and death." What stories am I being handed by my grandmother, Dorothy? She is ninety, has a sense of the ending of her life, a fear of it, perhaps, and surely this knowledge is present in everything she does and says—in the baby blankets stockpiled in her closet, in the Christmas stockings knitted with spaces left for new names and future dates, in assigning china sets to granddaughters, in the way she studies my children, Sam, Becky, and now Eliza, and their younger cousins, Willie and Ethan, with no end except to memorize their features. And now I listen to her urgently. This is where my children are from; she knows their history, my history, my mother's history. My memory seems unfit for the task of re- membering her stories, remembering her. I cannot wholly memorize my grandmother . . . already, I have forgotten some of the ways she has loved me, cared for me, listened to me, showed me how without making me feel small. I cannot listen hard enough, look carefully enough, memorize furi- ously enough, write quickly enough, to know my grandmother.

When I learn to listen to my students, when I learn to hear what their concerns are, as I come to know them as individuals rather than as an abstract group of students, I become a better teacher. Simply imposing a set of writing assignments on students and then judging their perform- ances does little to help them develop their self-confidence in themselves as thinkers or writers, and that is my primary concern. The theory of teaching implicit in this statement is based on the assumption that we have to know who our students are, that we have to know them well enough to build a curriculum that addresses both their concerns and ours as teachers. The theory of teaching is only implied, though, because what I know about teaching is based on my experiences—with students, with children, with writing. My knowledge is concrete. It is hard for me to write feelings and particulars into a theory, and yet the value of a theory is that it provides a framework for the particulars. It draws them together and makes them more readily translatable. I call my mother: "What is our theory?" "Focus on the children—find out where they are and nurture them along . . . focus on the child, not on the subject," she says.

Because of this focus on children first, John Dewey's ideas become an important touchstone for us as we venture together—mother and daughter, kindergarten and college teacher—into building a theory about learning and teaching. In *Education and Experience,* Dewey writes: "It is part of the educator's responsibility to see equally to two things: First, that the problem grows out of the conditions of the experience being had in the present, and that it is within the range of the capacity of the students; and, secondly, that it is such that it arouses in the learner an active quest for information and for production of new ideas" (79). From our perspective, five important claims about curriculum design are embedded in that passage. First, material needs to be presented as a problem—as something to be solved, as something about which students need to make decisions. Second, as Dewey states, these problems need to grow out of or be consistent with the students' experiences prior to coming to our classrooms or simultaneous with being in our classrooms. Third, the problems presented in our classes need to be within the range of the capacity of the students. They will be at varying points within that range at various times, depending on whether students need to be challenged or reassured. This requires, of course, that we know quite a bit about each individual learner. Fourth, the problems presented in classrooms need to be designed so as to lead learners to want to become engaged in the process of solving them. Fifth, the process of solving these problems needs to lead people to want to talk and write about what they are thinking and learning.

These five points speak to the needs of maintaining a flexible curriculum. If teachers are to fit a curriculum to the interests, experiences, needs, and abilities of our learners, we must know more about the learners than we typically do. And then we need to practice making connections between our concerns and curriculum goals and the concerns and goals of our students. Dewey points out that teachers of preschool, kindergarten, and early elementary school children will find it relatively easy to determine the range of past experiences and to find activities that connect in vital ways with it. This claim belies the individuality of our students, although it often is the case that younger students are more open about their out-of-class experiences or are less able to hide their out-of-class lives. Teachers of adults find it difficult to become acquainted with the people in our classes, because our situations make it relatively easy to focus on only a small part of our students' selves. For instance, as a college teacher, I often don't know where my students live, or what classes they are taking, or what they do when they aren't studying or in class. I don't usually know anything about the student's home life, and I rarely talk with people who know any more about the student than I do.

I only know any one of them as one of the twenty-two students enrolled in my three-hour writing class.

Barriers We Face: Marion and Emily

Even if we know that good teaching grows out of a waiting silence, out of attentive listening, out of focusing on students first and subjects second, it is hard to practice. We can invite students to write us their stories; we can try to help students find means of telling their stories; we can try to remember these stories. But one kindergarten teacher cannot listen attentively to fifty students. One college writing teacher cannot hope to get to know one hundred or more students in a single semester. The material circumstances in which we work make it impossible to be attentive to each student. Furthermore, because any individual story is full of important details, unfortunately, inevitably, some of its richness, like the richness of a grandmother's life, will be lost. Gordon Pradl writes: "Our responsibility as teacher-listeners never stops—there will always be one more story waiting to be told by a student. And deciphering its point, not merely pinning on a quick label, requires a great deal of energy and great deal of restraint" (47). We never have enough time or energy to listen to everybody. Inevitably, there will be a story that we do not have time to hear, or we find persons in our classroom with whom we cannot form a relationship, perhaps because they are hostile or withdrawn, perhaps because we are simply too tired. Then, when we begin to accept a certain percentage of loss, when we become realistic about what a teacher can do, we have created yet another barrier. Even when we are trying desperately to hold to the ideal of reaching each student, we may fail. We may misread our students, come to an overhasty conclusion about what they need from us. And finally, because attentive teaching is so personal, because it is teaching informed with both reason and love, it often feels awkward and is hard to describe.

MARION: June 11, 1990

Hello Everybody,
     School is over for awhile, so let me first tell you I'm sorry, sorry for thinking of William as a five-month old when he is nearly one-year old, sorry that I did not turn my student's mother's name in for being a wonderful volunteer at school and so she did not get a certificate, sorry that I forgot to teach the kindergarten about lowercase letters in their names

(but they can paint in the fashion of Matisse so that cancels that sorry), sorry that Sally Rabbit will not nibble on my shoestrings anymore or stretch out on the carpet, front paw under her chin, elbow bent to listen as I read good stories, sorry that I did not get those good letters and cards sent to Sam, Becky, and Eliza when they were going to be lonesome in New Hampshire, sorry that I did not get Ethan's infant gowns made, sorry that the pansies didn't get picked and have gone to seed, sorry that I didn't get the other closets emptied before Mr. W. came to paint.

On the piano at school yesterday, after everyone had left the room and the air was dusty and moist, on the piano where I would be sure to see it was the extra piece of light blue shoestring that belonged to Christopher's new sneaker. I had forgotten to tell him I found it under the ladder box and now he is gone for summer in his new jams and tank top and his ribbon for first-place standing long jump and first-place forty-yard dash. He is a perfect package of a well-built new six-year old. He is destined for prefirst because letters and numbers are not a high priority for him or his momma except when it is promotion time, and when we told momma that sometimes Christopher came in and fell asleep during our reading work and he told us he had to stay up late at night on account of his momma, when we told her that, she said what could she do? She had to mind her grandchildren and she had to keep Christopher with her and sometimes she did not get home until after midnight. . . .

I cleaned the trash out of the plan book last night and I got to September, and there was the note from Christie's mother reminding me that Christie was adopted at birth and that the family had been right up front with her from the start about how she was special and was picked from all the rest and so forth, a quite long letter, which seemed to have slipped my mind for nine months as I recalled with dismay that my series of letters to Christie's mom and her report card reports were one long stream of "believe in Christie, trust Christie, Christie is a fine little girl, take Christie's word for it, Christie is a very wonderful, very normal little girl . . . love her." Good grief, if I had remembered, I would have done it differently! It is too late; Christie too has left kindergarten.

Chantelle hovered like a bee around a newly opened morning glory. "Chantelle, what is on your mind?" "Here, Mrs. L.," she said, handing me a silk red rose. "Here," offering me a plastic comb or a bracelet. For the last week it has been so. Chantelle's mom did not come to her February conference because she was "sick." Chantelle was late for school because her "sitter was showing her how to put on makeup the right way." Chantelle likes to kiss Jimmy Swanson, on the lips, and winds her legs around so that when she points her toes she could be a mini-candidate for a centerfold. Chantelle is six, newly six. Her new baby sister's father is a professional basketball player, paying child support for the baby, not for Chantelle. Chantelle brought a paperback primer from a 1950 Catholic catechism to school yesterday. I told Chantelle I couldn't read it, another Jesus story, and we were still in public school. Chantelle seemed satisfied. And then I remembered in the night that we had extended the book exchange, bring a book, take a book, and I'll bet, now that it's too late, that Chantelle brought that expendable book to trade for a good one . . . and now there is no Monday to go back and hug her and say help yourself.

And Elaine J. Her mom is the bag lady you can spot picking through trash behind the old Zayre store. Fortunately, the one time she came into Hanson to see Elaine we were on a field trip. Her dad is illiterate, but he can come and sign the lunch form, says our school secretary. Elaine hovered too this week and held Sally Rabbit close. Every time I looked her way, Elaine was whispering in Sally's ear. Elaine told me that S., her DCFS designated homemaker, probably would take her to Disney World this summer if she could.

EMILY: journal notes:

I had been co-leading a discussion of some poems by Native American writers, including the one that follows, by Joseph Bruchac. After class, a man who had just finished a difficult semester of student teaching asked me quietly whether I ever became depressed, thinking about all the students whose lives I could not affect. He felt, he said, somewhat like the grandfather in the following poem, except that he felt overwhelmed by all the toads:

Birdfoot's Grampa

The old man
must have stopped our car
two dozen times to climb out
and gather into his hands
the small toads blinded
by our lights and leaping,
live drops of rain.

The rain was falling,
a mist about his white hair
and I kept saying
you can't save them all,
accept it, get back in
we've got places to go.

But, leathery hands full
of wet brown life,
knee deep in the summer
roadside grass,
he just smiled and said
they have places to go to
too.

                    —*Joseph Bruchac*

*In a hurry to get to my next class, I could think of no satisfactory response.
I adopted the pragmatic voice of the narrator in the poem: "You have to
learn to distance yourself. Try to leave your students at school and think
about other things when you get home. You'll get burned out if you don't
learn to let some go." The new teacher only looked at me in disbelief.*

MARION: journal notes:

*Things aren't always as they seem. Ronald's parents came to our first par-
enting workshop one evening at school. Ronald's dad took the lead in his
cooperative small group, participated enthusiastically. I was glad to see him,
told him he looked exactly like his son, and he grinned. In the Christmas
program, Ronald stood on the top of the risers and sang, "If you're happy
and you know it, clap your hands." Up in front of everyone, he clapped his
hands. Then his mom came into kindergarten to tell me that she and the
three kids were spending Christmas in the shelter, in seclusion, protected
from the father by a restraining order. So swept away were we—the teachers—with all the tinsel, the singing, the appearance at workshops, that we
hadn't seen the circles under Ronald's eyes. I should have known something
was wrong, because he raised his hand and then wouldn't know what to say.
He wanted to tell us something. If I had had time to sit down with him long
enough, we could have talked about it. At least his mom came in, and I
gave her a hug, and our principal gave her a hug, and they had a long talk.
We collected money for the family, and someone brought in clothes and stuff
for the kids. The custodian carried it to the car, and he gave the mom a
hug, too, and told her we are a family at this school. But I hadn't known
how much had been on Ronald's mind.*

EMILY: journal notes:

*The most important part of my teaching is the part that seems hardest to
justify. I'm glad I don't get evaluated on the way I conduct my writing conferences with students. Sometimes, for the student's sake or for my own, I
perform a little bit: I drop a grammatical term, begin a phrase with "re-*

search suggests" but most of the time, I think, the best work I do is the work
for which I have not been trained. I listen, I smile, I ask questions, I tease
a little bit when Adam tells me he is a little behind with his work and suggest
that he needs to experiment with a new socializing-studying ratio. I tell a
story about my kids. I try to establish some trust between us, so we can begin
to talk about the terribly important and terribly private work that is writing.
Madeleine Grumet calls these conversations "intimate communications,"
and she claims that they recapitulate the conversations we have had with
our mothers and with our children. The problem is, these conversations seem
too personal to be considered part of our work: "Though we secretly respect
this maternal pedagogy of ours, it seems personal to us, not quite defensible
in this public place, and we provide this nurturant labor without demanding
the recompense it deserves" (87). When I write my end-of-year account of
how I spent my time, I don't know how to inscribe this work in my list. How
do I write that I believe the students in my classes came to trust me? That
I came to know each of them individually? That I cared for them, and that
they came to care for each other?

Learning to Teach: Marion and Emily

One of the ways we can learn to be better teachers is by discovering
forms to describe what we do. In particular, we might begin by imagining
metaphors, because metaphors, faster than theory can lead us to imagine
teaching in a different way. They can help us to see and feel what we are
learning and what we know in new ways (Emig). We need to collect and
create metaphors for teaching in which teachers are in tune with and
attend to the needs of the people with whom they are involved. We have
already been given some good metaphors. In *Lives on the Boundary,*
Mike Rose gives us the metaphor of teaching as a romance:

> Teaching, I was coming to understand, was a kind of romance. You didn't
> just work with words or a chronicle of dates or facts about the suspension
> of protein in milk. You wooed kids with these things, invited a relation-
> ship of sorts, the terms of connection being the narrative, the historical
> event, the balance of casein and water. Maybe nothing was "intrinsically
> interesting." Knowledge gained its meaning, at least initially, through a
> touch on the shoulder, through a conversation. (102)

In *Caring,* Nel Noddings describes teaching as a form of caring, claiming
that caring, rather than pedagogy, is the essence of teaching: "The
teacher ... is necessarily one-caring if she is to be a teacher and not

simply a textbooklike source from which the student may or may not learn" (70). Henrietta Dombey casts teaching in a related light in "From Stories at Home and at School." Describing the interaction between a mother and her daughter as the daughter is learning to speak, she writes that Anna's mother plays a "supportive and self-effacing role: Anna is the conversational virtuoso while her mother remains the unobtrusive accompanist" (74). The accompanist, the one-caring, the suitor—all focus their attention on the other person, listening attentively, actively trying to engage the learner in an activity by making that person the center of attention. This image of teaching is radically different from one in which the teacher acts as the expert performer, the onstage entertainer, the one from whom knowledge issues.

EMILY: journal notes, 10/20/90:

> *Imagining, or remembering, that we are teaching other people's children who are as precious, as vulnerable, as important as our own children or grandchildren has helped me rethink my relationship with my students. When Sam started kindergarten this fall, I felt terrible. I knew the curriculum was wrong—too academic; I knew there would be too many kids in the class; I knew his teacher would never have time to listen to his lengthy stories, once he got the courage to share them with her. In my mind, the one thing that could save Sam from the perils of schooling would be his relationship with his teacher. If she liked him, and if he liked her, and if they could work together, he would be okay. As I met my own students this fall, most of whom were coming to college for the first time, I wondered what their parents' concerns were. Did they wonder whether the teachers at the University of Michigan would appreciate what their grown children had to offer? I came to feel that I owed my students the same kind of loving attention I desperately wanted for my own child.*

The sources for our metaphors will be our experiences, in and out of our classrooms. In "The American Scholar," Ralph Waldo Emerson reminds us that our ordinary experiences are valuable: "If it were only for a vocabulary, the scholar would be covetous of action. Life is our dictionary. Years are well spent in country labors; in town; in the insight into the trades and manufactures; in frank intercourse with many men and women; in science; in art; in the one end of mastering in all their facts a language by which to illustrate and embody our perceptions" (71). Emerson makes it sound easy to use our experiences as a dictionary; Alicia Ostriker reminds us that this is not necessarily so. We need to guard against adopting the position that some experiences, like the experiences of motherhood, of caring for another, are less important than others. In "A Wild Surmise: Motherhood and Poetry," Ostriker writes: "If the woman artist has been trained to believe that the activities of motherhood are trivial, tangential to the main issues of life, irrelevant to the great themes of literature, she should untrain herself. The training is misogynist, it protects and perpetuates systems of thought and feeling which prefer violence and death to love and birth, and it is a lie" (131).

EMILY: journal notes, 11/19/90:

My experience of motherhood, like my experience of teaching, is physical. I learn by doing things, by using my hands to change diapers, or to dig in the garden or to make food. If I were going to write a theory for teaching writing, it would have to include doing, feeling, thinking simultaneously. Mostly, it would have to be grounded. I watch the kids use their bodies to explore, to learn. Baby Eliza at the beach eats sand, rolls grains around with her tongue, tries to remove them with sandy hands. Toes touch cold water. She stoops, stares, backs too quickly, sits. Bodies and minds are one. A theory of teaching would have to say that we write who we are.

It's not enough to collect the metaphors about teaching that other people have created. All of us need to create our own. By describing teaching as a form of aesthetic practice, requiring both a studio "where the artist harvests silence" and the gallery where she serves the fruit to others, Grumet initiates a discussion about our need both to make and to share our perceptions: "Just as I would send the teacher to a room of her own where she can shed the preconceptions that blind her to the responses of her students, I would ask her to bring the forms that express her understanding of the child and the world to the children, to her sisters who are her colleagues, and to her sisters who are the mothers of the children" (94). As teachers, we need to share the forms that express our understanding of our students, ourselves, and the practice of teaching. We may find that forums already exist for this—that our seemingly staid professional organizations will welcome this kind of talk, at least up to a point. We may also find ourselves writing more letters or poems or stories, writing in journals or computer conferences, making time to talk with one another.

MARION: June 3, 1990:

Dear Emily and all others,

Josh was busy as I had a conference with his mom, M., and grandma. M. is pregnant ... showed me her new diamond ring ... "I am engaged. . . ." M. has a second child, Lexie, somewhere. My interest is Josh, a delightful earnest little boy who trembled when he spilled his milk and hid behind the ladder box. Josh can only speak about his love for Rex, as in Tyrannosaurus: "Rex will take care of it, Mrs. L." Rex was pictured with a huge syringe poked into him, and when questioned, Josh told me Rex was giving magic potions to help our crossing guard's wife get over her Alzheimer's, and then he told me that Rex is "getting stuff to make him happy."

Grandma told me Josh was smart, Josh knew his letters and sounds, Josh was okay. I commented that I thought Josh was tense, high-strung and preoccupied. Grandma replied that there was no pressure at her house, where Josh lives. She does have all white carpet and puts newspapers down whenever Josh eats. . . . Josh never sits long at a table. . . . Grandpa is his idol, the grandpa who says "don't try it if you can't do it right." Josh called over to us as we talked that he could take the hermit crab out of its shell. We kept talking.

Well, now it is Monday night. When I brought the hermit crabs home for their summer holiday, one of them indeed had been out of his shell for much too long a time, and hermit crabs shell-less are vulnerable, like kindergarten children without kindergarten teachers to say "Good morning" every day and "I like you a lot" and "Are you okay?" It is not owning children, though, it's mostly like being really interested.

Sharing Worlds: Marion and Emily

Creating a theory of teaching based on caring would radically change the nature of our classrooms and our schools. As Joan Tronto writes, "caring emphasizes concrete connections with others. . . . It evokes so much of the daily stuff of women's lives, and . . . it stands as a fundamental critique of abstract and often seemingly irrelevant moral (and educational) theory" (185). Once we accept the premise that teachers must be attentive to each person's needs, listen to each student's story, we become involved in the chaos of real lives. Grumet writes:

When I have typed the story that your child reads or have tied his shoe or found his scarf, when you have told my child a story of your own or have helped her catch the bus, other people's children become our own

children. This kind of contract . . . promises to extend a new tolerance
not only to other people's children but to other people as well. For as we
share the care of a child with her parent we engage in a mimetic and
empathic relation with them as well as with the child, gaining access to
their hope as well as to their habits of nurture. It is not enough to know
other people's children. We must know, share a world with, the other
people who love that child, wildly or tentatively, desperately, ambiva-
lently, or tenderly. (179)

As teachers, we need to come to know the people whose worlds we share
as best we can. We can start by listening and by watching. We can ask
our students and our children to help us figure out how to become better
teachers. We can share what we are learning with each other.

MARION: January 3, 1991:

Dear Em,
    It happened today, the first day back after Christmas vacation. A
grandmother had wrapped a tiny package for Sally Rabbit, and she had
attached a note to it: "Hope you like the color. Merry Christmas, Sally.
From Santa."
    Well, we passed the package around, pinched it, shook it, snooped
in all the ways kindergarten children know how to after a holiday of
practice. The consensus was that it was soft, it was squishy, it was small.
It was probably not a mirror, nor a rabbit ninja turtle . . . maybe a lovely
pillow. After all the ideas were shared, and it was a wonderful sharing
(the children were speaking in whole sentences), we opened the package. Four little felt boots fell out onto my lap, handsewn, two white ones
and two that were brown on one side and green on the other. Boots for
our favorite rabbit, Sally. The children were enchanted.
    Cassie hurried over, gathered Sally in her arms, and brought her
back to the circle. We tried the boots on. Sally was not as pleased as the
children. We got one on her right front paw but she kicked that off as
we secured the one on a back paw, much to the delight of her five-year-
old companions. In the midst of the fun and joy, the children happily
predicted the ways we could cause Sally to wear her boots and ruminated
about why she might not want to: "She is inside," "There is no snow
today," "She needs to put socks and shoes on first," "Rabbits don't never
need boots." As they were talking, the children were falling in love with
their pet rabbit all over again after the two-week holiday. Kindergarten
really begins to come together this time of year, and the annual magic
was happening again.

The moment seemed right. We passed out paper, and I suggested the children go to a seat and write a story about Sally Rabbit and her new boots. We had tried journals earlier in the year. The child who scribbled knew his writing could not compare with that of his sister in first grade: "It *is* scribbling, Mrs. Lardner." All of the stories about learning to creep, crawl, and then walk helped not at all. Christopher knew his writing looked wrong. But today with beloved Sally as the text, today after three months of growing in self-esteem in kindergarten, today in the excitement of coming home, back to our classroom, today we began doing writing without the pressures and foreboding that lingered last fall. We had good subject matter. We trusted each other. Today we could take chances, and we did. Ronald took paper and pencil and got right to work. Behind the dark glasses that he now wears, his thoughts spilled onto his paper: "I trst Sale." After school when his mom came to pick him up, he whispered in her ear. Mom looked up and grinned. "We'll have to ask them at the shelter. I don't know how they feel about having a rabbit for overnight."

For our children, the door has opened. We will write often, come to love it, to be successful. The writing was all over the page, the letters were frontwards and backwards, sometimes upside down, but we were writing. We had something to say, to record, and we did it. We're on a roll. Thanks to Sally, grandmother, four months of finding out who we are and that we are indeed each important. No one can stop us.

EMILY: journal notes, November 1990:

Conversation with Sam, who is five going on six and has been attending kindergarten since September, about teaching. My writing class seemed to be in the midst of a midsemester slump, so I asked Sam what he thought I could do to make my class more interesting. I asked him what he especially liked about kindergarten, and he told me that the best part about it was not needing to do things by himself. He also suggested that we try doing homework: "Homework would be a good idea; let them choose any homework they want, like zipping up their coats even if they know how, or tying their shoes, or learning to read." He thought for a while. "Ask them if they live in cities and if they don't have any pets. You could teach them how to have a pet." He paused, then asked: "Do you go on any field trips? That would be a good idea. You could go on a field trip to the museum, [or] to the apple orchard. But you need to be all separate into small little groups. . . . Ask the students if they'd like that. I bet they'd love that. Did any of your students ask you if they'd want to go on field trips?" Sam was right: my students would love to go on field trips, to gather information by making observations and by listening to people around them. Field trips aren't typically part of college

*writing classes, though they are part of his kindergarten curriculum. Why
don't we take field trips?*

*I asked Sam if he had any other ideas about how I might get my students
to like our class more. He told me that it was really important for me to help
the people who didn't want to do their work all by themselves. He asked me
if any of my students made mistakes or did things wrong, and when I said
yes, he told me that those were the students I was supposed to help. And the
strategy he suggested was not to tell them what to do but to show them: "The
easiest way is not to say or tell them what to do. You're supposed to show
them. . . . Do you ever do that? . . . Pick something out that you want them
to do and do it, and if they can't see it, just go around and show it to them.
And maybe if it's something you can hang up on the board, you put a tack
through it. And then if it falls down, you can just do this—you can go around
your whole class and show it to them, because then they'll be able to know
it better. Is there any more questions?"*

*Last year I taught a course on feminist issues in academic writing. We
spent time talking about what issues were feminist issues and what academic
writing meant. We talked and wrote a lot about writing—our own writing,
our experiences with writing courses, the relations between creative writing
and personal writing and academic writing. Toward the end of the course,
a student wrote this: "I want to teach composition, to allow people the expression of themselves, their questions, their convictions. I want to let people
believe in themselves enough to take the time to put forth their ideas and to
take responsibility for those ideas. I do not believe that English is an earth-
shattering topic. I don't care if anyone understands Beowulf or can identify
a dangling participle, but I do want to teach people how to express themselves, how to discover selves that can be let out on paper and accepted and
drawn upon. Writing is both a way in and a way out."*

MARION:

Dear Emily,

You asked how we began this dialogue, how this chapter came about.
I believe that the arrival of your dad's PC on our kitchen table is where
it all started. Finally overcoming the fears of a new technology, I found
I could create a group letter to you and your family and at the same time
send off the news to your sisters and brothers. Since my letters would
now appear in households where grandchildren and in-laws could read
them, I took special care in describing kindergarten, chickens, our pup-
pies, the garden, life in general around your former home.

The letter writing became lots of fun. The encouragement from you
and your sibs—"Mom, I am saving your letters," "You sure know how
to write"—encouraged me, just as I assume our encouragement of your

work from the time you were a little girl motivated you to do better and better. Isn't it curious that we circle, and as we circle in our lives and our writing, the same truths bob up? Feel secure; write about what you know; trust your audience.

As you told me about your grown-up students, and we shared our hopes for their success, and as I continued to spill over with my love and respect for five year olds as individuals with enormous potential, we compared teaching strategies and discovered that we were doing a lot that was the same. I was astonished to hear you say this. In too many teacher lunchrooms I have heard too many upper elementary teachers report the success of one of "their" students: "I taught her what she knows." Early childhood teachers understand that those early years are key, and to have a college professor agree that learning is a continuum was the hot fudge on the ice cream. When you and I agreed that we were part of a team with similar goals and similar practices, it became a great lot of fun to talk shop, which we continue to do, always trying to remember that other folks in our family—Sam, Becky, and Eliza; their cousins Willie and Ethan—along with the children in other people's families—Christopher, Christie, Chantelle, Elaine, Cassie, and Ronald, the kids in my classroom; and Elaine and Patty and Adam, the students you know—each need to believe that he or she is important, has ideas worth sharing, ideas worth listening to. We need to remember, and we need to celebrate.

BIBLIOGRAPHY

Bruchac, Joseph. "Birdfoot's Grampa." In *The Remembered Earth: An Anthology of Contemporary Native American Literature,* edited by Geary Hobson, 34. Albuquerque: Univ. of New Mexico Press, 1981.

Dewey, John. *Education and Experience.* New York: Macmillan, 1938.

Dombey, Henrietta. "From Stories at Home and at School." In *The Word for Teaching Is Learning,* edited by Lightfoot and Martin, 70–81.

Emerson, Ralph Waldo. "The American Scholar." In *Selections from Ralph Waldo Emerson,* edited by Stephen Wicher, 63–79. Boston: Houghton Mifflin, 1957.

Emig, Janet. "Children and Metaphor." In *The Web of Meaning: Essays on Writing, Teaching, Learning, and Thinking,* edited by Dixie Goswami and Maureen Butler, 97–108. Upper Montclair, N.J.: Boynton/Cook, 1983.

Grumet, Madeleine R. *Bitter Milk: Women and Teaching.* Amherst: Univ. Massachusetts Press, 1988.

Hall, Donald. "The Wild Heifers." In *String Too Short to Be Saved.*

Lightfoot, Martin, and Nancy Martin. *The Word for Teaching Is Learning: Essays for James Britton.* London: Heinemann, 1988.

Noddings, Nel. *Caring: A Feminine Approach to Ethics and Moral Education.* Berkeley and Los Angeles: Univ. of California Press, 1984.

Oliver, Mary. "The Wild Plum Trees." In *American Primitive,* 84. Boston: Little, Brown, 1983.

Ostriker, Alicia. "A Wild Surmise: Motherhood and Poetry." In *Writing Like a Woman.* Ann Arbor: Univ. of Michigan Press, 1983.

Palmer, Parker. *To Know as We Are Known: A Spirituality of Education.* San Francisco: Harper and Row, 1983.

Pradl, Gordon. "Learning Listening." In *The Word for Teaching Is Learning,* edited by Lightfoot and Martin, 33–48.

Rose, Mike. *Lives on the Boundary: The Struggles and Achievements of America's Underprepared.* New York: Free Press, 1989.

Tronto, Joan C. "Women and Caring: What Can Feminists Learn about Morality from Caring?" In *Gender/Body/Knowledge: Feminist Reconstructions of Being and Knowing,* edited by Alison M. Jaggar and Susan R. Bordo, 172–87. New Brunswick: Rutgers Univ. Press, 1989.

10

Composing the Multiple Self: Teen Mothers Rewrite Their Roles

Sara Dalmas Jonsberg, with Maria Salgado and the Women of The Next Step

The Next Step involves a group of women writing a new script for their lives—young women, whose lives have been bound to the feminine plot prescribed by their biology. They became mothers during their teens; now in their early twenties, they are struggling to make things different, to find a sense of dignity and purpose for themselves and their children, to get off welfare for good. It's hard for them to get where they want to go; all of them—before or because they became pregnant—dropped out of school for a few months or a few years. They went back, either to finish high school or to earn a General Education Development (GED) diploma, and they want to go on now, to learn more, earn more credentials, so they can get jobs that will have a future, that will be challenging and fun. They suspect that education is the key, but for them, the educational process has often been painful.

As teacher and researcher, I've been trying to figure out why that is, what makes school uncomfortable for so many girls and what we might change in order to make it feel better for them, for everyone. There are too many dropouts these days, girls *and* boys, at a time when the job market requires higher and higher levels of literacy and skill. The women I have worked with in The Next Step summer program for young mothers at Mount Holyoke College are helping me search for answers.

When I asked Maria to help me with this writing and with the work of my dissertation, I described my theoretical purpose this way: "It seems to me that girls have a part of their lives over here," (I shaped my hands as if to encircle a sphere), "that's what their families, or their culture or society or whatever, seem to want for them—being a girlfriend, being a mother, being dutiful and focused on other people's needs; and then there's another part over here that's what school wants—being a risk-taker, being independent and, in a way, *self*-centered. Many of us often feel caught between these two very different prescriptions for how to be, and it may feel sometimes as if we're being ground between two stones. Sometimes it may feel as though we are really several different people: one person for our families, another for our friends, another for school, and so on."

Her eyes lit up. "Yes," she said, "I have felt all of that. I know how it feels to be caught in between, to feel pushed and pulled and uncertain about what's right. I have felt, even now that I've made some decisions about my life, the confusion of being several things, several people, at the same time. I see what you mean, exactly. What you're saying makes sense." "If in school," I said to her, "we could talk and write about that confusion, that multiplicity, maybe girls would feel better about staying in school. That's what we tried to do this summer in the program," I said. I asked for her help in telling that story, and, with her consent, we began, with me as composer-compiler-commenter, Maria as coauthor-coresearcher-verifier of impressions.

What we have written is a sort of play. Milagros de Luz, our main character, is a composite of several real people. I chose the name because every one of the women in the program is to me a *miracle of light,* sparkling against the dull gray background of public opinion about teen parents, shining with a fierce and fiery determination. Maria thinks my invented name is a little corny, but we wanted her to have a Spanish name to represent the women in our program, most of whom are Puerto Rican. (However, adolescent childbearing is not a "minority problem"; the pregnancy rate for teens in the United States is as high for whites as for other ethnic groups [Sanders, 11].) In the pages that follow, Milagros talks about her life and about some of the things she discovered in the program during the summer. Her words are interspersed with those of some of the actual participants in the program. (These are given in italics.) These voices function as a chorus, echoing and elaborating on Milagros's thoughts and experience. Part of our summer curriculum—and the theoretical foundation for our pedagogy—is based on Jean Baker Miller's idea that, for women especially, the self is a multiple entity, defined by varying relationships (1984, 1986b; also, see Surrey).

Inspired by her descriptions of "mutually enhancing" relationships (p. 3, 1988), teachers and students in the program worked together to think and write and talk about relationships in our lives, about the various selves shaped by those relationships and the expectations they impose, about how and why relationships differ—why some feel good and others feel demeaning or frightening—and what those differences do to self-esteem. The teachers in the program hoped that, if our relationships with each other in this schoollike setting could be strengthening and affirming, they might provide a counterbalance to life forces that insist solely on a biological plot. Though there may not be a way to make the two spheres—what school wants and what society seems to want—one, maybe a means can be found to live more comfortably with complexity and contradiction.

The setting is the campus of a New England women's college, Mount Holyoke, in South Hadley, Massachusetts, from late June to early August. Young mothers aspiring to go on with their education spend four days a week here, from nine in the morning until three in the afternoon, engaged in writing, collaborative problem solving in mathematics, aerobic dancing, swimming, going on field trips, eating lunch, studying in the archives, meandering across campus, celebrating birthdays, visiting the career counseling office, and so on.

Milagros de Luz, our composite main voice, is a Puerto Rican woman in her early twenties, the mother of a three-year-old daughter. She completed her GED through the Care Center, a small alternative school for pregnant and parenting teens located in Skinnerville, the nearby industrial city where she lives. Elena, Ada, Nina, Nellie, Lisa, and Cindy are real women in the program; most, like Milagros are graduates of the Center and several are in possession of "real" high school diplomas. Initially this difference was a source of some friction, but ultimately it became no more than a silly tease. Only Cindy, among those who form the chorus here, is Anglo, as were several other women in the program; the rest are Puerto Rican. Sara and Rochelle are teachers, friends, and mentors. During the academic year, they are administrators at the college. Sara is also a doctoral student and miscellaneous worrier—Mama Sara, Maria calls her.

Self-in-Relation: Milagros and Friends

It is September, after the summer program has ended. Milagros is telling Sara about her background and her experience in the program.

Milagros: I was born right here, and I've known Skinnerville all my life. I've grown up here—in more ways than one—and it feels like home to me. My mother came here from Puerto Rico with my father when she was thirteen. They were married, and she had me when she was sixteen. My grandmother lives in Puerto Rico, and my mom has gone back there, too, which I think was a good decision for her. I feel good about her; I'm glad that she has finally found a way to be happy. She's more secure there somehow, more in control. Mainly because of the language, I think. She never really learned to speak English, so she was uncomfortable all the years she was here. To tell the truth, I think my mother knows English; she can certainly understand it. But she was always afraid to speak it, for fear she would make a mistake or whatever, for fear people would laugh at her.

As for me, I consider that my first language is English, but I learned to speak both English and Spanish as a child. I'd like to learn to write Spanish; I don't really know the grammar and the spelling. It's funny, because when you try to study Spanish in school, it's too easy, but it's too hard at the same time. What happens is that you don't really work at it, so you end up getting a *D,* which is crazy, because it's your language. I'd like to know it because that's a way of honoring where I come from. I'm proud of being Puerto Rican—it's something I have learned, mainly because of a course I took at the community college about diversity. I learned pride in that course, and I also learned to give a name to discrimination. I've had experiences that prove discrimination is there: for example, it has happened to me more than once that people—a landlord, for instance—may treat me one way on the phone (because I don't have a Spanish accent) and another way when they see me. But the funny thing is, it only makes me more determined to do what I want to do— and I feel proud of what I've accomplished so far, because it *is* harder.

I never really knew discrimination existed until, in one place we lived when I was younger, I was one of only a few Hispanics in the school. They didn't want us in the clubs or on the teams or anything like that. The kids made it hard, but the teachers made it hard also. It was like you were getting it from both sides, which can be totally frustrating; you feel like you have nowhere to turn.

What's really hard though is that some of us get kind of stuck in between. We're Hispanic, but we're American too. Especially single moms, I think, and especially if you're trying to make things different. Because you want both: you want to stay being Hispanic, because that's part of who you are. But if things are going to be different, you can't just do what your own mom did. You have to be more "American," if you know what I mean. Like reading my daughter a story: I never remember my mother picking me up and reading me a story. But I try to do that every day with my daughter. That's the way you make change, with little things like that, reading stories. Culturally, it may be weird to read to your kid. I'll bet 95 percent of the single moms going to college, especially Hispanic single moms, never experienced that when they were little, being read to. When you make the decision that things will be different, it separates you from what you've been used to, from your roots, I think you could say. And it's not easy; you feel lonely and scared sometimes.

Anyway, when I was little I liked school a lot. I still like school, as far as that goes, but it hasn't always been the best place to be. Especially when I went to the high school. It was so big and confusing; I felt really lost and alone.

LISA, journal entry, second day of the program:

> *My experience of loneliness was my first day in a new school. It was a junior high that was more like a high school. It had three floors and a lot of rooms. My mother signed me in, and that wasn't so bad. But then an office aide told my mother that she didn't have to walk me to class. I was devastated!!! Here I was, in a school full of strangers, and my mother wasn't even going to see me to class. She gave me a kiss on the cheek and went home. The office aide told me a room number and pointed in the direction of the room. Here I was, in a hallway, without a person in sight, and I was scared TO DEATH!!!*

MILAGROS: I got along okay, but mostly I would go to school to get out of the house. There was no reason to be in school, but it was even worse to be at home. Home was a pretty unhappy place. My father made things very hard for my mother, because of what he expected her to do; he wanted her to be totally devoted to taking care of him and to keeping house. He's the real reason, I think, that she never learned English. He wouldn't *let* her. He wouldn't let her go out, hardly ever, never alone. It used to make her angry, and I think it's what got to her finally, because she knew somehow that other women were doing things she couldn't do.

CINDY, journal entry, toward the end of the fourth week:

> *[My children's father] was very possessive and jealous. I stayed in the house most of the time to avoid arguments. My friends stopped coming over because*

he was a jerk when they came to visit; he made it uncomfortable for them. He abused me, what I mean is verbal abuse. There were also a few times when he slapped me. I couldn't argue back, because if I did it would make it worse. It began to be like a prison for me. We hardly went out. Once in a blue moon. To his family's house on Sundays. I was very unhappy. I was a very young mother, a homemaker, a housewife. It was hell for me.

But I finally did it, I finally got the courage to leave him. It was hard. I felt that I should stay with him because of the kids. To leave him made me feel really guilty. But I decided that the fights and arguments were affecting them too. I knew that I had to get away from him and get out on my own, no matter how hard it would be.

MILAGROS: I felt myself that I was missing something when I was young; I feel like I never really had my mother's love. But I can understand that now and feel sympathy for her. She grew up as one of ten kids, and that must have been hard; I think she never felt like she had much love either. And I can see now how hard it must have been for her, staying home all the time. It made me angry with my dad when I realized what it was like for her. But I want his love too. Even though I can really hate him sometimes if I let myself, I also love him. So that's another way of being stuck in between, between my parents.

I remember one time when they first split up, when my mother had finally decided to leave because she couldn't take it any more. I was living with her, you know, and I was writing him a letter. My mother found out, and it totally freaked her out. It was like if I loved her, I should hate him; she wanted me to take sides. But then—and now it's still true—I want them both. Not together necessarily—I can accept that, because I understand how it was for my mother. But I want to be connected to both of them and to have my daughter know them both as her grandparents. So, when my dad comes around to visit now, I'm glad. I like to have him know his granddaughter, and I want him to love her and her to love him.

I remember that day in the program when you asked us to write about a time when we felt really alone. I wrote about when my parents split up, about how I felt when my mother found me writing that letter to my dad and got so mad. She told me then, "Get out of this house," and I wrote about how that felt. I mean, it wasn't like some of the other girls, when their mothers got mad because they said they were pregnant; that wasn't the case with me. I didn't even have a boyfriend; I hadn't even been dating. I guess she wasn't mad at *me* really or anything I had done but, I think, at the situation. It was awful, because I didn't have any place to go or anybody to be with. I couldn't go to my dad. I was lost and alone and confused.

But what was amazing was that when I read what I had written out loud that day in the program, Ada said, "Oh my god! Listen to this!" And she read what she had written, and it was almost exactly the same. Not with the letter-writing part, but with how she felt when her parents split up. It blew me away, to think that here was somebody else, somebody I thought I knew, who had been through exactly the same thing. It was a long time ago that this happened, but the pain was still there, and suddenly that day it was better—just because I knew someone else had felt it too. I never realized that—that you could make something feel better just by sharing it.

NELLIE AND NINA, report on the program for their teachers at the high school, written during the fifth week:

> *We did writing, which was almost like English. We had journals which we would write in every day. We could write anything we wanted. We wrote about our feelings, about the program, how we felt that day. Every day, Sara and Rochelle would read the journals and write comments at the end. For example, if we wrote something personal, they would write back about a similar experience they had had. It really helped, because we didn't feel like we were alone, [we knew] that the same thing had happened to other people.*

MILAGROS: The writing in the program was really important, even though we kind of hated it at first. I remember we all looked at each other, like "Oh no!," when you handed out the journals and pens that first day. "Write," you said. You said you didn't want to hear it if we had nothing to say; if we had nothing to say, we were supposed to write that. You set a time, and we had to write that long, no matter what. And you wrote too, and so did Rochelle. And the room got so quiet—except for the gigglers, who all the time in the program seemed to have something to giggle about. But even they got quiet finally.

The funny thing about the writing was that once we got into it, we really got *into* it. Like that day the math teachers handed us blank paper because they wanted us to do something; but before they could tell us what to do we were all writing away, doing our own thing. That was pretty funny, because they were really surprised. I guess they were used to having people wait to see what was wanted. But not us. Give us paper, we write—whatever is on our minds.

That first day in my journal, I just wrote about the program, about what we had done that day and how it felt to be there. But the second day you said we had to write about loneliness. That was the beginning, you know, the beginning of trusting each other. I read mine—because I trusted you even if I didn't trust the other girls—and Ada read hers—I think because she was excited about how our stories connected. Nobody else read that day. Come to think of it, we never really read much out loud from our journals; you and Rochelle read them and wrote back, and we began passing them around sometimes, sharing with each other, even though we didn't want to share with the whole group.

Here's what's funny about that, about the journal writing. It ties in with what we did about relationships too, talking about relationships in the program, acting out and writing about people in our lives. The really first writing we did in the program—if you call it writing, not stories, not an assignment, but it *was* writing—was on our folders, on the outsides of our folders and our notebooks. Everybody put hearts with names in them, your name and his name. Everybody had a him. When we worked on the computers too, that first day, we were supposed to just write something for practice in using the machine. Everybody wrote about their boyfriend. They've got to do that, you know. *We*'ve got to do that. You want a guy; we all do. That seems like the most important thing. Partly maybe it's cultural—or people think it is, because of the machismo thing with us. But I don't think it's cultural; that's just the way it is with girls, what we've been taught or whatever. I think it's as true of white girls as it is of us, and the white girls in the program proved that to me. They were just as hung up in the who's-your-guy thing as we were. That's why we don't always trust each other: because *she* may take away your guy—since it always seems like she wants a guy more than she wants a friend.

So we talk and we write about *the* big relationship in our lives. Like it was all great, like it was just terrific, like he loves me and does this and this for me; *he*'s the only reason I'm happy.

ADA, journal entry, fourth week:

> *I never felt like I had a real close relationship with my parents, because I guess I never really talked to them, never told them my problems. When I met Robert, he made me feel so good that I could open up to him and tell him things. He always listened and gave me advice. He really cared about me.*

MILAGROS: But in our hearts, which we would let out sometimes in the journal writing, a lot of us are really scared about that relationship, scared he doesn't really like us, scared he's going to leave, scared of what he's thinking about.

ADA, journal entry, same week:

> *I feel like Robert doesn't love me anymore. Sure, we do things together, but sometimes I just feel like he's cheating on me. Sometimes I ask him and he gets angry, because it's a stupid question, he says. But to me it isn't. I worry, and I feel so alone sometimes, and so empty. The only one I really have is my baby.*

MILAGROS: To be honest with you, I think it's really crazy sometimes, because it's like there isn't any *us,* like if a girl didn't have a guy, she wouldn't even exist; she'd just be invisible. Sometimes I think that if other things were different we wouldn't have that "I've got to have a guy" thing so bad. If things had happened differently with my parents, I don't think I would have gotten pregnant, or if things had been different with school. It was when my parents split up that I got pregnant. I was confused and angry, and I dropped out of school. As I said before, I was there mainly to get out of the house, and when they split up, that didn't matter so much anymore. I wanted to hurt my mom too, to tell you the truth, pay her back for upsetting everything by leaving, for doing what I see now she *had* to do, get out of that house.

But not going to school just made me feel triple lonely. I met a guy, and the next thing we were living together, and the next thing I was pregnant. I thought about not having her, the baby, but I don't really believe in that. And besides, I really wanted her—somehow I knew she would make a difference in my life. I wanted a baby, someone who would really love me a lot, someone I could love and take care of. I like that, I like taking care of people, making them feel good, being close. So I thought a baby would be fine.

But that's when our relationship—her father's and mine—got terrible. He didn't want her, and I really did. I guess he just wasn't ready for the responsibility. I made the decision then to set out on my own—and to change what people think about teen parenting. I left him and came back here to live. I had the baby alone, and I've been living alone ever since. With my daughter, I mean, but otherwise alone. I've pretty much decided to keep it that way for a while.

Partly *because* I love my daughter so much. Maybe she ought to have a father, I don't know. But I'm determined now to wait on anything like that until someone comes along who really can accept and honor me for me, not because *he* needs something. It's hard to stick to that, though. There was this one time: a guy I had known for ages wanted to marry me. It was really tempting, the idea that we would settle down and he would take care of me and my daughter. But I could see finally that he just wasn't where I was. I realized that in a way he needed me more than I needed him. He hadn't grown up as much as I had, and I knew I would lose everything I had gained so far, for myself and for her.

I know guys have problems, too; they mess up in school, or they're unhappy at home, the same as for us. They also get hung up with being macho, pretending they're tough. And they use us sometimes to make themselves feel good. At least, that's what I think. Use us different ways, sometimes as a friend, someone to confide in, sometimes for other things. Being a daddy makes them feel like they've accomplished something. But lots of times they just can't deal with the hard parts.

CINDY, journal entry, fourth week:

> *[After I had met him at a party and gone out with him once], we began to see each other regularly. I fell for him very quickly. He was a smooth talker and said everything I wanted to hear. Until he got me pregnant; then it turned. He said everything I didn't want to hear. He said he was too young to be a daddy. I said, what about me? I was fifteen at the time. First he said, I'll be there for you. But within a month's time, he started avoiding me. I would call his house and he was never there. So I went my way with his child inside of me.*

MILAGROS: I don't want to sound like I don't like men. I don't blame them really. They're taught things, you know, the same way we are. I don't mean taught like in school—nobody sits you down and says this and this. But you learn somehow that girls do this and boys do that. And it seems like what *we*'re taught is to think about making them happy, doing things they want us to do instead of doing things for ourselves.

It's weird, because you're supposed to do things with guys and you're supposed to want to be a mommy, but then when you do, no one can deal with it.

NELLIE, journal entry, second day:

> *One of the times I felt really alone was when I was pregnant and I was in my English class in school. Everyone was talking about me and saying I was*

crazy to have a baby. I felt really out of place. It seemed like they thought I was no good just because I was pregnant. It made me feel real bad inside. The same thing happened in my other classes. I felt so bad, I just skipped the rest of the year after midterm. It seemed like people thought being pregnant was a curse.

MILAGROS: I'll tell you though what was really important about the writing in the program. Do you remember the portfolio of our children, that we wrote to share with each other? It was while I was writing that that I really understood how much my daughter is a part of me, how important she is. Never mind her father and the way he behaved to her and to me. Never mind what other people think. I know that it's because of her I want to make things different. It's because of her that I feel now like school is really important. Because I want to make it different for her. She'd be the third generation on welfare, and I want her to see that's not the way it is necessarily. So that's why I want to finish school and get a good job.

LISA, from "Portraits of Ourselves," fifth week:

I want to set an example for my daughter. I want her to know that obstacles can be conquered. Education is important in order to qualify for a good-paying job that you can also enjoy. I want her judgments along those lines to resist peer pressure; she can always have me in the back of her mind and say, "My mom did it and she had me." Maintaining a close relationship with my daughter is very important to me. I always think of it as she and I against the world.

MILAGROS: That's why I came to the program, to figure out how I'm going to do what I want to do.

ELENA, program evaluation:

The program isn't school. It's a room full of women that have experienced the same kind of discriminations of being a single parent, a woman, and/ or a minority. It's a place where you can share things that are deep, without feeling like a nuisance. But unlike school, the biggest difference is that it's a place where there are more positive than negative learnings. You're talked and taught to and not at.

NINA, program evaluation:

Well, I've found out that I'm not alone in this world, and yes, I do have people I can confide in. I never knew how important women really are and

*how much they are recognized in the world. It fascinates me greatly. I'm
proud of being a mother and definitely a woman, no matter how frustrating
it is having your period. Someday I hope I can work with teenage mothers,
not as a job but as a volunteer, so I can help them learn the things I have
learned.*

MARIA, program evaluation:

*This past six weeks have been a real turning point in my life. The women
in this program have made me grow up. I discovered a new person inside
of me that I've never believed was inside. I now know where my heart and
my mind are and belong. I also know that it's time for me to make decisions
and, like a woman, face the circumstances and consequences that may come
along.*

MILAGROS: I bet that all the girls would say the same thing—that the
most important thing about the program was that we began to understand we were women. Not girls. Well, yes, girls, too. But women. That's
really important. I don't know how to say it exactly. It's like women are
cultural too, themselves, Hispanic, black, American, white, whatever.
The same way I understand things sometimes about Puerto Ricans because I'm Puerto Rican, I saw that I can understand things about women
because we're all women. I never knew that before, or never really paid
attention to it anyway.

One thing that made it happen, I think, was studying in the college
archives. When we looked at those old diaries and letters and pictures,
I began to have a feeling—I don't know how to say it exactly—like I was
part of something bigger. Bigger than right here and now. We all felt
that way, I think. We kind of connected to all kinds of women, even the
ones that are dead and gone; it was like they were still alive, and we
entered their lives when we read about them. It made me feel proud,
proud to be a woman, which I certainly never felt before. Sharing what
we had learned in the Forum on Women was fun, and it made that feeling
stronger.

ELENA, from a written report read aloud during the fifth week for the
Forum on Women, in which members of the group shared results of
their work in the archives:

*Dolores Prida was born in Cuba in 1943 and came to the United States in
1961. Coming to New York from Cuba, she had to work from day one. She
worked in factories, speaking no English; she worked in a bakery, and then*

she did editing for a newspaper. She has not married and she has no children. . . .

Dolores Prida was a recipient of an honorary degree at this college last year. She says that this means more to her than an Obie or a Tony or even an Oscar. This "academy" award, a college degree, is a dream come true for her.

Dolores is a playwright whose work talks about what it's like to be a Hispanic in the United States. She began writing poems and short stories, but she concentrates now on plays. . . . She is very proud and happy of her work. After talking with her [on the phone], I know she will be a success, just like each of us.

MILAGROS: One thing about the program being all women was that we didn't feel afraid about talking or about asking questions. There was no competition, but instead we all helped each other out, and we got along really great. In math, for instance, the whole point was to work together. And in the writing, we didn't so much help each other, but the writing— about our children and ourselves, the "books" we made that we could all keep—was like making a gift of ourselves to each other; it was the writing that really brought us close together, made us a group. We began to feel like a family, a family that in some ways is better than your real one.

We really felt like a group on that next to the last day, when we shared our writing with the audience at the big presentation. People were crying—did you know that?—when Elena read about how she had tried to commit suicide. And they cheered when she pointed out that she had not succeeded.

ELENA, from "Portraits of Ourselves":

My name is Elena. I am twenty-one years old, born on July 18, 1969, in Hartford, Connecticut. I have two children, a son, age three years, and a daughter, age three months. These two children are my first reason for living; my second reason is for me.

I didn't always feel this way. When I was younger, I didn't think very much of myself. I didn't like school at all. I fought a lot, hoping to get expelled. I would wonder why I had to go. What was the reason for learning all these different things? To me, there was no reason. So, when I turned sixteen years old, I quit.

I thought I didn't fit in with others, and I thought, "What is the reason for living?" Being dead to me meant no school. Being dead also meant that I didn't have to obey my mother. It also meant not having to face problems.

I was so tired of life that I tried to commit suicide twice. But, as you can see, I didn't succeed. . . .

Gradually I have changed how I feel about myself. I got my GED at the Center, and I am now attending this program. I think I will be starting at the community college this fall. When I finish there, I would like to transfer to a four-year college (this one if I can). I am planning a better life for myself and my children. I know it's going to be a while, but I also know this: I AM GOING TO MAKE IT.

MILAGROS: We didn't all read for the audience, but I know I felt like the ones who did were speaking for all of us. When you work together on a show like that, you really feel like we're together, and together we are powerful, we can do anything we want. It was wonderful; that day of the show was one of the best days of my life.

I don't know. You try in your life to do the right thing. But it's not always easy to know what the right thing is. You want to be loved, to be close to somebody. First your parents—and then, as soon as you can, a guy who will supposedly take care of you. That's what we all want. So you find a guy, and guys want certain things, and pretty soon you find yourself having a kid and thinking that the kid will make you grown-up, make you able to do what you want to do and have what you want to have. But it's not that easy. You have to learn the hard way, or at least some of us do. Some of us never seem to learn. We keep thinking that the next guy who comes along will be the right one, the one who will make everything okay. But if we're lucky, we can discover finally that the only person who's really going to take care of you is you. But by then, you've probably dropped out of school, and then it's twice as hard to do what you want to do. For all of us in the program—*now* we know what we should have known maybe ten years ago: that school is impor-tant, that somehow if we had stuck it out a while back, it wouldn't be so hard now.

I wish we could make it so young kids could learn sooner some of the things we learned this summer. It makes me so sad to think that some of the kids I know in sixth grade now—kids I work with at the school where I'm a classroom assistant—are going to be pregnant within a year or two. They'll have such a hard time, have to go through so much. It's such a shame, because girls can do other things nowadays, and I wish we could help them know that.

Maybe if in school they could feel really part of something, like we did this summer, part of a group or part of something bigger. If they could *connect* to something, feel like they belonged. Or if they could feel like someone in school really cared, cared about how they were feeling, whether they were sad or mad or whether their parents were splitting up or whether their father had beat up their little brother the night before. If you could bring some of that stuff into the classroom—not like a counselor or anything, but like when you and Rochelle would read our journals and say, that happened to me one time, too. That helps a lot. I wish we could do that for little girls, so they'd think more about staying in school than they would about being with a guy. Not that they shouldn't have guys, I don't mean that. But if they could just want school and their own futures bad enough to wait, it would be so much easier for them, instead of struggling like we've had to struggle. Better for their kids when they do finally have them, too.

I wish sometimes things had happened in my life differently, but I don't know: maybe for me it just had to happen when I was older so I could understand it. There's no point in wishing; you just have to go on from where you are, and I do feel strong now. I feel like I can do what I want to do. We all will; it's harder doing it this way, but we're going to make it, I'm sure of that. Because somehow, some way, we'll find the courage to fight fear head on—which is most of all, I think, fear of lonesomeness, fear of the confusions that we have to face, fear of doing things differently.

MARIA, her poem, written during the sixth week of the program and read at the presentation:

Fear: Who Are You?

Are you the one that has ahold of my life?
Are you the one that cripples me when I'm down my path?
Are you the one that makes me go backwards when I'm so close to the
  mark?
Are you the one that keeps me in the place where I can no longer see the
  rainbow?
Are you the one that stares me in my face and says, "You're not going to
  pass this place?"
Are you the one that says, "Here's where you're at and you'll never get
  there?"
Well, yes, you probably are all those emotions and much more.

But I'll tell you who I am:
I'm the woman who will break the chain that you hold on to so tightly.
I'm the one who gets off the braces and continues on my way.

I'm the one that refuses from this day on to go back down the path where I started from.
I'm the one who will fight through the fog to see the shining light.
I'm the one who keeps my head up and looks at you and says, "Get out of my way."
I'm the one that will build that bridge to go through that gap to succeed.
I'm all that and much more. So, "Are you ready to fight, fear?"

Sara's Reflections at Summer's End

"What did you like best about the program?" we asked in an evaluative questionnaire on the last day. "The exercise and the writing," one student wrote: "I can't separate them, because for me they were both a way of getting over being angry."

Why angry? Why the terrible fear in Maria's poem? What's going on here? Valerie Walkerdine, the British educational theorist, has said (p. 47) that school is for girls a place of "persecutory pain," because they are confronted there with an excruciating choice: if they become what school wants them to be (autonomous, rational, competitive risk takers), they must give up what home and society seem to expect them to be (obedient, feeling-centered nurturers). In Valerie Walkerdine's post-structural terms, girls must choose or negotiate power positions within contradictory discourses. In everyday language, girls must decide between being good at school or being good at being a girl—or must figure out how to manage these opposites. Managing both, negotiating positions, is a lonely enterprise, because the fear and confusion it entails are rarely comprehended, either by the girl herself or by those around her.

It was this that my cupped hands intended to describe when I talked with Maria that day: two spheres, home-culture-society and school, grinding against each other, requiring impossible decisions. Being good at being a girl frequently means becoming a mother. It's a way out of confusion: the stories of young mothers suggest that getting pregnant often happens "accidentally on purpose," as a way out of conflict, as a way into the one role universally approved for females. Their stories suggest that knowing or not knowing about contraception is only a part of the problem, that reasons for the "problem" of teen pregnancy are much deeper—biological in origin, yes, but not so much at the level of individual sexual practices. Biological in the sense that women's destinies, at least many women's destinies, are circumscribed by the reproductive possibility, by the expectation that every girl, in order to find a self, must focus on the romance plot, forgoing or surrendering—as Carolyn Heil-brun elaborates in *Writing a Woman's Life*—the "quest" plot, the search-ing for interest and challenge and a sense of strength that can make loneliness into something else. Biological even more fundamentally, however, in a definition of the self in terms that seem to leave out the complexities of human relationships, that see growth and maturity as requiring separation, achieving autonomy. If we redraw how we think about the self, we have begun to write a new script for women—and for others who experience confusion and pain in a contradiction between what we think we are and what the world seems to expect us to be.

Mary Belenky and her colleagues perceive in the profound isolation of some of the women they interviewed—like the isolation of young mothers as boyfriends desert them, parents reject them, and friends turn away—a silence they interpret as absence of self. I would suggest that this felt silence may arise rather from confusion of selves, from the stress of contradictions. Silence is imposed because a sense of multiple selves born of interaction with others is denied by an image of self as unified. Silence is imposed because the centrality of relationship in women's lives is denied by a cultural tradition of self as independent, separated. Silence is imposed because it feels as though feelings have to come first, but we tend to set them aside because society sees them as less valuable, less important than the rational.

Surrounding the silence is a quantity of noise. The dominant dis-course makes itself heard in a complex of conversations, both spoken and written. Grandmotherly advice, child care handbooks, advertise-ments, magazine stories, television shows, movies, romance novels, vol-umes of history, psychology textbooks, all clamor away, teaching—to borrow and invert Dorothy Smith's phrase—a discourse of femininity, teaching what it means to be a woman. In the midst of this noise, what happens to a woman who wants to make things different? The task re-quires the learning and speaking of an alternative discourse, something feminist scholars and writers have been arguing from varying perspec-tives and at different levels of intensity for some time. How does it begin? Where do we start? It may need to begin with each of us, in the reflective act of creating a personal text, a written or spoken account of who we are and what we know. "To put it simply," Heilbrun says, "we must begin to tell the truth, in groups, to one another" (45). Our program made a space, a place of trust, where this telling of stories could happen.

It may be that a means of transforming the all-too-often painful ex-perience of schooling for girls is first their encouragement to a language of self-expression through writing and talking, the creation of personal texts. Such texts of the personal are inserted into the larger discourse to begin a dialogue of learning that gradually extends to public texts and events, literature and history, the "school stuff" that has traditionally defined knowledge. But the personal text comes first. Through it girls can find a center, a balance point from which to work. Through it they can, privately and in groups, address unequal power relations in their lives that upset the balance. Through it they can come to terms with the conflict and the pain of two spheres grinding together and begin constructing a new script for their lives.

It is not difficult to let this happen. When permission is given, when there is encouragement to wrestle through complexity, conflict, and the many shapes of fear, the voices and the selves emerge—in every young woman, many voices: the voice of daughter, of parent, of lover, of student, of victim, and of victor; Hispanic voice, American voice, childish voice, grown-up voice, whining voice, happy voice—voices ringing with anger and hurt and loneliness and love.

For the women in our program, writing was the key to finding affirmation and new direction. We wanted that to happen: we wanted writing to become a friend, a tool, a safe and reliable means of working things out—because we wanted to share what has been an important part of our own experience. And because they will need to feel confident about writing when they go on to college, as we hope they will do. In some future classroom they may meet a teacher who, plugging in an old definition of self, an old way of "doing school," will impose a reductive notion of "academic discourse" that is alienating. We hope our graduates will feel safe if that happens; we hope they will know that writing—like the multiple self—can have an array of shapes and goals.

First in the journals that initially only a teacher would read, then in daring to share with each other, and finally in the courage to stand before a larger audience, the women in our program wrote themselves out of isolation and into a world where voices like their own echoed all around. They came to grips with the confusion and distress of multiplicity by getting it out, getting it on paper, seeing it before them on the page. They learned to accept complexity in themselves by hearing it in their peers. Ultimately, they wrote themselves into a condition of mutual support, where trust in each other—a new and precious discovery—could gradually become trust in themselves, with all their complicated fears and hopes and dreams, a confidence that will permit Milagros's prediction that they're going to "make it" come true.

Special acknowledgment with thanks is due to the following participants in The Next Step program (summer 1990), who have kindly allowed excerpts from their writings to be used in this article: Kathy Chouinard, Marianella Garcia Indy Ramirez, Gloribell Ruiz, Luz Santiago, and Rosa Santiago.

BIBLIOGRAPHY

Belenky, Mary Field, Blythe McVicker Clinchy, Nancy Rule Goldberger, and Jill Matluck Tarule. *Women's Ways of Knowing: The Development of Self, Voice, and Mind.* New York: Basic Books, 1986.

Heilbrun, Carolyn G. *Writing a Woman's Life.* New York: W. W. Norton, 1988.

Miller, Jean Baker. *The Development of Women's Sense of Self.* Work in Progress 12. Wellesley, Mass: Stone Center for Developmental Services and Studies, Wellesley College, 1984.

———. *Toward a New Psychology of Women.* 2d ed. Boston: Beacon, 1986a.

———. *What Do We Mean by Relationships?* Work in Progress 22. Wellesley, Mass: Stone Center for Developmental Services and Studies, Wellesley College, 1986b.

———. *Connections, Disconnections, and Violations.* Work in Progress 33. Wellesley, Mass: Stone Center for Developmental Services and Studies, Wellesley College, 1988.

Sanders, Jane Levine. "Community Adolescent Resource and Education Center Evaluation." Unpublished manuscript, CARE Center, 1989.

Smith, Dorothy E. "Femininity as Discourse." In *Becoming Feminine: The Politics of Popular Culture,* edited by Leslie G. Roman and Linda K. Christian-Smith, 37–59. Philadelphia: Falmer, 1988.

Surrey, Janet. *Self-in-Relation: A Theory of Women's Development.* Work in Progress 13. Wellesley, Mass: Stone Center for Developmental Services and Studies, Wellesley College, 1985.

Walkerdine, Valerie. "On the Regulation of Speaking and Silence: Subjectivity, Class, and Gender in Contemporary Schooling." In *Schoolgirl Fictions,* 29–60. London: Verso, 1990.

II

. . . .

Rockshelf Further Forming: Women, Writing, and Teaching the Young

Christine Holm Kline

I sit at the table in my school district curriculum office with seven elementary teachers—women all—listening to their conversation as they make the transition from the hubbub of their morning in the classroom to the quiet of our afternoon writing meeting. The talk, wholly relaxed, is the unassuming talk of those comfortable with their expertise. An interlace begins. I listen. Adrienne Rich comes to mind, "the million tiny stitches . . ." Women's work, "world-protection, world-preservation, world-repair" (1979, 205). And, I think as I listen, world-composition.

Ann, a first-grade teacher, has mentioned a writing breakthrough one of her students has made. She holds up a large sheet of paper on which three stick figures are drawn above a five-sentence narrative. Leaning forward intently, she explains. The child Aaron has been reluctant all year, even with steady support and enthusiasm of classmates and teacher, to draw or write. This is his first voluntary effort. Ann is exhilarated. She describes the day it happened, the particular circumstance, Aaron's response to her response. Threaded through are thoughts about the reluctance of this otherwise capable, verbal child, superb reader, articulate and precocious. He's unusually tall, ungainly. She muses about his small-muscle difficulties. She speaks of his episodes of defiance and a seeming sorrow underneath; he is a child who will not be comforted.

Ann pauses to think about that for a minute and continues. She remembers the first day he smiled in spite of himself, the day he first did a drawing without prompting. She describes the visits from his parents.

They are tense about Aaron. They ask that more pressure be applied to "elevate" his performance. They intimate that Ann is not firm enough in her demands about his writing—both his handwriting, which is undeveloped, and his composition. Ann, pausing again, feels that Aaron needs steady encouragement, patient guidance and nurture.

Another teacher joins. Margaret shares her memory of Aaron's older brother and the pressure he always seemed to be under, his sporadic performance, tempers, resistance to physical activity; yet, too, moments of remarkably endearing behavior. She also describes an encounter with parents over a request for a summer supply of worksheets. She had firmly recommended play and good books. The response of the parents? Anger. The boy? Yes, she remembers that he, too, had an underlying sorrow.

Their talk loops and binds. Child-mind. Child-body. Child-psyche. Child-world. Threads laced, by knowing talk, into a seamless portrait. Beneath the details, an underlay of understanding. Rich comes to mind once again:

> minute, momentary life—slugs, moles, pheasants, gnats,
> spiders, moths, hummingbirds, groundhogs, butterflies—
> a lifetime is too narrow
> to understand it all, beginning with the huge
> rockshelves that underlie all that life.
>   *("Transcendental Etude," 265)*

Informal talk merges into meeting talk. We've been together for a year now; I, their supervisor, chairperson and fellow participant in a three-year staff-development project in writing. We've written together, read together, shared experiments in classrooms together, and shaped practices that we now plan to invite the staff to share. We talk of an expanded plan for the following year—how to involve the entire staff in our ongoing shaping of beliefs and practices.

A shift in the conversation. I listen. I hear disturbances. The comments from the women, tense, nubby:

> *We know what our kids are doing. We know that they're doing well, but the others won't. . . . They'll ask about covering the language and spelling book. Everyone expects that. Parents expect that. . . . How will we teach the skills? They have to do well on the Iowas. . . . Parents are not going to listen to us about the writing. They want numerical*

evidence. They don't give credence to teacher judgment. They won't accept our comments. . . . What if the administrators won't continue to support us? Shouldn't we have a document in place first? One that's been approved?

Rift. Anxiety. I remind them of the strength of administrative support, the history of strong parent support in this kind of effort. They will not be comforted. They have a history of their own and it gives little comfort.

A tear at their authority, a rift in their knowing. A fissure in the underlay. We are now talking about the wide world outside of our own circle, and we know, tacitly perhaps, but powerfully, who we are in the world. As teachers of young children—women all—we know that we are at the bottom of the barrel, the heap, on the bottom rung of the hierarchy. We know the truth of Adrienne Rich's recent statement—that we are part of a "horizontally segregated female ghetto of service and clerical work, cleaning, waitressing, domestic labor, nursing, elementary school teaching, behind-the-counter selling" (1976, xiv). We, college-educated, middle-class women. Educators. At the bottom. We know. And I know what I hear in the underlay. It is the most deeply disturbing of all. Acceptance of place.

But then, there are many who tell us. Voices, emanating from an interlock of layers above, come in chorus. The intertwining is a powerful one for teachers of the young, beginning with the world itself, which is ordered on a hierarchy of patriarchal values and dominated by patriarchal power. Women are subordinate. And in a world where women are subordinate, women-identified professions are indeed at the bottom of the hierarchy. When that woman-identified profession is also bound with another subordinate group in society—children—the inferior status becomes deeply moored. The voices from above chorus a language of reduction—immaturity, lack of intellect, inability—unexamined lyrics of dominance issuing over child and teacher alike.

Our social and political structures are based on a patriarchal hierarchy, and our language reflects it. The language shapes the way we think about the world. It forms our social, political, and intellectual structures. All arise from the patriarchal hierarchy. Ursula LeGuin describes this male-biased discourse as a "father tongue"; it tells us what to do (147). It assumes objectivity—claiming a distance between object and self. But as LeGuin states, when it further assumes rationality and identifies itself as both privileged and dominant, subordinates suffer isolation and a sense of inferiority (148–49).

With the dominant language being a "father tongue" and with its masculine mode giving form to our very thought, what of learning in the elementary schools? Language is both the dominant vehicle of learning and teaching and the major content of curriculum. What is actually being taught and learned? Who is in control? Here is the source of anxiety in my teachers' nubby talk. They may only vaguely know all the levels of inferiorization and its effects, but they most certainly know that, for a long time now, authority over their teaching and their students' language learning has been in other hands—distant and powerful hands. They also tacitly know that it is premised on the linear masculine hierarchical model of thought that does not match the actual making of meaning by students.

> *They'll ask about covering the language and spelling book. Everyone expects that.*
> *How will we teach the skills? They have to do well on the Iowas.*

Commercial instructional programs, composed of a basal reader, a language arts text, a spelling book, and in some districts, a vocabulary program, have for years dominated language instruction at the elementary level. The model for these programs is a linear sequence comprised of aspects of language that have been divided into separable, isolated units. The units are taught one at a time and tested in the same isolated fashion. Successful completion of the sequence in a text, as validated by the accompanying tests, signifies mastery of a given grade level and is the basis for major decisions about a child's placement in school.

> *Parents are not going to listen to us about the writing. They want numerical evidence.*

Further, materials are often designed to enhance success on commercially developed standardized tests. These tests are given yearly to children not only are the results used for placement, but they are published in local newspapers. Schools are judged; teachers are judged.

> *What if the administrators won't continue to support us? Shouldn't we have a document in place first? One that's been approved?*

Of course, the aspects of language that are separable and isolable are the surface features of language—spelling, mechanics and grammar in writing and decoding, word analysis and vocabulary in reading. The deeper structures of language—the construction and communication of coherent meaning—are neglected. The assumption is that the complex process of learning to represent the world symbolically can be achieved through practice and mastery of little pieces devoid of individual meaning making and the social contexts in which meaning making occurs. The assumption is, as Denny Taylor writes, that "human behavior (reading, writing, literacy, or whatever) can best be described in linear, hierarchical models" (186). Here, all meaning has been previously made; it must now be learned. Personally constructed meaning is subordinated.

This dominance is no small matter. Underscoring the predominance that commercial language programs and tests have in elementary schools and thus on language development, as much as 95 percent of language instruction is provided by such programs (Graves, 818). Lessons arising directly from the needs of children or from classroom, family, or world experiences are rare.

The immensity of this dominance came home to me several years ago when I conducted a study of the use of such texts in one district. The district used a basal reader, language arts text, and spelling text for the two-and-a-half hours of language arts instruction designated each day in the elementary program. It was expected that teachers would complete each of the texts by year's end.

James Moffett's five-aspect model for identifying the degree of sufficiency in all aspects of writing provided my analytical model (70–77). Moffett's scale begins at a baseline of handwriting. Next on the scale is transcription—the spelling and punctuation that "render vocalization patterns and intonation" or the direct copying of text (72). Paraphrasing is the next level—the synthesizing of another author's words, followed by crafting—the construction of good sentences and paragraphs and overall organization. Moffett includes in this level the assignment of any paper or story for which the explicit or implicit dominant purpose is proper crafting. The highest level on Moffett's scale is true authoring—the articulation of one's own thought: personal construction of meaning. Ongoing thought is shaped to communicate to self or others. When authoring occurs, all of the aspects of writing are being used.

What I found in my study was dismaying. Fewer than 1 percent of the learning activities sponsored authoring or the articulation of personal thought. Most of the activities consisted of transcriptions and the crafting of isolated sentences. What I did not count, and the number was significant, were the activities for which no writing of any kind was required—

merely the circling, underlining, or matching of isolated bits of language. Nor does the fracturing pertain only to the exercises and assignments. In basal readers, such reductionism has altered the very stories that children read. In first-grade readers, stories are written to serve readability and sentence length formulas and to include targeted individual skills. At older grade levels, stories of given authors are altered to meet these formulas. What of an original story, an authentic story, written to share experience, to ask questions of self and world? Gone. Sacrificed to formulas that isolate and quantify. Children are denied authentic stories. Teachers are denied choice of stories based on children's interest, needs, lives.

The assumption that something as complex as language, even ignoring the complex contexts in which it occurs and the complexity of the lives in which it lives, can be broken down, standardized, monitored, and controlled is hierarchical thinking. Such atomizing fulfills the function of program control, not the expansion and refinement of personally constructed meaning. Further, the programs control both learner and teacher. Should not language learning enable the learner to take control rather than submit to the control of others? Should not teachers have the responsibility for enabling the learner to do just that?

Not only is the language instruction of the teacher controlled but also the very language of teachers. Scripts are written in basal texts for the teacher, perhaps the ultimate denial of teacher control in teaching. It is important to experience what teachers experience in these programs. Here are two examples from a teacher's edition of a basal text [emphasis added]:

> Have pupils read pages 20–21 silently to find out what has happened to the seeds Millie planted. After reading, *ask:*
> —What has happened to the seeds Millie planted? (they have grown to become sunflowers)
> —Why do you think Grandpa tells Millie not to let farmers see her? (Answers may vary, but may include that farmers don't like groundhogs in their field). (Allington et al., 27)

or

> The *-ipe* word family. Write the word "stripe" on the board. *Say:*
> —The word "stripe" is in the same word family as another word you know, "pipe." (Write the word "pipe" under stripe). What is the name of the word family "stripe" and "pipe" belong to? (the *-ipe* word family. *Tell pupils* that the *i* in *ipe* is a long *i*. (123)

Small wonder the anxiety level regarding teachers' own knowledge, judgment, and authority. Sandra Gilbert and Susan Gubar comment on the anxiety of women—the "fragility or even the fictionality" of their autonomy or authority (769). For elementary schoolteachers, in language instruction as in so many other areas, this autonomy has quite literally been taken away. Though there is discomfort on the part of teachers and the expression of a nagging feeling that something has gone wrong, the programs and the assumptions on which they are based are rarely questioned. What has this to do with the place of elementary school teaching in the hierarchical scheme of things? What has it to do with the fact that most elementary school teachers are women and that women are subordinate? What are the consequences for the children they teach? I think about these questions. I think about what we, as educators in the field of language, have to say. I think about what we as feminists, in the field, have to say.

Other tables. Other talk. This time from the field. I listen. Disturbance. I hear the father tongue.

I've just finished a talk with a group of teachers—mostly secondary and college teachers. I've talked about the necessity of the self in writing—the importance of exploratory and personal writing for learners of all ages. Afterward, a high school English department chair grants that for younger children but worries that high school is, after all, more academic, and teachers must emphasize formal assignments.

At a conference on women's studies, I speak with the organizer of a woman's studies seminar for public schoolteachers sponsored by a noted woman's college. When I ask the organizer why elementary schoolteachers have been excluded, her reply? "It's scholarly." When I ask her to elaborate on a statement implying that elementary teachers have no life of mind, the reply? "Elementary teachers aren't really comfortable with scholarly matters."

I sit as a member of a deliberative body in a national language organization. We are discussing the selection of new members. We need an elementary schoolteacher. In the ensuing discussion, it becomes apparent that a professor involved in early language development will suffice. A professor is chosen. Her voice can be that of a primary teacher.

I sit at another table, at a local university, as we attempt to frame a new graduate program in elementary education to target returning students. The head of the current program, a woman with early childhood experience, talks repeatedly of the deficits that these returning students will have. They have been mothers at home, she cautions, and we'll have to build around the deficits. A secondary principal agrees that they know little of the world, therefore of content knowledge. I ask, this time more angrily, the accumulation of prejudice taking its toll, what they mean by deficits. I ask for a definition of content in full light of what children need to know and how they best come to know it. I ask what strengths these women might bring. A dead look. From the woman. From the secondary principal. From the other members.

Invisibility comes to mind. Tillie Olsen's invisible angel—"so lowly as to be invisible" (34)—who nonetheless, in education, has the responsibility for the minds and bodies of children for the bedrock years of learning. The hardest moment—the moment when I truly feel the invisibility—is when I speak of the above things to someone in the field, to those at the tables, and the response is that unseeing look, the nonrecognition of what they hear. It is worse, really, than the usual dismissal. The look of bemused tolerance on faces when an experience is related about a young child in the classroom or a piece of writing shown. Cute. A patronizing verbal pat on the head. Then dismissal—Not of the child, but of the teacher.

Elizabeth Meese writes of women writers as being "outsiders among the insiders" (5). As one surveys our own field, it is repeatedly apparent that teachers of the young are such outsiders whether one listens at tables or looks for visibility and representation in our work spheres or in our professional organizations.

> But in fact we were always like this,
> rootless, dismembered: knowing it makes the difference.
> *("Transcendental Etude," 267)*

Knowing. How do we begin stitching portraits of ourselves and our experience? How do we reveal our underlay of knowledge? How do we begin to re-member? How do we re-envision? I think of a session at a national conference last spring, where a young woman stepped forward and issued an eloquent plea to all of the teachers in the audience: "Where are the voices of teachers? We must each find our voice. If we do not speak we will not be heard." The sympathy in the response was palpable. The yearning was evident in so many faces. Yet it was clear we did not know what to do. We were not sure how to go about finding our voices. We know it begins with us, but we know, equally, that it does not begin with us alone. Searching voices need response. Growth does not occur in isolation. Searching voices, particularly those of subordinate groups, need an affirming response for growth to occur. Janet Emig posits that for growth, for learning, to occur we must be in environments that are "enabling"; that is, "safe, structured . . . unobtrusive," with participants who are themselves learners, providing vital feedback (139). Growth requires affirmation. As Galway Kinnell writes in his poem, "St. Francis and the Sow":

> for everything flowers, from within, of self-blessing;
> though sometimes it is necessary
> to re-teach a thing its loveliness,
> to put a hand on its brow
> of the flower
> and retell it in words and in touch
> it is lovely
> until it flowers again from within, of self-blessing.
>
> *(9)*

It begins with us, but not with us alone. If we do not find those who affirm us currently in the field of education, we can look to the field of women's studies and to the insights of feminist theory to affirm and offer guidelines. Surprisingly, few in our field have looked to feminist theory for insight on existing inequities. Nel Noddings writes: "Education is a blatantly hierarchical profession; professors of education are still mostly male, school administrators are overwhelmingly male, and school teachers are mostly female. . . . This situation should invite feminist criticism" (406). She attributes the lack of influence of feminist theory on educational thought to the dominance of two areas of inquiry: the continuing attention to gender differences, even though the usefulness of such knowledge is questioned; and the prominence of Marxist attention to race and class issues, which tend to ignore the importance of women's caretaking roles in society and to obscure women's oppression. Noddings calls for careful attention to feminist theory and to the life experiences of women (407–08).

Another major feminist theorist offers similar guidelines. Jean Baker Miller, in her recent edition of *Toward a New Psychology of Women,* applauds the tendency emerging in the literature on the psychology of women to describe women's lives in terms of the true lived experience, without assigning premature categories. The new insights often lead to changes in the language, thinking, and basic guiding assumptions of everyone: the entire landscape changes.

We can begin the searching conversation with these women. We can begin, as they suggest, by talking about our own lived lives, seeking the underlay that these experiences reveal. And we can do so in our own language—a language that not only closely reveals but invites and reflects. The language is what Ursula Le Guin describes as "mother tongue." It is a language mode closest to a lived life—a conversational narrative, in writing, where one attempts to capture the dailiness of experience. Mother tongue is the language of relation. It is part of a conversation—it offers experience as it feels its way toward ideas. It listens and responds (149–50).

I want to begin a searching conversation, in my own mother tongue, with women who not only affirm our own experiences, knowing that the personal is profoundly political, but urge us to talk, to question, to seek the underlay of what we know: to grow. The language we as women often use is beyond the confines of father tongue. It is a new landscape of language, with mother tongue at the heart; it is "native tongue." Native tongue can be "poetry, literature . . . but it can be speeches and science, any use of language when it is spoken, written, read, heard as art . . . the marriage of the public discourse and the private experience, making a power, a beautiful thing, the true discourse of reason" (151).

I want to have a searching conversation with the voices I hear in Rich's poem, "Transcendental Etude" (264–69). Her score, a song transcending categories, sparks my own. A search begins for intonation beyond known scales—just intonation—an echo that comes from the rockshelf underneath.

> rehearsing in her body, hearing-out in her blood
> a score touched off in her perhaps
> by some words, a few chords, from the stage:
> a tale only she can tell.
>
> *(266)*

I begin to trust the tale enough to tell it. I begin to trust the intonation that might reveal the rockshelf.

> *Vision begins to happen in such*
> *a life,*
> *as if a woman quietly walked away*

from the argument and jargon
in a room . . .

(76)

remembering.
re-membering.
I leave the room.
The party is large. Cocktails. Blazers.
Professionals.
Only several are teachers,
woman all.
My friend and I, outside, exchange stories.
She, too, an elementary teacher,
steely, bright.
She speaks of her conversation with three men.
They've teased. They want to know how
she can defend such an easy job,
small kids, small challenges,
short days, short years.
She wants to know, from them,
if it's so damn easy,
why they aren't in it too.
It hasn't too many males, she adds.
They laugh.
She does, too, sardonically.

My turn. My teacher story.
It's the usual, as is hers.
Talk with several new people.
Lawyer, curator, tax accountant,
professionals all.
We talk.
"Calcium Light Nights." Disappointment with Peter Martens.
City of Glass. Interest in Paul Auster.
Gretchen Dow Simpson's sheets on the *New Yorker* cover.
A query, at some point.
"What do you do?"
"An elementary teacher," I reply.
A pause. Then the statement.
"I'm surprised. I thought you were a professional.
How did you come to be a teacher?"
I know the implication.
They, of course, do too.
I apologize.

I've been apologizing for years
"It was not my intention," I reply,
"I have degrees—literature, history, in fact.
Graduate, in fact."
I laugh. "I guess I fell into it."

rhythms . . . moved to thoughtlessly.

I've been apologizing for years.
Rhythm of unquestioned acceptance.
Discomfort, yes, but more, shame.
No shame in the apology.
No anger at their assumptions.
Just a need to assert intelligence
in the presence of insults,
however benignly stated.
And yet,
with the apologies,
I've stayed in the classroom
for eighteen years.
The reasons for staying?
The reasons many women do.
It fits the expectations
of those around them,
the expectations of wifely role,
and yes, it fits and fills the call
of nurture and give.
Yet, with the discomfort
of being in a role, other-defined,
I feel the sweet pull of it,
a rounded satisfaction.
I hear in Rich
the completeness of those days:
life and its underlay.

But this evening . . .
the deer are still alive and free,
nibbling apples from early-laden boughs
so weighted, so englobed
with already yellowing fruit
they seem eternal, Hesperidean
in the clear-tuned, cricket- throbbing air.

Bright blue sun afternoon.
Long green playground, tumbling
with children, freed, for a time,

from the stout brick walls
of the school building just beyond.
The children are running,
I with them,
under a rainbow kite
stretched out on a spring breeze,
purchased, just for them, from a
San Francisco sidewalk vendor.
Laughing, grasping lightly the streamers—
bright physics—rippling text.
For now, the children are unconfined,
alive and free in the clear-tuned air.

The school hallway, a different text.
Just after lunch, I sit in a circle of
my fourth-grade girls. They are intense,
querulous, trying to sort out
the labyrinth called friendship,
now that it is more than play.
The intensity of alignments
shifting with nightly calls
and whispers,
imagined and unimagined.
Sorting it all out,
trying to claim true feelings
amid the desire to please,
to be pleasing.
Later that afternoon, Caroline,
writing
of her wish to be strong
and happy with her sturdy body,
her wish to play baseball,
"even if others whisper, 'boy.' "
Alive and free.

> *the immense*
> *fragility of all this sweetness,*
> *this green world already*
> *sentimentalized, photographed*
> *advertised to death. Yet, it persists,*
> *stubbornly beyond the fake Vermont . . .*
> *the sick Vermont of children*
> *conceived in apathy, grown to winters*
> *of rotgut violence,*

poverty gnashing its teeth like a
blind cat at their lives.
Still it persists. . . .

I hold Shana's hand between mine
while the DYFS social worker
pulls up her shirt,
asks her to pull down her pants
while she looks for bruises
on back, on buttocks.
"My mama don't beat me,"
Shana cries softly,
but she's compliant.
I gasp.
"Can't you explain? Proceed in a
more gentle way? She's only nine."

Her mama doesn't beat her,
but she drinks, and when she drinks
she sometimes forgets herself
and wanders.
She's a dreamer when she drinks.
She writes poems
and sometimes sends them in with Shana.
She adores her daughter.
She plaits her hair each morning,
each day more beautiful than the last.

"My mama's gonna be so mad,"
Shana worries as we walk hand in hand
back to the classroom.
"She won't be mad at you, honey."
"No, she'd never be mad at me."
She stays close by me in the afternoon,
where she knows a hug awaits if needed.
I walk her to the edge of the school grounds
at day's end.
"I'll be all right," she says,
"I'll tell my mama
that the lady's coming."
Narrow shoulders on a small figure
walking the long way home.
Shana writes poetry, too. Everyday.
She writes of friendship and love
and her mama.

I've sat on a stone fence above a great,
   soft, sloping field
of musing heifers, a farmstead
  slanting its planes calmly in the calm light,
a dead elm raising bleached arms
above a green so dense with life,
minute, momentary life—slugs, moles,
   pheasants, gnats,
spiders, moths, hummingbirds,
   groundhogs, butterflies—
a lifetime is too narrow
to understand it all, beginning
   with the huge
rockshelves that underlie all that life.

Thomas is writing about his beloved wolves,
objects of devoted study
for weeks now.
I'm gratified that the *New York Times*
once again comes through:
wolves in the *Science* section.
Thomas clasps it to his diminutive chest—
treasure.
Good coverage also, from the *Times,*
on our garbage barge.
Timely news, amid our monthlong study
of our own town's recycling journey.
It's Wednesday morning, the bell has rung.
We're about to gather, the children and I,
to discuss the recycling data
that we gathered yesterday,
circling our neighborhood,
fourth graders with tablets and pencils in hand,
charting the homes
that set out recycling bins.
But, before the session,
attendance to take,
and a schedule to give to Bob Crown,
parent and, each Wednesday,
volunteer craftsperson with the children;
the handcrafted book holders grow in number.
Martin's mother drops in,

forgotten lunchbox in hand, garbage story in tow.
Martin, it seems, inspects all trash nightly,
citing any recycling violation.
"My little garbage zealot," she laughs.
I laugh and reply,
"I hear he's recruiting other inspectors."
We both laugh.
Behind her, a special ed. teacher.
"Melinda's transmitter," she worries.
Melinda, profoundly hearing-impaired child,
wears a transmitter, I, a mike.
"It simply won't work in the auditorium.
She can't hear when she remains with you."
We agree, reluctantly, that she must sit
up front, with the kindergartners.
She hates to be apart from us.
She hates to be singled out.

Two children hand me notes from home.
Karen hands me a note of her own:
   Dear Mrs. Kline,
     Jesse said something
     really mean about me
     but I forgot!
       From,
       somebody named
       Karen.
I look around;
Jesse is late again.
He's always upset
when he arrives late.
Chloe is upset, too,
alone again, gazing out the window.
Her father, here for awhile,
has returned home to Canada.

We gather now.
We talk about our data.
What can we learn?
How can we best learn it?
Percentage of households that recycle.
How to determine percentage.
How to display information.
They determine how to determine it all.

They move into their small groups.
An hour later, we gather again,
to share
the knowledge in each graph—rich array.
Bob joins to admire.
We talk about the possible reasons
that families do recycle—and don't.
We decide to interview
both kinds of families
to see if our speculations
are true,
important information to have.
Our letter to the editor, we agree,
must be knowledgeable and persuasive:
searching conversations.

Afternoon reading,
Ursula Le Guin, Isaac Asimov
for the pleasure of science fiction
and the light it may bring
for upcoming projects
on recycling in the future.
Then there is
the individual research
on chosen aspects of recycling,
shared daily
as they learn about their precious earth.
Busy social scientists.

Time, also, for themselves each day,
time to write, to share.
They write stories of their lives,
stories of their dreams.
It's not surprising,
science fiction abounds.
They experiment freely,
nimbly crossing boundaries
between fiction and non.
Thomas proudly brings me the ending
of his ace report on wolves,
proud of the point he's made,
proud of the style with which he's made it.
(He's been experimenting with snappy endings,
"eye-catchers," he calls them).

"One hundred years ago," he writes,
"people thought of the wolf as a serious
threat. That is what you get from reading
Little Red Riding Hood over and over: false beliefs."

> *No one ever told us we had to study our lives*
> *make of our lives a study, as if learning*
>   *natural history*
> *or music, that we should begin*
> *with the simple exercises first*
> *and slowly go on trying*
> *the hard ones, practicing till strength*
> *and accuracy became one with the daring. . . .*
> *—And in fact we can't live like that:*
>   *we take on*
> *everything at once before we've even begun*
> *to read or mark time, we're forced to begin*
> *in the midst of the hardest movement.*

Nineteen sixty-nine.
A New Jersey suburb
a long way from Philadelphia,
the tatty old graduate apartment
on Baltimore Avenue,
comfortable demands of a doctoral
program at Penn.
I'm leaving. A move.
Husband's teaching position, yes,
but, there also,
a growing lack of heart for
studies in American Civ.
I begin a part-time job
while I determine my future.
A public school district,
a supplemental instructor.
I will provide one-on-one supplemental
instruction to children
who are educationally classified.
Two students, two hours a day.
Education courses unnecessary.
Low hourly wages, lack of benefits.
One can understand the lack of requirements,
women—all—in the ranks.
I am not sure what to do.

I'm to begin in the midst of it.
Pedagogy? An alien term.
I know that I have two students
with special needs
and two small desks
in the supply closet—our classroom.
I worry. I think of how I might possibly begin.
I can think only that good stories
might be the way to start—
good stories, just to read to them.
And I think
that perhaps I might simply listen
to their own stories.
Where to go from there?
I'm just not sure.

I comb the library—
the search for good stories.
I find them.
When we meet, Jay and I, Raymond and I,
I read aloud and I find
that we laugh over the good stories.
We read aloud together.
Together,
we begin to trace features and patterns.
We comb the library for other favorites.
We laugh, we talk, we trace. I discover
the lessons, large and small,
that good books can bring.

And I listen, simply listen,
to family stories, to sorrows,
to the frustration
at not being able
to read and write like the others.
I listen to Jay.
Soccer is his primary reason for being.
Soccer and his golden retriever, Sam.
We talk a lot about Sam.
John lives across from the school park.
I ask, one day,
if he'd like to take Sam
to the park to take some photographs.
"I've been thinking that we might make

a book about him," I say.
He grins.
We spend three afternoons
in the park—glorious green
for child and dog.
The two romp, while I follow,
with a little Instamatic.

Back in our room, typewriter ready,
Jay juggles photographs, telling stories.
I record on the typewriter. Later, he
revises the manuscript as he shifts photo
sequences and alters information.
The final typing. Layout of pages.
Bookbinding learned from a friend at Bank Street.
Reading and rehearsing for class presentation.
The presentation and applause.
Celebration at MacDonald's
with a chosen friend: Jay's mother.

I begin to write with Raymond, too.
I am lucky:
I have a supervisor who honors my efforts.
I honor her trust.
I begin to read more children's books—good stories.
I begin to read about reading and writing.

> *Everything else seems beyond us,*
> *we aren't ready for it, nothing that was said*
> *is true for us, caught naked in the argument,*
> *the counterpoint, trying to sightread*
> *what our fingers can't keep up with,*
>   *learn by heart*
> *what we can't even read. And yet*
> *it is this we were born to. We aren't*
>   *virtuosi*
> *or child prodigies, there are no prodigies*
> *in this realm, only a half-blind, stubborn*
> *cleaving to the timbre, the tones of*
>   *what we are*
> *—even when all the texts describe it*
>   *differently.*

Several years pass.
Undecided as to graduate work,

though a yearning is there,
undecided still,
about a future,
I decide, while deciding,
to teach full-time.
I'm savoring the transactions
with children
and the range of their learning.

A summer of methodology courses,
skills sequences, objectives,
little of the world.
I wonder where the good stories are.
A fall of student teaching.
Midyear, I enter
a class of twenty-eight third graders—
the shock of it,
twenty-eight stories multiplied
infinitesimally by the transactions
amongst the story makers.
I am unprepared.
Gone is the sustained attention
to one child at a time.
Simultaneity, multiplicity,
maelstrom, I think
during the exhausting first days.
I try to bring unity to the welter
of children and the welter
of skills, pretested, posttested,
in book after book for group after group,
three for math, three for reading,
three for spelling.
I seek a core, a center.
I read aloud each day.
Blessedly, it becomes
our one quiet time together, inviolate.
I buy journals,
they write each morning.
I write each evening,
to them, a moment alone with each.
Forty-five minutes each night,
before the paper marking begins.

Tentatively, we begin some projects together.
We build, we paint castles for social studies.
It seems to sponsor reading.
It seems to sponsor writing.
I know it sponsors togetherness.

We feast.
They love researching feasting.
They love eating with their fingers
as celebrating lords and ladies.
These experiences I try to squeeze
between the lessons
on prefix patterns
and the story starters
in the language book.
The starters pale
next to the stories
the children offer.
Fiction emerges
from their animal research.
Busy scientists, busy writers.
Pamela writes of a slow-witted whale:
"A-dopey Dick."
Juanita weaves
into the flight patterns
of her stalwart sparrow, Sara,
the plot patterns
of her search for home.
As I read their journals, their own true stories,
as I read their fiction, their own good stories,
I turn to what they tell me—*even when all*
the texts describe it differently.
I begin to look at their own texts.
I begin to look at the underlay.

> *And we're not performers, like Liszt*
> *competing*
> *against the world for speed and brilliance. . . .*
> *The longer I live, the more I mistrust*
> *theatricality, the false glamour cast*
> *by performance, the more I know*
> *its poverty beside*
> *the truths we are salvaging from*
> *the splitting-open of our lives.*

Years.
School families reappear in my life
with second and third children.
Threads.
Lines of learning, gathered in,
an increasing sense of coherence,
not always explicitly held,
of what learning
and learning language should be.
Personal for them,
constructed by them,
important to them,
connected with them,
shared among them,
celebrated by them.
Increasingly, certain projects,
investigations,
become the framework through which
talk, reading, writing, drawing
are woven.
Each child contributes uniquely, communally,
to the effort.
Experts all,
they flourish.

Just intonation.
The completeness of the days,
the weave of child, family, story,
the endless surprise of transactions,
the loop and bind
in a community of seekers:
searching conversations.

pulling the tenets of a life together
with no mere will to mastery,
only care for the many-lived, unending
forms in which she finds herself,
becoming now the sherd of broken glass
slicing light in a corner, dangerous
to flesh, now the plentiful, soft leaf
that wrapped round the throbbing finger,
soothes the wound,

and now the stone foundation,
rockshelf further
forming underneath everything
that grows.

(269)

BIBLIOGRAPHY

Allington, Richard, et al. *Sing and Dance.* Teacher's edition. Glenview, Ill.: Scott, Foresman, 1985.

Emig, Janet. "Non-Magical Thinking: Presenting Writing Developmentally in Schools." In *Writing: The Nature, Development, and Teaching of Written Communication.* Hillsdale, NJ: Lawrence Erlbaum, 1982. Rpt. in *The Web of Meaning: Essays on Writing, Teaching, Learning, and Thinking,* edited by Dixie Guswami and Maureen Butler. Upper Montclair, N.J.: Boynton/Cook, 1983.

Gilbert, Sandra, and Susan Gubar. "Sexchanges." *College English* 50 (1988): 768–85.

Graves, Donald. "Research Update: Language Arts Textbooks: A Writing Process Evaluation." *Language Arts* 54 (1977): 817–23.

Kinnell, Galway, "St. Francis and the Sow." In *Mortal Acts Mortal Words.* Boston: Houghton Mifflin, 1980.

Le Guin, Ursula. *Dancing at the Edge of the World: Thoughts on Words, Women, Places.* New York: Harper and Row, 1989.

Meese, Elizabeth. *Crossing the Double Cross: The Practice of Feminist Criticism.* Chapel Hill: Univ. of North Carolina Press, 1986.

Miller, Jean Baker. *Toward a New Psychology of Women.* 2d ed. Boston: Beacon, 1986.

Moffett, James. "Integrity in the Teaching of Writing." In *Coming on Center: Essays in English Education.* Portsmouth, N.H.: Heinemann, 1988.

Noddings, Nel. "Feminist Critique in the Professions." In *Review of Research in Education,* edited by Courtney Cazden, vol. 16. Washington, D.C.: American Education Research Association, 1990.

Olsen, Tillie. "One out of Twelve: Writers Who Are Women in Our Century." *College English* 34 (1972). Rpt. in *Silences.* New York: Dell, 1965.

Rich, Adrienne. Introduction to *Of Woman Born: Motherhood as Experience and Institution.* New York: W. W. Norton, 1976.

———. *On Lies, Secrets, and Silence: Selected Prose 1966–1978.* New York: W. W. Norton, 1979.

———. "Transcendental Etude." In *The Fact of a Doorframe, Poems Selected and New, 1950–1984.* New York: W. W. Norton, 1984.

Taylor, Denny. "Toward a Unified Theory of Literacy Learning and Instructional Practices." *Phi Delta Kappan* 71 (1989): 184–93.

Of Mice and Mothers: Mrs. Barbauld's "New Walk" and Gendered Codes in Children's Literature

Mitzi Myers

When I see the Parisian ladies covered with rouge and enslaved by fashion, cold to the claims of maternal tenderness . . . my thoughts . . . delight to contemplate . . . the mother endowed with talents and graces to draw the attention of polite circles, yet devoting her time and cares to her family and her children.

—*Anna Laetitia Barbauld*

Her whom I have heard him name with gratitude, "the mother of his mind," Mrs. Barbauld.

—*Lucy Aikin*

My gendered perspective on language and the literary canon converges from three directions. I am a teacher of writing and of juvenile and adolescent literature as well. I am also a feminist literary historian. My research has long been focused on late eighteenth- and early nineteenth-century women writers; for the last decade, I have been most concerned with early female authors of children's books and the relations between women and writing, language, and pedagogy implicit in their works. In the decade since Sandra M. Gilbert and Susan Gubar's *The Madwoman in the Attic* (1979) appeared, their nomination of John Milton as the patriarchal bogey fittest to join Satan in "bad eminence" and their concep-

256

Mitzi Myers

tualization of women's coming to writing—a female "anxiety of authorship" replacing the male Oedipal trauma of influence—have been so
often cited that they're now tantamount to feminist orthodoxies. This
chapter looks more closely at both, taking one pioneering writer for children, Anna Laetitia Aikin Barbauld (1743–1825) and responses to her
work as exemplary. Such contextualized analysis of a historical case has
implications for rethinking the contemporary status of the female teacher
in relation to language and institutionalized education. Although deplor-
ing the conjunction of teaching and mothering is the favorite sport of
much recent pedagogic critique, this chapter stresses the strengths of
this maternal legacy and posits its relevance to feminist pedagogy as an
alternative rhetorical tradition.

The male Romantics who recuperated Jean-Jacques Rousseau's misogyny did more to construct a literary climate inimical to female forms
of authorship than did their august seventeenth-century predecessor.
For one thing, they belonged to the first generation of male authors
confronted with female counterparts in sufficient numbers to be challenging. Despite what the amount of critical energy expended on famous
mid-nineteenth-century novelists might suggest, proportionately more
women were publishing in the latter years of the eighteenth century and
at the start of the nineteenth than in the later years of the period. Significantly, these female literary specialties were often explicitly teaching
genres. "Literature" at that time was not so strictly demarcated as it has
since become; it was not a hermetic realm sealed off and presided over
by a male elite. Rather, it elastically and eclectically included many prov-
inces of knowledge, valuing good writing in the educational, historical,
or religious treatise as well as in the poem or play. Increasing competition from women writers was not, of course, the only challenge romantic
male authors faced. The decades of the French Revolution brought many
other changes as well, including changes in publishing and in the literary
marketplace. This period's masculine reconstitution of "real" literature
as comprising certain kinds of writing generated by certain kinds of writers remains in place today, despite feminist efforts to diversify the female
authorial community by opening up the canon. The canon is still there—
Romantic literature pretty much equals male poetry—and so are the hierarchical standards that marginalize many kinds of writing, especially
educational writing and literary forms directed at a juvenile audience.

Historical female educators have not been much examined for their
formulations of authorship or their cultural resonance. Yet they must be,
if we are to rethink the female writing and reading subjects of the past

and to contest the assumptions about feminine authorship undergirding such popular paradigms as Gilbert and Gubar's anxiety model or Mary Poovey's *psychomachia* of proper lady versus woman writer. Neither schema adequately accounts for the authorial confidence and cultural impact of the late eighteenth- and early nineteenth-century female educator. After all, even an unfriendly male commentator admits that "children's literature, the first encounters with which are still deeply and often consciously involved with language acquisition, has proved itself to be a crucial element in the process of socialization" (Foulkes, 45). And children's acquisition of both language and literature has long been presided over by mother-teachers. Investigating scenes of instruction is crucial to understanding these historical educators as well as their youthful pupils; as Mary Jacobus notes, the "all-important question of women's access to knowledge and culture and to the power that goes with them" is frequently "explicitly thematized in terms of education" (1981, 213). The household education sponsored by early women teachers conjoins literary merit, innovative pedagogy grounded in children's everyday experience, and a maternal thinking both rational and affective. Educational provision was an enabling rationale for women's writing, as familial access to literacy and literature enabled their pupils. Women educators' rationale and methodology still offer much to enlighten us. If their erasure from history is disheartening, the strategies behind that devaluation are themselves instructive.

When Rousseau revolutionized eighteenth-century notions of childhood and children's education, he pioneered trends in teaching that still shape contemporary classroom practice—for example, learning by doing. He was, however, no friend to youthful reading and writing, especially on the part of girls. But *Émile*'s vignette of the vain little girl who rejects writing because she looks ungraceful in that posture and Rousseau's diatribe against early literacy as childhood's curse struck a raw nerve among the period's innovative women educators. They valued early reading and writing instruction as much as Rousseau and his heirs devalued both. He may have considered twelve early enough for male literacy and female literacy hardly worth consideration; but the women educators, like Anna Laetitia Barbauld, Sarah Trimmer, Hannah More, Mary Wollstonecraft, Ellenor Fenn, and Maria Edgeworth, who were instrumental in shaping late eighteenth-century reading and writing texts and educational provision felt otherwise. Self-consciously responding to Rousseau's devaluation of women's intellect, they adapted his theories to empower the juvenile reader and writer in a cultural community, rather than the isolated boy experientially learning from nature.

These women educators challenged the prevalent stress on classical learning and rote memorization, democratized vernacular instruction, and developed graded reading and writing texts, producing the first comprehensive body of literature tailored to every age, from toddlers to teenagers. Constituting an early network of quasi-professional female writers, the British women listed above, and many more like them, not only mothered youthful readers and writers but also enabled their own authorial careers via maternal imagery. Literacy instruction conjoining teaching and mothering provided a public voice for private women. Moreover, women used pedagogic genres not only to contribute to the civic welfare but also to represent their own status and concerns more frankly and safely than in less coded forms. Late eighteenth-century women's educational activities have traditionally been read repressively from an androcentric perspective conditioned by romantic definitions of the child and pedagogy. That judgment needs reassessment, for it was initially articulated by rival male authors. The birth of a pragmatic female teaching tradition occurred alongside valorizations of a romantic pedagogy and literature, tailored to construct subjectivities—individualist, autonomous, and masculine—rather than the relational selves in learning community that were women's goal. Because the romantic imagination overwrote female instruction, it is part of our academic history; women's work has been culturally forgotten.

Barbauld is among the most important of the late eighteenth century's many neglected female authors, a stellar figure among those women writers whose steadily increasing presence from the century's closing decades on has to be factored into revisionist literary, linguistic, and pedagogic history.[1] Barbauld's work spans genres from poetry, polemic, and literary criticism to educational essays and juvenile texts, and she was deft and progressive in most, achieving in her day a formidable reputation for both substance and style.[2] A case for her as a major eighteenth-century poet may no longer need making, since her retrieval is now well under way. But if writing Barbauld into the literary canon helps us rewrite literary history and women's studies, her rehabilitation is yet more significant in righting historical pedagogy. Her career as educator is unusually rich in revisionary possibility, for her Unitarian rationalism and reformism—the bourgeois progressivism so much a part of her religious and educational heritage—coexist in her instructional writing with a darker, complexly gendered self-reflexivity.

Thus dramatizing the multiple uses of educational genres to the female author, Barbauld airs important questions of how the period and the author construct the figure of the woman writer and of how the author herself overtly or covertly embodies woman in her text, as a mother, for example—or as a mouse. Situating revaluation of the interplay between gender and language within educational discourse, this chapter investigates the cultural context in which Barbauld's work emerged, considering how her instructional writing has been interpreted, especially by male critics, and suggesting a decoding of her textual practices applicable to other women writers of the period who similarly represent themselves as educators, as cultural mothers.[3]

Barbauld exemplifies the problematics of late eighteenth-century female authorship; the period both fostered and constrained female achievement. Generously educated thanks to her Unitarian background—a "veritable Lady Jane Grey!" gushed one editor—she enjoyed intellectual equality with a loving brother (Scott, 69). Great things were expected from the child prodigy who began reading at two in her *"wise book,"* but her most enduring literary legacies and revelatory testaments are arguably pedagogic instruction for the young and the closely related poetic microcosms that are my subject.[4] A daughter whose constrained relationship with her own mother marked her personality for life, Barbauld yearned so intensely for motherhood that, very early in her own marriage, she persuaded her more fertile brother to cede her one of his babies to rear, thus giving literary birth to the little Charles and his maternal instructor who played such a formative role in subsequent children's literature. Like her even more famous *Hymns in Prose for Children,* Barbauld's enormously influential series of *Lessons* for beginning readers were the products of hands-on educational experiment with a real child. Her remarkable Advertisement (to which I shall return) offers the originally private *Lessons* as a generous gift to the domestic teaching community, principally mothers: "This little publication was made for a particular child, but the public is welcome to the use of it" (1808, no page). "Probably three-fourths of the gentry of the three last generations have learnt to read by [the] assistance" of "'Little Charles,' as every household tenderly calls her Easy Lessons," Charlotte Yonge, a pioneer in historical criticism of children's literature as well as a Victorian best-selling author, observed in 1869—an assessment valid for two generations to come and transatlantically as well, judging from the extraordinary number of redactions and just plain thefts recorded in the listings of National Union Catalogue, the British Library, R. C. Alston, and Ian Michael (Yonge, 234).

The *Lessons* began their American career with a pirated edition by
B. F. Bache in Philadelphia only ten years after their first publication,
and in 1841 one enterprising publisher transformed part 3 of "Little
Charles" (*Lessons*) into "Little Marrian" and marketed Barbauld in Aunt
Mary's Library for Young Children, a nonsectarian series geared to
American youngsters. Sarah Josepha Hale also edited a collection of Barbauld material for American school libraries and praised her warmly in
Woman's Record, reprinting a key essay on education and terming the
Lessons "still . . . unrivalled among children's books" (197). It was a Bos-
tonian, Grace A. Ellis, who issued an 1874 life and selections updating
the 1825 *Works* to show Barbauld's accomplishments beyond her still
standard children's books (1:ix–x, 6–7, 86–87). A century after their publication, the *Hymns,* which had been translated into many languages and
published in every format, from sumptuous art books to cheap Sunday
School Association pamphlets, were even "more highly valued" in America than in England (Murch, 75). Because Barbauld's antiestablishment
Protestantism and her lucid style were particularly congenial to American tastes, she contributed significantly to this country's literacy
provision.

Much reprinted, translated, and imitated, even into the twentieth century, the *Lessons* founded a female tradition in writing and pedagogy.
Although her oeuvre was small, few works were more inspirational in
their day than Barbauld's *Lessons for Children* from two to four and her
Hymns (1781) or the *Evenings at Home* she coauthored with her brother.[5]
All were standard fixtures in Anglo-American juvenile libraries for more
than a century. Certain children's writers were far more significant in
shaping the nineteenth-century cultural climate than the canonically en-
shrined figures normally studied, yet those concerned with authorial
influence characteristically go to work as if only what one reads as an
adult matters. Psychological studies suggest otherwise; the things we
read as children, the early ways we learn of making sense of the world,
are deeply engraved in memory. William Hazlitt typically remarks that
his first literary recollections are of Barbauld, "with whose works I became acquainted before those of any other author, male or female, when
I was learning to spell words of one syllable in her story-books for children. . . . I wish I could repay my childish debt of gratitude in terms of
appropriate praise" (147). Anne Thackeray Ritchie similarly "first learnt
to read out of her little yellow books, of which the syllables rise up one
by one again with a remembrance of the hand patiently pointing to each
in turn . . . recalled and revived after a lifetime" (Thackeray, 1–2).

The great women writers for children who followed Barbauld in prose (like Maria Edgeworth) and poetry (like Ann Taylor and Jane Taylor, famed respectively for "My Mother" and "Twinkle, Twinkle, Little Star") praised her highly and developed further the tradition of domestic realism she began, a mode elastic enough to move from a quotidian mimetism of mother-child instructional interaction to a quasi-Wordsworthian Romanticism grounded in reverence for the common things of nature. Barbauld contributed the development of both high romantic poetry and its so-called antithesis, the period's realistic moral tale. At its liveliest, her work introduces a newly verisimilar and childsize perspective quickly made the most of in the more thoroughly developed fictions of Edgeworth, who went far beyond, but never failed to acknowledge her debt to, her illustrious predecessor. Barbauld's anecdotal dialogic format—the chitchat of mother and child as they go about their daily routine—and her implicit reformist critique of late eighteenth-century pedagogy—her privileging of the vernacular and experiential over the learned languages and rote memorization—energized much varied instructional exploration.

Barbauld provided a model for many other educational ventures: Sarah Trimmer and Hannah More's work with the charity and Sunday schools that became the main providers of working-class literacy through much of the nineteenth century; Lady Ellenor Fenn's ambitious series of readers and ingenious learning games for middle-class rational mothers; the multidecade, multivolume Edgeworth family project, grounded in the pioneering child study notebooks still among the Bodleian Library's manuscripts, anecdotes from which were incorporated into the influential 1798 manual for parents, *Practical Education*. All of this experimentation was directly and frankly inspired by Barbauld. A whole tradition of mother-teachers anticipated the reforms historians typically associate with Froebel, Pestalozzi, and Dewey.[6] Frances Burney D'Arblay, who supplies the quotation in my title, appraises this female educational innovation as a sister writer and a mother pragmatically concerned with teaching a child. She was flattered to be called on in 1798 by Mrs. Barbauld, "the authoress of the most useful books, next to Mrs. Trimmer's, that have been yet written for dear little children; though this for the world is probably her very secondary merit, her many pretty poems, and particularly songs, being generally esteemed. But many more have written those as well, and not a few better; for children's books she began the new walk, which has since been so well cultivated, to the great information as well as utility of parents" (D'Arblay, 5:419).

Barbauld's quite small body of juvenile work thus had remarkable literary and educational consequences; still more remarkable, both the original productions and their pedagogic progeny have been systematically misread by or erased from mainstream literary history. Even though the educational concept of authorship responsible for such texts was a justifying rationale for the majority of women before the twentieth century, the writing woman as teacher has not captured the imagination of feminist scholars, though her male contemporaries recognized her importance and feared her power. Pilloried by Lord Byron in *Don Juan* and twitted by the poet Samuel Rogers—"How strange it is that while we men are modestly content to amuse by our writings, women must be didactic"—a generation of exemplary educators achieved literary standing yet long failed to make the canonical cut (qtd. in Robinson, 436). Thus like a large body of sister teaching texts, Barbauld's juvenile works mostly survive, inaccurately summarized, in the backwaters of children's literature surveys, usually deplored for their pernicious effect on the emergent cultural construction of Romantic childhood, or in the margins of commentary on male high Romanticism, a minor inspiration for Blake or Wordsworth perhaps. Barbauld's writings for the young derive from the intersection of gender and pedagogy at a particular historical moment, yet they have never been situated within the appropriate matrix of female conceptualizations of authorship, childhood, and education.

Surveying Barbauld's educational output not only teaches us about the period's instructional provision but also offers lessons in construing its competing—and, I argue, gendered—models of the educator and the child and of literacy and literature itself. Moreover, it helps us with the ongoing feminist task of learning how to read historical women's writing, of analyzing what have been women's particular contributions and why and under what cultural circumstances these have been devalued or erased. Strikingly, too, it alerts us to the gendered codes in which women inscribe identity; alongside the poetic forms and masculine desires privileged by high Romanticism flourish multiple minor genres recording alternative female subjectivities and romanticisms. Reassessing women's early educational or "didactic" writing, then, offers a fresh take on a contested critical issue, the relation between language and the feminine, for what it means to write as a woman always depends on a particular historical and generic context. Before we can explore how Barbauld represents the world for a child reader and represents herself within that Lilliputian library, though, we need to consider how the female teacher has been constructed and *mis*represented by male interpreters and how the (en)gendering of the educator is central to the war between the sexes over the newly prized turf of literary childhood.

Charles Lamb's "Cursed Barbauld Crew," Gender Politics, and the Cultural Construction of the Woman Educator

It is indicative of this period's changing cultural construction of the woman writer that many of the poems in Barbauld's first publication (1773) were pronounced "inferior only to the works of Milton and Shakespeare" by the *Monthly Review*'s William Woodfall (54) and that she herself felt sufficiently comfortable as an established literary entity to play mentor to the young Samuel Taylor Coleridge in the 1790s, maternally chiding him in print for his boyish vagaries. Indeed, Ralph Griffiths, editor of the same influential journal, heralded a new literary era in 1798: "The polished period in which we live may be justly denominated the Age of ingenious and learned Ladies.... We need not to hesitate in concluding that the long agitated dispute between the two sexes is at length determined; and that it is no longer a question,—whether woman *is* or *is not* inferior to man in natural ability, or less capable of excelling in mental accomplishments" (442).

But if women's improved prospects bespoke authorial and authoritative opportunity, their literary access was nonetheless hedged with restriction.[7] Lately attentive to the public feminine influence Griffiths celebrates, revisionist literary historians are beginning to outline the rise of the woman novelist and poet: what used to be called the Romantic Period now includes more than Six Great Men and Jane Austen, but the record still ignores women's pedagogic and juvenile contributions. Critics of the Romantic period currently attempt to view their subjects historically, outside the universalist claims to truth and art promulgated by the male poets themselves; politics and gender, for example, are increasingly factored into studies of adult poetry. But Romantic ideology's essentializing of childhood, imagination, and education remains largely uninterrogated in studies of the juvenile market. Since this period's expansion of children's texts occurred alongside the related developments of the female writing and reading public and of masculine romanticism, giving women's educational contributions their due is crucial to revising literary history. Because Romanticism established high Literature as imaginative writing by males, simultaneously appropriating some feminine traditions and devaluing others, that revision is, in turn, crucial to revaluating historical female pedagogy.

Since Barbauld was both a respected adult writer and a juvenile innovator whose first (1773) and last (1826) publications span key transitions, her culture's reading of her as a female educator and her interpretation of her culture through educational writing are especially
illuminating. Woodfall's congratulations at the start of her career were
tempered with disappointment that her poems were insufficiently gendered, for "there is a sex in minds as well as in bodies." Educated more
by her father than by her mother, the poet as "*Woman*" had failed to
appear and instruct the critic in her peculiar specialty: the "pleasing passion, by which the ladies rule the world, and which they are thought so
perfectly to understand," together with the "particular distresses of some
female situations" (137, 133). Had Woodfall been less eager to equate
gendered writing with the "subject of Love," he might have discerned in
"The Mouse's Petition" for freedom a characteristic trope for female
distress that runs through Barbauld's oeuvre, along with the birds tor-
mented by bad boys, the hares torn to bits by hounds, the lambs devoured by wolves, and similar animal victims endemic in Georgian wom-
en's juvenilia.

But if women could be welcomed as instructors in love, authorities
within a limited literary space, their cultural work as actual educators of
the young provoked ambivalent responses still with us. Some men es-
teeming Barbauld's literary talents, like Dr. Samuel Johnson, Charles
James Fox, and Samuel Rogers in her own day and the editor of the 1989
Oxford anthology of women poets in ours, find her teaching trivial, the
teacher herself infantilized: "Education is as well known, and has long
been as well known, as ever it can be," Johnson pronounced, outraging
the period's progressives, who saw more to instruction than caning re-
calcitrant schoolboys into Latin memorization.

Endeavouring to make children prematurely wise is useless labour. . . .
Too much is expected from precocity, and too little performed. Miss
[Aikin] was an instance of early cultivation, but in what did it terminate?
In marrying a little Presbyterian parson, who keeps an infant boarding-
school, so that all her employment now is, "To suckle fools, and chronicle small-beer." She tells the children, "This is a cat, and that is a dog,
with four legs and a tail; see there! you are much better than a cat or a
dog, for you can speak." If I had bestowed such an education on a daughter, and had discovered that she thought of marrying such a fellow, I
would have sent her to the *Congress* [opprobrium indeed, considering
the speaker's politics]. (Boswell 2: 407–09)

Roger Lonsdale similarly, if less vividly, regrets Barbauld's educational writing and the eleven years at Palgrave boarding school that produced such an extraordinary number of social achievers: "Potentially the most versatile of women poets in the period, she accepted for many years a subordinate role in an eventually painful marriage, contenting herself with writing books for children."[8] Just as historians discount the reproductive work of women's bodies as not *real* work, so women's work as primary initiators into literacy, the elementary reproduction of culture itself, is devalued.

Two scathing critiques of Barbauld, both by early nineteenth-century critics, further complicate the masculine construct of didactic woman. The savagery of John Wilson Croker's notorious attack on Barbauld's *Eighteen Hundred and Eleven,* a politicized elegy for a decaying England, is shocking, even for the *Quarterly Review,* a journal often unkind to women writers and liberal thinkers. "Abandoning the superintendance of . . . the nursery" for political commentary, Barbauld has "wandered from the course in which she was respectable and useful"; her juvenile work though trivial, is yet "something better than harmless." A reader must doubt his claim that "it really is with no disposition to retaliate on the fair pedagogue of our former life, that . . . we have called her up to correct her exercise." The woman who undertakes to instruct "statesmen, and warriors" rather than " 'ovilia' " deserves a verbal birching; she has breached her teacher's contract. Revealingly, Croker's dominating image is that of the domestic schoolmarm "miserably mistak[ing] both her powers and her duty" in arrogating the public role of political commentator (309, 313).[9] Conservative distaste for Barbauld's liberal politics insufficiently explains Croker's *ad feminam* argument; an unfavorable review of the democratic William Roscoe in the same issue is conducted on an intellectual plane.

The masculine anxiety veiled by Croker's infantilization of his childhood instructress is unmasked in Charles Lamb's much cited demonization of Barbauld and Sarah Trimmer, the founding mothers of educational children's literature. William Taylor of Norwich's "mother of my mind," the benign maternal protector and fosterer, becomes, in the familiar binary opposition of fairy tale and juvenile nightmare, Lamb's wicked witch, repressive, emasculating—the disciplinary voice and "bad breast" of psychoanalytic theory. When female educators are noticed in histories of children's literature, the discussion is typically prefaced by Lamb's famous tirade against the "cursed Barbauld Crew," a quotable but very dubious assessment exemplifying the Romantic construct of the child and his reading. (The masculine pronoun is intentional, for Lamb's ideal juvenile reader, like Wordsworth's juvenile rover, is always a boy, mind and body untrammeled by maternal constraints.) No one ever fails to cite Lamb's heated dismissal of the writers who are my subject—and his criticism is usually treated as gospel. It is a locus classicus for male Romantic attitudes, usually a footnote to discussion of Wordsworth's attack on contemporary education (*Prelude,* bk. 5), always a staple in the juvenile literature survey's mythology of how romantic imagination— thanks to Blake and Wordsworth—ousted tedious Enlightenment instruction, the romantic youth schooled by Nature at last eluding those more pragmatic mothers with primers in hand. Lamb's much quoted letter to Coleridge was written on October 23, 1802:

> Mrs. Barbauld['s] stuff has banished all the old classics of the nursery. . . . Mrs. B's and Mrs. Trimmer's nonsense lay in piles about. Knowledge insignificant & vapid as Mrs. B's books convey, it seems, must come to a child in the *shape* of *knowledge,* & his empty noddle must be turned with conceit of his own powers, when he has learnt, that a Horse is an animal, & Billy is better than a Horse, & such like: instead of that beautiful Interest which made the child a man, while all the time he suspected himself to be no bigger than a child. Science has succeeded to Poetry no less in the little walks of Children than with Men.—: Is there no possibility of averting this sore evil? Think what you would have been now, if instead of being fed with Tales and old wives fables in childhood, you had been crammed with Geography & Natural History.? *Damn them.* I mean the cursed Barbauld Crew, those *Blights & Blasts* of all that is *Human* in man & child.[10]

Lamb's opinion is significant not only because it demonstrates a generation's fear of female competitors or the romantic cult of childhood's nostalgia for lost youth and pervasive valorization of instinctive juvenile wisdom. Seriously misrepresenting the content of late eighteenth-century women's texts, Lamb polarizes science and poetry, dichotomizes educators into the merely instructive and the mentally emancipatory, and reifies imagination as a separable mental faculty. He thus expresses in embryonic form ways of thinking about children, teaching, and literature that have long since been institutionalized in historical account and classroom practice: the privileging of an imaginative canon and its separation from all the cultural knowledge that had previously been thought of as literature; the binary opposition of scientific, empiricist ways of knowing and intuitive, imaginative insights; even the two-tiered structure of most modern English departments, with male-dominated imaginative literature on the upper deck and practical reading and writing instruction, taught most often by women and the untenured, relegated to the lower levels. Lamb may get almost every fact wrong, but his manifesto epitomizes the historical formation of attitudes that erased women's pedagogic contributions and that still marginalize writing instruction.

Barbauld's work as female educator and inculcator of primary literacy thus emerged in a contentious environment, different from yet not incongruent with our own. Late eighteenth-century women writers extolled maternal responsibility, claimed rationality for their sex, and functioned as semiprofessional teachers specially concerned with the pragmatic revision of childhood education. On the one hand, such work could be dismissed as trivial or condescended to as presumptuous.[11] On the other, it was deeply threatening, not only because of the mother's archetypal power but also because romantic men sought to appropriate for themselves both traditional feminine qualities of feeling and nurturance and the new literary territory of childhood. Much of the Romantic ideology that redefined literature from the late eighteenth century on was invested in the juvenile—like Wordsworth's self-aggrandizing little boys, autonomous amid nature, blessed with visionary gleams and transcendent truths.

Defining high Romantic art to a large extent defines the romantic view of children, which is so inwoven with all subsequent thinking about early education that it is difficult to recall that it is an ideology, a culturally conditioned tissue of assumptions—not a transhistorical, universal body of truths about The Child, who is in fact always an individual "he" or "she" living in a particular time and place. Historically, high Romanticism has been a masculine phenomenon canonizing poetry as the defining genre and visionary imagination as the defining epistemological mode. Erasing women's alternative romanticisms, their quotidian vision, their instructive romance of real life, it paid little attention to gender—the only good Romantic heroine is a dead one, like Lucy or Wordsworth's mother—or to prosaic genres that explore social development narratively or replace the male alone in nature with children, including females, in community. One sturdy Victorian lad, for example, recalls that he detested Blakean lambs and Wordsworthian reverie—"far removed from the spirit of lusty combative childhood"—and preferred women's juvenile tales for their vigorous action and recognizable social world: "It would be doing a service to Blake and Wordsworth to keep them hidden away from infant philistines." His response underscores how much venerated romantic writing is nostalgia *about* children rather than material *for* them (Jones, 25–29).

The romantic child, as fantasized through male identification with the maternal, makes the pragmatic teaching mother the Other; when not erased by death or marginalized as the peasant bearer of "old wives fables," she is enrolled in the "Monstrous Regiment" of female educators that haunts modern male historians of children's literature. "Shall we evoke Mrs. Barbauld?" asks one text widely used in survey classes: "Beware of what is to come; let us flee. There is a whole battalion of these fearsome women . . . who undertook to transform young girls [and boys] into essentially reasonable creatures."[12] But Lamb's "cursed Barbauld" was also Thomes De Quincey's "queen of all the bluestockings," who initiated him from the "silence" of infancy into language as symbolic system and whose prose *Hymns* "left upon my childish recollection a deep impression of solemn beauty and simplicity" (138, 144–45). At the heart of the gendered cultural construction of the woman educator and the romantic child are questions of language, power, and ways of knowing. As strikingly similar as their writers are different, Johnson's and Lamb's dismissive mimicries of Barbauld's juvenilia single out the concern with language and naming that informs her work, the referential format and mother-child intersubjectivity that recent investigators deem essential for the infant to enter the linguistic community (Bruner). Barbauld's primers not only influenced the initiation of children into elementary literacy for over a century but also assimilate with contemporary learning theory surprisingly well.

It is indicative that Barbauld's writings abound in riddles, allegories, mock heroics, and every variety of witty verbal indirection. Two of her best-known stories in *Evenings at Home* are "Things by Their Right Names" (a startlingly modern antiwar, antiheroic piece, beautifully capturing a saucy juvenile voice) and "A Lesson in the Art of Distinguishing" (another parent-child exchange that at one level exemplifies how scientific nomenclature insures referential accuracy but on another cleverly contrasts the dry abstractions of the father tongue with the descriptive particularities native to women and the young). Her posthumously collected *Legacy for Young Ladies* (1826) argues woman's special affinity for literature and the vernacular, "the real genius of our own tongue" (47), as well as her right to the classics ("On Female Studies" 47; "On the Classics"). It also contains one mother-daughter dialogue titled "A Lecture on the Use of Words," another beginning with a question about the meaning of "Pic-nic" and developing women's bent toward the conver-

sation that creates community, and still another, "A Letter from Grimal-
kin to Selima," that is simultaneously wise maternal advice to a young
kitten on her entrance into the world—culled from experience and the
best authorities like Locke and Edgeworth—and a hilariously purr-fect
feline deconstruction of it: "Remember that life is not to be spent in
running after your own tail" (198).[13] This pervasive interest in linguistic
coding and decoding thematic in Barbauld's work provides for her *Lessons* a structuring feminine epistemology and learning theory, a morality,
and an aesthetic, before part 4 turns the arbitrary relation between visual
and verbal literacy into a child's game at once sportive and sophisticated.
A picture of a horse denotes in any language, Charles figures out, but
words themselves are arbitrary, a social construct: if a culture had chosen
that "RAB should mean horse, it would" (102).

Barbauld's *Lessons* thus embody the process of learning to read the
world as a text—and of doing so through maternal mediation. She was
the first to conceptualize the act of writing a reader and the formation of
the child's subjectivity as coexistent, both products of the mother-child
dialogue that constitutes her text. It is a bonus that in her tutelage she
inscribes feminine subjectivity as well, instructing us in the subtle uses
of the educational stance for the woman writer. As teacher, Barbauld can
represent woman as the powerful mother who controls access to literacy
and culture, naming the world and defining reality, and, through the
analogical hierarchies of child-adult, animal-human, female-male, can simultaneously recreate the relative vulnerabilities of the female situation
encoded in the plights of the miniature, the unhoused, the entrapped.

Barbauld's Polysemic Lessons—Mother-Teachers and Mice, Microcosms and Mimesis, Literacy and Subjectivity

As Barbauld's case illustrates, women writers of the Romantic period
textualized the mother, the child, the learning process, and the relation
between emergent subjectivity and the cultural environment in significantly different ways from those we associate with the "egotistical sub-
lime" and epiphanic moment of masculine romanticism. What little positive critical attention Barbauld's juvenile works have received has been
devoted to positioning her as a not unworthy precursor of high Romanticism, to searching out parallels between the poetic prose and pastoral
vision of her *Hymns* and Blake's or Wordsworth's verse, a reading sometimes as sunnily Imagination-oriented as Lamb's is dourly instructive—
and as partial.[14] Victorians filled out the nondenominational *Hymns* with

their own preoccupations; some modern Romanticists find them service-
able as a glum backdrop to set off the achievements of androcentric
Romanticism, while others assimilate Barbauld to this normative male
tradition.[15] Her "poetics were Romantic" (Pickering 1975, 264). After all,
the *Hymns'* educative plot, their growth of a child's mind through the
formative influence of sensory impressions, their democratic celebration
of natural objects in rich variety—from the snowdrop, primrose, and
emerald-bodied insects to the roaring lion—their representation of nature as a language one learns, and their discovery of truths beyond ap-
pearances in trivial objects are readily subsumed under the romantic
rubric and valued because they presage Blake's *Songs* or Wordsworth's
Prelude or his "Immortality" ode. Although Barbauld was a "talented,
pious prig," for example, Blake "transmuted [her] tinsel into the gold of
authentic poetry" (De Sola Pinto, 84). Since the *Hymns* were composed
in metrical prose with an "ur-Wordsworthian quality," they "could easily
be recollected as verse," reasons one critic: "How ironic, then, if [they]
gave Wordsworth both his first poetic pleasure and the raw material for
his most finished poem!" (Zall 1970, 177–78). Critics have overlooked
the *Hymns'* contribution to adult romantic poetry because of preconceptions about Barbauld's instructive intent, argues another; Lamb is right
about her *Lessons* and other juvenile work, but the *Hymns* are different,
worth salvaging because they "expanded rather than limited children's
imaginations," because they affiliate with men's poems, not women's
teaching texts (Pickering 1981, 151).

But the *Hymns* belong to the same maternal agenda that produced
the *Lessons,* sharing the same practical teaching aims and many of the
same images. The lion, with which young Ernest Pontifex naughtily
mocked his father, for instance, turns up in both works (Butler, 99). The
Hymns' representation of nature's language—"Every field is like an open
book; every painted flower hath a lesson written on its leaves" (75)—
runs throughout the *Lessons.* All four parts open with references to the
child's reading, and each is structured not by a plot but by concrete
examples of his learning to decode nature's secrets, from cyclical sea-
sons to times of the day to her animal, mineral, and vegetable riches.
The *Lessons* abound in mother-child itineraries through the countryside,
in questions, lists, and analogies that demonstrate how to go about making sense of the world, how the child is similar to and different from what
it meets and sees and hears about. Helping Charles name the world,
giving him a voice (thematic in the *Hymns* as well), the mother's speech
is at first dominant, Charles's questions embedded in her replies, as a

child has been literally embedded in its mother's body: As the age-graded primer progresses, Charles's voice is heard more clearly, helped from orality to fuller literacy by the mother's tongue. If the infant mind is an acorn, "its powers . . . folded up" but "all there"—an impeccably Romantic organic image—it yet requires maternal nurture: "Instruction is the food of the mind . . . the dew and the rain and the rich soil" (1983, 124–25).[16]

As in the *Lessons,* the dominant images of the *Hymns* are parenthood, protection, and guardianship, recurrently imaged in mother and shepherd, tropes borrowed by Blake and illustrated in his *Songs* both textually and visually, as recent scholars have perceptively noted (Hirsch, 28–30, 183; Williams). Barbauld's "mother loveth her little child; she bringeth it up on her knees. . . . She teacheth it how to be good. . . . But who is the parent of the mother?" God is shepherd and parent; all the world alike belongs to his family. The Romantic prefigurations spelled out in Barbauld's preface and concretely realized in the *Hymns* are thus not a departure from the earlier, overtly instructive *Lessons* but an extension of them, both the outgrowth of a mother-teacher's experiential competence and imaginative engagement with Charles and the young boys of her school. Like the *Lessons,* they illustrate a sequential, interactive learning process, conversational and dialogic in the secular *Lessons,* antiphonal in the *Hymns* intended for juvenile "social worship" (14–16, v).

The eagerness to claim Barbauld for the male poetic tradition sometimes results in a more just recognition of her achievement than those of Lamb and his modern followers, but it also ignores the fact that her preface to the *Hymns* terms poetry an "elevated" form unsuitable for childish capacities and that her undeniable contribution to the late eighteenth-century stylistic revolution is not vatic poems but domestic verse and vernacular prose, a "real language" of mothers and children as they go about their daily routine. In the female tradition of Romanticism to which Barbauld's juvenilia belong, the imaginative is also the instructive, the microcosmic space of the teaching text also a mode of cultural commentary, and Science is not the binary opposite of Poetry, as Lamb would have it, but its ally. Barbauld typically concludes "The Manufacture of Paper," a dialogue for older children in *Evenings at Home,* by yoking its invention to literature itself, "show[ing] how the arts and sciences, like children of the same family, mutually assist and bring forward each other" (1793, vol. 2). If Barbauld's status as a woman and a religious Dissenter, inherently marginal to the establishment, reinforces her representation of gender and her educational innovation, it also informs her aesthetics, for her construction of the child and its world both participates in and dissents from Romanticism. Rather than the visionary revelation, the aggrandizing projection of self onto the world, the appropriation of divinity, hers is a quotidian Romanticism, delighting in the miniature, rooted in the domestic familiarities of everyday life.

Like the "new walk" it initiated, Barbauld's original Advertisement to the *Lessons* is disarmingly modest, yet revolutionary.[17] Although books "professedly written for children" abound, they don't really address a young reader's needs. "A grave remark, or a connected story" will not do for a first book, which needs to fit infant hands as well as infant minds: "*good paper, a clear and large type,* and *large spaces*" are essential. "Those only, who have actually taught young children, can be sensible how necessary these assistances are. . . . The task is humble, but not mean; for to lay the first stone of a noble building, and to plant the first idea in a human mind, can be no dishonour to any hand" (1808, no page). In trade parlance a "Lilliputian quarto," Charles's little book makes tangible a theory of learning and a way of telling the truths of women's lives. This microcosmic writing intended for juveniles brings us especially close to women's definitions and representations of reality, to their ways of making sense of the world and identifying what matters. And, far from being negligible, women's primary initiations of children into language and literature claim power for their miniature cultural constructions. This is what's important, they say. This is how things connect, these small details, these homely interactions and vernacular dialogues, this everyday round of daily life, engagingly ordinary and domestically located in place, time, and habitual action—mundane, yet metaphorically charged.

Juvenile trivia, as Barbauld reminds us again and again, emblematize larger issues at the same time that they deflate and contest high Romantic claims to the oracular and transcendent. "Written on a Marble," for example, finds in the game of taw a synecdoche:

> The world's something bigger,
> But just of this figure,
> . . . Your heroes are overgrown schoolboys
> Who scuffle for empires and toys,
> . . . And Pharsalia's plain,
> Though heaped with the slain,
> Was only a game at *taw*.
>
> *(1825, 1:148)*

A little girl's dollhouse tropes adult world making: Agatha must not delude herself that she owns

That toy, a Baby-house, alone;
... scarce a nation's wealth avails
To raise thy Baby-house, Versailles.
And Baby-houses oft appear
on British ground, of prince or peer.

(1:287–88)

When the mother's chat follows young Charles's actions just as he experiences that very moment's child life and learns from toy or task or season, domestic realism subsumes moral perspective and implies educational philosophy. Though meant for toddlers of two to four years, Barbauld's primer is diminutive in size and narrative strategy, not significance.

It is customary to assume that women take to children's literature and educational provision because writing for the young requires no training or capital, can be done at odd times at home, and is close enough to the socially sanctioned maternal role to incur no censure—not much of an achievement, but not much of a threat, either. (Historically and numerically, as *the Dictionary of National Biography* and *Cambridge Bibliography of English Literature* entries reveal, women have dominated this market, although juvenile works accepted as canonically important have usually been masculine—for example, those of Blake, Wordsworth, Lamb, Dickens, Thackeray, Ruskin, Carroll, Kipling, and Barrie.) Lamb's diatribe subverts this bland stereotype in one regard; the complex statements encoded in women's juvenile genres suggest that their choices are as problematic and ideologically charged as their reception. Writing for children is inherently duplicitous, an exercise in the simultaneous deployment of multiple discursive codes. Women writers for juveniles figure themselves as linguistically and culturally powerful, idealistic molders of young minds who also pragmatically warn to mind mother.

Yet they must not only nurture at the loftiest and most mundane levels but take the child's part, too, seeing with untutored eye, reliving what it was like to learn, and recalling what steps best sequence and facilitate that process. And they must write for an audience at once child and adult (the juvenile reader-listener, the parental buyer-reader) as well as embody in themselves this duality. Powerful, pedagogic, and playful, they grant the child linguistic and cultural access; within the safe space of the microcosm, mother-teachers can imagine for themselves and their readers humane possibility and a secure, ordered world. The mother in Barbauld's juvenile *Hymns* is likened to God: as she "moveth about the house with her finger on her lips, and stilleth every little noise, that her infant be not disturbed," so God hushes the world, that "his large family may sleep in peace" (32–33). Juvenile texts' teaching methodologies and narrative sequencing trope the access to language and knowledge that confers cultural power for woman teacher and child pupil alike.

But the textualizations of reality offered child readers by women teachers simultaneously call into question the narrative coherence and cultural authority they ostensibly confer, figuring through fables and similarly duplicitous genres alternative microcosmic constructions of the way the world works. Instructional issues thematized in women's writing are thus instructive in ways other than their mere content, what they are *about;* they literally exemplify women's "multiplicity of positionalities," their participation in a "tangle of distinct and variable relations of power and points of resistance" (de Lauretis, 131; Foucault, 92–96). Women writers act the pursued hare and caged mouse as well as the sheltering mother.

The *Lessons* nourish the "roots of literacy" by helping the child to be at home in the world, but they problematize that "secure home base" on almost every page in extraordinarily vivid prose (Hawkins, 1–14). And Barbauld seldom draws the easy moral we've been led to expect from early children's literature. The deaths just are. Cats torture mice and leave heaps of bloody feathers, partridges and pheasants fall prey to hunters, vicious boys starve robins (and get eaten by bears in return), a little female lamb evades her mother for a night's frolic, only to be seized by a mother wolf and carried to "a dismal dark den, all covered with bones and blood. . . . So the cubs took her, and growled over her a little while, and then tore her to pieces, and ate her up" (1808, pt 3:67).[18] The frantic hare pursued in part 1—"The horses are in a foam. See how they break down the farmers' fences"—returns toward the *Lessons'* close:

> When the huntsman sounds his horn, and the poor harmless Hare hears the Dogs coming, then it runs very swiftly. . . . Then the hounds come up, and tear her, and kill her. Then when she is dead, her little limbs, which moved so fast, grow quite stiff, and cannot move at all. A Snail could go faster than a hare when it is dead: and its poor little heart that beat so quick is quite still and cold; and its round full eyes are dull and dim; and its soft furry skin is all torn and bloody. It is good for nothing now but to be roasted. (pt. 1: 16; pt. 4: 115–18)

Barbauld's *Lessons* are recurrently, almost obsessively, punctuated by the deaths of small vulnerable animals, like those of the lamb and hare

above. Many animal tales and fables are overtly moralized, the pain subsumed within an overarching framework: only bad boys steal birds' nests
or torture cats; only wicked men beat their horses; if some creatures
were not killed by others or by man for food, the world would quickly
be overpopulated. Barbauld's implicit critiques leave the reader to get
the antiheroic point, a subtlety unusual in juvenile literature, then or now.
The animal victim was widely deployed by humanitarian writers for the
young, a late eighteenth-century update of the ancient fable tradition that
remained popular with the Victorians as well, but it was especially adapt-
able to women's concerns and their critique of masculine values. The
gender-coded animal is everywhere in Georgian female writing, for
adults as well as for children. Barbauld, like many other women, seems
especially drawn to mice (and cats) and often uses them to query established values. Her linguistic cat-and-mouse games suggest how complexly gender is implicated in generic choice and how frequently wom-
en's genres foreground the powers of language and instruction. Among
Barbauld's very earliest poems is "The Mouse's Petition, Found in the
Trap where he had been Confin'd all Night." Eloquently arguing an egalitarian case for bodily and intellectual liberty, the prisoner urges the
captor:

> If e'er thy breast with freedom glowed,
>   And spurned a tyrant's chain,
> Let not thy strong oppressive force
>   A free-born mouse detain!

Addressed "To Dr. [Joseph] Priestley," the mouse's instructive rhetoric
is prefaced by a Virgilian motto that makes overt a subtext for Barbauld's
animal anecdotes: "Parcere subjectis, & debellare superbos"—spare the
vanquished and subdue the proud (1977, 37–40).[19] The reprint in the
Works adds that the mouse was caged "for the sake of making experiments with different kinds of air" (1:35–38). A contemporaneous notice
elucidates Priestley's famous experiments with suffocating gases, des-
patching the "little victims of the domestic economy" routinely trapped.
Brought in at night, Barbauld's captive was set aside for next morning,
when it was found with its petition twisted among the wires of its cage.
The "poetical genius of the mouse prevail[ing]," it was thus set free (qtd.
in Ellis 1:34–35). Mock-heroic uses persiflage as camouflage; a charming
example of Barbauld's skill in this eighteenth-century genre, the poem
glosses the darker side of her juvenile texts in several ways. Since the

mouse world is microcosmic, a precariously domiciled populace within and subsidiary to a larger community, mice are readily available to satirize the human world they see, to constitute an alternative society, and to embody the plight of the displaced or marginal—the orphan and the poor, the juvenile and the feminine. Michel Foucault helps us think about how a mouse means, reminding us that "power is exercised from innumerable points," that it "comes from below," too (94).

It's ironic that Barbauld, like Maria Edgeworth, is often unproblematically aligned with bourgeois scientism and progress because of family affiliations, for women have coded self-reflexive voices as well as a civic discourse. Barbauld deeply valued Priestley, but the poem nevertheless contests the objective rationalism he stands for, delicately deflating what the world considers important. Eighteenth-century reviewers understood the petition as a rebuke to scientific inhumanity, but the mouse's prison has further implications. Its wires replicate broader cultural constraints, entombing the mouse, but also setting it free to speak its mind and question the hierarchical givens of everyday existence. Through language that blends logical argument and "feminine" sensibility, the mouse redefines reality and makes its audience see from its tiny vantage point.

The poem was quickly appropriated by youngsters, who often memorized it in childhood (Murch, 72). It also inspired several educational texts by women writers—who have been from the very start of children's literature remarkably subtle and skillful in assimilating fabular forms to a juvenile and female perspective—along with an anonymous and most unusual moralized fairy story: *The Curious Adventures of a Little White Mouse; or, A Bad Boy Changed, in a very Comical Manner, into A Good Boy* (c. 1780). Doubly indebted to Barbauld's petition, the story literalizes the mouse's entrapment until the child reforms and thus regains the freedom of human shape, then pirates Barbauld's poem in conclusion to underscore the point.[20] Barbauld herself brilliantly transferred the mouse theme to children's literature in the first volume (1792) of *Evenings at Home; or, The Juvenile Budget Opened. Consisting of a Variety of Miscellaneous Pieces, for the Instruction and Amusement of Young Persons,* which she coauthored with her brother, John Aikin. Five more volumes appeared between 1793 and 1796, and the collection was one of the most popular and frequently reprinted educational works for over a century, highly praised by many evaluators, including Maria Edgeworth.

The "Budget" in the title refers to the locked box of manuscripts from which the thirty evenings' entertainments are drawn, as described in the framing device. As do many of the pieces, the frame dramatizes the centrality of children and literacy in ascendant bourgeois ideology. Presided over by the mother, bestower of early literacy, the box contains offerings composed for the children by the family guests, and the youngsters both perform and consume what is drawn from it. The exemplary middle-class Fairborne family, their children, and their guests thus dedicate their evenings to the furtherance of cultural literacy. In the early editions, "The Young Mouse: A Fable" is their second treat; when the miscellany was finally revised by Aikin's daughter to make it age-graded, the little mouse took first place—and with good reason. Stylistically and thematically succinct, wonderfully colloquial and culturally resonant, the young mouse's tale is child's talk and woman's art, a tiny masterpiece with multiple meanings for multiple audiences. It is a fine early example of authentic juvenile speech in writing for children; the original punctuation, reproduced here, is one long breathless gush. It does not conclude with a moral tag, for it has embodied in the mouse's plight the intertwined patterns that weave through Barbauld's juvenilia: the need for nurture, shelter, home; the harsh reality of vulnerability, victimization, entrapment. But, like the "Petition," this story achieves a happy ending through language, teaching, and, since it is for children, maternal mediation. It is a parable about literacy as well as gender, childhood, and the inequalities of a hierarchical society. Though language cannot alter threat, communicative power can evade it. But let the heroine speak— or squeak—for herself.

A young Mouse lived in a cupboard where sweetmeats were kept: she dined every day upon biscuit, marmalade, or fine sugar. Never any little Mouse had lived so well. She had often ventured to peep at the family while they sat at supper; nay, she had sometimes stole down on the carpet, and picked up the crumbs, and nobody had ever hurt her. She would have been quite happy, but that she was sometimes frightened by the cat, and then she ran trembling to her hole behind the wainscot. One day she came running to her mother in great joy; Mother! said she, the good people of this family have built me a house to live in; it is in the cupboard: I am sure it is for me, for it is just big enough: the bottom is of wood, and it is covered all over with wires; and I dare say they have made it on purpose to screen me from that terrible cat, which ran after me so often: there is an entrance just big enough for me, but puss cannot follow; and they have been so good as to put in some toasted cheese, which smells so deliciously, that I should have run in directly and taken possession of my new house, but I thought I would tell you first that we might go in together, and both lodge there tonight, for it will hold us both.

My dear child, said the old Mouse, it is most happy that you did not go in, for this house is called a trap, and you would never have come out again, except to have been devoured, or put to death in some way or other. Though man has not so fierce a look as a cat, he is as much our enemy, and has still more cunning. (1792, 1:18–20)

Like that of the old Mouse and many other late eighteenth-century mother-teachers, Barbauld's educational writing is always firmly rooted in the pragmatics of familial and social literacy; teaching a very young Charles to read through simple vivid sentences about natural objects and domestic routines grounded her gradual expansion toward theory. Rather than abstraction imposed on experience, her influential and still strikingly modern essays on education were published only after years of teaching. "On Education" and "On Prejudice" depict the "education of circumstances—[the] insensible education" of home and parental example as far more significant than the schemes of schoolmen, and knowledge itself as associational, subjective, holistic, contextual—a cultural construct (1825, 2:305–37). Concerned with everyday child life, not romantic myth making, like Barbauld's teaching texts they combine high intelligence and homely, anecdotal language. The descriptive terms that come to mind are participatory, dialogic, vernacular, quotidian, empathetic, relational, nurturing—terms that still have implications for classroom practice, that belong to what Ursula Le Guin names "the mother tongue"—what we all learn as children but relinquish for the abstract and authoritative language of power (147–60). The argument for Barbauld's domestication of children's literature refers not just to its household content or the home-centered social productivity of such mother-teachers; it also argues for the inclusion of their "subliterary" works within a revised literary history and canon, to make them familiar, to give them a home—perhaps even to learn from them.

NOTES

I am grateful to the American Council of Learned Societies for the 1990 fellowship enabling me to complete the paper on which this chapter was based, and to the American Philosophical Society, for travel research funding.

1. Stuart Curran of the University of Pennsylvania has identified over six hundred women poets of the late eighteenth and early nineteenth centuries, most hitherto unnoted; for a brief overview of these poets, many of whom also wrote

for children, see Curran's fine essay. Since so much fiction and educational work was published anonymously, comparable numbers of women writers in other genres await discovery, especially in this period when household education was so much in vogue. Mothers often composed lessons and tales for their own youngsters and later published them. Because the fictive and the instructive were so tightly interwoven at this time, bibliographical surveys, like Ian Michael's on the teaching of English, only scratch the surface.

  2. Since most recent interest is focused on Barbauld as a poet for adults, it is important to emphasize her skills as prose writer and English educator. The second epigraph introducing this chapter, taken from Barbauld's niece Lucy Aikin, relates William Taylor of Norwich's encomium on Barbauld (Robberds, 2:570). Taylor was one of many among Barbauld's students at the Palgrave school who later became noted public figures. He was not the only one of her young pupils who regarded her training in composition as the "most valuable part" of his early education (Robberds, 1:8). "Of the excellence of her English prose style it is enough to say that I have heard it warmly praised both by [Sir James] Mackintosh and Macaulay," two of the early nineteenth century's outstanding stylists, Sir Henry Holland records in his *Recollections* (12). Even historians of children's literature unfriendly to the eighteenth-century moral tale concede the excellence of early women educators' prose styles; see, for example, F. J. Harvey Darton on Mrs. Barbauld and others (212–13). Reviewing the rise and development of children's literature, Charlotte Yonge, herself a noted nineteenth-century juvenile author, contrasts the "perfect precision and polish of language" in Barbauld and her brother's *Evenings at Home* with the "slovenly writing of the present day [1869]" (233). Barbauld's methods as an English teacher are detailed in Brodribb. William McCarthy of Iowa State University is working on an important biography of Barbauld utilizing new manuscript evidence, including fresh data on Barbauld's school and pupils.

  3. Late eighteenth-century women were better informed themselves and more concerned with responsible mothering and household education than their predecessors had been. Barbauld's celebration of enlightened English domesticity in the opening epigraph typifies women of her time, from radicals like Mary Wollstonecraft to conservatives like Hannah More (see Myers 1982, 1986). The question of what constitutes a proper education is the period's archetypal female literary theme, and women increasingly turned to actual instruction, both in the home and for pay. Teaching was a growth market, while professions open to women simultaneously dwindling. M. T. Clanchy shows that mothers figured in the iconography of reading as far back as the Middle Ages, but the late eighteenth-century educational vogue marks a genuine cultural shift. It is possible to teach reading without what we think of as full literacy, as Jennifer Monaghan's work on American women indicates, but these middle-class women were notably well educated. Unitarians, especially, affirmed liberal education for girls long before institutions were open to women (Watts).

  4. Lamenting the backwardness of her son's children (then under four), Barbauld's mother described her daughter's early literacy: "I once indeed knew a little girl who was as eager to learn as her instructors could be to teach her, and who at two years old could read sentences and little stories in her *wise book*

roundly, without spelling; and in half a year more could read as well as most women" (Le Breton, 23–24). Betsy Rodgers (156) supplies more information on Barbauld's mother's high expectations, but in fact, learning to read at two was not so atypical as she believes, judging from memoirs and the assumptions of many late eighteenth-century reading texts. The idea was not to force every child to read so early but to cater to those who were ready, depending on a mother's awareness of each child's individual development.

5. R. C. Alston's multivolume bibliography underestimates eighteenth-century women's contribution to education, both as subjects and writers; he includes few works about women's education and few from juvenile literature. In this period, lessons and stories overlap; readers, spellers, and fiction are very hard to separate. Many early books for home use by mother-teachers have been erased from educational history, which typically considers only institutional schooling.

6. It quickly became de rigueur for any writer or reviewer of a child's book to relate the work in question to Barbauld's; see, for example, the review of Harriet Mandeville's *Familiar Conversations.* For rare historical studies noticing early mother-teachers' contributions to primary education and national literacy, see Balibar, Gossman, and Zall. My book in progress on Maria Edgeworth explores in some detail the aesthetic and moral modes pioneered by Barbauld and developed by Edgeworth, relating these to a continuing tradition of women's writing, one by no means limited to texts for children. Georgian women writers for the young were not just innovators in juvenile authorship and educational practice, but also laid the groundwork for the major nineteenth-century female literary traditions.

7. Discussing a work on the female social condition and influence in 1804, the *Critical Review* illustrates this point with its ambivalent praise of Barbauld: "We think very highly of this lady's intellectual talents, . . . a strength of mind and originality of thought, very seldom found among her own sex, yet in a degree which would not perhaps have claimed any very distinguished notice in ours" (Rev. of *Women,* 458).

8. Lonsdale, xxxiii–xxxiv. Arbitrarily entered under 1775 before the publication of Barbauld's *Lessons,* Johnson's quotation is biographically accurate, his judgement probably reflecting his connection with Mrs. Thrale, another learned mother who spent much time in household teaching. Although Johnson's educational dicta were colored by his own miseries as a child prodigy, "Mrs. Barbauld . . . had his best praise," Hester Lynch Thrale (later Mrs. Piozzi) records. "No man was more struck . . . with voluntary descent from possible splendour to painful duty," not a reading of her teaching that Barbauld would have endorsed (Piozzi, 14). Like Johnson's praise, Lonsdale's defeatist summary belies the extraordinary energy Barbauld threw into her teaching and the inventiveness of her techniques, documented thoroughly in her letters and in records C. W. Brodribb cites. The poet Samuel Rogers records that the famous statesman Charles James Fox "thought Mrs. Barbauld's *Life of Richardson* admirable; and regretted that she wasted her talents in writing books for children (excellent as those books might be), now that there were so many pieces of that description" (95–

96), not recognizing that the proliferation was in great measure due to Barbauld's pioneering efforts.

9. Betsy Rodgers (142) attributes this review to Robert Southey but gives no reference; evidence for the authorship of Croker (who also savaged Maria Edgeworth and Frances Burney D'Arblay among others) is given in Shine and Shine (31). Because England's military fortunes were on the upswing, Barbauld's antiwar, antiheroic stance made her political prophecy of England's downfall doubly daring. Even Henry Crabb Robinson, who deeply revered Barbauld and her work, felt she exposed herself to the "charge of presumption" (64). The same stance informs much of her writing for children.

10. Marrs, 2:81–82. Byron's animus against the period's intellectual women may be better known than that of other Romantic men, but Lamb's hostility marks a whole generation of male authors newly contending against an ever increasing and very successful contingent of women writers, many of them professedly didactic. Much recent analysis of masculine Romantic poetry, such as Marlon Ross's, touches indirectly on this issue; Mary Jacobus on Wordsworth's usurpation of the mother's educative role represents a much needed start at relating childhood in adult poetry to the contemporary pedagogic issues with which it is intertwined (see esp. Jacobus 1989, chap. 9, " 'Behold the Parent Hen': Romantic Pedagogy and Sexual Difference"). For preliminary attempts toward a sociology of the period's authorship, see Tuchman and Haworth. Although a recent study of Lamb's youth claims that the women in his life "gave him an abiding respect for women as his equals," the period's literary men delighted in recording his witty castigations of women writers: "A female poet, or female author of any kind, ranks below an actress, I think" (Courtney, 17; Stoddard, 40). He spoke of literary women as "impudent, forward, unfeminine, and unhealthy in their minds. Instanced, amongst many others, Mrs. Barbauld, who was a torment and curse to her husband. 'Yet,' said Lamb, 'Letitia was only just tinted; she was not what the she-dogs now call an intellectual woman' " (Allsop, 1:218).

11. Educational discourse, which is probably most commonly (and negatively) gendered female these days, was much more highly charged at that time. One reviewer, for example, waxed indignant over Crespigny's *Letters of Advice from a Mother to Her Son:* "Among the peculiar characteristics of the present age of literature is the propensity of our female writers to publish sermons upon education, in the shape of letters, essays, and treatises.... To all such ... we have only to wish more sense, or more diffidence. 'I pray you, woman, being weak, seem so' " (Review of *Letters*).

12. (Muir, 82–99; Hazard, 37). Alan Richardson argues that, in moving from an age of reason to an age of feeling, male writers used memories and fantasies of identification with the mother "to colonize the conventionally feminine domain of sensibility" in their adult poetry; similar erasure and exploitation underlie much thinking about children's literature and education (13).

13. Barbauld's *Legacy* collects miscellaneous pieces from family papers, some written many years earlier. In addition to editing various educational anthologies like *The Female Speaker* (1811), Barbauld continually wrote out fables, riddles, and little tales for young family members and friends, some of which still exist in manuscript. Such writing for her, as for Edgeworth and other female educa-

tors, was affective and relational as well as instructive. Knitting family members together, it literally domesticated education. The preface to the *Speaker* characteristically extols the power of what we read in youth to shape subsequent life.

14. The editor of the Garland facsimile finds the *Hymns* "a stepping-stone between Enlightenment rationalism and Romanticism. The lesson the natural world teaches at first is that God is kind and good. . . . All things are bright and beautiful in Anna Barbauld's world of innocence. If elsewhere in the countryside, new factories are raising chimneys into a dark sky, we see no evidence here of Blake's 'satanic mills.' In the *Hymns* even the onset of winter fails to dull the radiance of this world where 'it is a pleasant thing to be alive' " (1977, viii–ix).

15. "Where in the long catalogue of children's books shall we find any to be compared with them? Many who heard them the first time at their mother's knee can trace to them their deepest, most precious convictions. . . . Still what a freshness and beauty in every page!" exclaimed an English biographer a century after publication of the *Hymns* (Murch, 75), and an American contemporary waxed still more enthusiastic, returning again and again to the "most charming prose hymns ever produced at any time," so "fascinating and simply unsurpassed" that they are as appropriate for a cultivated adult audience as for the very young, evaluations shared by Barbauld's niece Lucy Aikin as well (Murch, 75; Ellis, ix–x, 6–7, 97–99).

16. Bator's edition in *Masterworks* reprints three *Hymns* added to the expanded edition (10, 11, and 12). Since the *Hymns* were widely used in Sunday schools, they served many denominations; "A Forgotten Children's Book" describes a non-Barbauld expansion that attempted to graft sin and sectarianism onto the original (32–33).

17. Even authoritative histories and bibliographies give wildly variant dates for the *Lessons'* original publication; since no copies of the first printings survive and early reading texts are in general very rare, studies often simply hand down whatever their predecessors said. The initial publication dates can be reconstructed from Barbauld's letters and early reviews. Part 1, for children of two to three, and part 2, the first part for children of three, appeared in 1778; part 3, the second for children of three, was apparently published later in 1778, for it is listed as a 1778 imprint, and reviewed with part 4, for children of three to four, dated 1779. Since Charles was born in 1775 and came to the Barbaulds at two, the age-graded series correlated precisely with his growth. Most reprints consist of all four parts; quotes in text are from the 1808 reprint, one of many by Barbauld's publisher, the famous Joseph Johnson, notable not only for his liberal politics but for his pioneering of children's books. He was the publisher of Mary Wollstonecraft and Maria Edgeworth, and his house was a gathering place for radicals, including William Blake and William Godwin.

18. Sir Lawrence Jones, who detested the "nauseating" *Hymns* as much as he did Blake and Wordsworth, seems to be recalling this story, which did indeed worry other mother-teachers, in an "extraordinary case of the censor's blindness . . . a short tale . . . intended for very small children indeed, where 'the bones and blood' . . . are described with the relish we lately reserved for the sinking of a German U-boat. I daresay the child was eaten for an act of disobedience; but the moral is forgotten while the agreeable shudder abides" (33, 28).

19. Barbauld had become a close friend of Joseph Priestley and his wife in his days as a tutor (like Barbauld's father) at Warrington Academy, perhaps the most innovative of the Dissenters' many experiments in higher education. Barbauld's educational work at Palgrave school shares many aims with the college she knew so well. In addition to being a philosopher and scientist, famous for his experiments with electricity and the composition of air, Priestley was an educational innovator who broadened the traditional classical curriculum. He records in his *Autobiography* that, wanting to encourage ease in vernacular writing, he tried verse for himself as well as assigning it to his students and that some of his verses inspired Barbauld's efforts, many of her first poems being written "on occasions that occurred while she was [at his house]," among them the mouse's entrapment (89). Amusingly, Barbauld's mouse makes one kind of educational experiment critique another.

20. The University of California at Los Angeles owns an apparently unique first edition of *The Curious Adventures of a Little White Mouse;* it was later reprinted several times under slightly varying titles. Barbauld's female protest in "The Mouse's Petition" is naturalized as a modern child's poem in Iona Opie and Peter Opie's *Oxford Book of Children's Verse* (79–80). Some of Barbauld's poems are featured in recent anthologies, like Roger Lonsdale's, but the important new collection edited by William McCarthy and Elizabeth Kraft, *The Poems of Anna Laetitia Barbauld,* is the first inclusive edition ever; it prints all known poems, some formerly only in manuscript and many of them relevant to the issues of feminine aesthetics and pedagogy this chapter explores. The mouse's curious adventures reside in the Children's Book Collection, a division within Special Collections, University Research Library, University of California, Los Angeles. When this essay was written in 1990, Barbauld's writing for children had received very little scholarly consideration. That's already beginning to change: see, for example, Sarah Robbins, *"Lessons for Children* and Teaching Mothers." Bill McCarthy and I will be collaborating on a facsimile edition of Barbauld's *Lessons* in the future. When McCarthy's biography of Barbauld is completed, it will provide an invaluable context for assessing early women educators' contributions: Barbauld's private school pupils were extraordinarily distinguished, and her methods for teaching were innovative and fondly recalled.

BIBLIOGRAPHY

"A Forgotten Children's Book." *Hibbert Journal* 63.3 (1964): 27–34. [Aikin, Anna Laetitia.] *Poems.* London: Joseph Johnson, 1773. [Aikin, John, and Anna Laetitia Barbauld.] *Evenings at Home; or, The Juvenile Budget Opened. Consisting of a Variety of Miscellaneous Pieces, for the Instruction and Amusement of Young Persons.* 6 vols. London: J. Johnson, 1792–96.
Aikin, Dr. [John], and Mrs. [Anna Laetitia] Barbauld. *Evenings at Home; or, The Juvenile Budget Opened.* 15th ed. Edited by Arthur Aikin and Miss [Lucy] Aikin. London: Baldwin and Cradock; Longman, Rees; John Murray; Joseph Booker; Darton and Harvey; Hamilton, Adams; Smith, Elder; and Simpkin, Marshall, 1836.

[Allsop, Thomas, ed.] *Letters, Conversations and Recollections of S. T. Coleridge.* 2 vols. London: Edward Moxon, 1836.

Alston, R. C. *Spelling Books.* Vol. 4 of *A Bibliography of the English Language from the Invention of Printing to the Year 1800.* Bradford, England: Ernest Cummins, 1967.

Balibar, Renée. "National Language, Education, Literature." In *Literature, Politics, and Theory: Papers from the Essex Conference 1976–84,* edited by Francis Barker, Peter Hulme, Margaret Iversen, and Diana Loxley, 126–47. London: Methuen, 1986.

Barbauld, Anna Laetitia. [Published as Anna Laetitia Aikin]. *Poems.* London: J. Johnson, 1773.

———. [Published as John Aikin and Anna Laetitia Barbauld]. *Evenings at Home; or, The Juvenile Budget Opened. Consisting of a Variety of Miscellaneous Pieces, for the Instruction and Amusement of Young Persons.* 6 vols. London: J. Johnson, 1792–1796. Vol. 1, 1792, vol. 2, 1773. Later published as *Evenings at Home; or, The Juvenile Budget Opened,* by Dr. [John] Aikin and Mrs. [Anna Laetitia] Barbauld. 15th ed. Edited by Arthur Aikin and Miss [Lucy] Aikin. London: Baldwin and Cradock; Longman, Rees; John Murray; Joseph Booker; Darton and Harvey; Hamilton, Adams; Smith, Elder; and Simpkin, Marshall, 1836.

———. *Lessons for Children: In Four Parts.* 1778–1779. London: J. Johnson, 1808. Part 3 was later published as *Lessons for Children and Little Marrian,* in Aunt Mary's Library for Young Children. Boston: William Carter, [1841].

———. *The Female Speaker; or, Miscellaneous Pieces, in Prose and Verse, Selected from the Best Writers and Adapted to the Use of Young Women.* London: Johnson, 1811.

———. *The Works of Anna Laetitia Barbauld, with a Memoir.* 2 vols. Edited by Lucy Aikin. London: Longman, Hurst, Rees, Orme, Brown, and Green, 1825.

———. *A Legacy for Young Ladies, Consisting of Miscellaneous Pieces, in Prose and Verse.* Edited by Lucy Aikin. London: Longman, Hurst, Rees, Orme, Brown, and Green, 1826.

———. *Hymns in Prose for Children* [facsimile of 1781 1st ed.]. Edited by Miriam Kramnick. In *Classics of Children's Literature, 1621–1932.* New York: Garland, 1977.

———. *Hymns in Prose* [with 3 "Hymns" added after 1st ed.]. In vol. 3 of *Masterworks of Children's Literature,* edited by Robert Bator, 113–29. New York: Stonehill/Chelsea, 1983.

———. *The Poems of Anna Letitia Barbauld.* Edited by William McCarthy and Elizabeth Kraft. Athens: Univ. of Georgia Press, 1994.

Boswell, James. *Boswell's Life of Johnson.* Edited by George Birkbeck Hill. 6 vols. Oxford: Clarendon, 1887.

Brodribb, C. W. "Mrs. Barbauld's School." *Contemporary Review* 148 (Dec. 1935): 731–36.

Bruner, Jerome, with Rita Watson. *Child's Talk: Learning to Use Language.* New York: W. W. Norton, 1983.

Butler, Samuel. *The Way of All Flesh.* 1903. Edited by Royal A. Gettmann. New York: Holt, Rinehart, and Winston, 1960.

Byron, George Gordon, Lord. *Don Juan*. 1819–1824. Edited by Leslie A. Marchand. Boston: Houghton Mifflin, 1958.

Clanchy, M. T. "Learning to Read in the Middle Ages and the Role of Mothers." In *Studies in the History of Reading,* edited by Greg Brooks and A. K. Pugh, 33–39. Reading, G.B.: Centre for the Teaching of Reading, University of Reading School of Education, with the United Kingdom Reading Association, 1984.

Courtney, Winifred F. *Young Charles Lamb, 1775–1802*. New York and London: New York Univ. Press, 1982.

[Croker, John Wilson.] Review of *Eighteen Hundred and Eleven,* by Anna Laetitia Barbauld. *Quarterly Review* 7.14 (June 1812): 309–13.

The Curious Adventures of a Little White Mouse; or, A Bad Boy Changed, in a very Comical Manner, into A Good Boy. London: Printed, and Sold by all the Booksellers in Town and Country [c. 1780].

Curran, Stuart. "Romantic Poetry: The I Altered." In *Romanticism and Feminism,* edited by Anne K. Mellor, 185–207. Bloomington: Indiana Univ. Press, 1988.

Darton, F. J. Harvey. *Children's Books in England: Five Centuries of Social Life.* 1932. 3d ed., revised by Brian Alderson. Cambridge: Cambridge Univ. Press, 1982.

[D'Arblay, Frances Burney.] *Diary and Letters of Madame D'Arblay (1778–1840)*. Edited by Charlotte Barrett. 6 vols. London: Macmillan, 1905.

de Lauretis, Teresa. "Eccentric Subjects: Feminist Theory and Historical Consciousness." *Feminist Studies* 16.1 (Spring 1990): 115–50.

De Quincey, Thomas. *Autobiographic Sketches*. Boston: Houghton Mifflin; Cambridge: Riverside, 1876.

De Sola Pinto, Vivian. "William Blake, Isaac Watts, and Mrs. Barbauld." In *The Divine Vision: Studies in the Poetry and Art of William Blake.* 1957. Edited by Vivian De Sola Pinto, 67–87. 1957. New York: Haskell, 1968.

Edgeworth, Maria, and Richard Lovell Edgeworth. *Practical Education.* 2 vols. London: J. Johnson, 1798.

Ellis, Grace A. [later Oliver]. *A Memoir of Anna Laetitia Barbauld.* 2 vols. Boston: James R. Osgood, 1874.

Foucault, Michel. *The History of Sexuality: Volume 1, An Introduction.* Translated by Robert Hurley. New York: Vintage/Random House, 1980.

Foulkes, A. P. "Capitalist Integration Myths." In *Literature and Propaganda,* 45–54. London: Methuen, 1983.

Gilbert, Sandra M., and Susan Gubar. *The Madwoman in the Attic: The Woman Writer and the Nineteenth-Century Literary Imagination.* New Haven: Yale Univ. Press, 1979.

Gossman, Lionel. "Literature and Education." *New Literary History* 13.2 (Winter 1982): 341–71.

[Griffiths, Ralph.] Review of *Poetic Trifles,* by Elizabeth Moody. *Monthly Review* 2d ser. 27 (Dec. 1798): 442–47.

Hale, Mrs. S[arah] J[osepha], ed. *Things By Their Right Names, and Other Stories, Fables, and Moral Pieces . . . from the Writings of Mrs. Barbauld: With a Sketch of Her Life.* Boston: Marsh, Capen, Lyon, and Webb, 1840.

————. *Woman's Record; or, Sketches of All Distinguished Women . . . with Selections from Female Writers of Every Age.* 2d ed. rev. New York: Harper and Brothers, 1855.

Hawkins, David. "The Roots of Literacy." *Literacy in America. Daedalus* 119.2 (Spring 1990): 1–14.

Haworth, H. E. "Romantic Female Writers and the Critics." *Texas Studies in Literature and Language* 17.4 (Winter 1976): 725–36.

Hazard, Paul. *Books, Children, and Men.* Translated by Marguerite Mitchell. 1944. 5th ed. Boston: Horn Book, 1983.

Hazlitt, William. *Lectures on the English Poets* [1818] *and The Spirit of the Age: or Contemporary Portraits* [1825]. Everyman's Library. London: Dent, 1910; New York: Dutton, 1964.

Hirsch, E. D., Jr. *Innocence and Experience: An Introduction to Blake.* New Haven: Yale Univ. Press, 1964.

Holland, Sir Henry. *Recollections of Past Life.* New York: D. Appleton, 1875.

Hunt, Peter. "Examining Children's Literature: Children's Books at the University of Wales." *Signal* 62 (May 1990): 147–58.

Jacobus, Mary. "The Question of Language: Men of Maxims and *The Mill on the Floss.*" In *Writing and Sexual Difference,* edited by Elizabeth Abel, 207–22. *Critical Inquiry* 8.2 (Winter 1981).

————. *Romanticism, Writing, and Sexual Difference: Essays on* The Prelude. Oxford: Clarendon, 1989.

Jones, L[awrence] E., Sir. *A Victorian Boyhood.* London: Macmillan, 1955.

Le Breton, Anna Letitia. *Memoir of Mrs. Barbauld, including Letters and Notices of Her Family and Friends.* London: George Bell, 1874.

Le Guin, Ursula K. "Bryn Mawr Commencement Address (1986)." In *Dancing at the Edge of the World: Thoughts on Words, Women, Places,* 147–60. New York: Grove, 1989.

Lonsdale, Roger, ed. *Eighteenth-Century Women Poets: An Oxford Anthology.* Oxford: Oxford Univ. Press, 1989.

Marrs, Edwin W., Jr., ed. *The Letters of Charles and Mary Anne Lamb.* 3 vols. Ithaca: Cornell Univ. Press, 1976.

Michael, Ian. *The Teaching of English from the Sixteenth Century to 1870.* Cambridge: Cambridge Univ. Press, 1987.

Monaghan, E. Jennifer. "Literacy Instruction and Gender in Colonial New England." In *Reading in America: Literature and Social History,* edited by Cathy N. Davidson, 53–80. Baltimore: Johns Hopkins Univ. Press, 1989.

Muir, Percy. "A Monstrous Regiment." In *English Children's Books, 1600–1900,* 82–99. New York: Praeger, 1954.

Murch, Jerom. *Mrs. Barbauld and Her Contemporaries: Sketches of Some Literary and Scientific Englishwomen.* London: Longmans, Green, 1877.

Myers, Mitzi. "Reform or Ruin: 'A Revolution in Female Manners.'" In *Studies in Eighteenth-Century Culture,* vol. 11, edited by Harry C. Payne, 199–216. Madison: Univ. of Wisconsin Press, 1982.

————. "Impeccable Governesses, Rational Dames, and Moral Mothers: Mary Wollstonecraft and the Female Tradition in Georgian Children's Books." In

Children's Literature, vol. 14, edited by Margaret Higonnet and Barbara Rosen, 31–59. New Haven: Yale Univ. Press, 1986.

Opie, Iona, and Peter Opie, eds. *The Oxford Book of Children's Verse.* 1973. London: Oxford Univ. Press, 1980.

Pickering, Samuel F., Jr. "Mrs. Barbauld's *Hymns in Prose:* 'An Air-Blown Particle' of Romanticism?" *Southern Humanities Review,* Summer 1975: 259–68.

———. *John Locke and Children's Books in Eighteenth-Century England.* Knoxville: Univ. of Tennessee Press, 1981.

Piozzi, Hester Lynch [Thrale]. *Anecdotes of Samuel Johnson.* Edited by S. C. Roberts. 1925. New York: Books for Libraries/Arno, 1980.

Poovey, Mary. *The Proper Lady and the Woman Writer: Ideology as Style in the Works of Mary Wollstonecraft, Mary Shelley, and Jane Austen.* Chicago: University of Chicago Press, 1984.

Priestley, Joseph. *Autobiography of Joseph Priestley.* Edited by Jack Lindsay. Bath: Adams and Dart, 1970.

Review of *Familiar Conversations for the Use of Young Children . . . ,* by Harriet Mandeville. *Monthly Review* n.s., 2 (Oct. 1798): 329.

Review of *Lessons for Children . . . ,* by [Anna Laetitia Barbauld]. *Monthly Review* 59 (July 1778): 25–28.

Review of *Lessons for Children . . . ,* by [Anna Laetitia Barbauld]. *Critical Review* 46 (Aug. 1778): 160.

Review of *Lessons for Children . . . ,* by [Anna Laetitia Barbauld]. *Critical Review* 47 (April 1779): 320.

Review of *Lessons for Children . . . ,* by [Anna Laetitia Barbauld]. *Monthly Review* 60 (June 1779): 487–88.

Review of *Letters of Advice from a Mother to Her Son,* by Mrs. Crespigny. *Annual Review, and History of Literature for 1803* 2 (1804): 450.

Review of *Women: Their Condition and Influence in Society,* by Joseph Alexander Segur. *Critical Review* 3d ser., 2 (Aug. 1804): 457–[61].

Richardson, Alan. "Romanticism and the Colonization of the Feminine." In *Romanticism and Feminism,* edited by Anne K. Mellor, 13–25. Bloomington: Indiana Univ. Press, 1988.

Robberds, J. W., ed. *A Memoir of the Life and Writings of the Late William Taylor of Norwich.* 2 vols. London: John Murray, 1843.

Robbins, Sarah. "*Lessons for Children* and Teaching Mothers: Mrs. Barbauld's Primer for the Textual Construction of Middle-Class Domestic Pedagogy." *The Lion and the Unicorn* 17.2 (December 1993): 135–51.

Robinson, Henry Crabb. *Henry Crabb Robinson on Books and Their Writers.* Edited by Edith J. Morley. 3 vols. London: Dent, 1938.

Rodgers, Betsy. *Georgian Chronicle: Mrs. Barbauld and Her Family.* London: Methuen, 1958.

Rogers, Samuel. *Recollections of the Table-Talk of Samuel Rogers.* Edited by [W. Sharpe]. New York: D. Appleton, 1856.

Ross, Marlon. *The Contours of Masculine Desire: Romanticism and the Rise of Women's Poetry.* Oxford: Oxford Univ. Press, 1989.

Scott, Walter Sidney, ed. *Letters of Maria Edgeworth and Anna Laetitia Barbauld Selected from the Lushington Papers.* N.p.: Golden Cockerel, 1953.

Shine, Hill, and Helen Chadwick Shine. *The Quarterly Review under Gifford: Identification of Contributors 1809–1824.* Chapel Hill: Univ. of North Carolina Press, 1949.

Stoddard, Richard Henry, ed. *Personal Recollections of Lamb, Hazlitt, and Others.* Bric-a-Brac Series. New York: Scribner, Armstrong, 1875.

Taylor, Ann, and Jane Taylor. *Original Poems for Infant Minds and Rhymes for the Nursery.* 1804; 1805; 1806. 3 vols. in 1. Edited by Christina Duff Stewart. New York: Garland, 1976.

Thackeray, Miss [Anne Isabella]. (Mrs. Richmond Ritchie). *A Book of Sibyls: Mrs. Barbauld, Miss Edgeworth, Mrs. Opie, Miss Austen.* London: Smith, Elder, 1883.

Tuchman, Gaye, with Nina E. Fortin. *Edging Women Out: Victorian Novelists, Publishers, and Social Change.* New Haven: Yale Univ. Press, 1989.

Watts, Ruth E. "The Unitarian Contribution to the Development of Female Education, 1790–1850." *History of Education* 9.4 (Dec. 1980): 273–86.

Williams, Porter, Jr. "The Influence of Mrs. Barbauld's *Hymns in Prose for Children* upon Blake's *Songs of Innocence and Experience*." In *A Fair Day in the Affections: Literary Essays in Honour of Robert B. White, Jr.,* edited by Jack D. Durant and M. Thomas Hester, 131–46. Raleigh, N.C.: Winston, 1980.

[Woodfall, William.] Review of *Poems,* by Miss [Anna Laetitia] Aikin. *Monthly Review, or, Literary Journal* 48 (Jan.–Feb. 1773): 54–59, 133–37.

Yonge, Miss [Charlotte]. "Children's Literature of the Last Century: 1. Nursery Books of the Eighteenth Century." *Macmillan's Magazine* 20.117 (July 1869): 229–37.

Zall, Paul M. "Wordsworth's 'Ode' and Mrs. Barbauld's *Hymns*." *Wordsworth Circle* 1.4 (Autumn 1970): 177–79.

———. "The Cool World of Samuel Taylor Coleridge: Mrs. Barbauld's Crew and the Building of a Mass Reading Class." *Wordsworth Circle* 2.3 (Summer 1971): 74–79.

13

Becoming a Warrior: Lessons of the Feminist Workplace

Louise Wetherbee Phelps

Invitation to Power

> Composition is now perceived to be in a changing relation to its original carnivalesque status. . . . Composition is not the formerly accepted lower-class enterprise completing a higher mission within English, but it is not yet something else.
>
> —*Susan Miller*

> As the doors to the ivory tower have opened, we have lost both innocence and purity.
>
> —*Evelyn Fox Keller and Helene Moglen'*

The Meanings of Feminization

A number of feminist analyses posit feminization as a condition that afflicts composition as a discipline. Scholars analyzing composition as feminized draw attention to its historical lack of institutional power and seek to explicate (and condemn) this condition as a function of gender associations. (See, e.g., Connors, chap. 4, this vol., and 1990; Holbrook; Flynn 1991; Miller 1991a, 1991b.) They elaborate and document what is quickly accepted as a truism: we are a field dominated in numbers by women, concerned with a subject and a teaching practice perceived by many academics and the public as low-status, elementary, service-oriented, menial "women's work." As such, composition has suffered from minimal resources, intellectual invisibility to other fields, subordination to others' interests and goals, and a lack of institutional authority and control. This body of work suggests a kind of irresolvable, chicken-and-egg reciprocity between the low value ascribed to the content of composition (for instance, writing as ordinary language, children and students as audience and authors, practice as a disciplinary motive) and the overwhelming predominance of women doing the jobs of composition. This complex link provokes a gendered response even to the work of men teaching and researching writing, a response that dismisses in particular any values perceived as "feminine."

"Feminized" in this work, and for most of us intuitively, is almost synonymous with weakness, although Susan Miller has done a highly subtle analysis that reveals some of the ironies that mark this condition (1991a, 121–41; 1991b, 46–49). These include the fact that women's dominance of the profession in numbers and, some might argue, intellectual power has not translated without struggle into recognition, respect, access to journals, influence, and leadership positions within composition itself. Miller also points out the blurred gender coding that overloads "the figure of a composition teacher . . . with symbolic as well as actual functions," combining comforting and powerful, familial and public images of female writing teachers as nurse-mothers with that of the stern Miss Fidditch—disciplinarian, mother-power figure, sadomaschistic Barbarella (1991b, 47–48). These powerfully ambivalent attitudes and mixed messages toward women as writing teachers replicate cultural myths of womanhood that originate in family and home. As such, they are not merely external projections: they resonate with women's conflicted self-understandings of their teaching, described by Madeleine Grumet in terms of the passages and contradictions that link women's experiences of reproduction and nurture with curriculum. Together these images represent to Miller a "complexly feminized cultural call to identity imposed on teachers of composition" (49) that persists profoundly despite apparently successful attempts to redefine the field and resituate it politically in the academy. And so, as she documents, do feelings of stigma and alienation (1991a, 205–60).

As a writing program administrator, what I find incomplete or inadequate in these characterizations of feminization is that they fail to analyze the problem of empowerment or help us meet it when it actually comes—accompanied by its own paradoxes and discrepancies between appearance and reality, marked by lags, slippages, and regressions, but genuinely different for all that.[1] The meaning of composition's gendering is not immutably fixed but is susceptible to transformation (though not simple reversal) when its members, and particularly its women, begin to pursue their intellectual projects and enact their values with confidence and some measure of institutional support. Reimagining composition as a site for such enactments is, in part, the subject of new feminist pedagogies. But we are now seeing the rarer but potentially significant cases where institutional circumstances (not necessarily or even likely feminist in origins) create occasions for composition, through programmatic action, to join in and affect the broader policies and pragmatics of higher education itself.

Composition and rhetoric established a foothold in the academy in the 1980s, by tenuring and promoting its faculty and by developing successful undergraduate and graduate programs. Through writing across-the-curriculum programs and leadership in such areas of educational reform as pedagogies of active learning and evaluation of teaching, writing faculty have now begun to play a role in academic life beyond their own programs and universities. Women in composition studies are being appointed in larger numbers as writing program directors, graduate directors, department chairs, and deans, roles that position them to become future college presidents or heads of foundations. Men in composition face many of the same problems, as representatives of feminized disciplines and perhaps advocates of principles identified as feminine or feminist (see, e.g., Olson and Moxley, on the limited authority of writing program administrators). Those of us taking up these roles occupy an unstable niche that is neither outside nor genuinely inside the academic power structure but mixes features of both. More truly marginal than in the feminist sense, we are like animals of the tidal zone, neither sea nor land creatures. This, not feminization as we have known it, is the liminal condition we live in, the "now": "Our memories . . . blend the immediate past with the anticipation of the soon to be, and a living amalgam of these—not some infinitesimal pointlike instant forever fleeing out of reach—is our now" (Gleick, 124–25).

Implicit in any feminist critique of disenfranchisement is a utopian vision of empowerment: a future in which women have opportunities for leadership and influence, a future in which composition is not merely tolerated and contained but becomes a positive force in higher education. Yet analyses of composition as feminized can never fully anticipate the shift in the problem space that occurs when we begin to move into the tidal zone of power, nor the peculiar challenges of a transitional period. They do not contemplate the guilt and ambivalence and jealousies that will inevitably accompany accession to power; nor do they confront the radical transformation it requires in both strategies and moral under-standings. Academic feminists have preceded us: "Recognizing the strat-egies of marginality to be adaptive (although not devoid of the critical potential for subversion) we rushed openly to seize the opportunities offered and claim territory in those bastions of privilege from which we had been barred. Fallen creatures now, we look at one another's naked-ness in dismay" (Keller and Moglen, 494).

In short, our current understanding of the feminization of composi-tion provides neither ethical nor strategic guidance in "right action," either for women who, as senior faculty and administrators, must learn to exercise power wisely or for the field as it begins to acquire resources, centrality to an institution's mission, and the increased clout that goes with this position. Handling our own power, that is, coming to terms with the ineluctable authority of the writing teacher, is a central, unresolved problem for feminist classroom pedagogy. It becomes acute when the domains and forces involved are larger: programs, departments, insti-tutions, disciplines, and the winds of social change that are sweeping over all of them.

So far, I am begging an important question. When you are offered a position of power, there are many ways you can take it up—ways of being and acting that we must learn to choose, not just fall into, unthinking. Leadership "style" expresses how you conceive yourself in relation to the system that authorizes your position (legitimated, subversive, re-formist, conflicted, coopted. . . ?) and how you envision your responsi-bilities to and relationships with the people whose work and energies you direct, as distinct from the people, entities, and purposes this work serves. But you also have a choice not to take it up at all. You can refuse the appointment, as radical leftists might urge, arguing that to accept is to "buy into" an oppressive system of dominance, to be corrupted by the institution and the ideologies it both embodies and reproduces. To refuse in this spirit expresses despair over the possibility of evolutionary change or internal cultural transformation through a constructive project pur-sued from within. A logical corollary is the moral imperative to subvert any effort by others to do so. (Those who don't get their hands dirty have, at best, very ambivalent feelings for those who do.)

1986 and recurrently: *Why are you always bringing up money . . . limits . . . evaluation? I can't believe you're saying those things! You sound just like an administrator!*
   —Faculty friends[2]

Because this position is held implicitly or explicitly by many colleagues, including many of those we "direct" in our programs, it presents the most profound challenge to those of us actually trying to act on a utopian hope. I reject both the despair and the adversarial, deeply pessimistic characterization of American education and American society that many leftist intellectuals hold. But I am nonetheless compelled by the pervasiveness, sincerity, and idealism of those beliefs, and by my own conscience, to examine from an ethical perspective not only my own motives but also the implications of exercising power legitimated by institutional structures in what must always be an imperfect society. Because I think that for most Americans such decisions are local and context-specific, rather than apocalyptic, I will postpone a response in order to unfold that context and the highly particularized ethical issues it raised for me. For the moment, I will simply say this: if as feminists we are arguing for broadly distributed power and access, we must be prepared to imagine that one can ethically have visions, lead, and wield power despite the imperfectibility of institutions and the tragic limitations of human action.

But for composition and its women to accede to institutional power is an enormously complex business, an experience that pressures feminists to develop new understandings of power and virtue in the workplace that do not depend on purity or unalloyed innocence and are not predicated only on insights derived from the feminist "standpoint." Standpoint feminists argue that women's struggle against oppression positions them to develop understandings of social realities that are truer and less distorted than masculinist views and can presumably form the basis for founding new, morally superior social orders.[3] Feminists in composition make such assumptions when they imagine a safe, utopian social space (a classroom or a program) informed by culturally "feminine" principles like cooperation, dialogue, nonhierarchical structures, and "caring." But this position has its dangers, principally the fact that it doesn't provide a vision realistic enough to guide us through the minefield of ambiguities, complexities, and pain entailed in wielding power responsibly.

Imagine, then, that we do secure a less tenuous position in the academy, as we argue and struggle successfully on different campuses to demonstrate the centrality and synergistic value of our enterprise. Suppose, also, that this enterprise remains explicitly and visibly "gendered"—feminized in its position, feminist in some sense yet to be defined. Whatever the fate of this struggle—however still subject to the old ills of women and writing programs, however uncertain our perch in changing institutions—still, it has happened, for me and for others. And there is no going back.

From this perspective, accounts of the feminization of composition that gaze exclusively at the past or perpetually postpone a utopian future are dated as guides to action. A critical understanding of the past is vital to our future, especially since descriptions of the negative impact of feminization are still true, most of the time, most places. But if not interpreted and promulgated carefully, such descriptions could reify and even valorize our past condition as virtuous, with troubling consequences for our willingness to act in a flawed world. The point is not to discourage these important studies of feminization but to complement them with new feminist visions that are instructed by genuine, morally complex and practically messy experiments in building new orders—collective experiences of wielding power and accepting responsibility.

The Door Opens and We Find Pandora's Box

Pandora: The first mortal woman, fashioned from clay by Hephaestus, who intended that by her charms she should bring misery on the human race. Aphrodite gave her beauty and the art of healing; Apollo, the ability to sing; Athena, rich ornaments and skills in woman's work; the Graces, captivating charm; Hermes, eloquence; and Zeus gave her a beautiful box, which he forbade her to open. . . . When she opened the box given by Zeus, the plagues of mankind escaped and all that remained in the box was Elpis (hope).
—David Kravitz

In 1985 I was an assistant professor denied tenure by my department, watching a new regime unceremoniously dismantle the nationally respected doctoral program in which I taught composition and rhetoric. These linked events expressed the complex mix of fear, envy, and contempt that my largely male colleagues felt toward the field. People speculated about a general backlash in the mideighties against composition and rhetoric, as departments and universities across the country denied tenure to the cohort of composition professors hired six years before. The irrational processes and intense feelings surrounding many of these decisions suggested that academics were reacting to a perceived threat posed by the growing strength of composition and rhetoric. But threatening to what—to scholarly standards? traditional humanism? weak literature programs? other new paradigms for reorganizing English studies? departmental resources or institutional power? There were as many interpretations as there were schools.

One year later I was a tenured full professor and program director at another university, overseeing hundreds of instructors teaching writing to thousands of students, managing a budget of more than a million dollars. Fired because I was a scholar in composition and rhetoric, now I was hired for the same reason, selected over candidates with more administrative experience explicitly in order to assure that the future writing program would be intellectually grounded in the research and theory of the field.

That spring at conventions I marveled with my peers at the ironic game of musical chairs by which those denied tenure had moved into tenured senior positions elsewhere. Just one year before, we had anxiously exchanged information and experiences of job interviews; now we were leading searches ourselves, building undergraduate or graduate programs in writing and rhetoric. Inescapably, I understood my new leadership role as not merely personal but also political. Symbolically as well as substantively—by advertising the appointment as tenured, treating reform of writing instruction as a major initiative, having the new director report directly to the dean of arts and sciences—the university had, in hiring me, deliberately acknowledged composition and rhetoric as a scholarly field and invested some institutional power in its members and programmatic expressions.

From the beginning, then, my own responsibilities, ambitions, and opportunities were inextricably entangled with the fortunes of composition in the academy. Any sustained communal project regarded as significant for its institution—a teaching program as much as a research group, a technological venture, or an artistic collaborative—simultaneously realizes the intellectual processes and content of a field (its relation to ideas) and persuasively dramatizes these to students and other faculty, enabling members of that field collectively to gain respect and political power in their institution and within the national academic community. In the case of composition, we seemed in 1986 at a historic moment when programmatic inventions like writing across the curriculum and degrees certifying a generation of scholars genuinely trained in composition and rhetoric promised to legitimize the field and open the doors to the ivory tower. I felt myself representative, not singular, in my opportunity.

It wasn't so clear what being a woman had to do with all this.

Spring 1986: *On the plane carrying me toward my interview, I listened with growing dismay as a likeable future colleague described the structure* *of administration she and other women had already planned for the new writing program. She proudly showed me a chart of the organization: it showed a flat line marked off with four side-by-side directorial slots representing the director and three other faculty. This, she said, is the collegial model. We don't want the administrative model, which places the director at the top of a hierarchy. But what does it mean to be director, then? I asked. What authority would I have to make decisions? What's the difference between me and the other "directors"? None, she answered. You will just be first among equals.*

Spring 1986 and recurrently: *Women say to me suspiciously of a woman colleague: Watch out for her. She has a thing about power.*

Fall 1986: *The chancellor greeted me warmly at the door during his party to welcome new faculty. He shook my hand enthusiastically: I understand you're the one who's going to guarantee that every graduate of this university is literate!*

1988: *About fourteen people with administrative responsibilities in the Writing Program attend a professional development workshop in which a consultant earnestly administers a questionnaire on leadership style. The group includes several faculty directors, program coordinators who lead teacher groups, and staff directors. All but four are female. Your answers map you onto a color grid that labels your style as "analytic" (green), "nurturing" (blue), or "assertive-directive" (red). Almost everyone, including three of the males, falls mostly under "blue." I turn out red, with only two others—one male, one female. However, my answers are perversely mixed (you like to impose your views on other people—false; you like to subordinate your energies to other people's goals and visions—false; you talk better than you listen—true; you like to collaborate—true). So, depending on how I interpret dots all over the spectrum, I am ambiguously pink.*

If you had asked me in 1986, I would have readily acknowledged that as a woman catapulted from obscurity into a leadership role—and a peculiarly ill-defined and demanding one—I could expect problems with authority. But if I recognized this response to me as sexism, my sense of it was very subliminal and surfaced only occasionally. In retrospect this amazes me.

There were personal reasons I might have discounted or minimized such responses to the prospect of women in power. More important, though, identity is not singular, and I was a writing teacher before I was generic "woman." My political antennae were tuned to pick up shifts in attitudes toward composition itself, at a university where the euphoria of anticipated change was proportional to the disgracefully low position and official neglect of writing instruction in the past. I interpreted the anxieties of women colleagues sympathetically, as exhibiting the lingering effects and distortions created by that history, not by their gender or mine. It was evident from my interviews that pugnacious critics lurked in wait; that several other units resented the potential diversion of resources to a writing program and wanted to keep it under control; that it was delicate for a recent assistant professor and an outsider to "direct" colleagues, especially senior ones, in the very revolution they had fomented so successfully; that emotions among writing teachers ran deep and ambivalent about the unknown future. I didn't have to look far for plausible explanations of resistance to me as the symbol and instrument of change. So my reading of these challenges submerged gender in the situation of composition itself as it was exemplified at my institution: a past of profound subordination and neglect; a future of amorphous but exciting promise; the turbulence and chaos necessary to cross this gap; the resulting anxieties, inertia, tension, suspicion, and opposition to anyone charged with implementing such change. (I wonder how often women in composition have made this transference.)

What I missed here (just as well, since it might have paralyzed me with cynicism or despair) was the triple burden created for the woman leader in composition by the intertwinings of power with gender, teaching, and writing.

Feminists have shown that sexism—social structures and behaviors that exclude or stereotype or devalue or dominate women—doesn't apply only to individual women. It extends to their contributions as a group, to "women's work," to the point that women themselves, and society, have no names for some of their activities and do not recognize and define them as work (see, e.g., DeVault). Compositionists know that most university faculty see the teaching of writing as service, not "work"—that is, not intellectual work (the only kind that counts in the academy). I saw the connection, but incompletely. What I had yet to learn, on the bones, was the circuit of devaluation that runs from women in general to women's work to composition as a feminized discipline and back to the concrete institutional project—the writing program as an enterprise, and its people. The program as project is ignored as an intellectual force or set of ideas insofar as it is perceived as a bunch of women just doing a remedial service; dismissed or critiqued (as requiring structure and external control) insofar as its practices are perceived

as soft and feminine; vilified insofar as its values and leaders are perceived as dangerously, powerfully "feminist" or simply because it begins
to be too successful in a competitive environment. Such attitudes get an
extra jolt from the enormous ego investment most people have in their
own writing and in moralistic beliefs about what counts as "good writing."

Too often, these intense feelings are concentrated and discharged
malevolently on the embodied persons of the women, teachers and leaders alike, who construct their program and teach composition with bravery, fear, and ambivalence.

**1990, from a letter protesting peer evaluation by professional writ-
ing instructors (PWIs), mainly female:** *"The evaluators . . . are persons
of such minor intellectual, pedagogical, and executive attainments that they
have no tenable authority in matters of academic deliberation. They are
flunkies. . . . Considered as an intellectual enterprise, the Writing Program
is very widely agreed to be the shabbiest and shallowest sector of the whole
College."*
—a senior professor of English, male

1991, from a letter following an evaluation visit: *"I see the curriculum
in your program as thoughtfully planned, the support you give staff members
as extraordinary, the inventiveness of the staff as striking, and indeed the
teachers (from conversations, and student comments) as among the best
I've ever seen anywhere . . . the most creative and thoughtful . . . teaching
writing courses that foster such informative investigations that I genuinely
wish I could have had them when I was an undergraduate."*
—a senior scholar doing a national study of writing programs

1992, from a letter distributed during a program review: *"The PWIs
are largely ne'er-do-wells, who are middle-aged, otherwise unemployed, and
very susceptible to [the director's] promises of power and prestige."*
—a senior professor of English, female

1992, from the program review: *"The collaborative professional learning that goes on in the Program at all levels—among FTFs [full-time fac-
ulty], PWIs, and TAs [teaching assistants]—is a model of its own kind. The
result, in our opinion, has been the creation of a motivated, dedicated, and
professionally sophisticated and knowledgeable group of teachers. . . . The
PWIs . . . represent a talented and valuable resource for the University."*
—report from an external review team

In the face of all this that replays old gender themes, and sad ones, I want to insist that my experience as a writing program administrator calls for a feminist analysis of a different kind from any that I have found so far in the fast-developing feminism of composition and rhetoric.

Why a different analysis?

Simply because my concern as a feminist here is *not* with the historical denial of power to composition, and to women, and the adaptive strategies of weakness—"indirection, unobtrusiveness, and even invisibility"—that have been required to survive the realities of exclusion and devaluation (Keller and Moglen, 494). Admittedly, these concerns and the behaviors that provoke them (underestimation, paternalism, misunderstanding, indifference, denial of access, silencing, slander, harassment, personal abuse . . .) do not go away when the door opens a crack and we squeeze in. In trying to gain distance while writing this reflection over two years of transition from my role as writing program director, I have often been hurled back into the vortex of emotions such attitudes evoke: shock, indignation, anger, frustration, disappointment, loss of trust. Because dismissive and demeaning behaviors linger, recur, even intensify as women and their projects in composition grow stronger, and because good people still find such behaviors unremarkable and unworthy of censure or moral outrage, they have colored my work and my life as a writing program administrator dark beyond my (naive) expectations. Because they have hurt others I felt charged to protect and support, I will not forget or pass over them lightly in these reflections.[4]

1986: *I'm not worried about her ability to learn the administrative skills. But I doubt if she has the faintest comprehension how lonely it will be.*
—one administrator to another, about hiring me

Finally, though, these painful emotions are not at the core of my experience as a woman directing a writing program, nor should their distorting effects be allowed to define sourly the enterprise or the community. They are simply the penumbra. The core is joy: the fun, the ingenuity, the collaboration, the exhilaration when something works, the laughter, the leap, the learning. What compels my attention, my passion, and my intellectual interest as a feminist is the thrill of possibility in our accession to power; the moral, practical, and rhetorical complexities that we encounter in daily work on constructive projects in real-world contexts; the feminism that might arise in such a crucible. Like Pandora, I

must open the box. It's a myth that has always called for feminist rein-
terpretations.

Be careful what you wish: it might come true.
—*moral of a fairy-tale*

The sections that follow model some needed ways to measure feminists'
and compositionists' utopian visions against the rich density of practice
that develops when we get our wish. Such experience should not frus-
trate and embitter us with its flaws and failures, the gap it unfolds between hope and achievement, even though these are inevitable and dis-
illusioning. Rather, it teaches us to recalibrate and deepen our visions
themselves, to construct a more adequately complex and nuanced feminism.

Given the compass of this essay and the thickness of a communal
experience, there is much I've had to leave out. To clear up some potential misunderstandings about my purposes and claims, I'd like to acknowledge two kinds of deliberate omissions.

I present my program and my work as an administrator as an experiment in feminism. There are many ways one might take that claim:
autobiographically, to define myself as a feminist; empirically, requiring
proof; proudly, as a celebration of success; cynically, as a caution against
disillusion; prescriptively, as the basis for advice. However, I mean it in
none of these ways but rather as the phenomenological ground for exploring complexity and the hard choices it creates. Our program did
create many structures and practice many strategies that insiders and
outsiders alike have called feminist. We tried both to articulate and to
enact ideals that, in retrospect more than in prospect, I call feminist. But
I am not at all interested in documenting this claim systematically, and
certainly not in making it *heroically*. I am interested in talking about what
might be meant by *feminist* in this context and about the problems of
acting according to such principles even as we were composing or discovering and revising those principles and others were making their own
interpretations of our actions. Some strategies and principles will emerge
incidental to the exploration of complexity, focused on the moments
where ideals and realities converge and complicate our views of both.

For the record, here are a few disclaimers:

- These ideals I call feminist or utopian did not in some absolute
  sense predate the enterprise, certainly not in my mind; they are
  the continually composed, collective product of the experiment.

- They are incompletely and conflictually practiced, shot through with inconsistencies and subject always to alternate, "suspicious" interpretations (leadership as surveillance or exploitation, for example).
- Success and failure are highly relative judgments made from different perspectives on the same event, both in comparing intention to outcome and in judging the ideal itself as appropriate; the contrast is especially sharp between the sweeping perspective of central planners and the ethos created by the ways that program life is particularized and read in corridors, basements, classrooms, and offices, constantly diffusing images outward over student and faculty networks.
- Often the shape and outcomes of a feminist structure or practice are unexpected, whether good or bad—both outcomes and judgment being continually open to reinterpretation.

To say that our ideals or our practices have been influenced by gender is not necessarily a claim to virtue. I have been made acutely aware of some of the negative potentials in a woman-dominated culture, including the prevalence of gossip and indirectness over direct confrontation, the competition and envy that prevails among many academic women, the way women's divided, multiple commitments sometimes preclude ambition or limit engagement, and the tendency to consensus building that may suppress productive eccentricity or "crossness." These are some of the complexities that have been explicitly noted and discussed by members of our writing program but are little acknowledged in work that envisions feminist social orders.

My second omission has to do with theoretical perspectives that might be brought to bear on the work and experience examined here. Of course, any claim to feminist experimentation is subject to competing definitions and conceptions of feminism. Because my purposes here are pretheoretical and only foreshadow the possibilities for my own conceptions of feminism and power, I cannot conduct a dialogue either with other feminist theories (though I touch lightly and occasionally on these) or with theories of power and leadership in a variety of disciplines. To develop these observations in relation to such various systems of understanding is a considerable project, beyond the intent and scope of this work.

Constructing and Complicating the Feminist Workplace

There is no ground to till except what we stand on; only by learning
to apply feminist principles in particular instances does one make
change occur.
—*Nina Baym*

It's not as simple as you think.
—*motto hanging over my mother's desk*

The Composition Workplace Is Always Already Feminist

Most teachers of writing live in a workplace, often relatively self-contained, that is predominantly female and therefore has the potential to
become powerfully feminist. This premise is a little different from the
claim that composition is feminized in the senses described earlier. In
the first place, to understand composition as a workplace is to see it more
prosaically, more materially, and less academically than we normally do
in calling composition a feminized discipline. It brings to mind actual
spaces and people working at desks, in classrooms, in offices, reading
student papers, talking at computers and in mailrooms, and so on. It
implies such concerns as budget, pay, benefits, working conditions, labor, and employer-employee relations. In the second place, to call this
workplace always already "feminist" argues that women already have
some degree of power within it. Because of this potential energy within
feminization, it is only partly ironic to call the writing workplace "feminist" in the various interpretations women might give that term. In some
ways, we already have and have long had a feminist workplace in this
edgy, two-valued sense.

*The English language classroom is a place of power—specifically dis-
cursive power—for women.* In workplaces where writing is taught—elementary, high school, college, and even industry—women in large numbers not only work but also lead, albeit tacitly and without commensurate
recognition, status, and pay. A writing classroom headed by a woman
teacher is a microcosm where she sets the work agenda and exercises
various kinds of control, over who speaks and is heard, what writing or
talk is valued, what is read, who passes with what grades, and in what
terms (intellectual frameworks, social purposes, language) these things
are interpreted and understood.

Granted, many societal factors do shape and limit what women educators can do in classrooms: their own narrow training; the expectations

of their principals, directors, chairs, or supervisors; the school boards and parents with whom they work; available materials and prescribed textbooks; violence in schools; students' own competing agendas, and their personal histories; and social circumstances that outweigh anything teachers can do in the time they have with their pupils (see, e.g., Kline, chap. 11, this vol.). Nonetheless, they hold a special kind of power in that space and time each day. Despite feminist observations of women's alienation from language and Western rhetoric, American women teaching language arts, teaching English, stand within a long historical tradition that silently authorizes their power even while encapsulating it within male-dominated education (see Grumet; Monaghan; Myers, chap. 12, this vol.). One form that feminism in composition takes, influenced by radical pedagogy in education and cultural studies in English, is to exploit this latent classroom control to introduce feminist content and to mount cultural critiques of gender relations.[5]

Women are beginning to advocate as feminist many pedagogical principles and strategies long practiced in composition teaching. Many women in composition, including a number in this volume, increasingly emphasize "women's ways" of knowing, acting, speaking, writing, reading, and educating that some feminists have espoused for pedagogy or for the culture at large. Others have sharply disagreed.[6] Janet Emig and I call these women's ways (and alternate ones yet to be articulated) "feminine principles."[7]

The term *feminine* here refers initially to qualities identified culturally as "feminine in the deep classical sense—rooted in receptivity, relatedness, and responsiveness" (Noddings, 2). Clearly, much of the emergent feminism in composition speaks to the appropriation of these qualities for education; such principles are the basis for claims that process pedagogies of composition are feminist in their emphasis on relationship, responsiveness, peer collaboration, parentlike caring for students' development, sensitivity to difference and social context, and support for women's developmental needs. But this position raises troubling questions and easily provokes ambivalence and caution in its proponents as well as critique from other feminist perspectives (for celebrating qualities derived from marginalization or oppression, acting out roles provided for women by patriarchy, naturalizing culturally derived or imposed behaviors, and failing to analyze the intersections of gender with race, sexual orientation, or other aspects of identity, among other things).

By using the term *principles,* Janet and I tried to reframe this argument for composition (at this historical moment) by focusing on instances where stereotypically feminine qualities are deliberately chosen by women as values and enacted critically, regardless of whether their source is believed to be nature, the psychology of women's experience, direct cultural instruction and expectations, ideology, difference, or the effects of patriarchal oppression on victims. To speak of principles implies something worked for, not bestowed or imposed. By making such values or the appropriate expression of such values in practice the subject of definition and debate, one necessarily opens them and the concept of *femininity* (or *womanhood*, or *woman*, or other permutations of cultural idealization) to less stereotypical redefinition, cultural variety, and social change. From this more rhetoricized perspective, the attribute *feminine* is fluid, culturally and temporally contingent, and permanently subject to criticism, debate, experimentation, and a measure of personal choice. Once *femininity* is available as a concept rather than an essentialized feature of identity (and distinct from *feminism,* which is commonly defined not as an attribute but as an orientation to emancipatory activity on behalf of women), any number of stances becomes possible for a woman regarding her relation to being "feminine" as well as enacting the politics of feminism.

These two forms of feminism emerging in the composition classroom are of course inconsistent. One refers to women's controlling power as the designers and orchestrators of classroom work and, even, thought; the other, to women's ways of giving up authority—decentering—in order to empower learners to direct their own work and to think for themselves. But the very ability to choose to do the latter depends on authority of two kinds (themselves in tension): institutional authorization to teach and some degree of personal autonomy in pedagogical philosophy. This contradiction reflects to a certain extent a split practice, but much more significantly expresses an inescapable paradox in deploying culturally licensed power for social goods, including reform. Perhaps this paradox depends partly on an insufficiently differentiated notion of power, but it is also a philosophical knot whereby acting on behalf of students, even for their own good, seems to violate respect for the Other and to submit to becoming a hapless agent of institutional goals and ideological forces.[8]

Our feminism, like feminist movements in general, hesitates between the need for power and the distaste for it. That tension intensifies at the administrative level, where an individual is charged to "direct" the work of many teachers: in the words of my contract, "to provide conceptual leadership and timely implementation" for a programmatic enterprise. In the case of the teacher, the issue turns on the irony that, to pursue her goal of enhancing the student's freedom, growth, and energy, she must rely simultaneously on her own personal vision to control and choose for the student and on her role as transparent conduit of cultural authority. Unlike the director, though, her own actions are the medium for caring, and the student is the direct beneficiary.[9]

The problem is more complex for the "director" than for the teacher or editor because of the second- and even third-order responsibilities embedded in the charge. The director who envisions and enforces, however lightly, coherence for a programwide curriculum, or adjudicates student complaints, or hires and fires instructors is in these capacities putting teachers' energies to work as instruments of her own or the program's theories, aims, and commitments, which may have complex, mixed relations to the goals and interests of others at the institution (students, other faculty, administrators). If the teachers are themselves formally learners, the director is caught between conflicting obligations for "caring" (in Nel Noddings' term): to educatively "care for" graduate students while at the same time employing them to teach undergraduate students—in both cases authorized by and answerable to her institution.

Because women predominate in the composition workplace, improvements and new opportunities for leadership and learning can benefit them disproportionately and are more likely than elsewhere to reflect their specific needs and circumstances. The third and most precise sense in which a workplace might be defined as feminist echoes activist American concepts of feminism: it is a workplace specifically designed to benefit women by virtue of their working in it. Such a workplace would in its structures and conditions attempt to involve, recognize, support, and empower women; it would educate them for leadership. By understanding the workplace as ideally beneficent to all (teachers, staff, and administrators as well as students) I sought a way out of these dilemmas.

Utopian Dreams

> **Feminism per se does not require that gender be the most important factor; feminism is ultimately a practical decision about where to direct one's limited energies and powers in the effort to make a more livable world.**
>
> —*Nina Baym*

Consider my mixed motives for taking a job as director of a writing program, a decision I talked over at length with friends and family during the search process. Some reflect ambition and self-confidence. My father (who had been a hospital administrator) asked me whether I had the talents to run a writing program: if so, he said, you will have to do it eventually, so take the best chance when it comes. I answered yes, a decisive moment. (It is probably significant in feminist terms that I knew his serene and casual confidence in me was unshakable.) I relished the potential for major achievement in such an open-ended situation and understood, but wasn't frightened by, the commensurate possibility for failing on a grand scale. Intellectual curiosity—the prospect of what I could learn—and passion about ideas played an important role in my decision. I had strong convictions about literacy education based on study and personal practice, but I wanted to test and enrich these ideas by rooting them in the world of a concrete teaching community, where they would not only gain practical force and meaning but also evolve in collaboration with others. I anticipated and desired professional recognition for what might be accomplished, but the process, the experience of community, the intellectual growth, and the fate and appreciation of my ideas were probably more important to me in themselves than for the status they might bring. (Though I believe it is healthy for women and vital for feminism to acknowledge desires for territory and self-realization as well as the intellectual and utopian motives in ambition: see Phelps 1990; Laib).

Still, I was enormously ambivalent, and these reasons alone can't explain why I finally took the job. There were easier ways to disseminate my ideas and achieve professional recognition, through a quiet position somewhere doing graduate teaching and writing. (Most of my friends warned me that I was crazy to become an administrator at this moment in my career—or ever.) What tipped the scales was the combination of these incentives and an ethical sense that theorizing compels direct and committed engagement, with consequences. Ultimately, it was vaguely but genuinely a moral decision responding to the summons to take up responsibility toward others, to act on my convictions. It was not, however, self-consciously gendered in the sense either that I thought of these goals as derived from my gender (e.g., feminine in their relational emphasis) or that I directed them toward benefiting women (feminist in the political sense).

These motivational elements in an individual decision parallel the mixed goals of a programmatic enterprise. My charge from university administrators (itself the product of over two years of prior faculty inquiry and campus negotiation) was not simply to create an adequate or well-managed writing program but also to make it distinguished. I took that to mean intellectually vital, exciting, thoughtful; connected with the research and theory of the field; teeming with ideas and inventions; like a research center, based on continuing inquiry and capable of continued innovation and evolution rather than a static model that would soon stagnate and become boring for students and teachers alike. A program distinguished by intellectual quality and teachers' engagement should produce better instruction and outcomes for students. And, of course, it would enhance the prestige of my institution.

The intellectual work of a writing program has importance in itself (and to the discipline), but it is authorized and undertaken for the sake of (or at least in the context of) an overriding practical-moral purpose. The program charter expresses this charge: "to integrate writing with reading and critical thinking throughout the curriculum and to encourage continuing development of these abilities" ("Charter," 13). As a teaching program, ours exists to serve the university for the educational benefit of students, as the university exists to serve the good of society. The program only sometimes serves this goal through direct interaction with students—by instructing them in classes, through consultative teaching, or through cooperative action with other faculty—but its actions always have this ultimate outcome in mind. As clarified in the charter, which lays out provisionally some of the ways the writing program might accomplish its charge, the program just as often furthers its goal in a way one might call transitive—for example, by providing services for those who teach students (faculty development workshops, joint course development, and the like). In so doing it forms a complex relation to other units' goals for students' learning and writing in their own fields (complex because it is not a simple subsuming of writing teachers' energies to the principles and purposes of these fields and their faculty, nor should it attempt the reverse). The intellectual dimension of a writing program, if firmly asserted, transforms a subordinate relation into partnerships that embody both cooperation and negotiation of strong, perhaps irreconcilable differences.

Beyond transitivity, however, and partly because of it, an inquiry-based teaching program enlarges its functions in unexpected ways when some of its activities invite recontextualization as contributing to campus or national problems in education: for example, when it offers leadership in training of teaching assistants (TAs), pioneers ways of evaluating and supporting teaching, or brings together faculty across disciplines to share and solve common teaching problems. This is a different sense in which a writing program can "serve the university"—and the broader projects of American, even global, education.

1986, my second interview: *The administrator pulled out a piece of paper and sketched the organization of my university. It's pretty well organized, he said, vertically—it's simple enough so that you can get access to the top people without going through too many layers. But horizontally, there are all these units [thirteen colleges] that don't communicate well, don't cooperate, don't cohere into a "university." I have a vision! he said, drawing criss-crossing lines between the units, of using interdisciplinary programs to make these connections. The writing program can become connective tissue for the university.*

From the beginning, I perceived this power as latent in the logic of writing programs as a unique kind of programmatic enterprise. The possibility had already been foregrounded by the writing-across-the-curriculum movement, which emphasized in its early stages the transformational and integrative educational energies released by cross-disciplinary discussions of writing, teaching, and learning. These capabilities, however, depend as much on the administrative character of writing programs as on the content of their pedagogy. As organizations, writing programs combine a certain boundedness, recognizability, and clear definition as communities (delimited in space, in membership, in curricular purposes) with diffusion and interpenetration into the academic context through cross-curricular activity and communication with students, faculty, and administrators in many units and at all levels of the university hierarchy. The first feature makes writing programs relatively self-contained, cohesive, and observable in any innovations they practice; the second puts them as units in a position to exchange ideas with other subcommunities and to influence cross-institutional priorities—acting as partner, provocateur, demonstrator, catalyst, innovator, teacher, or mediator, among other roles (see Phelps 1991c).

Despite my inexperience as an administrator, I assumed that the single most critical factor in the success of a programmatic enterprise is smart, dedicated people: faculty and staff who are intellectually and morally engaged in working for shared goals. It seemed just common sense that if you want to implement something like writing instruction that is very complicated, requiring intelligence and improvisation, people doing the work need to be treated as agents, not automatons. (Later, I was repeatedly reminded that this "sense" is far from common in American schooling or among certain campus critics of writing programs, who want a "teacher-proof" curriculum.) This practical notion correlated with an ethical aversion to the domination of teachers by theory or by autocratic or paternalistic administration.

My most striking observations when I arrived were, first, the lack of communication among teachers and, second, their habitual subordination to a rigidly determined practice and its enforcers. The situation seemed to call both practically and morally for a massive effort to provide support for faculty development and to create an environment where talk and writing about teaching and learning could flourish. Reflecting these responses to the context, themes of agency, innovation, conversation, and community appear in my earliest speeches and talks with members of the program. (They refer primarily to the critical practice of teaching rather than teachers' participation in administration, which came a year or so later.) I refused to offer a new paradigm of writing instruction to play the same role as the old one: instead I tried to place teachers' own reflective thought and collaboration at the center of curriculum development and their intelligent, caring, and responsible interactions with students at the heart of learning.

From this vision of a writing program (originally, almost tacit) emerged a cluster of specific purposes, tasks, and strategies for administration. I gradually realized that my "conceptual leadership," insofar as it was utopian, would not lie in the curriculum theory or pedagogical strategies I introduced, even though these ideas did of course embody both values and intellectual principles (for example, the parallel notion that students are active agents, or stewards, of their own education). It lay rather in the idea of forming and orchestrating the activity of a teaching community in which people would be authorized and supported to teach flexibly within a broad framework of common goals, to invent curriculum together, to build a program that would finally have intellectual and educative value not only for the students taught but also for the university, the discipline, and for educational theory and practice. Within such a community, the specific range of teaching practices that fill in the framework in any particular course or teaching event, at any historical moment, would reflect not a director's singular "theory" of writing, or of composition pedagogy, but the inquiry and debate of teachers themselves (myself among them), with the cooperation of faculty in other disciplines, with reference to research in the field, and with the active participation of students in studying their own learning and the curriculum. Indeed, the framework itself would evolve through the critical action of the community, in interactions with learners themselves and with constituencies in the institutional context.

Now, factor in gender: most of the instructors were women; composition itself is feminized; I was a woman administrator; the Writing Program's full-time faculty consisted then of four women. And factor in the consequences and conditions of feminization: more than half the teachers were ill-paid, unappreciated, part-time instructors hired by the section on one-year contracts, teaching far less than full-time loads. They and the teaching assistants lived stereotypically crowded in a basement, without telephones, copying equipment, or secretarial help. They had tried, unsuccessfully, to unionize. Their disempowerment—having no control over curriculum, grading practices, teacher evaluation, or decision making in the program—had a strikingly different meaning when viewed through the lens of gender. And so did my own plans.

1983, remark made to part-time instructors when they tried to unionize: *Why should we raise your pay? I can find someone on the nearest street corner to do the job.*

—an administrator (as mythologized in institutional memory)

It was necessary for me to come to feminist terms with these conditions, this gendering of the writing program, and the ways they would create moral ambiguities and practical complexities for the purposes and approach I had conceived. This was the dilemma: my conception of a writing program required both practically and morally that teachers of the program be treated as primary agents of change in themselves, not as simply executing a director's will or serving as hapless instruments of ideology and institutional compulsion. Only they could invent and enact a curriculum and a pedagogy, by collectively becoming capable of this enterprise. That implied a broader political agency as well: opening teachers' access to programmatic decision-making and leadership roles. In asking or requiring (as a condition of employment) that program members take on this task, though, a director must learn the ironies of authority and decide how to ameliorate them. This interpretation of a director's role moved me into a more explicitly feminist position, since fulfilling my responsibilities to the largely female workers of the composition workplace, with sensitivity to the implications of gender, became over time an important goal in itself.

Steering Through the Minefield by a Moral Compass

Caring itself and the ethical ideal that strives to maintain and enhance it guide us in moral decisions and conduct.

The ethical self is an active relation between my actual self and a vision of my ideal self as one-caring and cared-for.

—*Nel Noddings*

Individuals don't always live up to their sense of morality.

—*Patrocinio Schweickart*

The central dilemma that I gradually realized I faced reflects the fact that agency (that is, both responsibility and authority) is not without heavy costs to those empowered. In enabling teachers to have more autonomy and control over their teaching, I also put pressure on them to learn, change, take risks, be more creative, face the unknown. They became accountable for their teaching in a different sense from before, a more dangerous position, given the demand for quality and excellence implicit in the program's goals for serving students and the need, in a research-based program, for constant self-assessment and improvement. However much the program supported and encouraged their professional development, some would be unable or unwilling to adapt. Many feared change, even change they themselves had planned and worked for.

Agency does not imply absolute power or freedom to do anything you please. Indeed, I discovered, there is a ratio between power and discipline: the greater your authority, the more visible and multiple the disciplines (rules, orders, structures) you must both accept for yourself and impose on others. This problem, which can be obscured or suppressed in the classroom (although it persists in teachers' conflicted feelings about grades and about their control of classroom talk), hits full force when teachers are given leadership roles as political agents of the program, rather than (as before) as subversives within it or legitimated opponents (e.g., teacher organizations set up to negotiate with "the administration"). Leadership involves more than generative ("maternal" or enabling) power—power to support and energize the development and work of others, the "cared-for"; more than rhetorical powers of persuasion. It requires leaders also to channel, constrain, and judge the actions of others, as I did in my role as an administrator, with sometimes highly unpleasant repercussions. What this means for teachers is that empowering them not simply pedagogically but politically, in such roles as supervisors and mentors of other teachers' work, peer evaluators, policy makers, grant proposers and administrators, writers, and public speakers, produces the same moral dilemmas, ambivalence, and discomfort for them as for a director, in a kind of cascade effect. Diffusion of power is diffusion of the problems of power: whether to accept leadership at all, how to construct one's relation to institutional authority, whether and how to evaluate peers or subordinates, how to live with the hard consequences of one's judgments and mistakes.

It quickly became evident to teachers (as, I think, it is not always to feminists and to reformers in general) that an increase in authority, voice, and autonomy is not an unqualified good in and of itself. It does not automatically bring wealth, leisure, increased status, or pleasure. It is certainly not, as some fantasize, independent of the reasons for which it comes into being, in this case broad programmatic and institutional goals that, no matter how much I invited the participation of all program members, had been shaped largely by others and by prior decisions, yet constituted obligations in the use of power.

Calls for improving the conditions of employment for postsecondary teachers of composition often emphasize professionalization, demanding that non-tenure-track instructors be allowed to join the faculty community, participate in departmental business, collaborate in developing curriculum, take part in assessment of their peers, have times and places to meet and to communicate with others, and even have opportunities and rewards for research.[10] A further irony our program illustrates is that these privileges may amount to exploitation if they become a condition of employment for teachers paid by the section or burdened with overly heavy loads along with the demands of graduate school. This is doubly the case for professional development—for instance, workshops, mentoring, and opportunities to attend conferences, to write and publish locally, and to take courses. Even if these are opportunities that individuals may legitimately decline (without overt penalty), such teachers will then find themselves disadvantaged, in skills and in political power, in comparison with those who take them up.

Many teachers in my program were angry, anxious, and resistant to expectations for professionalization. Even those many who describe their experiences in the program as personally transformational speak eloquently of the enormous pressures created by this abundance and intensity of stimuli and opportunities in the tightly budgeted economies of their lives. Although teachers' complaints often centered on the problem of rising expectations for commitment without adequate pay or released time (a conventional definition of exploitation), I suspect that even with such compensations the psychic cost of being caught up in utopian projects does not diminish; It is, perhaps, proportional to the potential growth and richness in the experience.

All the considerations that so complicate empowerment for part-time professional writing instructors become almost impossibly problematic for teachers who are graduate students misplaced in a writing program by the accidents of institutional history, as is common. In our case, TAs facing the difficult transition to graduate school, inexperienced yet feeling acutely their responsibilities to students sometimes only a few years younger, found themselves plunged into an ambitious project they thought irrelevant or even antithetical to their own intellectual interests in creative writing, critical theory, or cultural studies. Their situations, and the program's, were further conflicted by the differences and oppositions these teachers perceived among the various theories and practices at work in the different sites of their intellectual lives: their graduate courses, the writing courses they taught, the meetings and conferences through which the program tried to train, supervise, and offer them invitations to power. Inevitably these conflicts structured and colored their social relations and the psychology of their learning experiences as well.

Thus, every aspect of my vision of a writing program as utopian project is questionable (and was immediately questioned) as both impractical and at least potentially unethical. In treating teachers as moral agents—adults—and providing opportunities for curricular control and leadership, I exposed them, perhaps involuntarily, to new risks and pressures while possibly exploiting their capabilities and energy without adequate reward. From the other side, it could be (and was) argued that undergraduate students would suffer from the chaos and disorder created by inviting their teachers to take more power over curriculum and the circumstances of their professional lives.

1987, my remark to an instructor friend: *"I've just begun to understand what an incredible risk I took—assuming that any group of teachers who just happened to be here could become capable of collectively inventing a new writing program. And that they would want to."*

The thing is, the alternatives were worse, and I had made that democratic leap of faith. As I began to comprehend what a minefield of complexities lay in front of me, as we argued and examined these dilemmas daily in the program, I sought a compass for us to steer by.

To make the fine calibrations and reckonings required to balance multiple, conflicting responsibilities, I needed some way to understand my most fundamental, inescapable obligations to those whose work I supervised, in relation to the responsibilities more clearly charted for the program, and for myself, in its charge. Concepts of "caring" taken alone do not adequately account for these relations or resolve these conflicts, since they transcend one-on-one relations and become collective, institutional, and transitive. As events and crises unfolded, I began to feel that intuitively I was referring to some kind of moral compass and tried to make it more explicit (and debatable within the program). In retrospect it looks something like this.

In the immediate short-term situation, the faculty and staff of the writing program should not be harmed by their participation in it, at least not by the action or inaction of the program itself; and I should seek to maximize benefits to them resulting from their engagement in its common enterprise. I owed special consideration to part-time instructors, administrative assistants, and secretaries (largely women) who were in particularly vulnerable and ill-paid, subordinate positions; and I had special obligations to teaching assistants in their role as students, particularly young and inexperienced ones, many of them having come to teach there in order to attend graduate school without fully understanding or accepting the choice they were making, perhaps having little choice. I needed to be constantly mindful of the gender dimensions in the entire network of relations.

In the long term, I would try to change the underlying conditions that made the employment of these two teacher groups so morally troublesome: both had few alternatives to joining this project, while the program's definition (as a communal enterprise) and its ambitious goals demanded extraordinary effort and commitment. Ideally, those who participate should have foreknowledge of the program's project and viable alternatives to working there, ensuring to the greatest extent possible that they seek to engage wholeheartedly in the program project rather than have it thrust upon them by circumstances. The impossibility of ever ensuring the ideal case, though, creates the need to guard against totalitarian community by maintaining spaces and gaps in the workplace structures and demands that permit flexibility of commitment, distancing, and dissent. Yet the program must simultaneously find ways to preserve and forward its own project against internal subversions of its fundamental right to purpose, coherence, communal loyalties, and even existence.

One way to describe my practical utopianism—my feminism, as Nina Baym would define it—is that I tried to construct a program that would constantly move toward such a state of affairs while being extremely sensitive to the need for tolerance, compromise, compensation, and adjustment to the human experience of change.

Maturity is learning to live with complexities and ambiguities.
                                          —my mother, family maxim

Authority is necessary. Decisions must be made, difficult issues have to be dealt with. Employees need to be hired, disciplined, coached, and, occasionally, fired. The proper use of authority is one of the rarest management skills—and therefore one of the most valuable.
                                          —Andrew Grove, CEO

As I write this, I'm embarrassed to imagine an experienced executive reading it—my father, perhaps, or a woman vice president I admire. They are kind, but astonished at such angst. Bosses are paid to boss! These problems come with the territory—just get on with it and do your best!

I can only respond that soul-searching is inescapable in an environment so extraordinarily inhospitable to constructive foundings and to a woman's authority. A writing program is so emotionally charged by everyone's investments in writing, so central to the life of a university—yet so disdained— that its ethos is already highly problematic. Add to this a heterogeneous and partly involuntary population of teachers exposed to faculty critiques of power and oppression that provide seductively easy weapons to attack all authority and make suspect all invitations to join a communal enterprise. Add gender. It is a volatile mix that requires constant, explicit defense of one's ethical authority and justification of the program in the most basic sense—its right to try.

To meet the requirement that working in the program should not harm and should, if possible, benefit those participating in its implementation, a director must identify values that are within the capability of the program to provide. (See Noddings, on the requirement that an ethical ideal be realistic and attainable, in order not to be "diverted into abstraction and the endless solution of hypothetical problems" [109].) Four such benefits come to mind as most significant: material rewards and supports; enhanced agency, both in teaching and in broader political spheres; education, producing intellectual, personal, or professional growth; and the satisfactions and friendships of constructive communal action.

I am trying in this chapter to keep attention steadily not so much on the kinds of forces that we normally think of as frustrating change (for example, external critics, lack of resources, anemic support from administrators), although of course these are constantly operative, but on the internal complexities that accompany change and, especially, on those that follow from actually succeeding, or at least beginning to effect change. The effort to pursue each of these benefits is a long story, each showing the same relations between ideals, actions, and complex consequences that define the general dilemma. None is purer than another, either in conception or in execution; all reflect mixed purposes (which is to say they are feasible because they are synergistic with efficiency, economy, quality of instruction, and other program needs or goals). Each has elements or potential for coercion, each is subject to suspicious interpretations that reverse intention, each has unintended and undesirable consequences, each has limits and costs.

As an illustration, I will explore the paradoxes inherent in empowerment, a stereotypical goal of the feminist workplace. The concept of teachers and learners as agents is central to the social architecture of the writing program I directed and, in practice, is necessarily interlaced with the enactment of benefits for all constituencies served by writing programs. In focusing on empowering teachers, I am pulling out one strand in this pattern and, for teachers themselves, situating agency within an intricate system of tradeoffs and interactions that link empowerment with other rewards and their costs.

1991, from a dean's budget report: *"The Writing Program is costly, complex, and controversial."*

It is natural as a director to turn first to improving material conditions, because exploitive undercompensation and lack of environmental support is actively harmful. (There are in this benefit at least disciplinary guidelines and ways of deciding in a particular economic and regional context what minimal fairness requires.) The initial goals I set for realistic improvements were largely accomplished: among the most important were increased pay and benefits for part-time writing instructors, coupled with a merit pay system; improved facilities, including copying equipment and computers; support for professional travel; released time for program research and administrative or service responsibilities; slightly reduced teaching assistant loads; some access to funds for teacher research; and long-term contracts for part-time instructors. From a feminist point of view, these goods are noteworthy largely for the rhetorical strategies that achieved them. Instead of condemning exploitation and calling for justice and compassion, proposals stressed teachers' increased market value and the educational values (efficiency, quality, distinction) achieved by increased energy and skill on the part of program members. Economic benefits and material support were awarded teachers by higher-level administrators because they had become both competitively necessary and well deserved, because it was clear that improvements in the environment would generate desired values (better teaching), and because many people were rhetorically skillful and persistent in dramatizing those facts. In concert with these changes, part-time instructors were renamed "professional writing instructors" (PWIs) to accord them the dignity of acknowledgment and respect for their expertise (a significant benefit in itself).

Unfortunately, most writing program directors have little control over meeting this condition, since getting (and, even more, keeping) material benefits not already in the program is as much a matter of luck and local circumstances as one of commitment. (That is to say that ethical conduct lies, at least for a time, in seriously trying.) To the degree that WPAs do control and allocate internal resources, they must balance direct benefits to workers against obligations to the financial health and educational efficacy of the program and juggle priorities among competing needs and groups. (For example, how much money should be reallocated from, say, a tutoring budget to faculty travel? How should one balance travel funds for full-time faculty against those for graduate students? for professional writing instructors?)

Once material conditions improve, the response of those benefited is (as political leaders have repeatedly discovered) not simple satisfaction and appreciation, because the well of need is bottomless, and people judge leadership not by past accomplishment but by what they think will happen in the future. More objectively, economic benefits and material support will never be enough to offset the demands placed on people strained to the limit by a program as ambitious as this. Improvements are always relative and always fall short of the new goals that are quickly set once others are attained. That means that material benefits are necessary but insufficient compensation or incentive for people's work in this workplace.

Education can supplement minimal or barely adequate economic rewards and work environment with a benefit that is rarer and highly specific to a university and a writing program. It has the advantage of being achievable with relative ease, at least in theory: in many universities teachers and staff can take free courses and degrees; the program offers, in the course of normal operations, opportunities and hands-on training in computer skills, administration, and writing, among other things. (However, these benefits require released time and a substantive contribution of program resources—not so easy.) Insofar as graduate assistants are already students, the program is already organized to meet educational responsibilities for their growth and professionalization. (Indeed, the difference between the composition workplace and any company that offers educational benefits and in-house training is that every faculty or staff member in the writing program is an expert and self-conscious teacher and learner, and the whole discourse of the workplace focuses intensively on everyone's mutual education.) If the program is successful in creating a teaching-learning community, its faculty will teach one another and learn from collective inquiry with one another and with their students, not merely in formal contexts for professional development or teacher training set up by administrators. Finally, education has the great advantage of being internal to workers, and therefore a permanent benefit, something they can take away from this workplace and that, because it is transferable, makes them more autonomous. Teachers (and secretaries and work-study students—all workers in this feminist workplace) who exploit these opportunities for development will gain options: they will have more choices about staying there or moving on. For many, the program will be transitional; but others may stay because they enjoy learning as well as teaching.

Educational rewards nevertheless have their own problems and difficult consequences; for example, they can be perceived as coercive by those who did not seek them or have different goals for intellectual growth; they produce a constant turnover of the most skilled people; and they are gradual, relatively invisible to begin with, and impossible to assign consistent value. Nor can education be unambiguously "given" by an act of the program, in the sense that material rewards can be. Since programs can provide only the environment for learning, not learning itself, from one perspective education merely generates yet another form of work expected of program members. Education as a benefit can merge both helpfully and harmfully with the expectations for workers to continually increase their competence and raise standards for quality of performance. This can become a special problem when the constantly increasing expertise on the part of continuing teachers (who are in a sort of perpetual graduate program) contrasts more and more sharply with the steady-state inexperience of an equal number of new, inexperienced teachers entering the program each year, as TAs graduate.

As soon as I had articulated and initiated the participation of teachers in redesigning pedagogy, I began to extend the concept of teachers' agency in curriculum instruction to a more general political role in shaping the decision making of the program, including their own assessment. (I am drawing on a preliminary account written with Assistant Director Faith Plvan, called "The Social Architecture of the Writing Program.") I articulated these political goals explicitly in a programwide meeting (called the "perestroika [restructuring] meeting") using a diagram that visualized teachers as "the third force" in the program, whose critical practice, direct interaction with students, and sheer numbers should give them weight equivalent to the political force of full-time faculty (representing expertise and disciplinary credentials) on the one hand and administrators (representing institutional power) on the other. At the same time, the diagram blurred these distinctions by converting them from fixed group identities to roles—teaching, research, and leadership—that related groups by ratio rather than by exclusion, so that these identities overlapped for individuals. It took years of struggle to give this idea concrete meaning through rhetorical persuasion, reorganization of program activities, reallocation of resources, professional development, and creation of new structures to include teachers in responsible roles.

The complications and frustrations of this effort were of course manifold. There is no question but that the program created a radically new social architecture in which teachers have greatly enhanced political and curricular agency over the previous state of affairs. Yet the process was highly conflictual, and the perceptions of results are probably more mixed and ambivalent than those of any other aspect of the program intended to benefit members. Perhaps the most difficult aspects of the process itself were, first, crafting a new role for full-time faculty that did not simply introduce another layer of hierarchical compulsion; and second, for all program members, accepting and working with the coercive and institutional dimensions of their own power. However, one underlying feature of the situation explains many of these responses and problems, while provoking a counterintuitive way of conceptualizing and strategizing empowerment. This feature is the extreme heterogeneity of program members and the asymmetries in power that result.

Deconstruction by Asymmetries

Arguments about empowering students in the classroom often bifurcate into a romantic notion of power as unproblematically available to individuals or collaborative groups through their own action (aided by teachers' decentering authority) versus a deterministic view that power resides overwhelmingly in societal structures of dominance. Both these positions can be developed with great subtlety and careful qualification, and by stating them in extreme, perhaps unfair, terms I do not mean to reduce them to caricatures. However, it is a quick way to make my point that even at best these ways of characterizing the sources of power relative to a classroom setting are highly inadequate to interpret or guide the empowerment of teachers in a concretely located composition workplace. Clearly, the first view oversimplifies my problem, because it does not theorize the institutional component of power (the writing program is not a self-contained social system, and its members have sharply defined institutional identities). The second is unsatisfactory because it imagines no ethical position other than resistance; it fails to explain how teachers might accept the invitation to use power constructively as insiders, rather than subverting or opposing the program, perceived as a structure for controlling them.

I sought to create a social architecture that attempts to maximize dispersion of power among program members (sometimes spoken of, in the language of business, as a "flattened hierarchy") while accepting, and even exploiting, the consequences of the program's embeddedness in a concrete, particular institutional and historical context. Specifically, I assumed that inequalities of power as well as of hierarchy are inevitable in any large social organization, patriarchal or otherwise. The possibilities for sharing power among groups in the writing program are circumscribed by the specific social facts of its membership and the organization of the university as a political and bureaucratic workplace. I proposed to work with, rather than against, these real-world constraints. The effort was further complicated by the fact that both the romantic and the determinist theories of empowerment, as realized in feminist (feminine) pedagogy and some applications of critical theory, were already afoot (and in conflict) among teachers in the program, where they fostered a confused tangle of ideals and demands (for anarchy, radical individualism, reimposed Stalinist order, conversion of the whole program to radical pedagogy, organized resistance to the program's "theory" or its "surveillance" of teachers, etc.).

Underlying both these understandings of empowerment in composition (defining what Ann Berthoff might call the "killer dichotomy") is an assumption that is called feminist but actually owes much to models of society based on an ethic of justice or equality, where equality implies symmetry. This ideal is well articulated by John Trimbur in a critique of collaborative learning pedagogy:

> In Habermas' view we should represent consensus . . . as an aspiration to organize the conversation according to relations to non-domination. The anticipation of consensus projects, that is, what Habermas calls an *"ideal speech situation," a utopian discursive space that distributes symmetrically the opportunity to speak, to initiate discourse, to question, to give reasons, to do all those other things necessary to justify knowledge socially.* From this perspective, consensus becomes a necessary fiction of reciprocity and mutual recognition, the dream of conversation as perfect dialogue. Understood as a utopian desire, assembled from the partial and fragmentary forms of the current conversation, consensus does not appear as the end of the explanation of the conversation, but instead as a means of transforming it. (612; emphasis added)

Translated (uncritically) from speech to action, this can be taken to mean that any heterogeneity among people produces, in a given social structure and actual conversation, an asymmetry of power and that such an asymmetry is automatically undesirable and oppressive.[11] Whatever the concept of power is here (coercive force? assertive, territorial claim?), it seems to follow conservation principles that make power relations a zero-sum game. In composition, the tendency to conceive power this way is reinforced by the equation of power with the opportunity to speak: if one imagines a given period of time, say a classroom hour, in which silence may be filled by speech, it makes sense to think of dividing the hour ideally into equal parts, allocated equitably among the participants. (As critics like Evelyn Ashton-Jones have pointed out, though, that does not at all guarantee that each person can and will speak, or will be heard to equal effect and influence.) Since the hour is a finite resource, people who speak more than their share take time (power) away from others.

No one argues that such a utopian space exists, or ever will. But many do use the ideal of symmetry to define their goals and to organize their strategies for empowerment. The conception of ideal power relations as equality within any social space requires ethically that we try to construct such spaces as a level playing ground, in which central authority is diminished and more socially privileged members (e.g., males, full-time faculty, administrators) may need to be suppressed in order to give more power to the subordinate and vulnerable (females, PWIs, TAs, students).

I developed my own approach from an entirely different set of premises about the relations between asymmetries and power. It starts with a careful analysis of the actual asymmetries prevailing in the local context of the program.

The outstanding social fact of the program I inherited (like most writing programs and, probably, most workplaces) is that it is populated by groups of co-workers who are strongly heterogeneous and thus potentially asymmetric with respect to power. At first glance the asymmetries appear holistic, arranging the main players in the program (faculty administrators, full-time tenure-track faculty, professional writing instructors, and teaching assistants) in a stable hierarchy.[12] But in fact both individuals and groups are asymmetric along multiple, sometimes finely graded, dimensions (which have many interpretations besides their translation into power). Among these are title and status, pay and benefits, released time, contract length, credentials that authorize status (e.g., degrees), professionalism and interest in composition and rhetoric, investment of time and energy in program affairs beyond teaching itself, expertise in general areas or in specific issues, experience in general or in specific tasks, social and intellectual commitment to program goals, and personal qualities (e.g., charisma, eloquence, ability to inspire respect or fear).

Significant asymmetries can be clustered into three groups: (1) institutional authority (usually legitimated by academic credentials) and the symbols and rewards associated with it (status, pay, etc.), (2) attributes of competence, and (3) commitment or investment of oneself in the program. Instead of futile efforts to define people formally as equal, much less to account for or compensate for the social identities or histories of unequal access (including feminization) that lie behind their present configuration of asymmetries, my strategy was to create a social architecture that would permit a kind of deconstructive play with power relations. This play, most significantly, uses asymmetries from groups 2 and 3 to subvert those from group 1, while simultaneously (as in all deconstructive play) affirming the first (institutionally defined hierarchical power) as an invaluable, inescapable source of legitimation, order, potentially beneficent acculturative functions, and broader institutional influence.

This is possible because there is no simple equation of asymmetries with power (just as there is no single meaning here of power). For the purposes of this discussion, let me define *power* crudely as *influence in asserting one's priorities within the program or university.* While any of these variables may be scaled from positive to negative as a source of potential power, the asymmetries do not line up the same for any one person; all the dimensions for all individuals would have to be graphed to predict each person's prominence, prestige, persuasiveness, favored status, and so on (or whatever counted most toward power in the program). But such an evaluation would still not predict how these factors would operate in any given situation of decision making or setting priorities, where some would combine, like waves amplifying or interfering with one another. The possibilities are most open in small group situations, whose intimacy establishes a local, situation-specific equation of power that may enable personal qualities or competencies along with group dynamics to outweigh formal credentials and assigned or institutionally defined roles. The sum of all such specific occasions where power is exercised or views conflict and are resolved produces a flow of power in the program and a distribution of influence among its members.

Moreover, this process goes beyond the zero-sum game of redistribution to generate genuinely new, usable power. By any measure or definition I can think of, the social architecture of this program created new power: it generated or attracted energy, enabled novelty and change, created new order and legitimacy, and gave people more personal autonomy and scope for action. Such power apparently grows by converting existing energies (and infusing external ones like disciplinary theory or partnership with other units) into power-as-influence rather than by redistributing a finite internal pool of power-as-control. At the same time, these new individual powers combine to create new collective power—the ability for the program as a whole to influence others beyond itself, at the university, in the discipline, in higher education. Some of that power, by virtue of entitlement, gathers and is vested in the director as representative, spokesperson, and embodiment of this collective energy (another significant function of a strong executive office). At this new level of action, the director can reintroduce the strategy to diffuse it among program leaders, increasing their institutional voice; indeed, the program can practice the same deconstructions to generate and share power with external partners in broader domains—university, disciplinary, educational, and public spheres.

The social architecture that evolved to support these strategies of empowerment has three aspects: enabling conditions, structures, and exemplification. Access to information (a two-way flow) and an explicitly enunciated rhetoric of empowerment are the enabling conditions of the diffusion of power by deconstructive means. The first requires multiple channels of communication, both oral and written, formal and informal, through which those not defined as planners, administrators, or leaders have the fullest and fastest possible access to information relevant to decision making, while more centrally located individuals and groups are pressured by both structures and expectations to consult widely and frequently about decisions delegated to them. (This condition has technological implications, requiring widespread access to computers and communication networks.) It also has its negative side, including the inefficiency of broad consultation in crises; the time and energy costs imposed on people by intensive communication; and the related problem of how far to go in trying to replace gossip networks with more public argument and information sharing.

An enunciated rhetoric of empowerment requires the director to both articulate and encourage the development of self-conscious understandings and guidelines for the rhetoric and politics of social interactions in the program. For example, certain instructors proposed in administrative program texts that a rhetoric of "civility" or mutual respect should govern relations among different groups and individuals implementing the program. Various public and small-group settings like conferences, teaching groups, and publications were used to explore what that might mean, its justification, its dangers, its relation to pedagogy, and so on. A parallel discussion of the concept of "collegiality" informed the development by full-time faculty of promotion and tenure guidelines. The effort to establish this condition also included explicit administrative rhetoric acknowledging asymmetries of power, while inviting access by linking influence and autonomy in the program to competencies and concrete commitments.[13]

The second aspect of the process involves creating and revising structures and developing new traditions intended to fit this purpose to the larger one of implementing the curricular and broader educational goals of the program. The first step was to organize teachers into groups and recruit teacher leaders, called program coordinators, to run weekly group meetings and to advise and work with central planners. As primary mediators between central power (then largely in the hands of a tiny full-time faculty acting as a committee of the whole) and the perceptions and activities of various program groups, program coordinators were the key to developing teacher leadership and to sharing power widely in the program. Their contributions included modeling professional development as leaders and fostering it as mentors; defining the coordinator role by enacting, discussing, and writing about it; questioning the role and analyzing their tasks and teachers' responses from a political perspective; and serving as primary theorists and experimenters in new curriculum and pedagogy. Some other structural initiatives for diffusing power among teachers included a peer evaluation process for professional writing instructors; a summer planning team of TAs and PWIs to prepare orientation and organize mentorship plans for incoming new teachers; released-time appointments of teachers in leadership roles; the development of channels and forums for program publication and public speech; and a strategic planning process to develop a yearly program agenda, inviting participation by all members of the program.

A thread of collaboratively organized activity runs through all these plans, in two configurations: informal pairs (occasionally troikas), both symmetric (peers) and beneficially asymmetric (e.g., veteran PWI and inexperienced junior faculty member); and formalized teams, typically headed by an asymmetric pair or sometimes a symmetric pair with a faculty or staff adviser. The purpose of the latter asymmetry was to give every activity sponsored by the program (task force, committee, project group) institutionally legitimated representation at higher levels, in and outside the program. In practice, the first configuration has produced widespread voluntary co-teaching, defined broadly as almost any systematic, sustained cooperation in planning or implementing instruction, along with fluid mentorship networks. The team configuration continually subverts in the practice of small groups the stereotypical distinctions and conventionally hierarchical interpretations of relations among institutionally, theoretically, or politically identified program groups, even as these power differentials are constantly reinstituted by people's perceptions and behaviors.[14]

Exemplification refers to modeling and dramatizing these principles and strategies so that they can take hold strongly enough to enable people to consciously seek and practice their own empowerment for constructive purposes and to resist others' attempts to reinstate the old power arrangements or freeze new ones without qualification or blurring. (For, of course, those formerly or newly empowered, whether full-time faculty, program coordinators, or committee chairs, including the director, will always move in this direction, undermining even their own intentions to keep power constantly fluid and shifting.) Vectors of power develop in discussion groups (and there are few major decisions in this model that are not at some point informed, made, or approved by small groups). These vectors represent the way that the various asymmetries oppose or reinforce one another, which is highly complex and dynamic. Power builds and flows from a combination of the product of different asymmetries and the saliency of one or more over others, both within and among individuals. For example, a person may influence others by a combination of specific knowledge, charisma, and eloquence, even though someone else is more generally experienced and has higher rank or an assigned role. Or the joint commitment of three members of the group to writing a report will outweigh either personal qualities or official power in shaping the collective thought.

Although the three kinds of asymmetry most often challenge and deconstruct one another, if in group dynamics or a critical event they converge in a leader who is simultaneously high-ranked, articulate, knowledgeable, and hard-working, such a leader can exert overwhelming force. While this is not a bad thing in itself, the director and others who become program leaders need to constantly exemplify alternate possibilities by deferring to someone else's superior knowledge in one situation, asking others to chair a meeting or task force in which they participate, encouraging others to "delegate up," and so on. The idea is not to give up or hide the authority that resides in certain kinds of credentials and legitimation but to reveal what actually supports the effectivity of that authority in a given instance and to open the way for institutional power to yield to or synergize with experience, expertise, rhetorical power, or willingness to invest energy on the part of an ever increasing number of participants. Thus individuals may be perceived not just as having power in some general, undifferentiated and ahistorical sense but as being more or less successful in various situations in asserting their views, using their energies, shaping others' behaviors, and so on. At other times, exemplification requires explicit foregrounding of official authority with explanations of why it is appropriate and useful to invoke it and to assert it over other asymmetries or the collective will.

In the social architecture I envisioned (and I think this was true in practice), the number of times that individuals, including myself, invoked a sort of raw institutional power (I'm the boss!) to break a deadlock was small (and, after a few years, virtually never without awareness of the full range of views); the number of times they acted in terms of structured channels of legitimated power (e.g., when a decision was brought to them for final approval) was larger but carefully defined and circumscribed; the largest numbers of decisions arose from interactions of those asymmetries in ways too complicated to follow. I tried to strengthen the asymmetries that rested on merit or commitment against those resting on formal structures while preserving, defending, and using the symbolic power of the office in circumstances where it was most crucial to the survival or progress of the program or to the responsible fulfillment of its charge.

"Community"

Underlying the possibilities for programmatic action, the necessary ground for any utopian project, is a community. *Project* implies purposeful, jointly coherent constructive action, as does *program* (distinct from *department,* which often seems in the contemporary university to be a community only in the loosest sense). For the project to be successful and rewarding for them, its members must develop a sense of identification with the program as a community in more than a technical sense: as a self-organizing, dynamic social system that is relatively stable and secure in its identity, its people committed at least temporarily to the joint project as an institutional enterprise, its activities cooperative and linked by a common discourse and common topics of concern. (Thinking about international science as such a community, one realizes that *cooperative* does not imply an absence of struggle and conflict: see Bazerman; Polanyi.) This presumption of community is relevant to all teaching environments, even the individual and apparently isolated classroom; but a cohesive identity and purpose is doubly necessary if a program is to function effectively on the other levels suggested here, to speak to or intervene in educational matters beyond its own immediate domain of responsibilities.

It could be argued that, ideally, a utopian project or even a teaching program should not exist only for its own sake, to serve its members' needs or to glorify and enrich "the program," even though that is the constant temptation of all bureaucracies. (This point raises an interesting question, often on my mind as director: To what degree can one institutionalize a utopian vision? Or is any constructive cultural project a speedily self-consuming artifact—the very process of realizing it being the inevitable reinstitution of that which needs reform?) In actual life, in political life specifically, I think that institutions and programs, like nations, survive and thrive only when people develop a powerful sense of belonging and loyalty to them, and do indeed serve them partly for their own sake: as embodiment, however flawed and mixed, of noble human purposes, as homes or places of work and life, and as human families and collectivities that they love. If there is any single claim that feminists, in composition and elsewhere, seem to be making, it is that women's work in families and society (the invisible work of managing social interaction [DeVault; Fishman]) prepares them to understand and build such communities. Many of the "feminine principles" I have described here and tried to follow as a leader (collaborative work, consensus building, conversation, professional development, deconstructive use of asymmetries) enact a conception of relations as intrinsically rewarding.

I said earlier that belonging to a community in this sense is one benefit a writing program, or any utopian project, can offer to its participants and workers. But strangely, community appears to be the most problematic of all values associated with my vision of a writing program.[15] The very strength of the community created both attracts and repels newcomers. The rhetoric of the program promotes a constant inclusionary movement in which new people are invited in, so that the circle of insiders who constitute "the program" gets larger and larger, its members staying longer, growing more committed and also increasingly knowledgeable and powerful. The net result is that new people "thrown" (in the phenomenological sense) unwittingly into this community are caught in powerful currents that tend to sweep them into its discourse, its political structures and conflicts, and its curricular theories and lore. Many people, including those who joined this community intentionally, found it frightening in its strongly articulated and self-conscious identity, high energy, multiple activities and choices, insider discourse (disparaged as jargon), expectations for autonomy and responsibility, and sheer complexity. Some gradually assimilated and used these strengths; some withdrew into apathy or marginality; and some made the very idea of community the focus of their political dissent.

We are back to the point that power frightens people. Even the most benign power, and most especially collective power, is in part coercive, whether overtly, through rules and rulers, hegemonically, through structures tacitly assimilated, or interactionally, through rhetorical forces. Perhaps even constructive power made available to ourselves is frightening in the electricity it creates and the demands it generates. But does either concern really explain the profound alienation and skepticism in today's academy toward the very ideal of community? As a feminist, what am I to make of the fact that, of all aspects resisted in my own program's utopianism, it was the aspiration to communal spirit that stirred the fiercest hostility and provoked a virtual campaign of subversion? How does gender figure in these antipathies to an ideal of community articulated as "feminine principles" of empowerment, teamwork, free inquiry, democratic conversation, reflective practice, and civil rhetoric? How should we understand criticism that, rather than arguing against these principles, attacks the personal character of women leaders espousing them and the legitimacy of their authority to enact them? In my case, for example, such critics portrayed the cohesive strength of a teaching community as tyranny and the mutual trust and loyalty of program instructors as establishment of a cult.

Such critiques call into question the very possibility of leadership, especially a woman's leadership, in its inspirational and rhetorical function:

tellingly, they most bitterly targeted the director's public speech and writings, the rights of women to rhetoric (see Bizzell; Connors, chap. 4, this vol.). I do not think we can understand these responses apart from a much more profound analysis of American life in terms of its historic conflict between individualism and community and the relation of women, feminism, and rhetoric to that history. (For a start, see Bell et al.; Fox-Genovese.)

Lessons of the Feminist Workplace

The issue of power is assuredly among the most difficult that feminists face. Power is most often experienced as oppression, and hence the desire for it is frequently disavowed. Yet, insofar as power is the energy and control that gets things done, it is not only an ineluctable dimension of any situation, it is something that feminists require.

—*Nina Baym*

The Lesson of Organized Complexity

Women have always lived discontinuous and contingent lives, but men today are newly vulnerable, which turns women's traditional adaptations into a resource. Historically, even women who have devoted themselves to homemaking and childcare have had to put together a mosaic of activities and resolve conflicting demands on their time and attention. . . . As a result, the ability to shift from one preoccupation to another, to divide one's attention, to improvise in new circumstances, has always been important to women.

—*Mary Catherine Bateson*

The provisional analysis of asymmetry given earlier suggests that leadership can create in specific circumstances a productive polarity between centralized power and distributed internal power within a community, organized around a project (but folding into it and accommodating inconsistencies among many individuals' motives and projects). At this institutional site teachers have explored the possibilities and relations of autocratic order (before I came), near anarchy, and "thriving on chaos." The latter turns out to require a director managing organized complexity amid interruption, distraction, and conflict, improvising and shifting attention, weaving coherencies among multiple responsibilities, much as the traditional American maternal role and now the two-career family have required it of women or as the elementary "open classroom" ironically demands a more powerful yet more subtle teacher than the traditional classroom does, to prestructure and orchestrate its complex free play.

If empowerment of others within an organizational unit paradoxically requires and concentrates power in leaders; if it creates new power, but only through the ironic complementarities I've described; if it depends on a communal spirit that is severely in question—what are the implications for the utopian dreams of women, and composition, in taking up invitations to power?

I cannot judge whether mine is an account, or even an ideal, of a specifically feminist social order. But surely its surprises and puzzles, as in the lesson of organized complexity, teach that, if we are to pursue such projects in composition, our investigations are just beginning. I would like to see at least four kinds of studies:

Theoretical analysis: to reexamine the assumptions and ideas that are at work in feminist (and other) visions of new social orders and to develop fertile new concepts with which to interpret our goals, experiences, and actions. For example, in our current discussions power is an unanalyzed primitive; when you try to actually use it as a conceptual tool (as I did, slipping, sliding, and merging senses), you discover it is a portmanteau term that desperately needs unpacking; And that is the need with many other concepts as well: "Our working vocabulary . . . has to be coherent and adequate" (Langer, 17). Rather than tackle such huge, abstract, complex ideas directly, I find it more fruitful to work with midlevel terms that are empirically grounded, whether in pretheoretical experience or in disciplinary studies: terms like *agency* or *asymmetries.* For instance, there is need to adapt for academic practice a concept of morally legitimate power as defined by the executive "office" in the Elizabethan or American constitutional sense.

Empirical studies: to ground and test such concepts (and our utopian thought) in more complex descriptions and analyses of real-world workplaces relevant to our situations. We need, for instance, ethnographies, case studies, histories, and comparative studies of the dynamics of writing programs or similar academic communities (e.g., women's studies programs, or small secondary schools), to trace the intricacies of their heterogeneities and institutional differences and to compare their power structures and utopian possibilities with one another and with nonacademic workplaces. All this needs to be set within understandings of the academy at large as a workplace. These studies stand in scope and manageability between classroom dynamics and superstructural analyses and promise, I think, to help us mediate the two.

Rhetorical studies: to apply rhetorical frameworks to the texts, talk, and communication networks that operate within writing programs and across the contexts and communities (institutional, disciplinary, public) they participate in. Here is one of the most powerful contributions we can make to feminism. I hope to start with an analysis of the ethos of a WPA as a function of the complex relations that link self-image, ethical ideal, and reception (in the form of images and characterizations projected on the leader) with the "office," with the vision of the whole, and with the program dynamic itself as a product or composition in which the leader invests both caring and ego—and must learn to let go. We should also study the rhetoric and technologies by which some complex, partly temporary and partly continuing, communities are constructed and constantly resisted, deconstructed, revised, articulated, and understood. (Studying that process in the relatively small compass of a teaching community might help us to understand better how it works among all the constituencies of a college or university.)

Phenomenological studies: The subtext of my essay is phenomenological: What does it feel like to confront the ambiguities and conundrums of power? How do others experience my power? I have found the perceptions and attributions of others utterly terrifying: unexpected, enlarged and distorted beyond imagination—projections of fear and desire imposed on my unwilling self that make me imagine losing my ethical ideal, like the person who looks in a mirror and sees another face. How can we detoxify that experience, and how can phenomenologies of leadership (both active and receptive) help us to embrace power as enabling right action, rather than reject it because it will inevitably entangle us in moral ambiguity, error, and guilt? For women as well as for men, in oneself as in others, power presents terrible temptations to ego-centered behavior, to betrayal, cowardice, and corruption. However, the same is even more true for powerlessness.

1986 and recurrently: *You've changed. How can you be so hard-nosed . . . ungracious . . . relentless . . . overwhelming . . . impolitic . . . confrontational . . . authoritarian? It's not like you!*
—faculty friends

The Lesson of Bravery

Warriorship . . . is the tradition of human bravery, or the tradition of fearlessness.

> The key to warriorship . . . is not being afraid of who you are. . . .
> Shambhala vision teaches that, in the face of the world's great prob-
> lems, we can be heroic and kind at the same time.
>
> —*Chogyam Trungpa*

If anything is obvious when we examine the complexities of power sharing, it is the paradox that, while it expresses caring, it essentially depends
on the vision, institutional legitimation, willpower, and rhetorical skill of a
strong "executive"—an embodied person merged with an "office."

Remember I asked—and postponed answering—the more fundamental question, whether it is ever right to accept invitations to power in the
academy. Given the willingness to teach writing, to work in any institution
of american higher learning as a scholar or teacher, but especially in tenured positions of relative economic comfort and privilege, it seems to me
the fundamental choice has already been made; what remains is just responsibility and the specific conditions that make it right or possible to
take it.

1993, my response to the leftist critique of being an administrator:
All I can say is that, finally, I'm not willing to be infantilized.

But to the ethical question, how live with our own power, how use it
wisely, experience adds, how can we accept and develop our own
strength? How stop concealing it, fearing that we will be characterized as
bossy, egotistical, or ruthlessly ambitious—or that we are? How become
warriors unafraid of our own power?

> Real fearlessness is the product of tenderness. It comes from letting
> the world tickle your heart, your raw and beautiful heart. You are
> willing to open up, without resistance and shyness, and face the
> world.
>
> —*Chogyam Trungpa*

1986 and recurrently, to my family and friends: *Do I want to be a
woman administrator? a feminist administrator? or just a good administrator? What's the difference? I admire my father, husband, brother as leaders.
But can they be models for me, as a woman? Or is it only my feminine role
models, like my strong mother, aunts, grandmothers, who can show me how
to lead "as a woman"? When I turn to those models, they don't split along the
hard/soft, powerful/caring line. . . . Can I confound stereotypes? Does gender
allow me these choices at all?*

> The bravery of a warrior is like a lacquer cup. . . . If the cup drops
> it will bounce rather than break. It is soft and hard at the same time.
> —*Chogyam Trungpa*

1991: *My friend, an administrator, is small-boned, about five foot five, and
gentle looking. She was having a hard time getting a word in edgewise with
her boss, a six-foot ex-marine who stood towering over her, aggressively asserting his opinions. Finally she jumped up on a chair and looked him level
in the eye. There was a pause. All right, he said sheepishly, I get it. They sat
down knee to knee, eye to eye. She planted her feet solidly on the floor, palms
flat on her thighs, and leaned forward to stare at him. . . . He listened.*

    *What she wanted was to give a faculty member—accused of sexism—
another chance.*

NOTES

I have discussed the issues in this chapter profitably with more people than I can
name. Among those I owe special thanks for their ideas are Faith Plvan, Nance
Hahn, Patricia Stock, Janet Emig, Donna Marsh, and (for physics analogies) my
son Alex. Joan Carpenter is the best woman administrator I know and has generously shared her time in giving support and advice. Finally, I am grateful to my
husband, Fred, my parents, Virginia and Don Wetherbee, and my brother Harry
for providing me with my wisest counsel and best models for community and
leadership. They have all had a lot to put up with for seven years.

    1. Susan Miller is an exception in her clear understanding that feminization
has a double-edged meaning potential; she directly addresses the transitional state
between feminization and empowerment, analyzes the political and ethical choices
it presents, and proposes a stance. Our views are both tonally and substantially
different, however, and her solutions don't deal with the practical consequences
and complications of the concrete workplace.

    2. This chapter is partly a feminist experiment in form. Janet Emig and I hold
that feminist theory of practice, though informed by others' formal theories, should
be grounded in composition by reference to embodied, pretheoretical experience;
the naive view of experience is not primarily a cognitive error but a problem of
sentimentalizing ourselves. "To build an adequately complex theory, you must
render all these kinds of experience [personal lives, historical experience, collective experience, institutional experience] in a phenomenologically detailed, unsentimental, self-critical mode that accounts in some measure for the complexities of
lived life. . . . To access the complexities we often gloss over, we might start with
experiential vignettes that have the form of knots, tense, conflictual, paradoxical,
ambiguous, counterintuitive moments when stereotypes break down" (1991b, 4).
Toward this end, I use anecdotal material to evoke felt experience and create or
illuminate such knots. Blocked quotations weave into the text a chorus of scholarly,
popular, and personal voices in commentary.

3. Standpoint feminism is discussed extensively in works on feminist methodology: for example, Fonow and Cook; M. Gergen; Harding 1987, 1986; Malson et al.; Nielsen. See also essays by Hartsock; Smith. For brief critical reviews, see Harding 1987, 181–90.

4. Writing this chapter has recreated painful emotions and made me confront again the documents and memories that provoked them. If the point is to accept power and examine its paradoxes rather than allow oneself to be defined by victimization, it becomes difficult to know what to do with these experiences and the moral feelings they generate. Conflicts between the impulse to express indignation and the determination to minimize it are intensified by the recognition that, however vivid to oneself, these slights are trivial beside the privations, violence, and loss that afflict others around the world. I chose finally to acknowledge and represent these memories as a subtextual dimension of my argument (the strand of "knotty" reminiscences). In part, it was because I concluded that even humble problems are clues to how our society works; and the failure to remark or condemn unethical behavior in any situation is telling about the general moral climate. As Elizabeth Spelman says, "The [self-] censorship of anger is a way of short-circuiting, of censoring judgments about wrongdoing" (272) If anger is the "essential political emotion" (ibid.), then Spelman recommends we consider Aristotle's caution that "to get angry is easy. To do it to the right person, to the right extent, at the right time with the right motive, and in the right way—that is hard" (ibid., 270).

5. Although I am troubled by what I have directly observed of pedagogies that turn writing classrooms into arenas for feminist political work, I do not address those issues here, since this model does not translate in any obvious way to the programmatic level—that is, into a potential social order. The relevant comparison would be not to the feminist content and political purposes but to the methods and means of teaching and the relations proposed between the authority of teachers and the empowerment of students. See, e.g., Bizzell 1992; Crowley; Hairston; Lazere; Phelps 1992.

In composition, see, e.g., Ashton-Jones and Thomas; Caywood and Overing; Cooper; Flynn 1988; Hays, chap. 8, this vol.; Tedesco. On extradisciplinary sources, see Franke, chap. 17, this vol. For critiques, see Dingwaney and Needham; Jarratt.

7. Cf. Elizabeth Flynn's definition of feminism as "the use of feminine epistemological approaches" (1991, 143). Some feminists object to any (other than disparaging) use of the term *feminine*. But this rejection of the word is too close to rejection of the qualities it evokes and of women who exhibit or embrace them. In addition, feminists' assiduous avoidance of the word sometimes produces strained usages that contradict their own definitions. For example, Toril Moi claims, "It has long been established practice among most feminists to use 'feminine' (and 'masculine') to represent social constructs . . . and to reserve 'female' and 'male' for the purely biological aspects of sexual difference" (65), yet many oppose *masculine* to *feminist*. Consider also these phrases used by Nina Baym on the very same page: "Revalue such traditionally denigrated *female* attributes as compassion, empathy, nurturance"; "a society that values the *"female"* qualities while giving *biological females* access to the full range of human choices" [emphasis added] (60).

8. James Comas and Ronald Schleifer have analyzed this dilemma subtly as it applies to editing, drawing on concepts from Dewey and Kierkegaard, among others. "Kierkegaard makes clear the frustrating conundrum faced by the editor who acknowledges the institutional source of editorial authority and the resulting ethical imbalance in the author-editor-reader relationship" (67). The authors also turn to the concept of midwifery as a way out of this dilemma, a concept similar to Nel Nodding's "feminine" concept of caring or Max van Manen's "parental" notion of pedagogical tact (cf. Swearingen). But, they acknowledge, Kierkegaard's maieutic irony cannot finally ground editorship or leadership. We must proceed in the face of the knowledge that to make judgments of value (an ethical act) is necessarily also "an act of power and politics" (Comas and Schleifer, 68).

9. This difference between the director's and the teacher's position vis-à-vis students disappears if the feminist teacher subsumes writing pedagogy to her own utopian politics, teaching students not for their own individual sakes but in order to enlist them in the creation of a better society. See note 5, above.

10. See, especially, the Wyoming Conference Resolution and debates surrounding the Conference on College Composition and Communication (CCCC) Statement that evolved form it: Robertson et al.; CCCC Executive Committee; CCCC Committee; "Staffroom Interchange"; "Symposium."

11. See Carol Gilligan on an ethic of justice; Nina Chordas on composition's ill-defined use of the term *equality*. Patricinio Schweickart provides a useful critique of symmetric theories of power and valuable discussion, based on Noddings's theory of caring, of how asymmetries can be beneficent in teaching writing.

12. Although my focus is on differences in power among faculty and program administrators, a full description of the workplace would include secretaries and administrative staff, student workers, and technical staff, as well as other faculty, administrators, staff, and outsiders with whom program members interact. Most important, it would include undergraduate and graduate students taught by the program.

"There is, in any conceivable human community of this size, a distribution of institutional power. What matters is, what kind of power, how does it operate (under what constraints), and how can one achieve it. In this program, we have tried to make three things count as power that do not automatically come with a title or role: the power of ideas, the power of productive activity; and the power derived from accepting responsibility to our institutional commitments as well as to teachers and students in the program. . . . At the same time, we accept and respect the differentials in knowledge and commitment, and thus role, that characterize membership in the program because people are here for different reasons, for different lengths of time, and with different levels of energy to devote to this part of their lives; and we try to make those differentials workable, even advantageous, for the program and livable for all its members" (Phelps 1991a, 11–12). The broader notion of constructing a layer of reflection on the social relations was expressed in this and other quotations from Mary Catherine Bateson discussed with program members in my first month as director: "We designed a [conference] structure that would function on two levels, gathering a group of people to work together on particular themes, and always at the same time having a discussion of the process, a process in which interpersonal relationships as well as ideas are

336   Louise Wetherbee Phelps

interwoven" (1984, 223), a "double structure of the sort her father, Gregory, called a "metalogue."

14. These collaborative principles were set out in a program document, originally part of a successful argument to defend qualitative features of the program in planning budget cuts, later modified to present these features to teachers (Phelps 1991d). The list includes as already established, for example, principles of teaching community (coordinating groups and co-teaching), teachers' access to leadership roles, and the team structure.

15. *Community* has recently come under analysis as an ill-defined term in composition; at the same time, current critiques of collaborative learning call into question the often tacit notions of community and consensus that have thematized that pedagogy. See, e.g., Harris; Trimbur; Ashton-Jones, chap. 1, this vol.; Stewart. This chapter takes Harris's "specific and material view of community": that it is not simply (though it is) a community of discourse and that, "like a city, [it] allows for both consensus and conflict" (20).

BIBLIOGRAPHY

Ashton-Jones, Evelyn, and Dene Kay Thomas. "Composition, Collaboration, and Women's Way of Knowing: A Conversation with Mary Belenky." *Journal of Advanced Composition* 10 (1990): 275–92.

Bateson, Mary Catherine. *With a Daughter's Eye: A Memoir of Margaret Mead and Gregory Bateson.* New York: Washington Square Press, 1984.

———. *Composing a Life.* New York: Atlantic Monthly Press, 1989.

Baym, Nina. "The Feminist Teacher of Literature: Feminist or Teacher?" In *Gender in the Classroom,* edited by Gabriel and Smithson, 60–77. 1990.

Bazerman, Charles. *Shaping Written Knowledge: The Genre and Activity of the Experimental Article in Science.* Madison: Univ. of Wisconsin Press, 1988.

Belenky, Mary Field, Blythe McVicker Clinchy, Nancy Rule Goldberger, and Jill Matluck Tarule. *Women's Ways of Knowing: The Development of Self, Voice, and Mind.* New York: Basic Books, 1986.

Bellah, Robert N., Richard Madsen, William M. Sullivan, Ann Swidler, and Steven M. Tipton. *Habits of the Heart: Individualism and Commitment in American Life.* Berkeley and Los Angeles: Univ. of California Press, 1985.

Berthoff, Ann. "Killer Dichotomies: Reading In/Reading Out." In *Farther Along: Transforming Dichotomies in Rhetoric and Composition,* edited by Kate Ronald and Hephzibah Roskelly, 12–24. Portsmouth, N.H.: Heinemann, 1990.

Bizzell, Patricia. "The Politics of Teaching Virtue." *ADE Bulletin* 103 (1992): 4–7.

Brown, Amanda, and Andrea Constable, eds. *Teachers Sourcebook: A Guide to the Writing Program.* 4th ed. Syracuse: Syracuse University Writing Program, 1991.

Bullock, Richard, and John Trimbur, eds. *The Politics of Writing Instruction: Postsecondary.* Portsmouth, N.H.: Heinemann-Boynton/Cook, 1991.

Caywood, Cynthia L., and Gillian R. Overing, eds. *Teaching Writing: Pedagogy, Gender, and Equity.* Albany: State Univ. of New York Press, 1987.

CCCC Committee on Professional Standards for Quality Education. "CCCC Initiatives on the Wyoming Resolution: A Draft Report." *College Composition and Communication* 40 (1989): 61–72.

CCCC Executive Committee. "Statement of Principles and Standards for the Postsecondary Teaching of Writing." *College Composition and Communication* 40 (1989): 329–36.

"Charter for the Writing Program." In *Teachers' Sourcebook,* edited by Brown and Constable, 13–14. 1991.

Chordas, Nina. "Classrooms, Pedagogies, and the Rhetoric of Equality." *College Composition and Communication* 43 (1992): 214–24.

Comas, James, and Ronald Schleifer. "The Ethics of Publishing." *The Eighteenth Century: Theory and Interpretation* 29 (1988): 57–69.

Connors, Robert J. "Overwork/Underpay: Labor and Status of Composition Teachers Since 1880." *Rhetoric Review* 9 (1990): 108–27.

———. "Rhetoric in the Modern University: The Creation of an Underclass." In *Politics of Writing Instruction,* edited by Bullock and Trimbur, 55–84. 1991.

Cooper, Marilyn M. "Women's Ways of Writing." In *Writing as Social Action,* edited by Marilyn M. Cooper and Michael Holzman, 141–56. Portsmouth, N.H.: Heinemann-Boynton/Cook, 1989.

Crowley, Sharon. "Reimagining the Writing Scene: Curmudgeonly Remarks about *Contending with Words.*" In *Contending with Words,* edited by Harkin and Schilb, 189–97. 1991.

DeVault, Marjorie. *Feeding the Family: the Social Organization of Caring as Gendered Work.* Chicago: Univ. of Chicago Press, 1991.

Dingwaney, Anuradha, and Lawrence Needham. "Feminist Theory and Practice in the Writing Classroom: A Critique and a Prospectus." In *Constructing Rhetorical Education: From the Classroom to the Community,* edited by Marie Secor and Davida Charney, 6–25. Carbondale: Southern Illinois Univ. Press, 1992.

Fishman, Pamela. "Interaction: The Work Women Do." In *Women and Work: Problems and Perspectives,* edited by Rachel Kahn-Hut, Arlene Kaplan Daniels, and Richard Colvard, 170–80. New York: Oxford Univ. Press, 1982.

Flynn, Elizabeth A. "Composing as a Woman." *College Composition and Communication* 39 (1988): 423–35.

———. "Composition Studies from a Feminist Perspective." In *Politics of Writing Instruction,* edited by Bullock and Trimbur, 137–54. 1991.

Fonow, Mary Margaret, and Judith A. Cook, eds. *Beyond Methodology: Feminist Scholarship as Lived Research.* Bloomington: Indiana Univ. Press, 1991.

Fox-Genovese, Elizabeth. *Feminism Without Illusions: A Critique of Individualism.* Chapel Hill: Univ. of North Carolina Press, 1991.

Gabriel, Susan L., and Isaiah Smithson, eds. *Gender in the Classroom: Power and Pedagogy.* Urbana: Univ. of Illinois Press, 1990.

Gergen, Kenneth. "Feminist Critique of Science and the Challenge of Social Epistemology." In *Feminist Thought,* edited by M. Gergen, 27–48. 1988.

Gergen, Mary McCanney, ed. *Feminist Thought and the Structure of Knowledge.* New York: New York Univ. Press, 1988.

Gilligan, Carol. *In a Different Voice: Psychological Theory and Women's Development.* Cambridge: Harvard Univ. Press, 1982.

338   Louise Wetherbee Phelps

Gleick, James. *Genius: The Life and Science of Richard Feynman.* New York: Pantheon, 1992.

Grove, Andrew S. "Knowing When—and How—to Assert Your Authority." *Working Woman,* April 1993, 24f.

Grumet, Madeleine. *Bitter Milk: Women and Teaching.* Amherst: Univ. of Massachusetts Press, 1988.

Hairston, Maxine. "Diversity, Ideology, and Teaching Writing." *College Composition and Communication* 43 (1992): 179–93.

Harding, Sandra. *The Science Question in Feminism.* Ithaca: Cornell Univ. Press, 1986.

Harding, Sandra, ed. *Feminism and Methodology: Social Science Issues.* Bloomington: Indiana Univ. Press, 1987.

Harris, Joseph. "The Idea of Community in the Study of Writing." *College Composition and Communication* 40 (1989): 11–22.

Harkin, Patricia, and John Schilb, eds. *Contending with Words: Composition and Rhetoric in a Postmodern Age.* New York: MLA, 1991.

Harstock, Nancy C. M. "The Feminist Standpoint: Developing the Ground for a Specifically Feminist Historical Materialism." In *Feminism and Methodology,* edited by Harding, 157–80. 1987.

Holbrook, Sue Ellen. "Women's Work: The Feminizing of Composition." *Rhetoric Review* 9 (1991): 201–29.

Jarratt, Susan C. "Feminism and Composition: The Case for Conflict." In *Contending with Words,* edited by Harkin and Schilb, 105–23. 1991.

Keller, Evelyn Fox, and Helene Moglen. "Competition and Feminism: Conflicts for Academic Women." *Signs* 12 (1987): 493–511.

Laib, Nevin. "Territoriality in Rhetoric." *College English* 47 (1985): 579–93.

Langer, Susanne. *Mind: An Essay on Human Feeling.* Baltimore: Johns Hopkins Univ. Press, 1967.

Lazere, Donald. "Teaching the Political Conflicts: A Rhetorical Schema." *College Composition and Communication* 43 (1992): 194–213.

Malson, Micheline R., Jean F. O'Barr, Sarah Westphal-Wihl, and Mary Wyer, eds. *Feminist Theory in Practice and Process.* Chicago: Univ. of Chicago Press, 1989.

Miller, Susan. *Textual Carnivals: The Politics of Composition.* Carbondale: Southern Illinois Press, 1991a.

———. "The Feminization of Composition." In *Politics of Writing Instruction,* edited by Bullock and Trimbur, 39–53. 1991b.

Moi, Toril. *Sexual/Textual Politics: Feminist Literary Theory.* London: Routledge, 1985.

Monaghan, Jennifer. "Literacy Instruction and Gender in Colonial New England." In *Reading in America: Literature and Social History,* edited by Cathy N. Davidson, 53–80. Baltimore: John Hopkins Univ. Press, 1989.

Nielsen, Joyce McCarl, ed. *Feminist Research Methods: Exemplary Readings in the Social Sciences.* Boulder: Westview, 1990.

Noddings, Nel. *Caring: A Feminine Approach to Ethics and Moral Education.* Berkeley and Los Angeles: Univ. of California Press, 1984.

Olson, Garey A., and Joseph Moxley. "Directing Freshmen Composition: The Limits of Authority." *College Composition and Communication* 40 (1989): 51–60.

Phelps, Louise Wetherbee. "The Discourse of Controversy." Conference on Rhetoric and Literary Criticism, University of Waterloo, May 1990.

———. "The Institutional Logic of Writing Programs: Catalyst, Laboratory, and Pattern of Change." In *Politics of Writing Instruction,* edited by Bullock and Trimbur. 1991c.

———. "Keynote Speech." Syracuse: Syracuse University Writing Program, January 1991.

———. "Lessons of the Feminist Workplace." Presented at workshop, Reconsidering Composition Studies from a Feminist Perspective. Conference on College Composition and Communication, Boston, 1991b.

———. "Organizing Principles in the Writing Program." In *Teachers' Sourcebook,* edited by Brown and Constable, 26–31. 1991d.

———. "A Constrained Vision of the Writing Classroom." *ADE Bulletin* 103 (1992): 12–20. Rpt. in *Profession 93.* MLA, 1993: 46–54.

Phelps, Louise Wetherbee, and Faith Plvan. "The Social Architecture of the Writing Program." In *Windows on the Writing Program: The Syracuse Self-Study Portfolio,* edited by Louise Wetherbee Phelps and Charles Howell. Syracuse: Syracuse University Writing Program, 1992.

Polanyi, Michael. *Personal Knowledge: Toward a Post-Critical Philosophy.* Chicago, Univ. of Chicago Press, 1962.

Robertson, Linda R., Sharon Crowley, and Frank Lentricchia. "The Wyoming Conference Resolution Opposing Unfair Salaries and Working Conditions for Post-Secondary Teachers of Writing." *College English* 49 (1987): 274–80.

Schweickart, Patricinio P. "Reading, Teaching, and the Ethic of Care." In *Gender in the Classroom,* edited by Gabriel and Smithson. Urbana: Univ. of Illinois Press, 1990.

Smith, Dorothy. "Women's Perspective as a Radical Critique of Sociology." In *Feminism and Methodology,* edited by Harding, 84–96. Bloomington: Indiana Univ. Press, 1987.

Spelman, Elizabeth V. "Anger and Insubordination." In *Women, Knowledge, and Reality: Explorations in Feminist Philosophy,* edited by Ann Garry and Marilyn Pearsall, 262–73. Boston: Unwin Hyman, 1989.

"Staffroom Interchange." *College Composition and Communication* 40 (1989): 345–71.

Stewart, Donald. "Collaborative Learning and Composition: Boon or Bane?" *Rhetoric Review* 7 (1988): 58–83.

Swearingen, C. Jan. "The Rhetor as Eiron: Plato's Defense of Dialogue." *Pre/Text* 3 (1982): 289–336.

"Symposium on the 1991 'Progress Report from the CCCC Committee on Professional Standards.'" *College Composition and Communication* 43 (1992): 154–75.

Tedesco, Janis. "Women's Ways of Knowing/Women's Ways of Composing." *Rhetoric Review* 9 (1991): 246–56.

Trimbur, John. "Consensus and Difference in Collaborative Learning." *College English* 51 (1989): 602–16.

Trungpa, Chogyam. *Shambhala: The Sacred Path of the Warrior.* Edited by Carolyn Rose Gimian. Boston: Shambhala, 1984.

Van Manen, Max. *The Tact of Teaching: The Meaning of Pedagogical Thoughtfulness.* Albany: State Univ. of New York Press, 1991.

14

Between the Drafts

Nancy Sommers

I cannot think of my childhood without hearing voices, deep, heavily accented, instructive German voices.

I hear the voice of my father reading to me from *Struvelpater,* the German children's tale about a messy boy who refuses to cut his hair or his fingernails. Struvelpater's hair grows so long that birds nest in it, and his fingernails grow so long that his hands become useless. He fares better, though, than the other characters in the book who don't listen to their parents. Augustus, for instance, refuses to eat his soup for four days and becomes as thin as a thread; on the fifth day he is dead. Fidgety Philip tilts his dinner chair like a rocking horse until his chair falls backward; the hot food falls on top of him and suffocates him under the weight of the tablecloth. The story that frightened me most tells of Conrad, who couldn't stop sucking his thumb and whose mother warned him that a great, long, red-legged scissor-man would—and, yes, did—snip both his thumbs off.

As a child, I hated these horrid stories with their clear moral lessons exhorting me to listen to my parents: do the right thing, they said; obey authority, or else catastrophic things—dissipation, suffocation, loss of thumbs—will follow. As a child, I never wondered why my parents, who had escaped Nazi Germany in 1939, were so deferential to authority, so beholden to sanctioned sources of power. I guess it never occurred to them to reflect or to make any connections between generations of German children reading *Struvelpater,* being instructed from early childhood to honor and defer to the parental authority of the state, and the Nazis' easy rise to power.

I hear the voice of my grandmother instructing me that when I invite people to dinner, I should always cook two chickens even if only one is needed. Nothing more humiliating, she would say, than having your guests leave your dinner table hungry.

When I hear my mother's voice, it is usually reading to me from some kind of guidebook showing me how different *they,* the Americans, are from us, the German Jews of Terre Haute. My parents never left home without their passports; we had roots somewhere else. When we traveled westward every summer from our home in Indiana, our bible, the AAA tour guide gave us the officially sanctioned version of America. We attempted to "see" America from the windows of our 1958 two-tone green Oldsmobile. We were literally the tourists from Terre Haute described by Walker Percy in "The Loss of the Creature," people who could never experience the Grand Canyon because it had already been formulated for us by picture-postcards, tourist folders, guidebooks, and the words GRAND CANYON. Percy suggests that tourists never see the progressive movement of depths, patterns, colors, and shadows of the Grand Canyon, but rather measure their satisfaction by the degree to which the canyon conforms to the expectations in their minds. My mother's AAA guidebook directed us, told us what to see, how to see it, and how long it should take us to see it. We never stopped anywhere serendipitously, never lingered, never attempted to know a place.

As I look now at the black-and-white photographs of our trips, seeing myself in ponytail and pedal pushers, I am struck by how many of the photos are taken against the car or, at least, with the car close enough to be included in the photograph. I am not sure we really saw the Grand Canyon or the Painted Desert or the Petrified Forest, except from the security of a parking lot. We were traveling on a self-imposed visa that kept us close to our parked car; we lacked the freedom of our own authority and stuck close to each other and to the guidebook itself.

My parents' belief that there was a right and a wrong way to do everything extended to the way they taught us German. Wanting us to learn the correct way, not trusting their own native voices, they bought us language-learning records with the officially sanctioned voice of an expert language teacher; never mind that they themselves spoke fluent German.

It is 1959; I am eight years old. We sit in the olive-drab living room, the drapes closed so the neighbors won't see in. What those neighbors would have seen strikes me now as a scene out of a "Saturday Night Live" Coneheads skit. The children and their parental unit sit in stiff, good-for-your-posture chairs that my brother and I call "the electric chairs." The chairs are at odd angles so we all face the fireplace; we don't look at each other. I guess my parents never considered pulling the chairs around, facing each other, so we could just talk in German. My father had invested in the best 1959 technology he could find; he was proud of the time and money he had spent so that we could be instructed in the right way. I still see him there in that room removing the record from its purple package placing it on the hi-fi.

—Guten Tag.
—Wie geht es Dir?
—Wie geht es Werner/Helmut/Dieter?
—Werner ist heute krank.
—Oh, dass tut mir Leid.
—Gute Besserung.

We are disconnected voices worrying over the health of Werner, Dieter, and Helmut, foreign characters, mere names, who have no place in our own family. We go on and on with that dialogue until my brother passes gas or commits some other unspeakable offense, something that sets my father's German sensibility on edge, and he finally says, "We will continue another time." He releases us back into another life, where we speak English, forgetting for yet another week about the health of Werner, Helmut, or Dieter.

When I was in college, I thought I had the issue of authority all settled in my mind. My favorite T-shirt, the one I took the greatest pleasure in wearing, was one with the bold words QUESTION AUTHORITY inscribed across my chest. It seemed that easy. As we said then, either you were part of the problem or you were part of the solution; either you deferred to authority or you resisted it by questioning. Twenty years later, it doesn't seem that simple. I am beginning to get a better sense of my legacy, beginning to see just how complicated and how far-reaching is this business of authority. It extends into my life and touches my student's lives, reminding me again and again of the delicate relation between language and authority.

In 1989, thirty years after my German lessons at home, I'm having dinner with my daughters in an Italian restaurant. The waiter is flirting with eight-year-old Rachel, telling her she has the most beautiful name, that she is *una ragazza bellissima*. Intoxicated with this affectionate attention, she turns to me passionately and says, "Oh, Momma, Momma, can't we learn Italian?" I, too, for the moment am caught up in the brio of my daughter's passion. I say, "Yes, yes, we must learn Italian." We rush to our favorite bookstore where we find Italian language-learning tapes packaged in thirty-, sixty-, or ninety-day lessons; in our modesty, we buy the promise of fluent Italian in thirty lessons. Driving home together, we put the tape in our car tape player and begin lesson number one.

—Buon giorno.
—Come stai?
—Come stai Monica?

As we wend our way home, our Italian lessons quickly move beyond preliminaries. We stop worrying over the health of Monica, and suddenly we are in the midst of a dialogue about Signor Fellini who lives at 21 Broadway Street. We cannot follow the dialogue. Rachel, in great despair, betrayed by the promise of being a beautiful girl with a beautiful name speaking Italian in thirty lessons, begins to scream at me: "This isn't the way to learn a language. This isn't language at all. These are just words and sentences; this isn't about us; we don't live at 21 Broadway Street."

And I am back home in Indiana, hearing the disembodied voices of my family, learn a language out of the context of life.

In 1987, I gave a talk at the Conference on College Composition and Communication entitled "New Directions for Researching Revision." At the time, I liked the talk very much, because it gave me an opportunity to illustrate how revision, once a subject as interesting to our profession as an autopsy, had received new body and soul, almost celebrity status, in our time. Yet as interesting as revision had become, it seemed to me that our pedagogies and research methods were resting on some shaky, unquestioned assumptions. I had begun to see how students often sabotage their own best interests when they revise, searching for errors and assuming, like the eighteenth-century theory of words parodied in *Gulliver's Travels,* that words are a load of things to be carried around and exchanged. It seemed to me that, despite all those multiple drafts and all the peer workshops we were encouraging, we had left unexamined the most important fact of all: revision does not always guarantee improvement; successive drafts do not always lead to a clearer vision. You can't just change the words around and get the ideas right.

Here I am four years later, looking back on that now-abandoned talk, thinking of myself as a student writer and seeing that successive drafts have not led me to a clearer vision. I have been under the influence of a voice other than my own.

I live by the lyrical dream of change, of being made anew, always believing that a new vision is possible. I have been gripped, probably obsessed, with the subject of revision since graduate school. I have spent hundreds of hours studying manuscripts, looking for clues in the drafts of professional and student writers, looking for the figure in the carpet. The pleasures of this kind of literary detective work, this literary voyeurism, are the peeps behind the scenes, the glimpses of the process revealed in all its nakedness, of what Edgar Allan Poe called "the elaborate and vacillating crudities of thought, the true purposes seized only at the last moment, the cautious selections and rejections, the painful erasures."

My decision to study revision was not an innocent choice. It is deeply satisfying to believe that we are not locked into our original statements, that we might start and stop, erase, use the delete key in life, and be saved from the roughness of our early drafts. Words can be retracted; souls can be reincarnated. Such beliefs have informed my study of revision, and yet, in my own writing, I have always treated revision as an academic subject, not a personal one. Every time I have written about revision, I have set out to argue a thesis, present my research, accumulate my footnotes. By treating revision as an academic subject, by suggesting that I could learn something only by studying the drafts of other experienced writers, I kept myself clean and distant from any kind of scrutiny. No Struvelpater was I; no birds could nest in my hair; I kept my thumbs intact. I have been the bloodless academic, creating taxonomies, building a hierarchy from student writers to experienced writers, and never asking myself how I was being displaced from my own work. I never asked, "What does my absence *signify?*"

In that unrevised talk from CCCC, I had let Wayne Booth replace my father. Here are my words:

> Revision presents a unique opportunity to study what writers know. By studying writers' revisions, we can learn how writers locate themselves within a discourse tradition by developing a persona—a fictionalized self. Creating a persona involves placing the self in a textual community, seeing oneself within a discourse, and positing a self that shares or antagonizes the beliefs that a community of readers share. As Wayne Booth has written, "Every speaker makes a self with every word uttered. Even the most sincere statement implies a self that is at best a radical selection

from many possible roles. No one comes on in exactly the same way
with parents, teachers, classmates, lovers, and IRS inspectors."

What strikes me now, in this paragraph from my own talk, is that fic-
tionalized self I invented, that anemic researcher who set herself apart
from her most passionate convictions. I am a distant, imponderable, impersonal voice—inaccessible, humorless, and disguised like the packaged voice of Signor Fellini, giving lessons as if absolutely nothing depends on my work. I speak in an inherited academic voice; it isn't mine.

I simply wasn't there for my own talk. Just as my father hid behind
his language-learning records and my mother behind her guidebooks, I
disguised myself behind the authority of "the researcher," attempting to
bring in the weighty authority of Wayne Booth to justify my own statements, never gazing inward, never trusting my own authority as a writer.

Looking back on that talk, I know how deeply I was under the influence of a way of seeing: Foucault's "Discourse on Language," Barthes's
S/Z, Scholes's *Textual Power,* and Bartholomae's "Inventing the University" had become my tourist guides. I was so much under their influence
and so detached from my own voice that I remember standing in a su-
permarket parking lot holding two heavy bags of groceries, talking with
a colleague who was telling me about his teaching. Without any reference, except to locate my own authority somewhere else, I felt compelled
to suggest to him that he read Foucault. My daughter Alexandra, waiting
impatiently for me, eating chocolate while pounding on the hood of the
car with her new black patent-leather party shoes, spoke with her own
authority. She reminded me that I, too, had bumped on cars, eaten Her-
shey Bars, worn party shoes without straps, never read Foucault, and
knew, nevertheless, what to say on most occasions.

One of my colleagues put a telling cartoon on the wall of our photo-
copy room. It reads "Breakfast Theory: A morning methodology." The
cartoon describes two new cereals: Foucault Flakes and Post-Modern
Toasties. The slogan for Foucault Flakes reads: "It's French, so it must
be good for you. A breakfast commodity so complex that you need a
theoretical apparatus to digest it. You don't want to eat it; you'll just want
to read it. Breakfast as text." And Post-Modern Toasties: "More than just
a cereal, it's a commentary on the nature of cereal-ness, cerealism, and
the theory of cerealtivity. Free decoding ring inside."

I had swallowed the whole flake, undigested, as my morning methodology, but, alas, I never found the decoding ring. I was lost in the box.
Or, to use the metaphor of revision, I was stuck in a way of seeing:

reproducing the thoughts of others, using them as my guides, letting the poststructuralist vocabulary give authority to my text.

Successive drafts of my own talk did not lead to a clearer vision because it simply was not my vision. Like so many of my students, I was reproducing acceptable truths, imitating the gestures and rituals of the academy, lacking confidence in my own ideas and trust in my own language. I had surrendered my authority to someone else, to those other authorial voices.

Three years later, I am still wondering: Where does revision come from? Or, as I think about it now, what happens between the drafts? Something has to happen or else we are stuck doing mop-and-broom work, the janitorial work of polishing, cleaning, and fixing what is and always has been. What happens between drafts seems to be one of the great secrets of our profession.

Between drafts, I take lots of showers, hot showers, talking to myself as I watch the water play against the gestures of my hands. In the shower, I get lost in the steam. There I stand without my badges of authority. I begin an imagined conversation with my colleague, the one whom I told in the parking lot of the grocery store, "Oh, but you must read Foucault." I revise our conversation. This time I listen.

I understand why he showed so much disdain when I began to pay homage to Foucault. He had his own sources aplenty that nourished him. Yet he hadn't felt the need to speak through his sources or interject their names into our conversation. His teaching stories and experiences are his own; they give him the authority to speak.

As I get lost in the steam, I listen to his stories, and I begin to tell him mine. I tell him about my father not trusting his native voice to teach me German, about my mother not trusting her own eyes and reading to us from guidebooks, about my own claustrophobia in not being able to revise a talk about revision, about being drowned out by a chorus of authorial voices. And I surprise myself. Yes, I say, these stories of mine provide powerful evidence; they belong to me; I can use them to say what I must about revision.

I begin at last to have a conversation with all the voices I embody, and I wonder why so many issues are posed as either-or propositions. Either I stop sucking my thumb *or* the great red-legged scissor-man will cut it off. Either I cook two chickens *or* my guests will go away hungry. Either I accept authority *or* I question it. Either I have babies, in service to the species, *or* I write books, in service to the academy. Either I be personal *or* I be academic.

These either-or ways of seeing exclude life and real revision by push-ing us to safe positions, to what is known. They are safe positions that exclude each other and allow for no ambiguity or uncertainty. Only when I suspend myself between *either* and *or* can I move away from conven-tional boundaries and begin to see shapes and shadows and contours—ambiguity, uncertainty, discontinuity, moments when the seams of life just don't want to hold; days when I wake up to find, once again, that I don't have enough bread for the children's sandwiches or that there are no shoelaces for their gym shoes. My life is full of uncertainty; negoti-ating that uncertainty day to day gives me authority.

Maybe this is a woman's journey, maybe not, maybe it is just my own; but the journey between home and work, between being personal and being authoritative, between the drafts of my life, is a journey of learning how to be both personal and authoritative, both scholarly and reflective. It is a journey that leads me to embrace the experiences of my life and gives me the insight to transform these experiences into evidence. I begin to see discontinuous moments as sources of strength and knowl-edge. When my writing and my life actually come together, the safe positions of either-or will no longer pacify me, no longer contain me and hem me in.

Foucault still makes sense to me because his is an antiauthoritarian voice. It is a voice that speaks to me about a struggle I know: the nec-essary and inevitable struggle all writers face in finding a voice within and against the voices of institution and inclination, between conventions and desire, between limits and choices.

In that unrevised talk, I had actually misused my sources. What they were saying to me, if I had listened, was pretty simple; don't follow us, don't reproduce what we have produced, don't live life from secondary sources like us, don't disappear. I hear Bob Scholes's and David Bartho-lomae's voices telling me to answer them, to speak back to them, to use them and make them anew. They say, in a word, revise me. The language lesson starts to make sense, finally: by confronting these authorial voices, I find the power to understand and gain access to my own ideas. Against all the voices I embody—the voices heard, read, whispered to me from offstage—I must bring a voice of my own. I must enter the dialogue on my own authority, knowing that, though other voices have enabled mine, I can no longer subordinate mine to theirs.

The voices I embody encourage me to show up as a writer and to bring the courage of my own authority into my classroom. I have also learned about the dangers of submission from observing the struggles of my own students. When they write about their lives, they write with confidence. As soon as they begin to turn their attention toward outside sources, they too lose confidence, defer to the voice of the academy, and write in the voice of EVERYSTUDENT to an audience they think of as EVERYTEACHER. They disguise themselves in the weighty, imponderable voice of acquired authority: "In today's society . . ."; "Since the beginning of civilization mankind has . . ."; or, as one student wrote about authority itself, "In attempting to investigate the origins of authority of the group, we must first decide exactly what we mean by authority."

In my workshops with teachers, the issue of authority, or deciding exactly what we mean by authority, always seems to be at the center of many heated conversations. Some colleagues are convinced that our writing programs should be about teaching academic writing. They see such programs as the Welcome Wagon of the academy, the Holiday Inn where students lodge as they take holy orders. Some colleagues fear that if we don't control what students learn, don't teach them to write as scholars write, we aren't doing our job and some great red-legged scissor-man will cut off our thumbs. It is another either-or proposition: either we teach students to write academic essays, or we teach them to write personal essays—and then who knows what might happen? The world might become uncontrollable: students might start writing about their grandmother's death in an essay for a sociology course. Or even worse, something more uncontrollable, they might just write essays and publish them in professional journals, claiming the authority to tell stories about their families and their colleagues. The uncontrollable world of ambiguity and uncertainty opens up, my colleagues imagine, as soon as the academic embraces the personal.

But, of course, our students are not empty vessels waiting to be filled with authorial intent. Given the opportunity to speak their own authority as writers, given a turn in the conversation, students can claim their stories as primary source material and transform their experiences into evidence. They might, if given enough encouragement, be empowered not to serve the academy and accommodate it, not to write in the persona of EVERYSTUDENT, but rather to write essays that will change the academy. When we create opportunities for something to happen between the drafts, when we create writing exercises that allow students to work with sources of their own that can complicate and enrich their primary sources, they will find new ways to write scholarly essays that are exploratory, thoughtful, and reflective.

I want my students to know what writers know—to know something no researchers could ever find out, no matter how many times they pin my students to the table, no matter how many protocols they tape. I want my students to know how to bring their life and their writing together.

Sometimes when I cook a chicken and my children scuffle over the one wishbone, I wish I had listened to my grandmother and cooked two. Usually, the child who gets the short end of the wishbone dissolves into tears of frustration and failure. Interjecting my own authority as the earth mother from central casting, I try to make their lives better by asking: On whose authority is it that the short end can't get her wish? Why can't both of you, the long and the short ends, get your wishes?

My children, on cue, as if they too were brought in from central casting, roll their eyes as children are supposed to when their mothers attempt to impose a way of seeing. They won't let me control the situation by interpreting it for them. My interpretation serves my needs, temporarily, for sibling compromise and resolution. They don't buy my story because they know something about the sheer thrill of the pull; they are not going to let *me* deny *them*. They will have to revise my self-serving story about compromise, just as they will have to revise the other stories I tell them. Between the drafts, as they get outside my authority, they too will have to question and begin to see for themselves their own complicated legacy, their own trail of authority.

It is in the thrill of the pull between someone else's authority and our own, between submission and independence, that we must discover how to define ourselves. In the uncertainty of that struggle, we have a chance to find the voice of our own authority. Finding it, we can speak convincingly . . . at long last.

Reconfigurations and Responses

15

Issues and Discursive Practices

Janice M. Lauer

Two strands run through this collection of essays: the issues deemed important by these authors and the discursive practices used to elaborate them. The issues are either political or pedagogical; the discursive practices are heteroglossic and multimodal. I am drawn to reading the essays through this bifocal lens for two reasons. First, over the years, as rhetoric and composition has developed as a discipline, I have written about its complex problem domain and its multimodality, labeling these as distinctive features enabling us to study problems and issues that would otherwise elude us. A second impetus is my ongoing dialogue with graduate students who seek to know both the salient issues in the field and the ways they can be studied. Reading the essays through this lens exposes some gaps in both strands. My alternate table of contents creates titles in boldface for these missing or underrepresented issues and practices. All of the issues (both those suggested and those represented) can be studied in multiple ways, for example, historically, theoretically, empirically, interpretively, or by a rich mixture of modes, as many of the essays demonstrate.

Contents

13 **Women in Discourse Communities: Consensus and Resistance**

14 Becoming a Warrior: Lessons of the Feminist Workplace
    Louise Wetherbee Phelps

Theoretical analysis, multiple voices, personal anecdotes

Part II Pedagogical Issues

15 Teaching Other People's Children
    Emily Jessup and Marion Lardner

Narratives, journals, reflection, metaphors

16 Rockshelf Further Forming: Women, Writing, and Teaching the Young
    Christine Holm Kline

Contrasts, conversations
Poetry, student voices

17 **The Emergent Woman Writer: Adolescent Problems and Pedagogy**

18 Intellectual Parenting and a Developmental Feminist Pedagogy of Writing
    Janice Hays

Argument based on feminist and developmental theory and empirical studies

19 Discourse and Diversity: Experimental Writing Within the Academy
    Lillian Bridwell-Bowles

Examples of classroom and feminist writings

20 Collaboration, Conversation, and the Politics of Gender
    Evelyn Ashton-Jones

Critique of collaborative learning, citing research in conversational dynamics

21 **Gendered Inventional (or Revising) Strategies?**

22 **The Discursive Formation of Professional Women**

Political Issues

The essays in the collection that tackle political issues raise questions about power, authority, conflicting voices, and the gendered social formation of subjects in the culture and in the profession. One broad issue is addressed by Patricia Bizzell, who seeks a way to establish a new ethical authority in the culture without becoming foundationalist or essentialist. Her discursive practice, based on theory building and historical analysis, centers on setting a historical exemplar, Erasmus's Folly, whom she depicts as a woman, a mock and real rebel, who can speak, like the sophists, from the margins, taking a position different from the dominant discourse. Bizzell also uses a descriptive strategy to delineate the features of the ethical authority she hopes for, one that gains agreement by creating relation between rhetors' values, promoting mutual change, and being conscious of one's own values. Robert Connors uses historical discursive practices to examine the issue of power in English studies, in what might be viewed as a revisionist history. He argues that women's entry into higher education in the nineteenth century changed the essence of rhetorical education from challenge to nurturing, from the oral to the written, from argument to multimodal practices, from abstract, distanced subjects to personal ones, and from rhetoric to composition. Though he notes that composition is still marginalized by the academy, his historical description concludes that in the last three decades composition has been evolving into an academically equal discipline.

Three essays dramatize the issue of voice in the academy and in broader social contexts. Nancy Sommers rehearses the dissonance between her personal and academic voices. She uses representative anecdotes and two elaborated analogies from her childhood—her mother's travel guidebooks and her father's language-learning records—to narrate her struggle to reconcile these voices. Her own story becomes a representative anecdote for the theoretical and political problem of the subject in composition studies—caught between the shaping forces of culture and the drive to control and own discourse. Myrna Harrienger also deploys narrative to tell the story of the writing life of an ill elderly woman, exposing the disempowerment and loss imposed on her by the monologic discourse of medicine and by the effects of her illness. In this case study, Harrienger employs the discursive practice of argument by contrast, comparing the ordering influence of Grace's lifelong composing before and after her series of strokes. In the third essay, Sara Jonsberg, in collaboration with Marie Salgado and the women of The Next Step, composes a chorus of voices—teenage mothers who recount their struggles to negotiate power positions and to risk going beyond what society expects of them. Through their discourse, including images and anecdotes from their personal lives, they show how they came to write a new script for themselves in defiance of the dominant discourse. All three essays argue for new areas of investigation in composition studies, using images and multiple voices as powerful discursive practices to argue and elaborate these issues.

In a dialogic interview conducted by Mary Kay Crouch, Son Kim Vo shares her struggles to help Vietnamese women develop literacy and education in English yet maintain their own cultural values and roles as mothers and homemakers. Her own remarkable literacies and academic accomplishments, as well as her refugee work, serve as a model of how to negotiate the complexities and challenges that face these women. Louise Phelps probes the moral, practical, and rhetorical complexities of women administering writing programs. Through the use of theoretical analysis, rich intertextuality, personal anecdotes, and multiple voices, she demonstrates that responsibility and authority exact heavy costs for those empowered to construct and complicate the feminist workplace. She examines the ratio between power and discipline that the woman administrator has to develop and the social architecture that must support strategies of empowerment: enabling conditions, structures, and exemplification.

Many other political issues could be addressed here, through discussions of the gendered nature of current issues in English studies; analyses of the relationship between gender issues in the academy and in the larger culture; revisionist historical studies to recover women who have been marginalized in a largely male rhetorical history; empirical research (from case study and ethnography to experimental studies) to identify the gender practices and values within and outside the academy and their effects on the cultural codes by which we live, write, and teach; and cultural studies to examine the institutional structures that foster or inhibit women's writing. Other voices that need to be studied include those of women of color, women as citizens, and women in professions, other workplaces, and homes.

Pedagogical Issues

The authors of the remaining essays examine pedagogical issues, either advancing new feminist pedagogies, critiquing existing practices, or filling gaps in historical accounts of pedagogy. Emily Jessup and Marion Lardner sketch the contours of a feminist pedagogy for elementary schools. Using the practices of personal narrative, journals, reflections, and metaphors, they argue for the reciprocal influence of feminism and pedagogy, outlining a child-centered theory marked by listening and compassion balanced with objectivity. Christine Kline contrasts meaningful whole language instruction with impoverished workbook teaching. Against the harsh tones of the "father tongue," she records sensitive "mother tongue" voices: conversations of dedicated, knowledgeable, but frustrated elementary school teachers and her own resonant poetic voice, sharing her textual and teaching lives, interlaced with the poetry of Adrienne Rich and with the cries of her students, hungry for listeners and literacy.

Feminist pedagogies are also outlined for the college level. Janice Hays marshals research and theory in developmental psychology to argue for a pedagogy that helps students move from a dualist epistemology through the levels of multiplicitous-subjectivist and relativist-procedural ways of knowing to a committed, constructed knowledge. Her argument is based on feminist and developmental theory and on empirical studies. She contends that, through writing experiences, students can be guided to express gender and ethnically associated learning styles within different developmental positions. Lillian Bridwell-Bowles promotes teaching a variety of new writing forms and formats such as emotional writing, question-posing, columns, and visuals. She illustrates her ideas with examples from her own classroom and from feminist writers.

Evelyn Ashton-Jones, in contrast, problematizes collaborative learning, a pedagogy advocated by feminists; she argues that a hierarchy of gender profoundly inscribes group activity, influencing the writing of women. Citing studies in the dynamics of conversation between women and men, she questions whether women receive the benefits of collaboration ascribed to it by feminists and suggests that, instead, such collaboration may unwittingly collude in reproducing traditional gender structures.

Finally, two essays revise educational history by filling in gaps. Cinthia Gannett gives a historical account of the gendered heritage of journals, showing that males and females have had different attitudes toward them for at least a century. Her work underscores their value for women but also exposes their historical position as marginalized and mixed discourse. Mitzi Myers, through a contextualized historical case—the teaching career of Anna Barbauld in the early nineteenth century—demonstrates the way that educational histories erased the cultural impact of Barbauld and other female educators of the period. Lost were their notions of household education conjoining "literary merit, innovative pedagogy grounded in children's everyday experience, and a maternal thinking both rational and affective."

Other pedagogical issues could be included: the development of the adolescent woman writer; gendered differences in writing processes and strategies; the effectiveness of proposed feminist versus traditional pedagogies; the discursive development of professional women; and teacher research on local cultural codes of gender in the school, family, and neighborhood.

Despite these inevitable gaps, the essays here are a rich read. Especially powerful are their heteroglossic discursive practices (both within single essays and throughout the collection) that enable the authors to construct a complex account of the political and pedagogical issues implicated in feminine principles and women's experience in American composition and rhetoric. Throughout my reading of the essays, I was sensitive to their intertextuality, listening to the conversations in which the authors participated. To the bibliographies the essays cite, I add the following:

Allen, Prudence. *The Concept of Woman: The Aristotelian Revolution 750* B.C. *to 1250* A.D. Montreal: Eden, 1985.

Bradley, Patricia. "The Folk-Linguistics of Women's Speech: An Empirical Examination." *Communication Monographs* 48 (1981).

Campbell, Karlyn. *Man Cannot Speak for Her: A Critical Study of Early Feminist Rhetoric.* New York: Praeger, 1989.

Feldman, Saul. *Escape from the Doll's House: Women in Graduate and Professional School Education.* New York: McGraw-Hill, 1974.

Foss, Sonya K., Karen A. Foss, and Robert Trapp. "Challenges to the Rhetorical Tradition: The Feminist Challenge." In *Contemporary Perspectives on Rhetoric.* 2d ed., 275–87. Prospect Hills, Illinois: Waveland, 1991.

Fuss, Diana. *Essentially Speaking: Feminism, Nature, and Difference.* New York: Routledge, 1989.

Gallop, Jane. *The Daughter's Seduction: Feminism and Psychoanalysis.* Ithaca: Cornell Univ. Press, 1982.

Gray, Nancy. *Language Unbound: On Experimental Writing by Women.* Urbana: Univ. of Illinois Press, 1993.

Johnson, Barbara. *A World of Difference.* Baltimore: Johns Hopkins Univ. Press, 1988.

Lakoff, Robin. *Language and Woman's Place.* New York: Harper Colophon, 1975.

Meese, Elizabeth. *Re-Figuring Feminist Criticism.* Urbana: Univ. of Illinois Press, 1990.

Nilsen, Alleen. "Sexism in English: A Feminist View." In *Female Studies VI: Closer to the Ground: Women's Classes, Criticisms, Programs—1972,* edited by Nancy Hoffman, Cynthia Secor, and Adrian Tinsley, 102–09. Old Westbury, N.Y.: Clearinghouse on Women's Studies, 1972.

Robinson, Lou, and Camille Norton, eds. *Resurgent: New Writing by Women.* Urbana: Univ. of Illinois Press, 1993.

Rossi, Alice, and Calderwood, Ann, eds. *Academic Women on the Move.* New York: Russell Sage Foundation, 1973.

Spitzack, Carole, and Kathyrn Carter. "Women in Communication Studies." *Quarterly Journal of Speech* 73 (1987): 401–23.

Women's Studies in Communication 11 (1988).

Yaeger, Patricia. *Honey-Mad Women: Emancipatory Strategies in Women's Writing.* New York: Columbia Univ. Press, 1988.

16

Mapping the Scene of Learning Through the Lens of Drama

Edward L. Rocklin

Dramatic Form as a Perspective

When Louise Wetherbee Phelps and Janet Emig invited me to respond to this volume, they made clear the contribution they hoped my participation would make. My professional identity is itself the product of the conversation between composition and drama, embodied in an effort to bring what we have learned about teaching writing to drama and literature classes and to bring what we have learned about teaching drama in performance to the challenges of designing new pedagogies in all the disciplines of English. Teaching has been a defining event in my own development; I have used drama as my primary conceptual tool for designing classes and have formulated the project of articulating a poetics of pedagogy.

This essay does not address the relation of the perspective I offer to feminism, feminist theory, feminist literary and theatrical criticism, or feminist practice. However, my approach shares a number of beliefs with many versions of feminism: (1) that the personal is political; (2) that pedagogy must be as much our concern as theory and content; and (3) that we must think as carefully, rigorously, and self-critically about what we do with our students as about other aspects of our practice. As well, my focus on drama as a tool for thinking coincides with a focus on the classroom as a shaping arena in the emergence of feminism in composition studies.

The concept of dramatic form as one perspective uses the constitutive elements of the dramatic event as a lens through which to look at the

enactment of feminism in the writings that comprise this volume. I read
the essays, that is, both as contributions to an emerging feminism in the
field of composition and as reflections on the complex relation between
feminism and pedagogy that, explicitly or implicitly, appears central to
many feminists and certainly to many, although not all, of the writers in
this volume. I perceive six elements that constitute the lens, or perhaps
the facets of the lens, for ordering and rereading this volume. My alternate table of contents has been organized according to these elements.
(This list is not exhaustive but represents those constitutive elements
that are relevant for the present project.)

Contents

The Enabling Conventions

The Copresence of Actor and Spectator

The Movement Through Time

The Objective Form of Presentation: The Apparent Absence of a Narrator

The Verbal and Written Mediums: Conversation, Dialogue, Written Texts

The Script

In the words of Raymond Williams and Alan Dessen, the enabling conventions are "the terms upon which author, performers and audience agree to meet, so that the performance may be carried on."[1] When seen through this lens, the essays in this volume by Robert Connors, Janice Hays, and Mitzi Myers appear as explorations of the conventions that enable us to constitute and participate in the scene of learning, for these authors explore the terms on which teachers and students agree to meet so that education may be enacted. The essay by Phelps, in turn, expands this focus, for she explores how an encompassing institution such as a large university authorizes not only a class but a program, and thereby creates the terms on which a program director, a varying array of instructors, and students meet and, through the performance of interlock-

ing scenes and whole drama, not only create but also transform the very
program that initially brings them together. Connors presents a historical account focused on the gendered nature of teacher-student and
teacher-teacher relations as these are embodied in the long history of
the teaching of rhetoric and in the recent transformations from rhetoric
to composition. Hays offers a possible further transformation, even as
Myers presents us with a case study of one particular figure who sought
to transform these relations through her own practice. And Phelps's analysis not only anatomizes how challenging it is to transform a pedagogic
vision into an active program, but also unpacks some of the tensions and
paradoxes that inhere both in gaining power and attempting to empower
others.

    Connors suggests that the original American model of education in
rhetoric was the (apparent) conclusion of a two-thousand-year evolution
of a highly gendered paradigm, in which the apprentice sought to equal
or overthrow the patriarchal instructor in order to gain his own authority;
and that the end of the nineteenth century saw "the change of student-
teacher relationships in rhetoric courses, from challenging and judgmental to nurturing and personalized, a change still in process today."
Connors describes a paradoxical paradigm shift in which one set of conventions "overthrew" an older set—the newer set explicitly opposed to
the model of agonistic contest it agonistically overthrew. This shift is
strikingly embodied in the contrast between the earlier agonistic relation, whose permanent hostility erupted in moments of direct physical
confrontation, and the modern "irenic" relation, in which the teacher is
seen as coach, facilitator, and enabler. And yet there is an irony here,
for implicit in Connors's account is a recognition of the seemingly inevitable presence of "contest" in efforts to extend feminist projects. What
seems to be emerging is an imperative to rethink the complex relation
of agonistic and irenic approaches—an imperative evident in other essays in this volume.

    In terms of the complex narrative offered by Connors, Janice Hays
constructs a role for the teacher that combines the traditionally gendered
activities of nurturing and challenging in a positive, gender-neutral enabling convention. Hays extends the idea of nurturing through the (traditional) undergraduate years, defining it specifically as the nurturing of
the student's maturing ability to confront and grow from intellectual challenges. At the same time, Hays articulates the danger that women teachers may simply be trapped into the all-nurturing half of the model. Hays
also implicitly sketches one of the many challenges confronting male

faculty who seek to construct a revised identity for themselves as teachers: this is the challenge of teaching students to challenge the teacher without letting insecurity drive the teacher back to authoritarian styles of pedagogy (although this is a challenge presumably not limited to male teachers).

"Of Mice and Mothers: Mrs. Barbauld's 'New Walk' and Gendered Codes in Children's Literature," by Mitzi Myers, explores one writer's efforts to revise the enabling conventions by combining the roles of writer and teacher. Seen in this way, and placed after the essay by Janice Hays, this is an account of a woman writer who served as an "intellectual parent" in a variety of ways, not only to her own and other people's children but also to adults, by modeling what literature for children could do. Whereas in this essay I use drama to emphasize the powerful connections of feminism with what might be called the "genre of pedagogy," Myers concentrates on a concept of pedagogic genres and, with it, "the birth of a pragmatic female teaching tradition" focused on constructing "relational selves" (thus her work connects with that of Sara Jonsberg). Barbauld, as cultural mother and shaper of "the domestic teaching community," is offered as one model of an intellectual parent. Myers suggests one direction in which we might extend the project of this book by looking for "a female tradition in writing and pedagogy" and indicates how we might begin to recognize a whole tradition of mother-teachers—a tradition embodied in the Emily Jessup and Marion Lardner in the next section of my table of contents. Furthermore, Myers raises a question as to why "the writing woman as teacher has not captured the imagination of feminist scholars." Here is another cue for further exploration, both historical and self-reflective.

Even in the conjunction of its key words, *warrior* and *feminist,* Louise Wetherbee Phelps's "Becoming a Warrior: Lessons of the Feminist Workplace" illuminates the paradoxes that Connors begins to suggest. Indeed, Phelps can be seen as seeking to articulate some enabling conventions for a new stage in the evolution of composition and rhetoric, a stage in which "we begin to move into the tidal zone of power." Her essay shows that those who attempt to create a more irenic model of gaining, wielding, sharing, and transforming power in the university not only will have to develop the skills of a warrior to deal with the agonistic nature of the larger institution but also will become involved in a complex interplay of irenic and agonistic encounters with their peers and those they seek to empower. That is, the very actions by which we propose to create a more cooperative scene of education will not only be contested but also inevitably precipitate contests between those who propose and those who must enact such transformed (and transforming) relations. As is true of other writers in this volume—Ashton-Jones, Bizzell, and Sommers, in particular—Phelps notes that to gain power is to gain responsibilities and pains we may not have imagined. Conversely, she reminds us that we maintain our purity or freedom from such responsibility and pain only at the cost of being marginal actors. Further, a fundamental proposition of the essay is that we must rethink the enabling conventions themselves: specifically, through creating new forms of what Phelps calls "social architecture" we will be able to initiate a process that "goes beyond the zero-sum game of redistribution to generate genuinely new, usable power."

The Copresence of Actor and Spectator

In drama, the copresence of actors and spectators encompasses several complex phenomena. First, it points to the fact that actors, or more precisely actors' bodies, are the medium of performance: the words of the script become embodied in their performance. Second, this mutual presence ensures that no two performances are identical, as the actors must respond to the nuances of a given enactment. Third, spectators are both present to the actors, and hence shape their performance, and present to each other, and hence shape one another's response. Correspondingly, students and teachers are the medium of education, and this element comes into focus in the three essays placed in this section of my table of contents.

In "Teaching Other People's Children," Emily Jessup and Marion Lardner show us how the copresence of teacher and student is crucially embodied in the opportunity to observe and listen to students. They illuminate how we must think about ourselves as spectators of our own participation, because we must learn to observe how we are listening— and, as they poignantly show, how we are forgetting to listen—to our students. In particular, Emily Jessup offers a crucial articulation of the place of listening in the act of composing: "For me, this is what teaching, especially teaching writing, is about. I write best when I know someone else will pay attention to what I'm trying to say. My most important need as a writer is an attentive reader; my most basic need as a learner is an attentive teacher." As they well know, their revision of the teacher's role would, if seriously carried out, transform the whole drama of education. Indeed, it would be an incredible enterprise actually to reshape even a single school system to enact a program such as that implicit in the Jessup and Lardner and Hays essays.

Another radically different role for the teacher is offered by Patricia Bizzell. While it is obvious that Bizzell is thinking of the women rhetor as critic, conference presenter, and intellectual among her peers, in exploring the role of the fool as articulated in Erasmus's *Praise of Folly* Bizzell offers a cue for beginning to think about the complex, multilayered performances we give as teachers: as people who balance several roles, some visible to our students, some visible only to ourselves, some perhaps invisible even to us, at least when we are performing. And while the idea of the teacher as rhetor assuming the role of the fool is at first sight radically divergent from the concept of "intellectual parent" presented by Janice Hays, Bizzell's sketch illuminates some deep tensions and untapped potentials in our role or, as Renaissance thinkers might call it, our office. For example, it is crucial that the fool is, as Goneril says of Lear's fool, *licensed,* and licensed in a way that is radically different from the responsibility given to a parent. We might want to explore how teachers are licensed, not only in terms of each state's credentialing but also in terms of the tacit enabling conventions. The crucial point is to recognize that we have not yet taken advantage of the full range of actions we are licensed to perform and invite our students to perform.

Whereas Bizzell wants to invent a new model in order to dissolve prevailing gendered constraints on the role of the teacher, in her work, "Collaboration, Conversation, and the Politics of Gender," Evelyn Ashton-Jones shows us how a practice that apparently liberates the students from the teacher in the role of authority may nonetheless perpetuate comparable gendered constraints between and within the students. Much previous feminist writing on composition pedagogy, says Ashton-Jones, simply asserts that collaborative groups dissolve hierarchy and thereby function in inherently feminist ways: thus, collaborative learning is seen as an integral part of feminist pedagogy and a practice that produces the results sought by feminists, simply by virtue of its structured action. But "it takes a logical leap of questionable validity to conclude that removing the teacher-authority from the scene of meaning making effectively removes all traces of the patriarchal presence. . . . The feminist valorization of collaborative learning, then, seems to me surprising, because . . . it does not acknowledge the role that gender may play in group dynamics." Ashton-Jones insists that ignoring this aspect of gendered conversation is obviously a mistake and that, if we continue to ignore the gendered nature of how students perform in collaborative groups, we will miss how "the work of social hierarchies goes on, embodied in the participants, in the process of interaction itself, and in the pedagogy being employed."

Thus Ashton-Jones can be seen as qualifying Connors's claim that composition already is the most feminized discipline outside of women's studies and challenging the tacit assumption that this is a paradigm shift that automatically dissolves other forces perpetuating male dominance. Nonetheless, it seems to me that her final imperative is not to stop using collaborative groups but rather to use them as laboratories for feminist change, making the group a place where we might foreground the issues delineated in her essay. As much as any piece in this volume, the essay by Ashton-Jones also offers a sense of a key moment in the unfolding feminist articulation of an appropriate pedagogy. We encounter a self-reflective voice offering a critique of the more optimistic premises on which earlier writers began to articulate a feminist pedagogy of composition. Further self-reflective critique is, I assume, an outcome the editors of this volume hope to stimulate.

The Movement Through Time

A third constitutive element in drama is the play's double movement through time. It is double because the spectator, unlike the reader, cannot stop the experience in order to return to earlier moments and because this experience of time as unstoppable parallels the human subjugation to time that is also enacted within the world of the play. This apparent limitation in drama is, of course, really one source of its great power: drama can produce a vivid sense of the movement through time of a whole life, compressed into the movement through time in a few hours. "Writing a Life: The Composing of Grace," by Myrna Harrienger, beautifully illuminates the need for and difficulty in capturing composition as "a life-defining practice": "Because Grace's writing extends over the . . . years of her adulthood, it illustrates what often eludes shorter-term studies, namely, the enormous potential of rhetoric, especially in its written form, to construct, empower, and validate the ordinary life. Written discourse was central to Grace's mode of life, her self-concept, and her sense of worth and defined her relationship with the persons and events of her lived experience." Although Grace is not herself a feminist, nor is she seen as teacher or student, her life as presented instructs us in the ways people use writing to compose an identity moving through time. Moreover, Harrienger lets us glimpse a model of how someone might construct the sort of complex identity that a number of other contributors to this volume—Bridwell-Bowles, Jonsberg, Kline, and Sommers, for example—are also concerned with constructing and helping students to construct. Certainly, an essay such as that by Jonsberg, Salgado, and the women of The Next Step can be seen as presenting the initial stages of the same use of writing as "a life-defining practice" of which Grace shows us the later stages.

The Objective Form of Presentation: The Apparent Absence of a Narrator

Interesting aspects come into focus when I look at "Between the Drafts," by Nancy Sommers, through the lens of the apparent absence of an authoritative narrator, one of the most striking features of drama as compared with prose fiction. That is, we can discern an analogy between the apparently unnarrated form of drama and the unnarrated form of human existence and then recognize that, just as the play, at least in the classic Western forms of drama, has an author who invites us to reconstruct that missing point of view, so there exist external or cultural narrators who, in some ways, function as authoritative voices in our lives. These narrators are, as Sommers phrases it, "off-stage . . . authorial voices," and in her case, she now sees them as having shaped both her childhood and a major stage of her own academic career. Her list includes such life-scripting off-stage narrators as family members, children's books, academic authorities, and dissertation directors as well as the voices of influential critics who become our discursive mentors. Sommers illuminates the paradoxical relation of our own creativity to authorities whose shaping impact on our lives we do not fully understand. "I was so much under [the influence of Foucault, Scholes, Barthes, and Bartholomae that] . . . I was stuck in a way of seeing. . . . I had surrendered my authority to someone else, to those other authorial voices." The paradox is neatly embodied in the slogan from her college days, QUESTION AUTHORITY. She elegantly demonstrates that we must first use the authority of others to gain our own authority so that we may, in turn, question that authority.

Expressed in another way, Sommers spotlights two apparently conflicting meanings of the phrase *to listen to:* we listen to others as authorities and obey, but we can also listen as receptive and responsive fellow participants, taking in and hearing others' stories so as to encourage them to grow beyond their present story. In this sense, she also emphasizes the way in which *to listen* can be *to disobey* or, rather, to obey another imperative, namely the imperative to let our listening to another's voice liberate new versions of our own voices. What we may do between the drafts is not to hear commands but to listen for cues. And, certainly, learning to distinguish between listening for cues and listening for commands, thereby achieving a balance between scripted and improvised acts, is essential to the art of teaching.

The Verbal and Written Mediums: Conversation, Dialogue, Written Texts

Cinthia Gannett's "The Stories of Our Lives Become Our Lives: Journals, Diaries, and Academic Discourse" is the first of three essays that can be seen as focusing our attention on the verbal medium in the classroom and in writing. These essays raise questions about the role of gender in the emergence of a writer's or a student-writer's identity and about the process by which student-writers gain authority from and through experience. Journals are so pervasive that they can seem to be as canonical a part of the emerging discipline of composition as the collaborative groups analyzed by Ashton-Jones. Like groups, journals are both scripted tools and a means for encouraging dialogue in speech and writing.

Gannett suggests two ways we could reshape our pedagogy. First, we might make explicit and validate the female tradition of diary keeping as a valuable means for learning to write, for inquiry, and for connecting the personal with the public in ways that the male-shaped tradition seeks to keep separate. Second, we might have men and women in our classes write in both traditions, so as to increase their range as thinkers and writers, and encourage dialogue that is both within and across the gendered roles. "Indeed, it might be educational for men, particularly white, middle-class men, to work in discourse forms not historically of their making. It might help them become more multilingual, expand their language conventions and, thus, their worldview, as well as that of the academy itself."

In a number of ways, Christine Holm Kline's "Rockshelf Further Forming: Women, Writing, and Teaching the Young" meshes with Gannet's essay by exploring other aspects of how "gender can inform reading and writing" and also enacts the imperative to compose in novel ways, offering us finally a long piece in dialogue with the poetry of Adrienne Rich. Like Jonsberg, Kline's objective is to change the nature of the play: as Jonsberg suggests how we might revise the plots for school, so Kline suggests how we might revise the scripts for teachers. She does this, in part, through this exploratory type of authoring in her own writing.

Kline's essay leads directly to Lillian Bridwell-Bowles' "Discourse and Diversity: Experimental Writing Within the Academy," since Bridwell-Bowles seeks to enact precisely the project of having students invent new ways of authoring: "I have invited students to imagine the possibilities for new forms of discourse. . . . I do this because I believe that writing classes (and the whole field of composition studies) must employ richer visions of texts and composing processes."

Furthermore, when she cites Adrienne Rich to express a desire for change that is not merely revolutionary but transformative, Bowles articulates a point that weaves through this volume and is certainly in the minds of the editors: namely, that one primary objective—or perhaps a primary result, whether it is an objective or not—of a feminist project is to transform the disciplines in which feminists operate, the departments in which they work, and the classrooms they shape and conduct. That is, whereas most members of traditional literature-centered English departments think that hiring a specialist in composition and rhetoric or hiring a feminist instructor is an additive process, like adding a specialist in Jane Austen or Toni Morrison, it is clear that the people so hired usually aim to have a transformative effect. So Bridwell-Bowles seeks to transform the premises of her discipline, the underlying logic of her department, and the practice of her students as thinkers and writers.

The Script

"What we have written is a sort of play" say Sara Jonsberg and Marie Salgado of the essay "Composing the Multiple Self: Teen Mothers Rewrite Their Roles," composed with the women of The Next Step. I place this essay and Mary Kay Crouch's interview with Son Kim Vo together, looking at them through the lens of the script, because they show women collaborating in writing new scripts for themselves, in which they seek to make sense of their multiple selves and their multiple roles. In both works, we follow a process by which women collaborate in inventing new plots to counter the biological plot and the various cultural plots they inherit through their families and communities. This is a pedagogy that asks the essential question, Which plot do girls and women choose? Which plots are they offered in school so that they can make a choice rather than live out the dominant gendered plots their culture seems to mandate they follow? Or, put another way, How can teachers open a space in which students discover that they can choose more than the biological plot?

> Biological in the sense that women's destinies . . . are circumscribed by the reproductive possibility, by the expectations that every girl, in order to find a self, must focus on the romance plot, forgoing or surrendering— as Carolyn Heilbrun elaborates in *Writing a Woman's Life*—the quest plot, the searching for interest and challenge and a sense of strength that can make loneliness into something else. . . . We have begun to write a new script for women.

Implicit in this essay is the imperative for people who work in educational institutions to construct new scripts to support the quest plot for women, instead of the romance plot. Indeed, in these essays as a whole we recognize a variety of teachers all seeking to construct new identities: not so much to abandon all authority as to reconstitute their authority, even as they also recast themselves in the roles of ally and mentor, and to help students also discover writing as a friend, an ally, a dialogue partner. Much of what we hear throughout this volume is an account of helping students write soliloquies that they need to share: "we wanted writing to become a friend."

The interview with Son Kim Vo conducted by Mary Kay Crouch functions as a powerful ally to Jonsberg and Salgado's essay, especially when seen as concerned with the issue of the larger cultural scripts within which we conduct our classrooms. Both these essays show us women grappling with "the problems and disjunctions of living in two cultures," and both show us people attempting to revise the gendered scripts of a dominant culture to make room for outsiders to the world presupposed by those scripts. "In this culture, women traditionally hold a special place as the moral educators of the family, ensuring that the children learn about filial piety, respect for elders, honesty, and so on." The interview makes clear how Son herself, in moving between a number of different educational systems—Vietnamese, French-model Vietnamese, and American—not only has become multilingual and multicultural but has become someone who at once fulfills and radically transforms the role of women in her home culture. Strikingly, the interview creates a deep but positive irony: Son fulfills the traditional role of moral educator in part by resisting passing on the traditional roles. She resists simply passing on a traditional content and seeks instead to compose a new one, shaped by both her oppositional relation to her own Vietnamese culture and her attempt to transform that culture as it collides with American culture. She seeks to replace that traditional content with a new content of active professional women and yet, at the same time, to preserve the authority of the educator-mother, transformed now into the authority of educator-mother and professional woman.

If we look at the ways Son has envisioned a complex culture-transforming role for herself, we can imagine her as extending the drama recorded in the essay by Jonsberg and Salgado: when juxtaposed, they seem to propose a developmental sequence, as if Salgado might go on to assume Jonsberg's role and work with future Salgados because, like Son, she has become a culture and gender mediator for other women. That is also, I think, a drama in which this book participates. It is a drama in which we seek to radically revise the enabling conventions that compose education, in part through the acts of composing in which we and our students are engaged.

NOTE

1. The quotation is from Raymond Williams, who offers his definition of *convention* in *Drama from Ibsen to Brecht* (London: Penguin, 1968), 12–16. His work is cited and extended by Alan C. Dessen in *Elizabethan Stage Conventions and Modern Interpreters* (Cambridge: Cambridge University Press, 1986), ch. 1, esp. 10–11.

17

Writing into Unmapped Territory: The Practice of Lateral Citation

David Franke

Those who take turns speaking and listening, representing others and being represented by them, learn not just who these others are but who they themselves may be, not just what others may mean, but what they themselves may mean among others

—*Don Bialostosky*

There are few things more difficult to account for than acts of the imagination: they rarely document themselves and seem always to toy with the boundaries of our conventions and expectations. But accounting for a special kind of imagination is my subject here. Working with Louise Phelps as a research assistant on this volume, I observed how all the authors who submitted abstracts and essays to this collection imaginatively sited their projects at the place where women's experience, feminism, and composition intersect. Each essay appeals to a different set of methodologies, assumptions, and goals, a variety that I view as an effect of writing in the almost complete absence of any available set of "standard" words to sanction the claims one can make about "feminine principles and women's experience in American composition and rhetoric."

It is not that the essays have no intellectual tradition but that they have many, and there is no accepted method of interrelating them. Writing in this situation, writing into unmapped territory, the authors are creatively engaged in a dialectic: their sources define their projects, just as each project leads them to certain sources. Tracing this dialectic allows us to understand better the context writers have drawn around themselves, one that shows us the practices and principles they consider constitutive of this emerging community.

With Louise Phelps, I read and catalogued the abstracts and manuscripts in the long process of editing this book, reading drafts and watching the way each one evolved. From the beginning, I was impressed by the degree of risk and commitment reflected in the book's submissions, as the authors tried to make new claims based on their reading and experience. These imaginative decisions—reflected both in the early abstracts' citations and later in the finished manuscripts—inspired me to look more closely at the process. I did not expect the complexity of this task; in fact, identifying each work's influences quickly and disappointingly became almost impossible. But the ways that the writers identified their antecedents led me to a surprise, a particular rhetoric of attribution I have called *lateral citation*. Our authors' textual conversations with others, as revealed in their references and bibliographies, suggest a less hierarchical and less traditional method of citation, one that emphasizes collaboration and connection over argument and defense; that is, an author's identity is often established by connection with others rather than argument against them. I have called this form of citation *lateral* to contrast it with more conventional practices of *vertical citation,* and see it as a feminine/feminist practice characterizing this volume.

If we see citation as the written equivalent of conversation—as voices interweaving, questioning and declaring—we can see how it is studded with interesting questions of who gets to speak and how the voices of others get represented. My cue for this was Nancy Sommers's essay, which explicitly connects citation to issues of authority, contest, and power. I was taken by this passage:

> I was so much under their influence [Barthes, Scholes, Foucault] and so detached from my own voice that I remember standing in a supermarket parking lot, holding two heavy bags of groceries, talking with a colleague who was telling me about his teaching. Without any reference, except to locate my own authority somewhere else, I felt compelled to suggest to him that he read Foucault. My daughter Alexandra, waiting impatiently for me, eating chocolate while pounding on the hood of the car with her new black patent-leather party shoes, spoke with her own authority. She reminded me that I, too, had bumped on cars, eaten Hershey Bars, worn party shoes without straps, never read Foucault, and knew, nevertheless, what to say on most occasions. (Chap. 14, this vol.)

Perhaps what struck me about this paragraph was that it described much of what I have felt as a graduate student: the inability to find or defend one's own voice, which results in the panicky search, "without any reference," to "locate my own authority somewhere else." It also described for me the difficulty of placing one's own intellectual and personal experience on the level with those of published or "real" authors. Sommers's reflection on this moment became emblematic for me not only of my own work in graduate school but also of this entire volume. As they attempt to articulate their projects, many of the authors here find issues of authority, imprimatur, and power wrapped up in the act of citing others. It soon became clear to me that issues surrounding what is cited and how it is cited, often overlooked as part of a mere conventional or scholarly gesture, are inextricably entangled with women's experience, feminism, and feminine principles.

My first attempts to make sense of this complex issue were interesting failures: my reflection on them, like Sommers's reflection, might speak to some of the issues of feminist/feminine authority and power that are central to this book.

In the early abstracts, I began looking for clues about how the writers had positioned their work in relation to that of others, many of whom were working out of related fields. I wanted to get a better sense of how our authors imagined the context that surrounded their projects and (if the abstract culminated in a published manuscript) how that context would be quilted to surround the book as a whole. The abstracts promised to be an especially rich source for this information, because there writers have to explicitly declare their sources—and what they think those sources mean—in order to guide the editors in the placement of the essays. The task seemed simple: I would count the number of times a particular writer had been cited and add them up; if Carol Gilligan appeared more often than Helen Cixous, for example, this different ratio of sources would imply an entirely different set of commitments and assumptions underlying this book.

But this early inquiry was a complete failure. I quickly found that there were very few times when an author, a work, and an explanation of that work were all found together in the same abstract, and I needed all three parts in order to determine what the author understood by the reference. Adrienne Rich, for example, appeared frequently. But a numerical list of the times her name appeared would be misleading, for she is cited as an American educator, a lesbian, a feminist, a poet, an essayist, and a scholar. Her influence on the volume would seem to be illustrated

David Franke

by a list of how many times her name had appeared, but in reality such a list would convey very little specific information about why she had been cited. I also found myself unable to account for which of Rich's works—or parts thereof—were important. I barely considered the difficult possibility that Rich might have been cited only to be disagreed with, and I had yet to ask how Rich's works were interpreted after being cited. The more I asked myself these questions, the more they seemed to undermine my attempts to identify the abstracts' intellectual antecedents.

Some of the abstracts' strongest influences were invisible, assumed or internalized. Just as one does not cite Thomas Jefferson when the *Miranda* rights are read, the authors here did not identify some of their most prominent influences. Conversely, weak or circumstantial influences could appear important because they found a niche in frequent, conventional acknowledgments. What a citation meant became more and more difficult to pin down: the original environment from which a citation is drawn and the contemporary arguments that promote it and qualify it have a strong hand in determining exactly what borrowed words mean when they appear in a finished work. Tone (the author's relationship with the audience) and stance (the author's relationship with the subject) are also deeply influential in the original context but nearly impossible to account for when uprooted from that context. The quotation that begins this piece is an example of this problem. (The line is quoted in Daniel R. Schwarz's "Humanistic Formalism: A Theoretical Defense.") Where is its tone and stance drawn from? From the Schwarz essay? From Don Bialostosky? From its position as an epigraph at the head of this essay? The answer is probably that all three contribute. Sometimes peeling an idea from one context and pasting it into another does not seem to be a problem; in other cases its meaning is deeply dependent on its origins—as with *ecriture feminine,* where the original context is another language.

I found my lists of influences getting longer and longer, more elaborate and annotated as I attempted to account for all the details and differences in the ways that influential sources were imagined. It soon became clear that, because of the complex assumptions, beliefs, arguments, and conclusions attached to every citation, this sort of inquiry would require enormous space to do properly—it was a dissertation or two—and there was no guarantee that I would ever find a way to make sense of the influences on the volume, regardless of how baroque my annotations became.

I had to find a way to reduce the complexity of my data. A chart was the next step (no doubt the promise of coming to some sure conclusions—and getting the paper done by its deadline—helped make the use of a rather positivistic device more attractive). I decided to categorize the citations, grouping similar references together, which I hoped would allow me to generalize by focusing on schools of thought and yet keep the analysis specific enough to make some accurate, if tentative, conclusions about the sources that served as wellsprings for the abstracts. Early enthusiasm led to a chart of citations in the abstracts that looked something like this:

American composition scholarship	105 entries
Various	62 entries
American feminist psychological-sociological school	49 entries
Other American feminisms	36 entries
American critical theory (Bloom, reader-response)	34 entries
Continental critical theory	21 entries
French feminisms	17 entries
Research in the gendered use of language	16 entries
Historians	6 entriers
Women writing: Writing by women	4 entries
Histories of composition or of English	3 entries

The same problems I had with the abstracts, of course, accompanied this chart. In fact, by choosing (somewhat arbitrarily) what I felt to be important and appropriate categories and ignoring the way citations were used in the abstracts' context, I had only multiplied the problems. Furthermore, I had no way to know how the abstracts' authors themselves would have constructed these pigeonholes—though I could be sure they would disagree with me and with one another. It became clear to me that this chart caused more problems that it solved. Aside from the significant strength of the category I titled American composition, scholarship the greatest influence was the heading various. This meant only one thing clearly, that sources were chosen using an eclectic and unpredictable logic. I am no statistician, but it was clear to me that if the second-largest category is undefinable, something is wrong with the method, data, or assumptions that ground the investigation.

The chart did yield one valuable result. It pointed out the presence of many references to what I called the American feminist psychological-sociological school, comprising works by such commonly associated authors as Jean Baker Miller (*Toward a New Psychology of Women*), Carol Gilligan (*In a Different Voice*), Nel Noddings (*Caring*), Nancy Chodorow (*Mothering*), and Mary Belenky and her colleagues (*Women's Ways of Knowing*). Usually, this school of inquiry—the largest coherent category after the vexing various grouping—was claimed by this book's writers to enable a reexamination of human development, teaching, or learning in terms of gender. As a group, these authors were taken to suggest significant differences in gendered perceptions of ethics, identity, and relationships with others; many of them claim that men and women reason differently. These works suggest that women's responses to knowledge and meaning may differ from men's but are not therefore less valuable. Though not all of their claims harmonize, they were often identified as a set of voices that support attention to the development of the self from within the context and community of others (rather than in contest against it). I noted with surprise that, rather than a more traditional and competitive relation to others, this school often suggests that one's community allows one to become whole; Cinthia Gannett's essay in this volume, for example, echoes these claims when she shows how participation "heals" its members.

This discovery marks the moment when my inquiry took a turn for the better. I found the strong showing of influence under the feminist psychology heading made an interesting fit with my growing awareness of how the writers for this volume constructed their community in citation and reference. I took into account, of course, that the manuscripts I was working from were chosen by the editors for certain features—these pieces did not form an "objective" cross-section of emergent feminist theory and practice in composition and rhetoric. Looking at the abstracts and then the incoming manuscripts for this particular collection, I soon started to notice a pattern. Feeling, as well as referenced and defended ratiocination, seemed to be respected as a valid way of knowing; some essays cited little or not at all, depending for support on the authors' personal accounts of affective interconnection with others. Those writers who did cite, such as Christine Holm Kline, often found a way to connect with others who were asking the same questions about authority and experience. Kline observes how difficult it is to obtain respect for the knowing that comes from experience rather than from an authority's sanction. She applauds Jean Baker Miller and Nel Noddings for their articulation of what she, too, has felt deeply: the need for the reality of women's lives to appear in otherwise theoretical accounts of teaching and learning. When it did appear, citation—an act, in part, of appealing to another's voice for sanction—was often full of acknowledged ambivalence. Sommers's suspicion (in an earlier version of her chapter) of the "off-stage authorial voices" that "enabled and then, finally, constrained [her] way of seeing" is emblematic. Of course, I did not discover any rigid law regarding citation: some essays, such as Janice Hays's (ironically, one that speaks most pointedly about this psychological school), were quite comfortable with citation as a way of plotting an argument and structuring a vision.

My guess was that the feminist psychology school had great influence in the revised manuscripts, though this influence became harder to see as the essays were modified. That is, the abstracts often explicitly identified Belenky and her colleagues as claiming that the individual is best understood as an integral part of a community rather than a force opposed to it. But later, in the essays, when it was less necessary to identify one's antecedents for the editor, this claim had become manifest less as an explicit theory and more as a practice. When colleagues were identified by citation, they were often imagined not as competitors but as parallel voices. There is a sort of flattened hierarchy, too, when citation was used to look to the past: the (preceding) authority is not often seen as terribly different, writing from on high or down through the ages to the present. The hierarchy we expect in the academic convention of citation is not often emphasized here. The majority of influences in this volume are welcomed as opportunities to share power and to extend community, the practice I have called lateral, as opposed to vertical, citation. Lateral citation is clearly evident in Cinthia Gannett's essay, which ends with a long series of citations from other people's journals, each offering a new view on their use. That one's sources make competing claims is accepted; but, instead of teasing out the differing status of these various claims, Gannett connects them in a lateral, or nonhierarchical, fashion. The effect is that voices are joined together; a web of perspectives replaces any single superior perspective that judges the "proper" and "improper" use of journals or thinking about journals. This does not mean that in her essay she refuses to disagree with others or avoids critical evaluation. It means only that she is trying to make her point as a contributor to an ongoing conversation, borrowing from others who have gone before her and extending the discourse beyond her.

As Sara Jonsberg and Marie Salgado write in "Composing the Multiple Self: Teen Mothers Rewrite Their Roles," Jean Baker Miller's understanding (*Toward a New Psychology of Women*) of the "self in relation" allows us to see how writing works to encourage identity through a nonhierarchical relation to others. The authors openly show how this works: Milagros is the central character of the play, and the other voices are like "a chorus, echoing and elaborating on Milagros's thoughts and experience." Because in this model the authors join the student writers in a "chorus," they need not cite experts for validation. The self is confirmed by engaging with others, and the others are validated in the same way.

This reciprocity is again evident when an essay's subjects are also contributors to that same study. With Jonsberg and Salgado's piece, the women of The Next Step, not professional scholars, are coauthors (and an implicit audience). No "authoritative" citations are used to explain what the Next Step women "really" mean or experience. In drafts of Emily Jessup and Marion Lardner's chapter, the contributors are kindergarten children, and the authors establish authority from their status as teachers and parents; they, not outside experts, interpret the children's and teachers' experiences. Such a perspective, which sees the person studied as a participant in the study rather than merely a subject of it, solicits reflection from within the community rather than from some distant, objective perspective or point in time. Jessup and Lardner's work, for example, seems to continue unfolding what is happening *right now* in the course of the essay. The researcher and her subjects are not separated, even for analytical purposes. To the extent that citation incorporates an analytic distance and to some extent estranges (both useful maneuvers in certain situations), it does not often appear in this volume (but see chaps. 8 and 12 to the contrary). I have identified one attribute of lateral citation as the author's seeming willingness to use her discourse as an opportunity to connect with others. In none of the pieces here is anyone "dissected." The writers often cite others who have tried to articulate similar ideas, not because it is necessary in order to prove their case but because it represents and supports other workers who are trying to communicate about these topics. Myrna Harrienger shows this wonderfully when she simply points the way to fellow researchers, asking them to join her, laterally, in her investigation.

I suspect that writers using lateral citation are trying to create community not only because it "feels right" but for the more pragmatic reason that it helps them imagine an audience for their work and to invite peers to join them. Once there is a coherent body of scholarship, once it is possible to craft a critical lens to focus on women's experience, they will be able to reevaluate their own teaching and learning practices from within. In the present, there is no ongoing conversation complex enough to bring together, securely, women's experience, feminism, and composition. But that may change.

As I see it, the feminist psychological school, at least as it is represented in this volume, defends and practices the often undervalued claim that meaning and responsibility come from community rather than from an isolated self. This claim is reflected in one of the functions of citation in this volume: to make meaning among others and even for others. Take, for instance, the complex negotiation of community in Evelyn Ashton-Jones's chapter "Collaboration, Conversation, and the Politics of Gender." The author clearly does not accept the limits and implications of others' theories about how communities of writers work. Using a much less utopian view, she argues for attention to the micropolitics of gendered inequality that may arise in any small group where men and women work together. But she does not lose sight of the necessity of seeing herself as a participant in a conversation with other scholars, some of whom she disagrees with. Fishman, Trimbur, Bruffee—all are woven into the conversation, not dismissed or put down. They become legitimate members of a community of researchers who are, like Ashton-Jones, trying to make sense of a difficult subject. In such a case, meaningful claims become an event of community, not merely a defense against outsiders.

The authors in this volume often seem to act on the belief that the meaning of a citation comes from sharing it, not from some inherent meaning fixed in the passage cited. Without explicitly turning to literary theory for support, they are comfortable with the intertextuality of their work. For some, it is a way to acknowledge a personal exchange, as when Harrienger mentions how others have shared observations that leave her "incredulous" and "struck." The community she cites is not one that helps her defend her concepts from others but one that enables her to come to terms with her own psychological understanding and personal experience. As a writer, then, she uses others to build up resonance and clarity and to enable her to connect with her own experience. In a similar situation, Sommers struggles with the work of Michel Foucault, both rejecting and incorporating it as she works to articulate her felt experience (as opposed to her intellectual conclusions). She exemplifies the uneasiness of working with a theorist who, some claim, can magically erase the reality of daily experience with a theoretical prestidigitation but who also "makes sense to me because his is an antiauthoritarian voice. It is a voice that speaks to me about a struggle I know," a struggle she identifies with that of "all writers." When cited as a member of a community engaged in a shared struggle, Foucault again becomes real. He is suddenly understood by Sommers as a "voice" and not a mere mechanical arrangement of concepts. Connection, not the power to control or dictate, makes Foucault useful and meaningful, and it is only to make this point that he is cited at all.

What excited me about this project was watching the way citation moved from an obligatory scholarly gesture to a rich practice, embodying the commitments that the authors here identify as they imaginatively create their own textual communities, interlacing feminism, personal experience, and composition. Identifying one's intellectual predecessors is hard enough in an inchoate field such as the one this book represents, but negotiating the competing claims these predecessors offer—without losing one's own voice or limiting oneself to traditional, vertical citation— is much harder, especially because so few of the writers here seem to feel comfortable with making one's own voice heard by shouting down the claims of others. Though it was never possible for me to account for the contextual depth and intricacy that presage the works collected here, I was pleased to find that connection, not competition, is not only theorized in this volume as a feminist/feminine activity but is also enacted in such seemingly traditional practices as citation.

Note: The author thanks Nance Hahn for her help and careful reading.

In Search of Ways In:
Reflection and Response

Jacqueline Jones Royster

This volume offers its readers perspectives on women, writing, and learning that have at least two distinctions. First, in articulating their field of inquiry, Louise Wetherbee Phelps and Janet Emig lay out a territory, as David Franke indicates in the preceding reflection that is little known and essentially uncharted. They make room for us to think in ways that we have not thought before, to consider dimensions of lives and experiences that have not been adequately considered before, and to discover insights about human potential and endeavor that are likely to place us farther along the road to understanding ourselves as human beings.

Second, the various and sundry ways that the contributing authors follow through in presenting their discoveries and insights signal quite boldly that more could be recovered, reconstructed, and incorporated into what we know and what we are coming to understand. The collection serves, therefore, as a clarion call for teachers, scholars, and researchers to look again, to look more closely, to look more carefully. This collection whets the appetite and fires the imagination, opening up a world of possibilities that, until now, have remained largely untapped and untouched.

By including in this volume a section for reconfiguration and response, Phelps and Emig have carved out critical space for a dialectical experience and set in motions reverberations that seem particularly appropriate, given the multidimensional nature of the inquiry itself. Fundamentally, Phelps and Emig relinquished a significant part of their authority as editors to those of us who were invited to participate in this section, by presenting the essays in alphabetical order by authors' names instead of by the usual system of themes, categories, or rubrics of one sort or another. While I recognize, certainly, that even something as seemingly innocuous as an alphabetical listing serves, in and of itself, as a construction of knowledge, this particular arrangement was ultimately liberating for me. I can not imagine a more powerful or more synergetic way to encourage the breadth and depth of consideration that this territory deserves.

As a reader, this alphabetically ordered collection allowed me to read without being particularly constrained by the ways in which Phelps and Emig might have been envisioning relations and entanglements. I was not called upon to respond or react to their versions of meaning or truth. The alphabetical scheme allowed the diachronic to be mixed with the synchronic, the pedagogical with the theoretical, personal narratives with propositions of research and scholarship, and so on. In effect, the editors invited us to say what we would say if we were not "directed" to say anything in particular. By framing the task in this fashion, they created, whether by design or by chance, a virtual whirlwind of ideas, thoughts, experiences, and, potentially, of responses, also. What I was able to enjoy by this rendering of the task was, on one level, the wonderful chaos of it all. On another level, I was able to choose to read these essays both singularly and collectively by placing them within the context of my own work and my own lived experiences and not just within the context of a popularized academic discourse. As Nancy Sommers suggests in her essay, I set aside the dispassionate stance of the academic observer, a stance that seems to result too often in a disavowing of the passionate and the personal. Instead, I chose to embrace my passions as a black feminist teacher and scholar and to respond in keeping with classical traditions within the African-American community.

In my reading of this volume, the pages "called," and I "responded." The words "spoke." I filtered them through my systems of belief, and I held them and their creators accountable for the ways in which their renderings rang true or not in the company of my own. This time, however, I was able to practice this way of responding by the invitation of the editors rather than by what others might perceive as contrariness, or tendencies to be defiant or to resist conventions. By what I interpreted to be a request that I act according to my own inclinations, I invoked the long-standing authority, as bell hooks has articulated this tradition so well, of women of African descent to "talk back." I claimed the privilege of showing my alternative ways of seeing, thinking, believing, and doubting without battle, negotiations, or intrigue.

When an open invitation to think, talk, and respond is extended, it carries with it the potential to be interpreted in ways that simply cannot be controlled by whoever is doing the inviting. Seemingly, though, a volume that seeks, as this one does, to unpack the intersection of feminine principles, women's experiences, and rhetoric and composition would need to take such a chance. How else can we discover the unknown and the unseen? How else can we tweak our suspicions that there might actually be something more that we do not already know, that can not show itself using the paradigms that have historically prevailed or even currently hold sway in academic circles?

If, as suggested by the essays of Evelyn Ashton-Jones, Myrna Harrienger, Janice Hays, Patricia Bizzell, and others in this volume, those who are practicing and refining feminist principles are in effect remaking knowledge and, certainly, reconsidering the ways in which we construct communities, operate within them, and use the knowledge made by them, then the high-risk endeavor of inviting teachers, scholars, and even students to participate as they will in the making of collective sense seems quite appropriate. As Lillian Bridwell-Bowles posits, we are searching, or should be, not for the tried, the true, and the few but for the multiple ways that we might actually manage to "break the boundaries of textual space" and blossom forth with amazing critical and creative thought.

Basically, however, in reading this volume, I read actively, and, as evident in this accounting of it, the process was rewarding. I was able to notice, not by a particular conceptual filter but by juxtaposition, by virtually seeing one idea next to another, an identifiable matrix of concerns that complemented my own, concerns that defy, to some extent, neatly categorized points of departure. I identified a resonance in the need to recover the distinctions of individual experiences; to find better ways to talk about these experiences; to resist hierarchies and binary thinking; to account for the impact of power, privilege, and authority on individuals and groups; and to find systems and arrangements that better allow sense to emerge, to be uncovered or created and then incorporated variously, using a range of disciplinary or interdisciplinary lenses.

I noticed also that there were some observable distinctions as well between my priorities and the priorities of this collection. Across the spectrum of women's lives as I have come to know this spectrum, I saw that the particularities of the human condition matter. I noticed that history and ongoing experience matter, that we see in accord with our lives, whether we admit it or not. Ultimately, therefore, I acknowledge the considerable extent to which my response to this collage of insights, observations, and experiences reflects not just a community of discourse in which I operate but my own pathway to research, teaching, and scholarship.

As I come to this work, I bring with me a profound interest, from both a personal and scholarly perspective, in the rhetorical history of women of African descent. Over the years, I have found feminist studies, African diaspora studies, and literacy studies to be an unbeatable combination in helping to ferret out this dimension of their realities. Even so, I have learned to expect precious little in scholarship that directly mirrors my own perspectives or priorities or that embrace my guiding questions or points of focus. So I was neither surprised nor disappointed that women of African descent, though present in the ways that our experiences overlap in particular territories with others, are not a bold image in this collage. Several examples come to mind.

Evelyn Ashton-Jones presents gender as a salient variable in group dynamics and in the reproduction of an ideology of gender. She clearly acknowledges that gender is not the only perspective of difference to be considered in such analyses and makes reference to other research that takes into account perspectives on race, ethnicity, class, age, sexual orientation, and occupation. Still, I feel discontent. I am reminded of a book title, *All the Women Are White, All the Blacks Are Men, But Some of Us Are Brave,* and I feel compelled to leave much of the multiplicity of myself outside of the Ashton-Jones door, in fairness to the parameters and priorities that she has set.

In the essays by Janice Hays and Mitzi Myers, I am struck by the powerful images of parenting and mothering, images of feminist teaching that seem to constitute a vibrant thread as we dig more deeply into theory and practice to imagine and document how ideology and practice actually come together in classrooms. What lingers, though, is a concern that "parenting" and even "mothering" are many-splendored things. Variables other than gender often matter. History, human condition, systems of belief, and preferred patterns of behavior often matter. So, what does the image of mother or parent mean in classrooms, when we factor in other dimensions of ourselves? What is the same? What might vary? How do my images of parenting and teaching match these experiences and propositions? Do I mean the same thing when I say the same thing?

Another example of how African American women are not boldly present is the essay by Robert Connors. Connors presents provocative insights about how the presence of women in academic settings changed the culture of educational environments. He does not look, however, at the particular experiences of women or of groups of women (e.g., African American women) as these changes were being wrought. We have, as in the case of the other examples, an instructive account, but we also have what I call a "Meanwhile, back on the farm . . ." situation. What stands out for me in such instances, when the essays are so well documented and well constructed, is the ever present sense that I am consistently called upon to read my life between these lines, before the story, around it, or simultaneously with it, rather than in it.

In other words, this volume does not really include in its talk (as compared with its responses) the black woman's voice or vision, and I find myself, as Anna Julia Cooper must have found herself in 1892, wondering "when and where I enter." Cooper says, "Only the Black Woman can say 'when and where I enter, in the quiet, undisputed dignity of my womanhood, without violence and without suing or special patronage, then and there the whole Negro race enters with me' " (31). Despite the century that has passed since 1892, I have come to understand that, like Cooper, I still must make my own door, my own place. What has changed over the last century is that African American women do not have to sue quite as often to be heard. Even if we may not be talking, we are sometimes talking back and, occasionally, by invitation instead of by suing.

What does the apparent inevitability of this dilemma mean for authors and editors? One thing that it seems to mean is that none of us can claim a case for much of anything with the rendering of just one set of experiences. Something always goes untreated, unconsidered, unincorporated. That, after all, is the situation that has allowed the "studies" fields to emerge in the first place. Clearly, there is a slew of "stuff" that can be taken into account in any given viewpoint, especially when we are talking about language and learning. While, with each run through a territory, we must inevitably choose a path, we need more than one crossing to see what is really going on. Always, we need sensibilities that acknowledge converging actions, reactions, and realities. The more pathways we create, the more dialectical the analysis, and the more we take in the periphery of our own vision and experiences, the greater the chance we have of accounting more adequately and more sensitively to complex worlds.

So, at this point in the inquiry, what options do we have? In my estimation, the task at hand is not to indict Phelps and Emig, or Ashton-Jones, or Connors, or any of the other authors for what they were either unable to do in a single essay and volume, or chose not to do. At the same time, I hope that the information base is becoming such that any author or editor feels compelled to reference his or her line of thought within the company of other choices that could have been made. I hope that all authors and editors will be held accountable when they do not do so. However, the essence of the task of authorship or editorship in a complex world seems to be, first and foremost, to acknowledge that lines inevitably get drawn and that the drawing of them matters in the construction of the meaning and in the opening and closing of possibilities.

Phelps and Emig have stepped forward with a collection that recasts the continuing conversation of "woman's sphere." The collection seeks to center abstractions in the lives, experiences, and insights of the lived experiences of women across lines that seek to divide—race, class, ethnicity, sexual preference, age, place, physical condition. Their presentation, however, does not represent the totality of women's experience. Nor should it. We now need other articles, collections of articles, accountings of teaching, research, and scholarship that can talk back to them and can fill in other dimensions of this dynamic territory. We need to keep prying the inquiry open, to keep extending the conversation, casting and recasting, to find other "ways in" to a territory that is so richly endowed with a multiplicity of experiences and so deeply deserving of attention, thought, and more thought.

In search of wisdom, I turn again to Anna Julia Cooper. In 1892, Cooper considered herself and other black women to be "barometers" in the interest of equity and justice. She appealed, therefore, to those with power and authority to embrace a full chorus of voices from wherever they might come and to acknowledge the value of more than a single eye. She says:

> It is not the intelligent woman vs. the ignorant woman; nor the white woman vs. the black, the brown, and the red,—it is not even the cause of woman vs. man. Nay, 'tis woman's strongest vindication for speaking that *the world needs to hear her voice*. It would be subversive of every human interest that the cry of one-half the human family be stifled. Woman in stepping from the pedestal of statue-like inactivity in the domestic shrine, and daring to think and move and speak,—to undertake to help shape, mold, and direct the thought of her age, is merely completing the circle of the world's vision. . . . The world has had to limp along with the wobbling gait and one-sided hesitancy of a man with one eye. Suddenly the bandage is removed from the other eye and the whole body is filled with light. It sees a circle where before it saw a segment. The darkened eye restored, every member rejoices with it. (121–22)

From my point of view, our blind spots are still rather pervasive, and the cost to us as human beings still seems quite dear. The imperative, therefore, regardless of what this current volume is or is not able to do, is to proceed as tenaciously as we can to keep removing bandages, restoring vision, raising voices from wherever they come, and insisting on critical and creative responses that will keep us thinking and keep the inquiry open.

BIBLIOGRAPHY

Cooper, Anna Julia. *A Voice from the South.* New York: Oxford Univ. Press, 1988.
Hooks, Bell. *Talking Back: Thinking Feminist, Thinking Black.* Boston: South End, 1989.
Hull, Gloria T., Patricia Bell-Scott, and Barbara Smith. *All the Women Are White, All the Blacks Are Men, But Some of Us Are Brave.* Old Westbury: Feminist Press, 1982.

19

Reality Check at the Crossroads

Mary M. Salibrici

My student, Alicia, announces her trouble on the very first day, when I ask students to write a short paragraph about prior composition experiences. She has been plagued with having nothing to say: "An opinion paper obviously requires an opinion from the writer. Many times, I felt I did not know enough about the subject to be personally comfortable with developing a strong opinion required for the assignment." Completing papers for college has become a frustrating, conflicting experience; her attempts to sound knowledgeable on "rape, drug abuse and social welfare" have failed: "Without a real opinion on certain subjects, my papers always lacked direction and a sense of organization. Of course, my [first year] writing teacher quickly discovered this and graded accordingly." Alicia is hesitant and anxious at the prospect of having to write again: "The mere thought of more writing classes is quite intimidating to me." In her mind, she is unable even to begin writing without any knowledge of the topic at hand.

My concern for Alicia on this opening day of class is twofold: first, can I help her overcome this enormous obstacle by showing her that she does in fact have ideas of her own and will also be able to acquire and invent new ideas as our course progresses; and second, can I help her become successful at translating these ideas into the kind of academic discourse that is continually expected of her as a college student? She does know something; but she lacks a process for expressing what she knows and for expanding and connecting her ideas to academic discourse. She needs to develop a sense of her own ability to use a method that will enable her to become expert on a topic, an ability to use writing practices to build knowledge and, therefore, confidence. I

393

seek a way of teaching her that will build upon her potential to express and create knowledge, a classroom organized to help her enact her own ability to be expert. In a writing class where her ideas are given time to form, develop, and be articulated, where there is space to work them out and critique them, where there is an opportunity to reveal them and debate them at the same time, would Alicia find the ideas and the language she needs? Would she then feel stronger as a writer?

A pedagogy that elicits responses and then carefully complicates those responses in terms of personal knowledge is, in fact, the most effective way to develop a student voice dynamic enough to stand up by itself and, at the same time, take its place coherently within a particular discourse community. The academic language I am imagining is not suspended in an idiosyncratic world of personal experience, but it may begin with subjective responses and from there learn to communicate in a manner valuable for a larger community. Our subjectivities (which lead us to speak in the first place), our ways of reading, may of course be fictions; but, fact or fiction, we have to start with them, if we are to learn how they may or may not relate to the world at large. We do not encourage our students to take their places within the broader academic community by asking them to erase themselves from their own singular material presence in it.

As I develop my writing course to meet the needs of a student like Alicia, then, I consider the value I am placing on her individual experience of reading and her ability to discover and convey knowledge; I consider the way I am designing a student-centered classroom. I know this: my students come to me expecting some help in this task that faces them—to write intelligent academic prose in a variety of places before they graduate. They need to find a way to express what they know within the constraints placed upon them by different discourse communities.

Signposts on the Roadway . . . Detours, Direct Routes, Dead Ends?

My initial intention, however, before I articulate my position regarding the work Alicia must do, is to discuss the relation between her dilemma as a writer and the practical solutions offered by several current feminist pedagogical strategies. Alicia needs to find that intersection between what she knows and the demands of academic scholarship. What might feminist approaches offer her in this desire to become a more confident academic writer? What do they suggest to me as I try to develop a classroom experience that will ultimately enable her to situate herself comfortably within the academy—to be comfortable, that is, with conventions and the concurrent sense of her own expertise? In their reflections in this volume, Louise Wetherbee Phelps and Janet Emig describe experience in a way that unleashes new dimensions for the word. They comment:

> Implicit in these reflections is the need to complicate and deepen the descriptive notion of experience before it gets to the point of theoretical interpretation or formulation. In other words, one should not take a simplistic notion of experience and oppose it to a sophisticated one of theory. In the first place, experience refers not merely to personal lives but to historical experience, collective experience, institutional experience, literary experience—all ways that our direct personal understandings rest on the interactivity and intersubjectivity of human life and are thus endlessly complicated by others.

My classroom models this description of experience; I witness Alicia building on experiences that she has room to tinker with in my classroom, sorting through the knowledge she brings with her, the diverse readings we debate as a whole class, as well as her small group experiences, to arrive finally at a more sophisticated position on our topic of inquiry.

Lillian Bridwell-Bowles, in "Discourse and Diversity: Experimental Writing Within the Academy," searches for a writing classroom experience that will open the way to experimentation with diverse forms to enrich our visions of what can constitute a text. If language represents culture, if culture is indeed pluralistic, and if a dominant, singular culture maintains the correct discourse, then "we need new processes and forms if we are to express ways of thinking that have been outside the dominant culture." Bridwell-Bowles's image of this new form includes several alternatives familiar to existing feminist pedagogy, including "a more personal voice, an expanded use of metaphor, a less rigid methodological framework." She argues that new patterns must emerge to challenge the old ones, and that, in fact, the old patterns of argument "run counter to new theories of socially constructed knowledge and social change." Indeed, she sees the future as modifying these old structures with more personal, nonlinear, and emotional ones, as the poststructuralist revolution causes us to rethink the constraints of our cultural inheritances. For Bridwell-Bowles, then, feminist pedagogy allows for experimental discourse in a way that fills her "with optimism about the possibilities for a liberating discourse."

What will this liberating discourse look like in the writing classroom? Bridwell-Bowles cites several examples of experimental forms, including

personal and emotional writing, writing through multiplicity by weaving
together on the page different sources or simply other voices, language
play, and searching for modes that uncover our own differences as women,
despite our common gender identity. She further recommends confronting class barriers and writing in a style truer to identities defined by race,
gender, class, or ethnic background. Searching for and using these experimental forms has, Bridwell-Bowles asserts, "reinvigorated me as a
reader, a teacher, and a writer."

At the heart of Bridwell-Bowles's position about experimentation in
the writing classroom is the familiar feminist dichotomy between a
writer-based private voice and a reader-based public voice. To cross over
to the personal is to violate standard principles of academic scholarship
that value a more objective, certainly nonidiosyncratic and authoritative,
universal voice. One of her students attempts to write a paper on the
struggles of feminist reading and writing, and Bridwell-Bowles describes
her response to the student's hesitancy about excising the objective distance from her language: "Throughout the essay, she weaves her concerns with audience into challenging questions about the material she
has read. It truly is private writing, or 'writer-based prose' in the jargon
of composition, but as I had told her earlier, that was what the course
was about: making external knowledge personal. I encouraged her to
think ... that not all academic writing has to be 'reader-based.' " Her
response implies that traditional discourse excludes the personal and is
essentially reader-based, while experimental forms learned through new
pedagogies will transform our writing selves into more authentic and
more empowered beings. Bridwell-Bowles hopes that, in response to
these options, her students will be transformed by a resistance to the
dominant discourse and will make scholarship a reflection of their personalized experience of knowledge, finding other avenues to rhetorical
authority in the academy. What if, however, academic discourse itself is
not the problem? What if our students, those like Alicia, make it very
clear that taking part in an academic community through its standard
discourse is of paramount importance?

Bridwell-Bowles delineates several experimental genres with the potential to help students uncover what they know and feel themselves. If
Alicia were in the writing classroom of Lillian Bridwell-Bowles, I could
imagine her discovering a personal oasis after some of her early composition encounters. Through personal and emotional writing or writing
without argument, for instance, Alicia would probably get in touch with
feelings and experiences leading her to believe that she has quite a bit

to say . . . about herself. Perhaps that is, indeed, an essential beginning. Yet the problem still exists: How does Alicia learn to translate her sense of self, her knowledge, to the world in terms of knowledge about that world? Once she begins discovering her own ideas in personal and emotional writing, she still must work to make her ideas relevant or connect them credibly to the academy; in fact, she *wants* to be able to maintain herself in the academy. Bridwell-Bowles leaves Alicia, therefore, with several experimental genres but with no clear-cut route to make the academic crossover.

Cinthia Gannett's essay, "The Stories of Our Lives Become Our Lives: Journals, Diaries, and Academic Discourse," also interested me at the outset because her title takes up the notion of personal and public writing in a way that might intersect with my goal to help Alicia become a confident college writer. Gannett is interested in how journals can operate in the writing classroom, despite reservations expressed by many in the field that journals may not foster intellectual discipline as well as academic writing tasks might. Like Bridwell-Bowles, she addresses the tensions between the muted voices of those in marginalized discourse communities and those voices that traditionally dominate public and academic life. Her intention is to reclaim the forms of the journal and the diary as a way to access and strengthen the vocal cords of those muted female voices.

True, journals and diaries have historically been the accepted genre for women who did not see themselves operating in the public realm, a realm that Gannett describes as frequently distorting or eliding women's experiences, "making it difficult for women to name or know themselves or the world as they see it." The journal becomes, then, the most accessible vehicle for those on the margins; "women have used it to 'read' and 'write' themselves, to listen to and develop their own possible voices." Gannett confronts typically male responses to journal keeping as being like writing in a diary, as a place for "self-disclosing introspection," which they "tended to shun . . . seeing it explicitly as gender-inappropriate behavior." Her women students, on the other hand, while not always sure why it belonged in a college classroom, took more easily to writing in a journal and "integrated their academic writing with writing on family and friends and domestic and social relationships, in keeping with the older women's journal traditions of maintaining domestic verbal networks and chronicling family and social history."

Of critical interest to Gannett is her discovery that "the men's and women's attitudes about keeping personal journals carried over into attitudes about keeping class journals." Of the males who had kept school journals before, only 20 percent gave positive reactions to the experience, while of the women, 67 percent were positive in their reactions to using a journal for school writing. Gannett explores the idea of journal writing, then, to clearly examine it as another symbol of women's difference and as a symbol of empowerment for their otherwise muted voices. She believes that academic language has always been singular in nature and aggressively male, but at the same time she sees ways that this nature can be modified, now that more women teachers and scholars have entered the academic domain than ever before. Yet she is cautious in this advocacy, since she must reconcile her hope with the "enormous literature on gender, teaching styles, and classroom dynamics ... [that] shows that, in many classrooms, unconscious discourse patterns that derogate and mute women are still common." Still, I am thinking about the academic discourse reference in Gannett's title and wondering again about Alicia. Gannett's feminist pedagogy has inspired me to reconsider how effectively journal writing can help my student see the connection between life and learning: "Many students, but particularly marginalized students, and especially women, have found the journal a place to connect with possible literary, public, and academic possibilities for their own voices. By voice, I refer not simply to the expressivist notion of *personal voice* but rather to the effort to *give voice* in the difficult social and historical conditions that have governed the possible voices for women and other muted groups." Gannett wants to connect keeping class journals and developing or giving voice within rhetorical conventions of the academy. But what I do not understand from her work is how a female tradition of writing in personal journals can help students bridge the gap or make the leap to academic discourse still required of them, as it is required of Alicia. I agree with Gannett that women's voices are muted, that, in fact, we do not know our own strength in being able to join in the academic conversation. But while Alicia will learn to give voice to herself within the journal, Gannett does not explain how this will help her learn to speak in the academy.

Approaching the Crossroads: Alicia's Reality

Let us get back to embodied theory in the real world of Alicia and the work she has to do. The first day of class introduces her to my syllabus and the goals for the semester, describing the course as the site for a workshop atmosphere with plenty of freewriting, drafting, revising, and conferencing. Students' "critical reading and writing skills will develop and improve over time and in different ways" for the purpose of equipping them with the skills of "thinking, reading, and writing" their way through the university. To establish these skills, I explain that we will look at "a particular theme together and in various ways," exploring the notion "that what you say is governed to a large extent by who you are, why you are saying it, and to whom you are speaking." An informal reading-journal requirement asks students to write an entry for each reading assignment based on personal reactions to the readings, a place "to experiment with ideas in a free, unrestricted way." Additionally, there will be formal writing assignments that "will be typed, polished in both idea and form, with close attention paid to audience and purpose."

Along with the typical strategies found in many classrooms described by feminist or process-oriented pedagogy (small groups, collaboration, journals, conferencing), my course depends on another very important component—that Alicia will confront difficult academic language by studying one topic over an extended period of time and expressing herself introspectively and individualistically in reading-journal entries on that topic. As the course progresses, she will develop and begin to believe in her own expertise. Once she discovers herself articulating her own ideas and comprehends how much she is learning with each new reading, she will gradually feel that she owns her words, academic or otherwise. Her language will represent, in whatever form it occurs, an opinion that she has taken time to formulate and analyze. She will have something to say, both privately and publicly; but that public expression, until now so threatening to her, will become the strong representation of a private voice situating itself in a community discourse, having found the shared territory where it can connect. In fact, she will have become an academic reader and writer by the end of the course.

Over a six-week period, we read a variety of materials relating to the case of Julius and Ethel Rosenberg and stage a mock retrial of their case, with students taking on the roles of attorney, witness, reporter, and judge. Like most students in the class, Alicia has never heard of the Rosenbergs. You can imagine her dismay as she figures out that, instead of having to write this time about "rape, drug abuse and social welfare," she will now be required to do analysis of historical events she knows nothing about. We begin with two weeks of discussion before the first formal paper is due, and students are asked to submit reading-journal entries each day that an assigned reading is due.

Selections from Alicia's early reading-journal entries reflect the hesitant voice introduced to me on the first day. Of the excerpt from Louis

Nizer's *Implosion Conspiracy,* an extremely emotional exploration of the Rosenberg case, she says:

> *The writing style angered me to a point because I thought he was sensationalizing another person's suffering. Granted, this was an extremely moving trial, but until I can understand more about the actual facts behind the case, I will be hesitant to form an opinion.*

By the second reading, a lengthy selection from *The Rosenberg File* by Ronald Radosh and Joyce Milton, she tentatively agrees that there is a lot to be learned, while she holds back from committing herself to any conclusion about the case. I like her reluctance here; she doesn't want to position herself until she has more of the facts:

> *I found this article quite informative. At the same time though, I felt the authors assumed the reader knew more about the events surrounding the case. . . . It's obvious that whatever was going on was quite involved. It's scary to think such "undercover" events actually took place and most likely still are taking place today. . . . If [the Rosenbergs] were guilty like all the rest, why didn't they admit to their acts just like all these other people. . . . I couldn't stop thinking that the Rosenbergs proclaimed their innocence adamantly to the end.*

Each time she writes a journal entry for me, I can respond with questions and comments on the case, moving her in directions she needs to go, probing her surface thoughts to indicate where her ideas may have great potential for further analysis. For this response, in fact, I ask her why she thinks the Rosenbergs did not cooperate. Could they have been protecting others? Were they simply not guilty? What exactly makes her think that these undercover events might still be going on today? What does her experience tell her about this? Has she read or heard things that suggest these ideas to her? Where do they come from? Each response from me will cause her to reflect on what she wrote spontaneously after reading, as well as help her make further, more complex connections when the case unfolds even more in future readings.

By the third journal entry, after another lengthy reading selection from *The Rosenberg File,* Alicia's language is actually taking shape around a question that seems significant to her:

> *I am beginning to feel that something definitely happened in this espionage case involving Julius Rosenberg. Nothing was really mentioned about Ethel. . . . Am I to believe that she was guilty by association?*

In addition to formulating this question about Ethel, which could prove to be a fruitful academic topic, Alicia is using her journal entries to describe the case and its intricacies as her understanding of it develops:

> *I don't think that conspiring to commit espionage deserves such a severe penalty. The government was obviously trying to make an example out of someone. I don't feel that the Rosenbergs were the proper choice. What happened to Gold and Fuchs? They admitted to their parts in everything and they still didn't get the death penalty. The anti-communist sentiment was obviously stronger than what I can perceive from the readings for such an example to be made from the Rosenbergs alone.*

Here I can help with some of her questions, commenting on further material she might wish to read or clarifying a passage she appears to misunderstand, while continuing to direct her toward areas she finds provocative. She now, for example, has two areas of concern: the lack of a case against Ethel and the desire by the government to make an example of the Rosenbergs. In fact, by her fourth entry, on an article entitled "The Hidden Rosenberg File" by Ronald Radosh and Sol Stern, she reveals:

> *After reading this article, I think I can finally form an opinion on the Rosenbergs' case. I feel that from what I've read, Julius was indeed involved in espionage. As for his wife Ethel, I feel she could only be guilty by association. I don't think she understood as much as it is thought. The magnitude of this case is beginning to become overwhelming.*

Overwhelming, indeed. In a subsequent entry she vents this frustration again about the mounting and conflicting information she is reading about the case:

> *I am really beginning to get extremely frustrated because it seems everytime I read something new, my 'opinion' on the case changes. I just don't know how to separate each reading and analyze it.*

Yet in a revealing turnabout within the very same entry, she actually represents in her own language how much control she has, how her expertise is developing to such an extent that

> *I've developed some new thoughts on the case. It appears that the FBI could have stumbled onto a huge spy ring with the discovery of Klaus Fuchs. It must be noted that Harry Gold admitted to being the infamous Raymond*

before Klaus Fuchs "suggested" that he was. I think that Fuchs saw an opportunity to keep the larger spy ring uncovered. In doing that, he figured the FBI would be put on a totally different track.

This hardly sounds like the language of a confused student suffering from a lack of expertise, suffering from nothing to say. On the contrary, Alicia has reached the point in the course where her attentive reading and active class discussion finally causes her language to overflow with ideas. By the time she has the opportunity to read a Court of Appeals document on the case, she is actually arguing with the judge in her journal entry:

How can he say that the Rosenbergs caused the Communist aggression in Korea? He makes it seem as if the Rosenbergs were the sole people behind the aggression. . . . If Greenglass was involved in this spying ring (which he admitted to) why didn't Judge Kaufman impose a more severe penalty like he wanted to?

What brought Alicia to this point, so distant from her opening day tension? I would argue that the use of this introspective, loosely structured, and personal reading journal writing (as predicted by feminist pedagogical theories) is indeed the key to her development of confident and complex language use. However, the productivity of these entries comes specifically from the way the assignment was structured and allowed to develop over time, in conjunction with a teacher's continual input of information and interpretation through structuring class discussions and responding to journal writing. The reading journal allowed Alicia to enter the discussion in a way that accepted her level of understanding at the outset and then, through carefully placed questions and comments, prodded her into complicating the issues she herself had raised. Alicia had time to get to know her subject and to get to know what she believed about it, which finally gave her the confidence to speak intelligently about it in a sustained academic analysis. My written dialogues with her in the journal, the numerous class discussions elicited from the contrastive readings, as well as the readings themselves standing in opposition to each other, created an atmosphere of great motivation for a student like Alicia. She was in the act of discovering something important about herself: the life-knowledge that she had begun to articulate interacted with read-knowledge to produce academic writing with form and life. The academic analysis she ultimately wrote was as much a part of her authentic language as her writing in every journal entry.

Another Option on the Roadway

Janice Hays, in "Intellectual Parenting and a Developmental Feminist Pedagogy of Writing," considers the idea that expressing the personal voice through the kinds of genres suggested by Bridwell-Bowles and Gannett should actually serve as the beginning phase in a plan that takes college writers to more intellectual complexity, a complexity that Hays suggests is not achieved by learners in this country until their graduate school education. Achieving this more complex stage of intellectual growth means that the writer will recognize the tension between the constant flux of personal context and responsibility to the larger community: "The person holds this knowledge in tension with the recognition that such commitments must be rethought again and again in the light of new knowledge, experience, and constructions of meaning." In terms of the writing classroom in particular, Hays identifies a style of teaching she calls "intellectual parenting," one that is "attuned to students' needs, 'holding' them when to do so is appropriate, urging them to progress when they need urging, and entering with them into the interpersonal process of making meaning."

While Hays does not abandon the nonlinear, associative types of writing advocated by Bridwell-Bowles and Gannett, she recognizes the need to "help students compose discourse that constructs meaning, expressed with sound reasoning and the concerned voice of the writer, in those forms appropriate to the kind of writing in question and to its context, occasion, and audience." In fact, as she describes the kind of alienation that exists for far too many female college students, she advocates a style of teaching that tries "to integrate reason and emotion, self and other, concrete particularities and abstract generalizations along varying points of a continuum extending between these polarities."

Hays speaks in convincing tones about my student's dilemma. Alicia must learn to write academic discourse, yet with some awareness of her own rhetorical authority. Hays's feminist pedagogy suggests that

> since women students are often alienated by what they perceive as the excessively abstract and impersonal thrust of academic knowledge, it is crucial for the instructor to help them find personal points of connection with what they are studying; this is true in every subject and at every level of development. Probably most, if not all, of our own academic work has begun with some question or problem related to our own lives; only later in the scholarly process do we generalize about the issue and deal with it at a more public level. *We need to make students aware of this*

connection between the private and the public and encourage them to take
advantage of it, instead of pretending that we investigate areas of knowledge
with complete objectivity, in a personal vacuum. [Emphasis added]

Hays agrees that our culture reinforces the dominance of procedural
knowing, the type of knowing that allows a person to be positioned within
society and establish a career, the type of knowing represented in the
male discourse taken to task by Bridwell-Bowles and Gannett. Hays
would caution feminists, however, about the tendency of their critique
to go "too far when it asserts that the values of procedural knowledge
are exclusively masculine values and, therefore, to be eschewed." As she
correctly reminds us, "many women want an opportunity to perform in
public domains, and indeed, securing such opportunities has been a major goal of the women's movement. It is when procedural knowledge
becomes the end point, not a way station, of development that its orientations need to be questioned. We need to encourage women to struggle toward autonomy rather than avoid it."

Of course, I hear Alicia's words as I read Hays here. She wants to
take a place in the public domain of the academy, but her work thus far
has inhibited her from doing so. She is in search of that flexible voice, a
language that will help transport her back and forth between what she
knows as truth and what she needs to do to represent herself to the
community. Hays's feminist pedagogy recognizes Alicia's dilemma and
bolsters her desire as it describes a classroom that "will support students
as they develop rational skills, learn procedures that enable them to
achieve intellectual and professional mastery, and make judgments about
a wide range of issues, judgments that are both intellectually sound and
ethically committed, both reasoned and caring." Alicia needs to traverse
that bridge between the personal and the public as her needs dictate,
sometimes even straddling it, one foot on each side. And, as Hays clearly
recognizes, there is really no choice between the dominance of public
academic discourse and the expressiveness of personal writing. Alicia
needs them both, and sometimes she needs them both at once. But there
is the danger of dichotomizing the private and the public to the point
that they seem to exist separately and without need of each other.

Checking In Back at the Checkpoint

By the end of the Rosenberg unit and because of her interest in our
mock trial, Alicia was moved to consider the influence of communism

on the Rosenbergs during the 1930s in a formal, analytical essay. This final work, the culmination of several weeks of reading and writing about the case in a research-oriented way, illustrates her ability to analyze her own judgments and those of secondary sources with a focus on the following thesis: "The communist rhetoric of the Thirties was extremely influential for Julius and Ethel because of their impoverished backgrounds. It was this rhetoric that would dictate the outcome of their lives." A section of her introduction leading to this position shows Alicia's growing ability to synthesize material:

> The first half of this century was an incredible time of change for the United States. The nation was involved in World War I from 1917 to 1918. The U.S. prospered during the Roaring Twenties and saw that come to a screeching halt with the stock market crash in 1929. The Great Depression was not far behind. It took a second world war during the Forties to re-establish the U.S. on firm social and economic grounds. Then, with this new stability, the nation saw the "Red Scare" develop right before its eyes. These were tremendously stressful times for people to go through.

She proceeds to explain the early lives of the Rosenbergs, their poverty and disenchantment with the capitalist system, and the way the communist vision eventually influenced them. She analyzes the notion that the communist vision that inspired many Americans to political resistance during the Depression continued to inspire the Rosenbergs and turned them into fanatics, even during the 1950s, when to be associated with communism meant the blacklist or, in their case, death. She concludes:

> The power of Communist language during the 1930s was very influential in shaping the outcome of the Rosenbergs' lives. The Great Depression was a very impressionable time when Julius and Ethel were first exposed to Communism. The different rhetorical languages they were exposed to, from the Mooney pamphlet to the DAILY WORKER, shaped their entire lives. The persuasive power of the evident languages was strong enough to interfere with their basic judgments. By 1953, the Rosenbergs were so fanatical about the Communist Party that they died for it in the electric chair.

I would argue that Alicia's ability to write academically in this assignment is not built on a dichotomy between the private writing of her journal and the public discourse she used in the formal assignments. To see these as separate spheres is to lose sight of the dynamic interplay throughout the unit between what she was exploring first for herself, in personalized writing, and second for the wider community of our class, in more objective language. The language that looks and sounds objective is actually permeated by the subjective at the same time. We may describe these spheres individually, if necessary, to understand what is working for Alicia, but we cannot separate them. Alicia's own ideas are not exclusively personal anymore. They incorporate the voices of other writers from the diverse number of readings, my dialogue with her in the journal entries, and other students in the classroom giving constant expression to their ideas in discussion, as well as public knowledge about the Rosenberg case itself. The case, then, serves as a metaphor for critical analysis. I immersed Alicia in its concrete and contrastive nature; through journals, discussion, and finally a mock trial, she found that she was capable of inventing her own critical analysis, one that operates from an expanded knowledge base and uses a specific framework for interpretation. She learned how to weave together her personal understanding with the conventions of public, academic discourse.

My course allows for multiple perspectives and creates a space where various roles can be played out in the discovery of language. I want all my students to understand that language is theirs to own, even as their language is also populated by the voices of others. Feminist pedagogical strategies clearly have their limitations, some of which are noted earlier in this essay. Limiting students to the personal voice, for instance, is by itself obviously restrictive, when we consider the rest of the work students have to do. At the same time, it is feminist pedagogy that currently seems to be taking the most productive route away from rigid, objectified, almost solidified and lifeless discourse forms toward something more dynamic and invested, while still public. It is feminism, after all, that proclaims that the personal is political and is willing to critique each side of that equation. That, to me, is the heart of the most potent feminist pedagogy that articulates goals so promising for composition. It looks closely at the intricate particles of the personal without losing sight of the overall wave pattern making up the public domain.

Note: I would like to acknowledge and thank my student Alicia Staley for generously permitting me to use the written work she composed in my spring 1992 writing class as the central focus for this article. Alicia's developing confidence includes plans to continue writing and to tell her own story someday. I look forward to that moment as her teacher and her friend.

20

Editors' Reflections: Vision and Interpretation

Louise Wetherbee Phelps, with Janet Emig

Titling the Volume

Our title for this volume has surprised and disconcerted many people, including some of our contributors. It grew out of our earliest conversation about doing this book together, when Janet and I first talked about our own complex experiences of femininity within our professional lives in composition and rhetoric and imagined how they might be the same or different for others. We used *feminine principles* then as a rubric for the kinds of thinking about writing, teaching, rhetoric, and gender often discussed quietly among women but seldom published in books and journals of the field, and almost never linked to feminism as a social movement or academic study. From this seed our title grew, reinterpreted and reshaped over time to fit the content that emerged unpredictably from more than one hundred abstracts, even as that content gave varied meaning to the ambiguous possibilities of the term *feminine principles.*

Meanwhile, exactly contemporaneous with our editing project, feminism broke through dramatically into the public discourse of composition and rhetoric, notably with the 1988 publication of Elizabeth Flynn's "Composing Like a Woman" and the rapid proliferation of gender-related sessions at the Conference on College Composition and Communication (the 4Cs) between 1987 and 1989.[1] We present our own collection now as one landmark in this development and, perhaps, a synecdoche for the feminism still emergent in the field. This volume, in its rather idiosyncratic range and eclecticism, provides a window on a uniquely transitional moment when everything is yet to be decided. Our title is one way we have tried to capture our own vision of that emergent feminism and its potential contributions, and so we begin our reflections there.

The title deliberately sets up two terms (*feminine principles* and *women's experience*), a context (American composition and rhetoric), and an empty space (feminism). At the time of conceiving this volume, we knew of only a few scattered articles that raised gender issues about our field (a major exception was Cynthia Caywood and Gillian Overing's 1987 collection exploring connections between feminism and the teaching of writing as process). Our volume was intended to pose the question, How and what might feminism in composition and rhetoric come to be? We did not assume that it already existed, or that it would take some particular form. We anticipated, in fact, that much work put forward in composition as feminist might be judged something else (or less) by mainstream academic feminists, especially if they applied standards of "advanced feminism" from various theoretical perspectives (materialist feminist, say, or poststructuralist feminist). We thought that some of the work we wanted to value might be from some perspectives prereflectively feminist—for example, accounts, of women's experience or practices as writers, readers, learners, and teachers. Rather than prejudge, we decided to problematize feminism as a construct in composition by omitting the word from the title. In so doing, we left open the question of attributing "feminist" positions to all contributors, or to their female subjects, as well as the definitions that might be proposed and argued for a new feminism of composition.

Janet and I first used *feminine principles* during that early conversation in discovering one of our commonalities: that we both understood our own gender as incorporating and holding in dynamic tension the complementary principles defined in our culture as feminine and masculine. Our own feminism, as we began to think of it relative to composition and rhetoric, depended powerfully on constantly negotiating this balance within ourselves—for example, in our complicated experiences of taking on leadership roles within institutions and professional organizations. However, we quickly perceived the usefully unorthodox ambiguities and openness to redefinition of both *feminine* and *principles*.

In the context of titling our volume (with feminism as an empty space yet to be filled, to be characterized and debated), we envisioned *feminine principles* as protofeminist possibilities in the work and discourse of women in the field. Here we imagined reexamining the past work of women scholars and teachers in composition and rhetoric to discover organizing principles—values, qualities, ideals (for example, the ideal of a dialogic rhetoric)—that are often claimed for feminism but are not explicitly framed in that work as feminist in the usual, political sense—indeed, may not be linked there to women or gender at all. We suggest that these cases embody or enact culturally feminine values (on the part of both men and women) but not necessarily feminist positions. In fact, much of what is called, in our volume and elsewhere *feminist* seems to us to be claims and disclaimers about the contested feminine—women's different ways of knowing, writing, teaching, learning, and so on. (See, e.g., Flynn 1988; Cooper; Jessup and Lardner, chap. 9, this vol.; Caywood and Overing.) Part of the task these authors face is to decide how these problematic claims might constitute or contribute to feminism in composition and rhetoric as an intellectual study or a political stance (and why that would be significant or useful for either composition studies or rhetoric). One important way they do that is to define or redefine "feminine" attributes as principled choices: not so much claimed about women as chosen by women, proposed for women and perhaps men, offered as a basis for constructing new models for writing, learning, teaching, and rhetoric.

As we reflect on feminine principles in the volume, we see many of our contributors as trying to characterize and value women's differences—as teachers, for example, or writers. One positive outcome of such an effort can be to recuperate and extend what Mitzi Myers calls historically "female conceptualizations of authorship, childhood, and education" and other ideas central to composition studies or rhetoric. This is a powerful strategy, but one with important limitations (see Dingwaney and Needham for a thoughtful critique; see, also, Jarratt 1991b). We hope that teachers and scholars developing feminism in composition and rhetoric will address the contradictions among claims about feminine principles that show up among our contributors and elsewhere: for example, between the social values of dialogue, community, or collaboration on the one hand and, on the other, individualistic emphases on personal experience, identity, voice, and subjective knowledge. Our own reservations about this approach diminish when such conceptualizations, characterizations, and evaluations have a strongly historical cast, as they do in Myers's work.

We added *women's experience* to our title in recognition of the extraordinary importance we came to attach to narrative or poetic renderings of a collective experience that has been silent, ignored, or uninterpreted in constructing understandings of our field. Reading composition and rhetoric through the lens of gender is revelatory, rendering dramatically visible the extent to which our contemporary field and its contents (subjects, texts, processes, practices) have been shaped by the historic masculinity of rhetoric and the feminization of composition.[2] Composition must come to grips with this fact through its scholarship, borrowing frameworks from feminists in other fields and inventing new ones to analyze the material conditions and social forces that molded the development of rhetoric and composition as educational disciplines and produced their current structure as intersecting institutional and discursive practices. But it is equally important to gain access to this gendered history and present it phenomenologically, in terms of what it means and how it was and is still felt in women's (and men's, and children's) experience.

Experience is, of course, a problematic term for many poststructuralist feminists, who dismiss appeals to experience as unreconstructed essentialism. Certainly, relying on the authority of personal experience can produce naive (that is, inexplicitly or uncritically theorized) accounts or formulations of feminist writing or feminist pedagogy, as we observed in some proposals submitted for the book. Yet these may be the very pieces by or about outsiders to our academic categories and worlds whose complexity and materiality challenge simplistic abstractions and enlarge sympathies and understanding beyond our own personal experiences. In choosing to include some of these in the volume, we *insist* on experience, especially the representation of daily activity, as a source of feminist theory in composition and rhetoric. We have honored here, and urge feminist theory developing in composition to honor, individuals' eloquent stories as fundamental supplements to more abstract structural information and analysis as well as sources of theoretical concepts and insights in their own right. (In practice, individuals' stories often turn out to be interdependent, multivoiced stories, like those evoked by Cinthia Gannett and Lillian Bridwell-Bowles and told by Christine Kline, Emily Jessup and Marion Lardner, and Sara Jonsberg with Marie Salgado and the women of The Next Step.)

The urge to express and reflect on life experience is not unique to feminism in composition; it marks the early stages of most feminist movements. But there is a difference with theoretical import for a feminist treatment of experience in composition and rhetoric: the centrality of writing to this work. I learned this at the age of fifteen (in a formative encounter with the healing power of writing), when my mother wrote for her family a book-length memoir of her difficult childhood. Called

"Rites of Passage," it begins with two epigraphs quoted from Isak Dinesen: "All sorrows can be borne if you put them into a story or tell a story about them," and "I will tell you my story. Perhaps I shall understand it all better when I can, at last, give words to it." Any writing class potentially affords an opportunity for women to compose their lives—reconstructing and recuperating them as experience that can ground insight and future action. For this reason, composition can never transcend experience as a component and source of feminism. Rather, any conceivable feminism in composition must offer a theoretical account of this composing function and the ethical issues it raises, not only in students' writing but in teachers' facilitative or responsive relation to it; in researchers' or teachers' representations of other women's experience as culturally and individually diverse writers and learners; and in our own writing, our conception of writing, our relation to it (see, in this vol., Sommers, Bridwell-Bowles, Bizzell; see also Gannett 1990).

It is probably unavoidable as feminism in composition begins that it overemphasizes its own stories: those of academic women who live in or on the fringes of composition and rhetoric as a profession, along with their students. Despite our desire to blur the edges where that academic world impinges on others (the public schools, the lives of students, the workplace), despite a wide-ranging call for papers, despite the unorthodoxy of some of our choices, the volume remains reluctantly limited by its academic provenance. Even in that domain, Janet and I consider the volume insufficiently polyphonic: not diverse enough in our writers' ethnic, religious, national, linguistic, class, and racial backgrounds (though we didn't always know these) and in their workplace roles and contexts (for example, the level of schooling and age of students, the type of institution, the region, the mix of students). We strongly regret that students are only sketchily present in these essays, either as authors or as subjects (e.g., Bridwell-Bowles; Jonsberg with Salgado and the women of The Next Step). In American composition and rhetoric, diversity and difference become multidimensional issues, because they apply not only to scholars but to teachers of writing in American schools—rich, poor, private, public, urban, rural, and suburban; and not only to scholars and teachers (professionals in the field) but to their students, who of course represent the whole rainbow spectrum of American life. Inevitably we had to give up any goal of expansive representation or coverage: the American range is too rich and the volume finite. Rather, through this volume we (and our "Response" contributors) invite our colleagues to capture in future work both sides of such heterogeneity—the tensions, discord, and struggle as well as the vitality and human potential.

Obviously, we think feminists in composition and rhetoric should aspire to study comprehensively, and to sponsor, the connections among American women's writings, their cultures, and their lives—in work and at play, in religious practices, community service, leisure, and home life (see, e.g., Crouch, with Vo). But in doing so, they tend to erase clear boundaries between academic feminism and popular understandings expressed in ordinary varieties of language. That is so partly because the ethics of feminist methodologies and the unique position of the writer in composition and rhetoric make it hard to preserve distinctions between ourselves (as authors, teachers, or researchers within a discipline) and our subjects. In our volume the two tend to merge, sometimes uncomfortably, in experiments with genre and coauthorship. A certain tension results, in a work that situates its contributions "in" *composition and rhetoric*—that is, that declares a disciplinary identity and attempts to imagine forms of feminism specific to an academic field.

Our inclusion of such pieces reflects, however, a sense that this irony is internal to composition and rhetoric and constitutive for its potential feminism. This is one important way that the volume has been shaped tacitly by the conceptions of the field that Janet and I brought to the book, jointly and separately, and which have in turn been reshaped by it. This vision was not a conscious agenda, nor one we want to argue here. But we want to acknowledge that influence in a few respects that seem significant.

It is not a given, even for our own colleagues, that composition and rhetoric qualifies as an academic discipline. We make that assumption, while believing it is a field that may transgress orthodox notions of both *academic* and *discipline* (cf. Harkin; Bartholomae). As a discipline, its concerns and perspectives on the intersections of women and writing with feminism will be distinctive. That premise allowed us to exclude certain kinds of contributions that bring together women, writing, and feminism from other perspectives. The obvious example is literary criticism or literary history of women's texts, but many other disciplines take up the conjunction of women and writing in the course of feminist projects: recuperating women's contributions to science or philosophy, for instance, or studying gender differences in language use, or reconstructing social history from women's journals and letters. What operated tacitly in our editing process will become a task for feminism in composition and rhetoric: to specify the way further variables (for example, an emphasis on teaching and learning, or a specifically rhetorical mode of analysis) distinctively mark a feminist study as native to composition and rhetoric.

More important than this selective function, though, the visions of composition and rhetoric Janet and I brought to the project were similarly generous in imagining its reach and scope. We had in our own past work defined composition and rhetoric as a domain of scholarship and practice not limited to freshman or college writing, to writing or texts in a literal sense, to English departments, to literature as a disciplinary partner, to academic discourse and academic settings, to a single form of inquiry, and so on (e.g., Emig 1983; Phelps 1986, 1988). But the more capacious one's conception of the field, the more problematic its coherence and the more salient its internal contradictions and tensions. If one imagines then constructing feminism, and constructing this volume, across such an inclusive domain of responsibilities, topics, subjects, sites, and modes of inquiry, some of its features become explicable: for example, the tension between professionalism and populism already mentioned (which draws nonacademics into this volume as authors); an eccentric range of genres, modalities for inquiry, and disciplinary affiliations (see Franke); the impossibility of comprehensiveness coupled with the sense of fissures and gaps that our contributors address in their reconfigurations and responses.

Many of the expansions we would argue in principle for composition and rhetoric spring from a shared developmental orientation uncommon in current scholarship. Janet and I share a theory of human development (and of gender as a component of identity) that emphasizes interactions among biological, psychosocial, ideological, symbolic, and material influences (cf. Hays). Viewing learning as epigenetic, spanning birth to death, we think it impossible to understand or teach writing profoundly as an adult form of literacy except in context of that entire span—a position that among other things leads us to regard teachers of writing and language arts at all levels as intellectual colleagues. We have tried imaginatively, if not actually or adequately, to compass that developmental range from the very young to the very old. Perhaps one contribution of feminism to composition and rhetoric will be the generational resonance that women create when they link and overlap families, pedagogy, writing, and history. In the volume we feel that resonance keenly in essays that portray, examine critically, and value relations among different generations of teachers, families, and students (Jessup and Lardner; Kline; Sommers); incorporate feminine principles (an ethic of care) into models of pedagogy often portrayed analogically as parental (Hays); describe women's traditions as writers-educators and caretakers of literacy with important public roles and voices (e.g., Gannett; Myers; Crouch, with Vo).

Developmental theories of writing (and gender) are often understood wrongly as promoting biological or psychological perspectives *in opposition to* theories that emphasize context (social, historical, ideological, and material forces) or to those that highlight the symbolic mediation of all experience. True, our emphasis as developmentalists on embodiment does weigh against such theories in the extreme and, as feminists, leads us to value experience as an important though not absolute source of knowledge. But the developmental perspective (interpreted interactionally) also implies a broad charge to composition and rhetoric for the study of culture, language, and history.

The more we reread the essays in our volume, the more we feel the need for a stronger historical base, not only to explain the ways writing is currently taught in the academy and regarded in the culture but to reconceptualize it more fully as a native American field. History is beginning to flower in composition studies, and with it an emphasis on gender as a social force in its origins and development. We applaud in this work a growing attention to doing archival history that, while it is informed by and generates broad theories and is sensitive to interpretive issues in historiography, does not allow theory and metatheory to overwhelm or replace data. Robert Connors's work here (and that of Sue Ellen Holbrook, C. Jan Swearingen, Susan Miller, and others elsewhere) connecting the rise of composition (and the decline of rhetoric) with coeducation and feminism only begin to tease out the complicated, heterogeneous, multicausal relations among composition, literacy, education, rhetoric, and gender as they developed in nineteenth-century America, are rooted in earlier history, and structure our current field. The nature, causes, effects, motives, and meanings of these relations are already controversial and need more solid grounding in both archival evidence and a broader historical perspective that takes into account events, ideas, and forces (for example, wars, economic conditions, immigration, racial and ethnic conflicts, religious revivals, technological inventions, cultural myths) besides education itself.

Working on the volume has reinforced our sense of the significance to composition and rhetoric of its American provenance. Historical studies and, even more, theories in composition have never adequately recognized that the context for the field's formation is American society and politics, including feminist movements and their connections with abolition and civil rights; the American historical experience, including the contributions of women—native, pioneer, slave, immigrant; American cultural life, including gender myths like that of the separate spheres and the cult of true womanhood; American letters, including women's belles lettres and personal writing as it is being reclaimed in literary and historical studies, their writing for children, other women, and public life, their impact as a readership; and especially American education, including the central role of women as teachers of democratic literacy and the development of women's colleges and coeducation. Such studies need to examine the complicated gender relations of composition not only to Anglo-American, classically based rhetoric (and alternative, minority European traditions), but also to the rhetorics and language experiences of African Americans, Native Americans, and immigrant peoples. For composition (more broadly, language arts) was the crossroads at which these languages, rhetorics, literacies, races, and cultures met, in the schools where children became "American" by speaking and writing American English. Today it is happening in colleges and graduate schools as well. (See Slevin, on the crosscultural and conflictual nature of all teaching of "English" from the earliest colonial days.) From this perspective, British and European discourse traditions (like those evoked by Robert Connors and Mitzi Myers) are only one piece of the history that scholars must trace to understand the contemporary discipline of composition and rhetoric—and the issues, problems, and practices it studies—as distinctively American. Theorists in the field need to turn from an overawed dependence on continental influences to the American intellectual traditions (in literature, philosophy, science and technology, political science) and material history that have for good or for ill invisibly shaped composition and rhetoric and whose revisions to account for gender and multicultural sources and influences should inform our own revisionism. Janet's and my own visions of teaching and scholarship in writing have been decisively shaped by American philosophical pragmatism from Dewey, James, and Peirce to Rorty, and by American philosophers Susanne Langer and Nel Noddings.

Feminism as an Empty Space

We omitted *feminism* from our title in part to dramatize the astonishing absence of explicit feminism from our field before 1988. I called this phenomenon "the dog that didn't bark in the night": the significant non-event that no one had noticed (Phelps 1990). Even more puzzling, this phenomenon was not remarked when feminist issues and pieces did begin to emerge at conventions and in journals, as if taking up such questions were not itself historically situated. Authors writing now about feminism in composition often act as if they are addressing it because they just happened to be reading some feminist psychology or literary theory and realized (as in the case of other disciplinary borrowings) that it might be relevant and useful to composition and rhetoric.

Granted, our field has always been very bad about recognizing the historicity of its own interest in particular external sources, treating them as personal discoveries driven by the field's own internal questions or even an individual scholar's idiosyncratic reading taste. But in this instance, as the case unfolds compellingly for composition as a deeply feminized field and the complexity of its historic entanglements with gendered dichotomies and gender politics becomes evident, it is hard to explain the failure to ask, Where have its feminists been? Why does feminism become discursive now, not before? Why, especially, do women scholars and teachers speak their feminism now—about the most blatantly feminist issues, like collaborative authorship, or the role of affect in writing and learning, or conflicts about authority and leadership—when they did not even a year before? (Compare, for example, Ede and Lunsford 1983 with Lunsford and Ede 1990.) After all, didn't each of us (women scholars and teachers, that is) know these things about composition and rhetoric in our hearts? For we read them now with no surprise, just nods of recognition.

In the long conversations between Janet and me so vital to our collaboration on this project, we have speculated endlessly about this fascinating question. We have read the stories in this volume and elsewhere about the lives of women who teach and study writing; and we have told our own, tracing our own decisions and the choices that led us on such different paths to editing this book together (in Janet's case, a story taken by others as emblematic: see R. Gerald Nelms's case study of her academic life, based on oral history). We have listened and joined in as students, colleagues, and friends argued: about what it means to be feminist, whether they identify themselves as feminists, what is or is not feminist about their life history, their teaching, their writing; about conjunctions and polarization between academic and popular feminism, as these relate to our own histories; about the feminization of composition and what that has meant and still means in terms of the class structure of the academy itself. Collecting and reflecting on such arguments and stories, and relating them to historical and theoretical analyses of our field as gendered, we may begin to understand what has delayed the expression of feminism in composition and rhetoric.

Small wonder that feminism as a newly explicit feature of our field is not a coherent phenomenon. In this respect, this book is representative, and we would argue that the incoherence of both is perhaps one of their most interesting and promising features. Peggy McIntosh, among others, has described the standard progression for feminism as it has developed in other academic fields: from discovering and celebrating "great women" of the past to redefining or reconstructing the discipline (its topics and its own history) to "include us all" (3–4). One might have imagined that either composition would recapitulate this history, starting with the reclamation of women's invisible contributions coupled with a critique of androcentrism (see Flynn 1988), or it would assimilate these earlier phases and begin at the point of advanced feminism, with (let's say) debates about essentialism or the problematic conjunctions of feminism with Marxism or poststructuralism, gender with race, class, and sexuality. Instead, we have in composition and rhetoric a delightful disorder that I have described as an "Olduvai Gorge":

> Feminism emerges to the eye and hand of the archeologist in 1990 as if the feminist turn opened up a rift in space that provides us simultaneous access to all phases and times of feminism at once. On the one hand, they are already there, hidden and obscurely related in the jumbled deposits and faults of our history; on the other, they will only be revealed by digging carefully in our past and aligning present work with historical moments in the development of feminist studies. (Phelps 1990, 13)

In part, this variety reflects the characteristically eclectic and often undiscriminating ways that composition borrows and assimilates work from other disciplines (and in this respect, feminism is to composition and rhetoric another authoritative discourse, or rather many competing ones). But there is an important difference from those earlier appropriations, coupled with an even more important difference between composition and other fields in the way it constructs feminism as a strand of the discipline. In most other fields, women introduced women, and feminist issues, into a prior male discourse; there is a necessary violence to the ways they broke down that discourse and "added women"—compelling the field to acknowledge them historically and to welcome them as present agents in developing, applying, writing, and teaching its

418 Louise Wetherbee Phelps, with Janet Emig

knowledge. These changes both enabled and were brought about by
analyses of traditional topics and issues in each discipline in terms of
gender and from feminist perspectives, generating in the process new
questions, topics, and issues along with transformations (in some cases)
of its research modes and epistemology. Composition, however, was feminized in its very origins, and has developed in terms of an enormously
conflicted and complicated practical and political history of gendered
relations to masculinist discourse and power (as well as to the racial,
ethnic, class, and language issues only now being taken up in other
feminisms). If women in composition and rhetoric simply overlay the
field with other, borrowed feminisms (some singularly unsuited for uncritical importation into such a quintessentially American context), they
will deny the heritage of an indigenous though subterranean feminism
that awaits critical articulation and elaboration.

The Encounter with Feminism/the Construction of Feminism

From these essays, and even more the abstracts from which they were
drawn, and from the feminist work in the field that is coming out at an
accelerating rate (several composition journals have devoted special issues to gender), we discern the promise of productive relations in two
modes: the encounter of composition and rhetoric with other feminisms
and, more important, the construction of feminism from indigenous
sources and traditions in the field—experiential, practical, intellectual,
discursive, and historical. We want to sketch out a list of these possibilities that is by no means exhaustive, but is also perhaps not obvious,
since it draws on absences as much as on feminist work already begun
here and elsewhere.

*Using feminism as a tool for addressing problems in composition and
rhetoric:* This is the familiar paradigm whereby the field draws on concepts
in other fields to rethink aspects of its own theories and practices. Here
feminism implies a cross-disciplinary body of scholarly work that, however
diverse, constitutes a conversation and a shared set of issues and problems
along with a considerable knowledge base and well-articulated values and
positions. (See Bridwell-Bowles, Ashton-Jones in this volume; Ritchie;
Worsham, for examples.) These theories and their values instruct composition and rhetoric in how to build its own theories and practices of
feminism and how to evaluate others' positions in the terms provided.

*Treating gender as a missing dimension of the self-understanding of
composition and rhetoric:* This approach may draw on the work of other

fields analogically but as a source of questions more than of answers. The assumption that gender matters generates an immense number of topics for research, indeed whole genres of study. Among these are, for example, appreciations and revisionist readings of women scholars; studies of the reception, criticism, citation, and use of women's scholarship or leadership and its appropriation (sometimes unacknowledged) by male colleagues; development of new concepts taking into account women's questions, problems, and perspectives (for example, a concept of legitimate and ethical power [Phelps, chap. 12, this vol.]; embodiment [Emig 1983] as it relates to discourse; or childhood [Myers, chap. 11, this vol.]); and of course all the historical studies we have already called for.

Experimenting with and theorizing genres and forms of discourse for women or in terms of feminist concerns and women's styles: Our volume is particularly suggestive in this regard (see, also, *College Composition and Communication* 43 (1992)), including as it does multivoiced and multitextured discourse of several kinds, blending poetry, narrative prose, classic academic argument, journal, and drama. Such experiments with organization, style, and genre serve a feminist purpose in opening up academic discourse to alternate and mixed modes that represent through their form the contemporary complexity, density, and intertwining of personal and professional experience that mark women's lived lives. Composition and rhetoric is of all disciplines perhaps best suited to lead this feminist project, through critical examination of feminist critiques of male discourse and feminist utopian rhetorics in the light of practical knowledge and rhetorical expertise. Composition can ground such critiques and utopian theories uniquely in experiments with genre by both female and male student writers; in studies of how people learn, invent, experience, resist, choose, and adapt genres (see Bridwell-Bowles; Harrienger); and also in historical and rhetorical studies of the discourse traditions (both talk and writing) from which any genre must develop (see Myers; Gannett).

Studying relations among pedagogy, gender, and language: Again, composition and rhetoric is uniquely positioned by its history, expert knowledge, and current responsibilities to develop and test new theories of teaching and learning that take into account both teachers' and students' gender (see Bridwell-Bowles; Ashton-Jones; Hays; Myers) without overlooking the complexity of relations between gender and other features of social identity, such as ethnicity, native language, and home culture, with which teachers of literacy have long been concerned.

Studying feminisms from the perspective of rhetoric: This seems to us one of the most fruitful possibilities in the encounter between feminism and our field. The rhetoric of feminism is a little-studied but uniquely significant aspect of its intellectual projects; since most academic feminisms make their political and ethical commitments constitutive, they see their persuasive purposes as prior to the search for knowledge. Chris Weedon's statement is representative: "Feminism is a politics ... directed at changing existing power relations between women and men in society. . . . [Political questions] should be the motivating force behind feminist theory which must always be answerable to the needs of women in our struggle to transform patriarchy" (1–2). (Bizzell addresses one interesting rhetorical problem women, and feminists, face, and speculates on how to turn it into an advantage.)

Comparing composition and rhetoric with feminism: We are struck by the many parallels between these two if thought of as disciplines or fields of scholarship and practice. The first thing they share is the sense in which they are problematically unitary as "disciplines," with their scholarship diffusely dispersed throughout traditional academic fields and professions. Some other points of comparison are their utopianism (grounded in social missions), their experiences of cross-class cooperation and conflict, and their pragmatic concern with language from the user's perspective. This point merits some careful exploration (see Ray; Phelps 1990).

Final Thoughts

In thinking about the possible contributions of composition and rhetoric to feminism, Janet and I are impressed generally with the potential for theorists and teachers in our field to deal with multiple variables. Given the responsibilities and problems it inherits of dealing with literacy as the alchemy for an extraordinarily complex democracy of peoples and languages, a history that already encompasses gender practically, if not theoretically, this should not surprise us. Any teacher of writing—especially in today's public schools—is a magician in dealing with multiplicity and complexity.

It is a little easier to understand the absence of gender in the scholarship of composition and rhetoric if we see it as part of a matrix of variables (race, class, and native language are others) that, although they remain largely latent as theoretical issues, are vividly salient and problematic in its practices. To confirm this hypothesis we have only to listen in on teachers' conversations and classroom discourse. Tellingly, even recent composition scholarship often invokes ideas like gender or class as crystallized meanings, treating them as authoritative, unanalyzable terms rather than debatable concepts needing definition and argument.

Ideally, investigations in composition begin with the phenomenal fact of a complex relation (a textual transaction, a student conference, a course design, the status of part-time instructors in an institution, the rhetoric of assessment) and examine the way internally complex elements like gender enter into its dynamic, rather than starting with discrete simple factors and analyzing them as causes, effects, motives, or attributes. Such an approach to feminism will likely be quicker to perceive other aspects of social identity as interactional with gender, given their copresence in the matrix of practice that is part of the field's collective historical experience.

The job of someone writing out of this rich interaction is a form of bricolage in which the bits and pieces writers bring into conjunction are each huge, complex domains of human life. Janet and I saw the difficulty and excitement of this task in editing the volume, advising writers on revision while trying to compose the volume as an intelligible array of pieces forming emergent feminism in the field. We came to think of the writers in each essay, and ourselves in the volume as a whole, as trying to capture the dynamic of a matrix of forces by creating a nexus point where they and we (the writers, editors, and readers) could understand multiple variables by observing how they collide, merge, and interact. Here, such a nexus brings together women as subjects and agents with gender, feminism, writing, rhetoric, education, literacy, and (usually) some concept or experience used to focus and connect them. (Rocklin's reconfiguration of the volume is a heroic effort on this score.) This work (like the discipline of composition and rhetoric itself) is always threatened by centrifugal forces; again and again, the pieces flew apart. Two of our authors who did it best told us this was the hardest piece of writing they had ever done (and they were rather proud of it). If individual pieces do not always achieve such virtuosity (and some didn't even try), together they contribute to the volume's effort to create kaleidoscopically something of the grand effect. We think familiarity with the challenge and exhilaration of this juggling act (in a piece of writing, in teaching) is one of the values composition offers to feminism.

At the same time, introducing and foregrounding gender as a significant variable puts pressure on the project to compose composition and rhetoric itself and has sharpened our own sense of the field as intersectional, multivariate, and subject to both centrifugal and centripetal forces (cf. James Zebroski, on composing, and Jim Corder, on rhetoric as intersectional). The parallels between writing feminism, editing this volume, and composing a field of multiple variables are reciprocally suggestive, especially in the problems they identify.

In closing, consider once more the matter of experience and theory. Implicit in these reflections is the need to complicate and deepen the descriptive notion of experience before it gets to the point of theoretical interpretation or formulation. In other words, one should not take a simplistic notion of experience and oppose it to a sophisticated one of theory. In the first place, experience refers not merely to personal lives but to historical experience, collective experience, institutional experience, literary experience—all ways that direct personal understandings rest on the interactivity and intersubjectivity of human life and are thus endlessly complicated by others. To build an adequately complex theory or to test proposed ones, scholars must render all these kinds of experience in a phenomenologically detailed, unsentimental, self-critical mode that accounts in some measure for the complexities of lived lives. From this perspective, naivete is not simple ignorance—the failure to be informed about theory or to take into account feminist critiques of essentialism and centered subjectivity. Naivete is sentimentalizing ourselves, failing to be honest and adequate to the ambiguities, difficulties, and ambivalence of our observations and analyses of experience. To access these complexities, I have suggested starting with vignettes that have the form of knots—tense, conflictual, paradoxical, ambiguous, counterintuitive moments when stereotypes about gender break down (Phelps, chap. 13, this vol.).

Both Janet and I did serious reading in feminist scholarship as we worked on this project, some of it with great pleasure and profit. We hope to do much more. But, finally, we must urge that such reading is not the primary basis for constructing feminism in composition and rhetoric.[3] In editing the book together, Janet and I confirmed what we independently believed when we started: that feminist theory in composition cannot spring derivatively from other academic feminism but must grow from the hearts and heads of women in their work within this field. (This is not to exclude our male colleages from helping us in this task but to affirm that without women's experience there could be no feminism.) For Janet and me personally, this means that it is living as a woman and specifically, as a teacher, scholar, administrator, a professional in composition that allows such reading to instruct each of us. Our reflective practices enable us to bring to those texts our own questions and needs, to learn from them, to interpret and transact with them. The passions generated by these experiences drive our search for and our shaping of theoretical understandings, which in turn foster rhetorical and practical action in the world.

The same relation between experience and theory we propose for ourselves should hold for the discipline. From one perspective, feminist scholarship is yet another body of knowledge, a network of interrelated texts and arguments, to which composition looks for enlightenment and inspiration. The danger here is of taking up the same submissive posture to feminist scholarship with which composition has encountered other fields in the past, most recently, critical theory. When we ask, How can academic feminism change us? we are asking the wrong question, one that immediately positions us as passive, a blank page without prior feminist meanings, waiting to be inscribed. In short, composing feminism like a woman.

Prior to any relation between composition and other feminisms is this question: What do we learn by appreciating our own native feminism, by looking to our own, peculiarly American historical and personal experience—heterogeneous and heteroglot, abounding in possibility and conflict—as its source? From this starting point we can read feminist scholarship with antennae tuned. We can probe its texts to find connections—ideas that illuminate, challenge, and connect synergistically with our own home-grown purposes, insights, nascent positions. But more important, we encounter feminist theories then in a different spirit, on different terms and footing, with the right question about the relation: What can American composition and rhetoric contribute to feminist scholarship by reclaiming its own heritage, its own stories and dramas, its own ideals, by reexamining its own practices, its own political and rhetorical action ... by formulating from these its own concepts and theories?

NOTES

1. In March 1987, we count five sessions on feminism or gender at CCCC plus a postconvention workshop on integrating the scholarship on women into the composition classroom. In 1988, the number increases to thirteen sessions, and in 1989, with twenty-five sessions and a research-oriented preconvention workshop, "Women and Writing" is added to the topic index for concurrent sessions.

2. This historical work has just begun: see Holbrook 1991a, 1991b; Miller; Flynn 1990, 1991; Swearingen; Jarratt 1990, 1991a; Connors chap. 4, this vol.;

1991. Because of its length, we were unable to use in the volume Sue Ellen Holbrook's historical essay on the gendering of nineteenth- and early twentieth-century composition, "Manful Enterprise, Feminine Subject: Expressions of Gender in the History of English Composition 1880–1950"; but our thinking about this issue was informed by her rich store of archival data.

3. With rare exceptions we have confined our citations in this reflection to authors and writings in composition and rhetoric, in part to make our point that the field should develop feminism primarily from its grass roots, not by imitation.

BIBLIOGRAPHY

Ashton-Jones, ed. *Gender, Culture, and Ideology*. Special issue of *Journal of Advanced Composition* 10 (1990).

Bartholomae, David. "Freshman English, Composition, and CCCC." *College Composition and Communication* 40 (1989): 38–50.

Bullock, Richard, and John Trimbur, eds. *The Politics of Writing Instruction: Postsecondary*. Portsmouth, N.H.: Heinemann-Boynton/Cook, 1991.

Caywood, Cynthia L., and Gillian R. Overing, eds. *Teaching Writing: Pedagogy, Gender, and Equity*. Albany: State University of New York Press, 1987.

Connors, Robert J. "Rhetoric in the Modern University: The Creation of an Underclass." In *Politics of Writing Instructions*, edited by Bullock and Trimbur, 55–84. 1991.

Cooper, Marilyn M. "Women's Ways of Writing." In Marilyn M. Cooper and Michael Holzman, *Writing as Social Action*, 141–56. Portsmouth, N.H.: Heinemann-Boynton/Cook, 1989.

Corder, Jim. "A New Introduction to Psychoanalysis Taken as a Version of Modern Rhetoric." *Pre/Text* 5 (1984): 137–69.

Dingwaney, Anuradha, and Lawrence Needham. "Feminist Theory and Practice in the Writing Classroom: A Critique and a Prospectus." In *Constructing Rhetorical Education: From the Classroom to the Community*, edited by Marie Secor and Davida Charney, 6–25. Carbondale: Southern Illinois Univ. Press, 1992.

Ede, Lisa, and Andrea Lunsford. "Why Write . . . Together?" *Rhetoric Review* 1 (1983): 150–57.

Emig, Janet. *The Web of Meaning: Essays on Writing, Teaching, Learning, and Thinking*. Edited by Dixie Goswami and Maureen Butler. Upper Montcalir, N.J.: Boynton/Cook, 1983.

Flynn, Elizabeth A. "Composing as a Woman." *College Composition and Communication* 39 (1988): 423–35.

———. "Foremothers of Composition Studies." Presented at the annual meeting of the Modern Language Association, Chicago, 1990.

———. "Composition Studies from a Feminist Perspective." In *Politics of Writing Instructions*, edited by Bullock and Trimbur, 55–84. 1991.

Gannett, Cinthia. "Who's Afraid of Virginia Woolf's Diaries: Writing to Heal and Academic Discourse." Presented at the annual meeting of the Modern Language Association, Chicago, 1990.

Harkin, Patricia. "The Postdisciplinary Politics of Lore." In *Contending with Words,* edited by Harkin and Schlib, 124–38.

Harkin, Patricia, and John Schlib. *Contending with Words: Composition and Rhetoric in a Postmodern Age.* New York: Modern Language Association, 1991.

Holbrook, Sue Ellen. "Manful Enterprise, Feminine Subject: Expressions of Gender in the History of English Composition 1880–1950." Unpublished essay, 1991a.

——. "Women's Work: The Feminizing of Composition." *Rhetoric Review* 9 (1991): 201–29.

Jarratt, Susan C. "The First Sophists and Feminism: Discourse of the 'Other.' " *Hypatia* 5 (1990): 27–41.

——. "Feminism and Composition: The Case for Conflict." In *Contending with Words,* edited by Harkin and Schlib, 105–23. 1991b.

——. *Rereading the Sophists: Classical Rhetoric Prefigured.* Carbondale: Southern Univ. Press, 1991.

Lunsford, Andrea A., and Lisa Ede. "Rhetoric in a New Key: Women and Collaboration." *Rhetoric Review* 8 (1990): 234–41.

McIntosh, Peggy. *Interactive Phases of Curricular Revision: A Feminist Perspective.* Working Paper 124. Wellesley, Mass.: Center for Research on Women, Wellesley College, 1983.

Miller, Susan. "The Feminization of Composition." In *Politics of Writing Instructions,* edited by Bullock and Trimbur, 39–53. 1991.

Nelms, R. Gerald. "A Case History Approach to Composition Studies: Edward P. J. Corbett and Janet Emig." Athens: Ohio State Univ. Press, 1990.

——. *Composition as a Human Science: Contributions to the Self-Understanding of a Discipline.* New York: Oxford Univ. Press, 1988.

Phelps, Louise Wetherbee. "The Domain of Composition." *Rhetoric Review* 4 (1986): 182–95.

——. *"A Meditation on Composing:* Emergent Feminism in Composition Studies." Presented at the annual meeting of the Modern Language Association, Chicago, 1990.

Ray, Ruth. *The Practice of Theory: Teacher Research in Composition.* Urbana, Ill.: NCTE, 1993.

Ritchie, Joy S. "Confronting the 'Essential' Problem: Reconnecting Feminist Theory and Pedagogy." *Journal of American Composition* 10 (1990): 249–73.

Slevin, James. "Introducing English: The Politics of Seventeenth-Century Colonial Education." Association of Departments of English, Skidmore College, 1991.

Swearingen, C. Jan. "Discourse, Difference, and Gender: Walter Ong's Contributions to Feminist Language Studies." In *Media, Consciousness, and Culture: Studies of Walter Ong's Contributions to Rhetoric, Communication, and Criticism,* edited by Bruce E. Gronbeck, Thomas J. Farrell, and Paul Soukup. Newbury Park, Calif.: Sage, 1991.

Weedon, Chris. *Feminist Practice and Post Structuralist Theory.* New York: Blackwell, 1987.

Worsham, Lynn. "Writing against Writing: The Predicament of Ecriture Féminine in Composition Studies." In *Contending with Words,* edited by Harkin and Schlib, 82–104.

Zebroski, James Thomas. *Thinking and Theory.* Portsmouth, N.H.: Heinemann-Boynton/Cook, 1993.

Notes on Contributors

Evelyn Ashton-Jones teaches writing and composition at the University of Southern Mississippi, where she also directs the Writing Center. Her interests include cultural studies, social theories of literacy, and feminist perspectives on language and discourse. She is coauthor of *The Gender Reader* (1991) and is guest editor of a special issue on gender, culture, and ideology published by the *Journal of Advanced Composition* (1990). Her work has appeared in the *Journal of Education, College English, Composition and communication, Writing Center Journal, Writing Program Administration,* and *Teaching English in the Two-Year College.* She currently serves as co-editor of the *Journal of Advanced Composition.*

Patricia Bizzell is Professor of English and Director of Writing Programs at the College of the Holy Cross. She has published *Academic Discourse and Critical Consciousness* (1992), with an introduction that discusses the influence of her family life on her work; and, with her husband, Bruce Herzberg, *The Rhetorical Tradition: Reading from Classical to Contemporary Times* (1990; winner of the NCTE Outstanding Book Award), which attempts to include women's contributions. Her essay in this volume reflects her ongoing interest in problems of classroom authority and their relation to issues of basic writing and cultural literacy.

Lillian Bridwell-Bowles is Associate Professor of English and Director of the Center for Interdisciplinary Studies of Writing, and a Faculty Affiliate in Women's Studies at the University of Minnesota, Twin Cities. In addition, she is Co-director of the Minnesota Writing Project and Immediate Past Chair of the Conference of College Composition and Communication. Her research interests include rhetorical theory, especially the historical treatment of women's speech and writing in rhetorical theory and by women rhetoricians; linguistics, particularly gender issues; issues of race, class, and gender in writing instruction; composing processes, especially those of women; and analyses of "new," experimental, or undervalued textual forms, alternatives to conventional rhetorical patterns.

Robert J. Connors is Professor of English and Director of the Writing Center at the University of New Hampshire. He has published many articles on rhetorical history and theory and, with Lisa Ede and Andrea Lunsford, co-edited *Essays on Classical Rhetoric and Modern Discourse.* He co-authored *The St. Martin's Handbook* with Andrea Lunsford and *The St. Martin's Guide to Teaching Writing* with Cherl Glenn. He is editor of *The Selected Essays of Edward P. J. Corbett.* In 1982 he received the CCCC's Richard Braddock Award and was co-recipient of the Mina P. Shaughnessy Award given by the MLA in 1985. He is currently editing a collection of articles on composition history and a monograph on the development of modern composition teaching and studies, *Composition-Rhetoric.*

Mary Kay Crouch is an Associate Professor of English at California State University, Fullerton, whose field of study is composition and rhetoric. One of the founders of the journal *The Writing Instructor,* she has published articles in that journal, in *College Composition and Communication,* and has essays on assessment by writing portfolio in two book collections. Her interest in Vietnamese literacy stems from her association with Son Vo; her efforts to meet the language needs of Vietnamese and other Asian students on campus; and the teaching, service, and social activities she is involved with in the Little Saigon community in Orange County. With Dr. Vo she developed an ESL training workshop for university teachers that was presented in Hanoi and Ho Chi Minh City in 1991. They and other Fullerton colleagues have been invited by Vietnam's Ministry of Education to suggest ways of restructuring the nation's system of higher education.

David Franke is a graduate student at Syracuse University and an adjunct faculty member in the Writing Program. As a research assistant for Louise Phelps, he helped organize the manuscripts and early correspondence for this volume. He was one of the first coordinators (teaching-group leaders) for the Syracuse Writing Program and continues this work, primarily with first-year teaching assistants. His in-process dissertation takes up a phenomenological "governing gaze," reflecting on the experience of these newcomers as they try to name and organize their encounter with a community and discourse unfamiliar to them. As in his chapter for this book, he is interested in examining how thinkers "map" their experience, creating new claims and practices as they proceed.

Cinthia Gannett is Associate Professor of English and Women's Studies and Coordinator of the Writing Program at the University of New Hampshire. She is the author of *Gender and the Journal: Diaries and Academic Discourse* (1992) and various articles on journals and academic discourse. She writes, teaches, and presents programs on feminist research in composition, journals, writing across the curriculum, and the role of grammar in the composition classroom. She is currently researching unpublished women's diaries in New Hampshire for a project called "Unlocking the Diary."

Myrna Harrienger teaches undergraduate composition and graduate courses in rhetoric and composition at Texas Tech University. Her Ph.D. dissertation, "Medicine as Dialogic Rhetoric and the Elderly Ill Woman," breaks ground for rhetoric and composition, including within its scope the literacy events of the elderly and elderly ill, especially women. Supported by a NCTE grant and a Purdue fellowship, that work was motivated by Myrna's involvement in the illness experiences of elderly women and her conviction that rhetoric and composition can empower and reposition persons in areas outside academia or the workplace. She continues to focus on the literate practices of the elderly and the positions assigned to them by society and such institutional rhetorics as medicine.

Janice Hays is Professor of English at the University of Colorado, where she teaches rhetoric and composition, creative writing, and women's studies. She also holds an MFA in writing (poetry) from Vermont College, has published one chapbook and numerous poems, and has a second manuscript ready for publication. She conducts research on writing and intellectual development, most recently on writing and intellectual development and stylistic substructures linked to gender and race. She has published numerous articles on these topics, and is currently working primarily in the field of creative writing and poetry.

Emily Jessup (Decker) is the Associate Director for Assessment at the University of Michigan. She designed and now manages the assessment of writing portfolios from about 5,000 incoming students for the purpose of placing them in appropriate writing courses. More important are the curricular changes that will result from getting a clear sense of the needs and abilities of entering writers, as well as the advantages of better articulation between high school and college writing programs. With Kitty Geissler, she is co-editor of an anthology entitled *Valuing Diversity in Composition Research* and is writing a book on feminism and composition for the Prentice-Hall Series on Literacy and Culture.

Sara Dalmas Jonsberg, a member of the English faculty at Montclair State College, holds a B.A. from Mount Holyoke College, a master's degree from Johns Hopkins University, and an Ed.D. from the University of Massachusetts. Founder and coordinator between 1989 and 1991 of The Next Step, a summer program for young mothers at Mount Holyoke College, she is interested in how women take charge of their own learning and living. Personal writing, she believes, is an important tool for understanding and transforming relations to oneself and others.

Christine Holm Kline, an Associate Professor of Education at the University of Puget Sound in Washington, was until recently a language arts curriculm supervisor in a K–8 school district in New Jersey. As a former elementary school teacher, New Jersey Writing Project trainer, and curriculm staff development specialist, she has been interested in women's issues as an integral part of language learning and teaching.

Marion Lardner has spent her professional career in early childhood education as a public school teacher of grades K–3. She has used science to stimulate children's writing as they observe, learn to predict, and express their interpretations of the world. At professional conferences she has made gardening a focus for science teaching and teaching children's writing. Her articles have appeared in such diverse publications as the eighth North American Prairie Conference newsletter and the *American Horticulturalist.* In 1992 she received the Presidential Science Award for Illinois elementary science teachers.

Janice M. Lauer is Professor of English at Purdue University, where she directs the graduate program in rhetoric and composition and teaches composition theory and classical rhetoric. She is an author of *Four Worlds of Writing Composition Research: Empirical Designs,* and of articles on invention, persuasive writing, classical rhetoric, and composition studies as a discipline. She is the editor of the composition/rhetoric entries in the *Encyclopedia of English Studies and Language Arts* and the forthcoming *Composition Studies: Conversations and Controversies,* a data bank of composition essays. She directed a national Rhetoric Seminar for thirteen summers, chaired the College Section of the NCTE, and was on the executive committees of CCCC, the MLA Group on the History and Theory of Rhetoric, and the Rhetoric Society of America. She currently coordinates a consortium of doctoral programs in rhetoric and composition.

Mitzi Myers teaches writing and children's and adolescent literature at the University of California, Los Angeles. She has published extensively on historical children's literature and on eighteenth- and nineteenth-century women writers, including Mary Wollstonecraft, Hannah More, Harriet Martineau, and Maria Edgeworth. She is currently completing *Romancing the Family: Maria Edgeworth and the Scene of Instruction,* which examines, among other topics, literacy narratives, the intertextuality of Edgeworth's work for children and adults, and the blurred boundaries between "pedagogy" and "literature." She is especially interested in these areas and in this anthology because they offer a gendered approach to cultural studies that foregrounds the mother-teacher.

Louise Wetherbee Phelps is Professor of Writing and English at Syracuse University, where she served from 1986 to 1992 as founding director of a university writing program. As a scholar-teacher in composition and rhetoric, she explores the complex relations among theoretical concepts, experience, and ethical action from a contextualist perspective informed by feminism. As an administrator, she attempted to enact these relations and her own "feminine principles" in a program organized as an inclusive teaching-learning community. She is author of *Composition as a Human Science* (1988) and many essays in journals and collections. In 1993–1994 she was a Fellow of the American Council of Education, studying leadership in higher education and serving an internship at Towson State University. Her current interests include graduate education, faculty development, ethical and rhetorical dimensions of administration, and efforts to reshape the values and practice of academic culture.

Jacqueline Jones Royster, Associate Professor of English at Ohio State University, is a founding member of the editorial team of *Sage: A Scholarly Journal on Black Women.* In addition to their semiannual journal, the team has published an anthology, *Double-Stitch: Black Women Write About Mothers and Daughters.* Royster is the author of various articles in literacy studies and women's studies and is consulting author for composition of *Writer's Choice 6–8.* Currently, she is completing a work entitled *Traces of a Stream: Literacy and Social Change Among African American Women.*

Edward L. Rocklin is Professor of English in the English and Foreign Languages Department, California State Polytechnic University, Pomona. He has just completed a book on teaching Shakespeare's plays through performance and has begun a related project, tentatively entitled *Being in Action Together,* which will use the drama-based frame employed in his response essay to develop an integrated pedagogy for literature and composition courses, as well as for courses in other disciplines such as history and philosophy. Like the editors, he also sees the classroom as a place that has not only its own poetics but its own ethics—an ethics that grows directly out of the implicit pedagogic commitment between students and teachers. Rocklin is also one of seven Postsecondary Fellows of the American Council of Learned Societies who are participating in a nationwide collaboration to improve teaching in the public schools.

Maria Salgado earned a GED through The Care Center, a community resource for parenting teens in Holyoke, Massachusetts, and has studied at Holyoke Community College. For two summers she participated in The Next Step program at Mount Holyoke College and worked as a classroom assistant at the Holyoke Magnet Middle School. She coordinated after-school activities with teens through the New Bridges program and is currently a community organizer with Nueva Esperanza in Holyoke. She is a frequent writer of prose and poetry and is currently working with her friend Sara Jonsberg on a volume of story and reflection.

Mary M. Salibrici is a writing instructor at Syracuse University, where she is involved in teacher training and projects concerned with writing across the curriculum, in addition to classroom teaching.

Nancy Sommers is Director of the Expository Writing Program at Harvard University. She has also directed the composition program at the University of Oklahoma and taught in the English Department at Rutgers University, where she was a Henry Rutgers Research Fellow. She has published widely on the theory and practice of teaching writing and has co-authored five college writing textbooks. She received the National Council of Teachers of English Promising Research Award for her work on revision and the Richard Braddock Award in 1983 and in 1993. Recently she published a study of undergraduate writing at Harvard.

Pittsburgh Series in Composition, Literacy, and Culture

David Bartholomae and Jean Ferguson Carr, Editors

The Origins of Composition Studies in the American College 1875–1925: A Documentary History
John C. Brereton, Editor

The Powers of Literacy: A Genre Approach to Teaching Writing
Bill Cope and Mary Kalantzis, Editors

Pre/Text: The First Decade
Victor Vitanza, Editor

Reclaiming Rhetorica: Women in the Rhetorical Tradition
Andrea A. Lunsford, Editor

'Round My Way: Authority and Double-Consciousness in Three Urban High School Writers
Eli C. Goldblatt

Word Perfect: Literacy in the Computer Age
Myron C. Tuman

Writing Science: Literacy and Discursive Power
M. A. K. Halliday and J. R. Martin